# SUNDAY

## IN

# NEW YORK

*Written by Karen Cure*

*Edited and conceived by*
*Andrew A. Anspach*

Fodor's Travel Publications, Inc.
New York and London

### Fodor's Sunday in New York

**Editors:** Holly Hughes, Andrew A. Anspach
**Contributors:** Laura Broadwell, Suzanne Brown, Susan Spano Wells
**Art Director:** Fabrizio La Rocca
**Cartographer:** David Lindroth

**Cover Illustration:** Steven Guarnaccia

### About the Author

Karen Cure has lived in New York City since 1973. She is the author of *Mini Vacations USA*, *The Travel Catalogue*, *An Old-fashioned Christmas*, and numerous articles for magazines including *Travel & Leisure* and *Diversion*. She has contributed to many major guidebook series and has traveled all over the world, but still believes that there's no place like home.

### Special Sales

# Contents

## 6 Sports, Games, and the Urban Outdoors *143*

## 7 Performing Arts *177*

## Index *203*

## Maps

# Foreword

Sunday is the day to see New York at its best—not just because there are so many wonderful things to do, but because Sunday is a perfect day to do them. On Sunday tensions lift. Moods lighten. Gone is the weekday frenzy, the emotional gridlock of a city hard at work.

On Sunday streets are busy but not crowded, and the people you meet are just there because they want to be. Unlike on weekdays, traffic moves along at a pleasant pace, and free curbside parking or reasonable garage rates are available almost everywhere. Getting around is no longer a major undertaking, and everything seems within easy reach. Sightseeing, dining, shopping, sports, the arts—whatever your pleasure, Sunday is the day to enjoy it.

The focus is on Sunday, but most of the guide is equally valuable for planning Saturdays, too. Whether you're a visitor from Vitebsk, a neighbor from New Canaan, or a hard-core New Yorker who calls the city home, this book provides a detailed—and eye-opening—survey of all there is to do and see on weekends.

You'll find the popular attractions—"musts" for first-time visitors—as well as surprises even seasoned New Yorkers don't know about. There's chess, bridge, and croquet; boccie, baseball, and bowling—even sailing and golf. There are walks through salt marshes and gardens. There are guided architecture tours and trips to some of the world's greatest museums, as well as to many smaller ones showcasing specialized collections and art from all over the world. It's all here, along with where to get a pedicure, have an article translated, buy a pair of riding boots. Kids? There are suggestions on what to see and do with children that will transform just another family outing into a day of fun and adventure.

A series of maps at the back of the book will help you find your way around Manhattan's neighborhoods and orient yourself in the four other boroughs. With this book you'll see Sunday as an excellent time for getting things done, and also for enjoying the city's bountiful pleasures—enough to fill a lifetime of Sundays.

*Andrew A. Anspach*
*Executive Producer, WNYC Public Radio*
*Managing Director, Algonquin Hotel (1956–86)*

# 1 Essential Information

## Visitor Information

The **New York Convention and Visitors Bureau** at 58th Street and Eighth Avenue provides a wealth of free information, including brochures, subway and bus maps, listings of hotels and weekend hotel packages, information about performing arts events, and discount coupons for Broadway shows. *2 Columbus Circle, New York, NY 10019, tel. 212/397–8222. Open weekdays only.*

The **New York Division of Tourism** offers a free series of *I Love New York* booklets, which include a number of New York City attractions and tour packages. *1 Commerce Plaza, Albany, NY 12245, tel. 518/474–4116 or 800/225–5697.*

**Fund for the Borough of Brooklyn** has several excellent publications about the borough. *16 Court St., Room 900, Brooklyn, NY 11241, tel. 718/802–9025.*

**Office of the Queens Borough President** publishes *Queens Neighborhoods*, which covers Astoria, Flushing, and Long Island City attractions and restaurants. *120–55 Queens Blvd., Kew Gardens, NY 11424, tel. 718/520–3220.*

## Useful Phone Numbers

**Transportation** **Amtrak** (tel. 800/872–7245).
**Long Island Railroad** (tel. 718/454–5477).
**Metro-North trains** (tel. 212/532–4900).

*Local* **Metropolitan Transit Authority,** for local bus and subway information (tel. 718/330–1234).
**New Jersey Transit** (tel. 201/460–8444).
**PATH trains** (tel. 212/466–7649).
**Port Authority Bus Terminal** (tel. 212/564–8484).

*Tri-state* **Port Authority Bridges and Tunnels** (tel. 212/360–3000).

**Entertainment** **Bryant Park Music and Dance Half-Price Tickets Booth** (tel. 212/382–2323).
**Lincoln Center** (tel. 212/877–2011).
**Madison Square Garden** (tel. 212/563–8300).
**NYC On Stage,** for comprehensive updates on performing arts events (tel. 212/587–1111).
**Park Events** hotline (tel. 212/360–1333).

## Getting to New York City

**By Car** From New Jersey, the **Lincoln Tunnel** (I–495), **Holland Tunnel,** and **George Washington Bridge** (I–95) connect Manhattan to the New Jersey Turnpike system and points west. The Lincoln Tunnel leads to midtown Manhattan, the Holland Tunnel to lower Manhattan, and the George Washington Bridge to upper Manhattan. For each of the three crossings a toll ($3 for cars) is assessed eastbound into New York, but not westbound.

From Long Island, the **Queens–Midtown Tunnel** (I–495) and **Triborough Bridge** (I–278) are the most direct links to Manhattan. Both connect with the east side, but the tunnel comes out in midtown, while the Triborough Bridge enters uptown. Both require tolls ($2.50 for cars) in both directions.

From upstate New York and central Westchester County, the city is accessible via the **New York (Dewey) Thruway** (I–87), a toll road that becomes the **Major Deegan Expressway** through the Bronx. Enter Manhattan via the Triborough Bridge ($2.50 toll). From western Westchester County, the **Sawmill River Parkway** (25¢ toll) leads to the **Henry Hudson Parkway**, which enters Manhattan at the **Henry Hudson Bridge** ($1.25 toll).

From New England, the **Connecticut Turnpike** (I–95) connects to the **New England Thruway** (I–95, toll road) and then the **Bruckner Expressway** (I–278). Take the Bruckner to the **Triborough Bridge** ($2.50 toll) or to the **Cross Bronx Expressway**, which crosses upper Manhattan to the west side.

Getting in and out of the city may be easier if you avoid late-afternoon Sunday traffic. In summer, in particular, New Yorkers returning from weekend getaways often clog the Long Island Expressway, the Lincoln and Midtown tunnels, and the Triborough and George Washington bridges.

**By Train**  **Amtrak** trains between Boston and Washington arrive and depart from Pennsylvania Station (31st to 33rd Sts., between 7th and 8th Aves.).

The **Long Island Railroad,** with service from all over Long Island, also uses Penn Station, as does **New Jersey Transit,** which offers frequent service from the north and central regions of the state. **Metro-North** trains from the northern suburbs and from Connecticut as far east as New Haven stop at Grand Central Terminal (42nd St. and Vanderbilt Ave., between Lexington and Madison Aves.).

All three commuter lines operate weekend schedules.

**PATH trains** serve Hoboken, Jersey City, Newark, and Harrison, New Jersey, from the World Trade Center and from stops along Sixth Avenue at Christopher, 9th, 14th, 23rd, and 33rd streets. Trains run every 20 to 30 minutes on weekends; the fare is $1. In New Jersey, PATH trains connect with seven major New Jersey Transit commuter lines at Hoboken, Broad Street (Newark), and Penn (Newark) stations.

**By Bus**  All long-haul and commuter bus lines feed into the **Port Authority Terminal,** a mammoth multilevel structure between 40th and 42nd streets and Eighth and Ninth avenues. Though it was modernized recently and is kept fairly clean and well-patrolled, Port Authority is not the best place to spend much time because of the large number of homeless it attracts. Especially at night, don't plan to linger here any longer than necessary.

The **George Washington Bridge Bus Station** is located at Fort Washington Avenue and Broadway between 178th and 179th streets in the Washington Heights section of Manhattan. Six bus lines, serving northern New Jersey and New York's Rockland County, operate Sunday from 5 AM to 1 AM. The terminal connects with the 175th Street subway station and the Eighth Avenue A subway.

## Getting Around

**By Subway**  The 300-mile subway system is the fastest and cheapest way to get around the city. Unless otherwise noted, all the destinations in this book are accessible by subway and a short walk.

On Sundays, you can always get a seat, though the trains may be surprisingly full—many people head for the beach or the park or some explorable neighborhood in the late morning, and many more, laden with packages from Macy's or Loehmann's or the Lower East Side, pile into the trains homeward bound in the afternoon. It's an affable group. Now that most cars are sheathed in glossy, graffiti-free stainless steel, the experience is not at all unpleasant.

Trains run 24 hours a day. A single fare is $1.15, regardless of the distance you travel. Children under six travel free; those six and older pay full fare. If you plan a day of traveling around the city by public transportation, buy enough tokens to last. One token permits unlimited transfers within the system until you exit, and tokens can also be used on buses.

Maps are posted at both ends of most subway cars and outside token booths, but are rarely posted on the platforms themselves. Some token booths have a few to hand out on request (no charge). The New York Convention and Visitors Bureau also has subway maps. For route information, call 718/330–1234. For safety reasons, don't linger on deserted platforms or enter empty cars, and if the train isn't crowded, ride in the same car as the conductor (in the middle of the train).

From midday on, when the subway's busy, children may enjoy standing at the front window of the first car of the train. With the tunnel lights racing toward you and the track shining in the gloomy distance, it's great fun—for all ages.

**By Bus** When New York's streets and avenues are practically traffic-free, as on Sunday mornings, buses may actually go so fast you can scarcely take in the scenery. Later in the day, the pace is more "leisurely," and you can enjoy the cityscape sliding by. Even with a great many New Yorkers out and about, it's easy to get a seat. Bus fare—which is $1.15, the same as subway fare—must be paid with a token or cash, but no bills or pennies. This includes one transfer that will permit you to ride at no charge on an intersecting bus route; ask the driver for the transfer slip as you board. Children six and up pay adult fares, as in the subways; those under six ride free.

Most routes follow the Manhattan grid: up or down the north–south avenues, east and west on the major crosstown streets. Bus maps are occasionally available in subway token booths but never on buses. The best places to pick one up are the Convention and Visitors Bureau at Columbus Circle or the information kiosks in Grand Central Terminal and Penn Station.

Guide-A-Rides, which show a specific route's map and schedules, are posted at many bus stops in Manhattan and at major stops in the other boroughs.

**By Taxi** Taxis are usually easy to hail on the street on Sundays. Only the ones with the rooftop number lit are available. Taxis cost $1.50 for the first ⅕ of a mile, 25¢ for each ⅕ mile thereafter, and 20¢ for each minute not in motion, plus a 50¢ weekend surcharge, and the 15% tip that all cabbies expect. Still, New York taxis are mile-for-mile less expensive than those in many cities. A short trip for two or more people may cost less than public transportation for the group, since you pay by the ride, not per person.

**By Car**  Driving around Manhattan is one of Sunday's great pleasures. The blocks slip by, almost too quickly; one neighborhood slowly gives way to the next. You get a sense of how it all fits together, and you can really get around.

Two major north–south arteries run the length of the island. The **West Side Highway** skirts the Hudson River from Battery Park (where it's known as West Street), through midtown to the upper West Side (where it becomes the Henry Hudson Parkway north of 72nd Street), and past the George Washington Bridge.

The **Franklin D. Roosevelt Drive** (or FDR Drive) runs along the East River from Battery Park into upper Manhattan, and it connects with the Triborough Bridge, the Midtown Tunnel, and the Queensboro Bridge.

Most major cross-streets in Manhattan (including 14th, 23rd, 34th, 42nd, 59th, 72nd) connect with either the West Side Highway or FDR Drive.

## Manhattan Orientation

Above 14th Street, Manhattan streets form a regular grid pattern. Consecutively numbered streets run east and west (crosstown), while broad avenues, most of them also numbered, run north or south. Fifth Avenue is the east-west dividing line for street addresses; in both directions, they increase in regular increments from there. For example, on 55th Street, the addresses 1–99 East 55th Street are between Fifth, Madison, and Park (the equivalent of Fourth) avenues, 100–199 East 55th would be between Park and Third avenues, and so on; the addresses 1–99 West 55th Street are between Fifth and Sixth avenues, 100–199 West 55th would be between Sixth and Seventh avenues, and so forth. Above 59th Street, where Central Park interrupts the grid, West Side addresses start numbering at Central Park West, an extension of Eighth Avenue. Avenue addresses are much less regular; consult the Manhattan Address Locator in this chapter. South of 14th Street, you'd do best to use a map.

## Parking

Forget what you've heard about parking in Manhattan. Most on-street parking restrictions are lifted on Sundays, so you will not feel, as you may on weekdays, that all 12,000 miles of the city's curb space are consumed by crosswalks, bus stops, driveways, fire hydrants, loading docks, and parking zones for every special-interest group but your own. With many New Yorkers and their cars away for the weekend, you'll have much less competition than during the week.

Street parking is easy on Sundays west of Eighth Avenue and east of Lexington Avenue in midtown. It's somewhat tougher in Greenwich Village and on the Upper West and Upper East sides, as well as in the core of midtown—between Lexington and Eighth Avenues and 42nd and 60th streets. But even here, persistence yields its reward: 10 feet of open curb and not a hydrant in sight.

# Manhattan Address Locator

To locate avenue addresses, take the address, cancel the last figure, divide by 2, add or subtract the key number below. The answer is the nearest numbered cross street, approximately. To find addresses on numbered cross streets, remember that numbers increase east or west from 5th Ave., which runs north–south.

**Ave. A**... *add 3*
**Ave. B**...*add 3*
**Ave. C**...*add 3*
**Ave. D**...*add 3*
**1st Ave.**...*add 3*
**2nd Ave.**...*add 3*
**3rd Ave.**...*add 10*
**4th Ave.**...*add 8*
**5th Ave.**
Up to 200...*add 13*
Up to 400...*add 16*
Up to 600...*add 18*
Up to 775...*add 20*
From 775 to 1286... *cancel last figure and subt. 18*
**Ave. of the Americas**...*subt. 12*
**7th Ave.**...*add 12*
Above 110th St... *add 20*
**8th Ave.**...*add 9*
**9th Ave.**...*add 13*
**10th Ave.**...*add 14*
**Amsterdam Ave.**
...*add 59*
**Audubon Ave.**
...*add 165*
**Broadway (23–192 Sts.)**...*subt. 30*
**Columbus Ave.**
...*add 60*
**Convent Ave.**...*add 127*

**Central Park West**...
*divide house number by 10 and add 60*
**Edgecombe Ave.**
...*add 134*
**Ft. Washington Ave.**
...*add 158*
**Lenox Ave.**...*add 110*
**Lexington Ave.**...*add 22*
**Madison Ave.**...*add 27*
**Manhattan Ave.**
...*add 100*
**Park Ave.**...*add 34*
**Park Ave. South**
...*add 8*
**Pleasant Ave.**...*add 101*
**Riverside Drive**...
*divide house number by 10 and add 72 up to 165 Street*
**St. Nicholas Ave.**
...*add 110*
**Wadsworth Ave.**
...*add 173*
**West End Ave.**
...*add 59*
**York Ave.**...*add 4*

In addition, many garages throughout the city cut their rates on Sundays. Garage rates may range from $6 to $21 per day, usually about $10 for all day on Sunday.

The following garages are open on Sunday and are located near shopping and tourist attractions.

**Upper West Side** **Berkley Garage** (201 W. 75th St., tel. 212/874–0581).
**Term Parking Garage** (200 W. 79th St., tel. 212/874–9149).
**Tower Parking** (60 W. 66th St., tel. 212/874–8639).

**Upper East Side** **CGMC Garage** (301 E. 79th St., tel. 212/650–1936).
**FAS Garage** (184 E. 73rd St., tel. 212/650–9625).
**Kinney Garage** (15 E. 60th St., tel. 212/832–9750).

**Midtown–West Side** **Broadway Hippodrome** (1633 Broadway, tel. 212/997–9522).
**Edison Park Fast** (355 W. 34th St., tel. 212/502–5362).
**Eighth Avenue and 53rd Street Garage** (888 8th Ave., tel. 212/974–9470).
**Square Plus** (306 W. 44th St., tel. 212/247–5807).

**Midtown–East Side** **Carlton Parking Garage** (443 E. 49th St., tel. 212/688–7666).
**Continental Garage** (237 E. 40th St., tel. 212/599–9485).
**Murray's Park Garage** (230 Lexington Ave. at 34th St., tel. 212/684–9312).
**Square Parking** (206 E. 59th St., tel. 212/650–9220).

**West Side below 23rd Street** **All Market Garage** (166 Perry St. at West St., tel. 212/741–9773).
**Minetta Garage** (122 W. 3rd St. at 6th Ave., tel. 212/777–3530).
**Roxy Parking** (422 W. 15th St., tel. 212/243–7909).
**61 Parking Corp.** (623 Hudson St. at Jane St., tel. 212/243–6303).

**East Side below 23rd Street** **PAT Garage** (12 E. 13th St. at 5th Ave., tel. 212/255–5966).
**Square Parking** (70 E. 10th St. at 4th Ave., tel. 212/254–3870).

## Weekend Hotel Packages

Many midtown hotels offer special packages that turn a weekend in the city into a wonderful minivacation. These include deluxe suite accommodations, free parking, champagne, luxury chocolates, use of health-club facilities, museum tickets, and/or shopping vouchers—and at bargain room rates. Reserve in advance. The following hotels frequently offer such packages; phone or write for current prices and availability.

**Algonquin** (59 W. 44th St., 10036, tel. 212/840–6800).
**Bedford** (118 E. 40th St., 10016, tel. 212/697–4800 or 800/221–6881).
**Beekman Tower** (3 Mitchell Pl., 10017, tel. 212/355–7300 or 800/ME–SUITE).
**Beverly** (125 E. 50th St., 10022, tel. 212/753–2700).
**Doral Court** (130 E. 39th St., 10016, tel. 212/685–1100 or 800/223–0945).
**Doral Inn** (541 Lexington Ave., 10022, tel. 212/755–1200 or 800/223–5823).
**Doral Park** (70 Park Ave., 10016, tel. 212/687–7050 or 800/847–4135).
**Doral Tuscany** (120 E. 39th St., 10016, tel. 212/686–1600 or 800/847–4078).
**Dorset** (30 W. 54th St., 10019, tel. 212/247–7300 or 800/227–2348).

**Drake** (440 Park Ave., 10022, tel. 212/421–0900 or 800/DRAKE–NY).

**Essex House** (160 Central Park South, 10019, tel. 212/247–0300 or 800/NIKKO–US).

**Grand Hyatt New York** (Park Ave. at 42nd St., 10017, tel. 212/883–1234 or 800/228–9000).

**Halloran House** (525 Lexington Ave., 10017, tel. 212/755–4000 or 800/223–0939).

**Helmsley Middletowne** (148 E. 48th St., 10017, tel. 212/755–3000 or 800/221–4982).

**Helmsley Park Lane** (36 Central Park South, 10019, tel. 212/371–4000 or 800/221–4982).

**Helmsley Windsor** (100 W. 58th St., 10019, tel. 212/265–2100 or 800/221–4982).

**Inter-Continental New York** (111 E. 48th St., 10017, tel. 212/755–5900 or 800/332–4246).

**Le Parker Meridien** (118 W. 57th St., 10019, tel. 212/245–5000 or 800/543–4300).

**Marriott Marquis** (1535 Broadway, 10036, tel. 212/398–1900 or 800/228–9290).

**Mayfair Regent** (610 Park Ave., 10021, tel. 212/288–0800 or 800/223–0542).

**New York Helmsley** (212 E. 42nd St., 10017, tel. 212/490–8900 or 800/221–4982).

**Omni Berkshire Place** (21 E. 52nd St., 10022, tel. 212/753–5800 or 800/THE–OMNI).

**Salisbury** (123 W. 57th St., 10019, tel. 212/246–1300 or 800/223–0680).

**Sheraton-Park Hotel** (45 Park Ave. at 37th St., 10016, tel. 212/685–7676 or 800/325–3535).

**United Nations Plaza Hotel** (44th St. at 1st Ave., 10017, tel. 212/355–3400 or 800/228–9000).

**Vista International** (3 World Trade Center, 10048, tel. 212/938–9100 or 800/258–0505).

**Waldorf-Astoria Hotel** (301 Park Ave., 10022, tel. 212/355–3000 or 800/HILTONS).

**The Westbury** (15 E. 69th St., 10021, tel. 212/535–2000).

## Activities for Children

The **Parents' League of New York** (115 E. 82nd St., 10028, tel. 212/737–7385) offers a splendid listing of events and services for children. *New York Family,* a magazine published eight times a year (New York Family Publications, 420 E. 79th St., Suite 9E, 10021, tel. 212/744–0309) and the weekly *Big Apple Parents' Paper* (Buffalo-Bunyip, Inc., 67 Wall St., Suite 2411, 10005, tel. 212/323–8070) are excellent sources of information for activities geared to youngsters. Several local publications, including the *Village Voice, New York* magazine, *7 Days,* and the Friday edition of the *New York Times,* also offer up-to-date calendars of happenings for kids.

Before you set out to explore the Big Apple, keep two things in mind. First, children under six travel free on subways and buses; kids six and older must pay the full fare. Second, clean rest rooms are often difficult to find; your best bet is to use the rest rooms at museums, department stores, shopping atriums, hotels, and restaurants as you patronize them.

## Churches

Even in secular New York City, churchgoing is very much
a part of Sunday. Beyond moral uplift, Sunday services offer
an opportunity to study gracious architecture, listen to
sacred music, and rub shoulders genteelly with other New
Yorkers.

**Baptist**    **Abyssinian Baptist Church** (132 W. 138th St., tel. 212/862–
7474), a Harlem institution, is known for gospel music and fiery
sermons. The Adam Clayton Powells, father and son, were min-
isters here. Services: 11 AM.

**Roman Catholic**    **St. Ignatius Loyola** (Park Ave. at 84th St., tel. 212/288–3588)
has an austere exterior and an interior exuberantly orna-
mented with mosaics, columns, and Tiffany glass. Services:
7:30 AM, 9:30 AM, 11 AM, 12:30 PM, 7:30 PM.

**St. Malachy's** (239 W. 49th St., tel. 212/489–1340), known as
the Actor's Chapel, schedules masses around theater matinees
and evening performances. Services: Saturday 5 PM, Sunday
9 AM, 11 AM, 12:30 PM, 5 PM.

**St. Patrick's Cathedral** (5th Ave. at 50th St., tel. 212/753–2261)
is the soaring Gothic cathedral where Cardinal O'Connor celebrates the 10:15 mass almost every Sunday. Services: 7 AM,
8 AM, 9 AM, 10:15 AM, noon, 1 PM, 4 PM, 5:30 PM.

**St. Vincent Ferrer** (869 Lexington Ave. at 66th St., tel. 212/
744–2080) is an immense church with splendid stained glass
and a carved altar wall. Services: 7 AM, 8:30 AM, 10 AM, 11:30 AM,
1 PM, 4:30 PM.

**Christian Science**    **Second Church of Christ Scientist** (Central Park West at 68th
St., tel. 212/877–6100), a plain green-domed structure built in
1900, is one of the fixtures of the neighborhood. Services:
11 AM.

**Third Church of Disciples of Christ** (Park Ave. at 63rd St., tel.
212/234–8181) is a Georgian structure built in 1920. Services:
10 AM.

**Church of Christ**    **Manhattan Church of Christ** (48 E. 80th St., tel. 212/737–4900),
built in 1965 of cast concrete with a stained glass facade, is conveniently near the Metropolitan Museum. Services: 11 AM.

**Eastern Orthodox**    **Archdiocesan Cathedral of the Holy Trinity** (319 E. 74th St., tel.
212/288–3215), with its golden mosaics and gilded paintings,
makes a Sunday service almost like a trip to Greece. Services:
10:30 AM.

**Episcopal**    **Calvary Episcopal** (Park Ave. at 21st St., tel. 212/475–1216) is a
lovely Gramercy Park church designed by James Renwick, who
also did St. Patrick's Cathedral. Services: 11 AM.

**Cathedral of St. John the Divine** (112th St. at Amsterdam Ave.,
tel. 212/316–6350) is the world's largest Gothic cathedral,
though still under construction. Yuletide holidays set the Cathedral abuzz, and the annual blessing of the animals, part of
the celebration of St. Francis Day, is a New York spectacle.
There are tours at 12:45 on Sunday. Services: 8 AM, 9 AM, 9:30 AM
(Spanish), 11 AM, 7 PM.

**Church of the Incarnation** (Madison Ave. at 35th St., tel. 212/
689–6350) occupies an early Gothic Revival building con-

structed in 1882 by Marc Eidlitz. There are sculptures by Augustus Saint-Gaudens, carvings from the Daniel Chester French atelier, and fine stained-glass windows. Services: 8 AM, 11 AM.

**Church of the Transfiguration** (1 E. 29th St., tel. 212/684–6770), known as the "Little Church Around the Corner," got its name in 1870, when one Joseph Jefferson, put off by another institution while arranging a funeral for an actor-friend, was told that there was a "little church around the corner where they do that sort of thing." The church is now a national historic landmark. Services: 8, 9, 11 AM.

**Grace Church** (802 Broadway at 10th St., tel. 212/254–2000), topped by an elegant steeple, is another Renwick-designed church. Services: 9, 11 AM; call for summer hours.

**St. Ann and the Holy Trinity Episcopal Church** (Clinton and Montague Sts., Brooklyn, tel. 718/875–6960) has Sunday services that may feature drama, dance, or music ranging from string quartets to steel drums; Palm Sunday services begin on the Promenade and process up Montague Street to the church. Services: 11 AM.

**St. Bartholomew's** (Park Ave. at 51st St., tel. 212/751–1616) is a grandiose Byzantine-Romanesque structure with rose windows and mosaics. Services: 9, 11 AM.

**St. James's** (Madison Ave. at 71st St., tel. 212/288–4100) is a brownstone Gothic structure with fine stained glass. One of the city's wealthier congregations worships here. Services: 8, 9, 11:15 AM.

**St. Mark's in the Bowery** (2nd Ave. at 10th St., tel. 212/674–6377), one of the city's most historic churches, occupies a part of Peter Stuyvesant's old estate and is intimately involved in the life of this bohemian corner of the Village. Services: 10:30 AM.

**St. Michael's Church** (225 W. 99th, tel. 212/222–2700), which houses one of the nation's largest collections of works by Louis Comfort Tiffany, also boasts a youthful congregation and a lively roster of choral eucharists and festival services. Services: 8:45, 11 AM.

**St. Thomas Church** (5th Ave. at 53rd St., tel. 212/757–7013) has a fine rose window, an altar wall full of sculptures, and a noted boys' choir. Services: 9, 11 AM.

**Trinity Church** (Broadway at Wall St., tel. 212/602–0800), chartered in 1697, now occupies a mid-19th-century Gothic building by Richard Upjohn. The reddish sandstone has blackened with time, as the silhouette has become one of the icons of New York. Services: 9, 11:15 AM.

**Interdenominational** **Judson Memorial Church** (55 Washington Sq. S at the corner of Thompson St., tel. 212/477–0351) is an NYU-area landmark, designed by Stanford White with stained glass windows by John LaFarge and statuary by Augustus Saint Gaudens. It is listed in the National Register of Historic Places. Services: 11 AM.

**Riverside Church** (Riverside Dr. at 122nd St., tel. 212/222–5900), built in 1930 by John D. Rockefeller, Jr., and inspired by the cathedral at Chartres, features an awesome 215-foot-long nave. Services: 10:45 AM.

**Lutheran** **Holy Trinity Lutheran Church** (Central Park West at 65th St., tel. 212/877–6815), a neo-French Gothic structure completed in 1903, evokes Paris's Sainte Chapelle. Services: 11 AM, 5 PM.

**St. Peter's Lutheran Church** (Lexington Ave. at 54th St., tel. 212/935–2200) is a lively, contemporary church located in the Citicorp Center. There are Louise Nevelson sculptures inside. Services: 8:45 AM, 11 AM, 5 PM.

**Methodist** **Christ Church United Methodist** (Park Ave. at 60th St., tel. 212/838–3036), built in 1932, is part Romanesque, part Byzantine, and very imposing. Services: 11 AM.

**John Street United Methodist Church** (44 John St., between William and Nassau Sts., tel. 212/269–0014) houses the oldest Methodist Society in America, organized in 1766. The current structure, built in Greek Revival style in 1841, is simple and pristine with white pews trimmed in dark wood. Services: 11 AM.

**Mormon** **Church of Latter-Day Saints** (2 Lincoln Sq., Broadway at 65th, tel. 212/595–1825) is opposite Lincoln Center. Services: 9 AM, 11 AM, 3 PM.

**Presbyterian** **Fifth Avenue Presbyterian** (5th Ave. at 55th St., tel. 212/247–0490) features almost-opalescent stained glass windows, some by Louis Comfort Tiffany, others by Maitland Armstrong. Services: 11 AM.

**First Presbyterian Church** (5th Ave. at 12th St., tel. 212/675–6150) provides restful sanctuary in a structure surrounded by an ornate old cast-iron fence and a fine green yard and gardens. Services: 11 AM.

**Madison Avenue Presbyterian Church** (917 Madison Ave., at 73rd St., tel. 212/288–8920), a wonderful Gothic structure built in 1899, has a fine music program. Services: 9:30, 11:15 AM.

**Quaker** **Society of Friends** (15 Rutherford Pl., between 2nd and 3rd Ave., tel. 212/777–8866). Sunday meetings are also held in Brooklyn and at Columbia University. Telephone for details. Services: 9:30, 11 AM.

**Reformed Church** **Marble Collegiate Church** (5th Ave. at 29th St., tel. 212/686–
**in America** 2770) held the New World's first communion service on April 7, 1628, in a dusty room above a grist mill on what is now William Street, and has been going strong ever since. In more recent times, it was famous for its minister, Norman Vincent Peale. Services: 11:15 AM.

**West End Collegiate** (386 West End Ave. at 77th St., tel. 212/787–1566) looks like something out of Amsterdam, with its stepped-gable facade. It's simple and unprepossessing inside, with massive timbers and turn-of-the century murals. Services: 11 AM.

**Unitarian** **Church of All Souls** (1157 Lexington Ave. at 80th St., tel. 212/535–5530) has an eminently civilized congregation. Services: 10, 11:15 AM.

**Community Church of New York** (40 E. 35th St., tel. 212/683–4988), traditionally very liberal, is where the late Michael Harrington used to be the minister. Services: 11 AM.

**The Universalist Church** (Central Park West at 76th St., tel. 212/595–8410) is a neo-gothic church built in 1898 on designs by William Potter. Services: 11 AM.

## Seasonal Pleasures

New York is a city for all seasons. Each month brings a new crop of special happenings in museums, parks, and other institutions, as well as sports events and much more. Many of these are noted in Chapter 7. Look for updated announcements in local publications, in particular *New York* magazine, *7 Days*, the *Village Voice*, and Friday's "Weekend" section in the *New York Times*. Here's a selection of some seasonal pleasures worth looking into.

**Winter**  In wintertime the great indoors beckons and the performing arts calendar is usually full. But don't forget about the city's great outdoors, too. There's ice skating in the parks and at Rockefeller Center. The Bronx Zoo, delightfully uncrowded, offers the opportunity to see animals in their winter coats. For a taste of the flowers to come, take in the spring preview in the Enid Haupt Conservatory at the Bronx's New York Botanical Garden; the warm and steamy air is a flash of summer.

**Early Jan.: National Boat Show** will awaken the sailor in you. Jacob K. Javits Convention Center, tel. 212/684–6622.

**Mid-Jan.:** The **Winter Antiques Show** is one of the top events of its kind in the country. Seventh Regiment Armory, Park Ave. at 67th St., tel. 212/665–5250.

**Feb.: Chinese New Year** is celebrated with special banquets at nearly every Chinese restaurant in the city, and Chinatown's narrow streets are ankle deep with red firecracker paper.

**Mid-Feb.: Westminster Kennel Club Dog Show** offers a fascinating showcase for top-of-the-line pooches. Madison Square Garden, tel. 212/563–8300.

**Early Mar.: International Cat Show** is a feline lover's delight. Madison Square Garden, tel. 212/563–8300.

**Mid-Mar.: Ringling Bros. Barnum & Bailey Circus,** begins its glittering run here. Madison Square Garden, tel. 212/563–8300.

**Late Mar.: Greek Independence Day Parade** struts a fabulous show of native costumes. Fifth Ave. from 62nd to 79th Sts.

**Spring**  Nature wakes up with a floral show that fairly takes the breath away. Daffodils and forsythia gild Central Park as well as the botanical gardens; the New York Botanical Garden in the Bronx is especially wonderful, particularly the Murray Liasson Narcissus Collection and Daffodil Hill. April brings the neon blaze of azaleas, and May means a pink blizzard of flowering cherry trees, singularly beautiful along the Hudson River in Riverside Park, around the Central Park Reservoir, and in the Brooklyn Botanic Garden.

**Mar. or Apr.: Easter festivities** occur all over town. Masses of flowers turn Macy's ground floor into an exquisitely fragrant wonderland; the Waldorf-Astoria displays an elaborate chocolate sculpture worth going out of your way to see. On Easter Sunday, exhibitionists don extravagant or improbable hats and saunter down Fifth Avenue in the annual Easter Parade.

**May: You Gotta Have Park** is a special weekend when thousands of volunteers—citizens and celebrities—pitch in to clean up

Central Park in a great show of community spirit, and a good time is had by all.

**Mid- to late May: Ninth Avenue International Food Festival** features food and merchandise from 32 countries. Ninth Ave. south of 57th St., tel. 212/581–7217.

**Late May to early June: Washington Square Art Show** fills Washington Square Park and adjacent side streets in Greenwich Village. Tel. 212/982–6255.

**Summer** As the hot weather settles in, so does the season of street fairs and block parties. In June, roses bloom by the thousands at the Brooklyn Botanic Garden and at the Bronx's New York Botanical Garden. Later on, perennials come into their own in these two gardens, as well as in Central Park's Conservatory Garden and the Community Garden in Riverside Park near 90th Street. Water babies sun at the beaches, fans pray for homers at Yankee and Shea stadiums, theater goers enjoy Shakespeare in the parks, and music lovers savor the Museum of Modern Art's Summergarden concerts. (For more on the foregoing, *see* Chapters 6 and 7.) One more seasonal note: Many Manhattan businesses temporarily curtail Sunday hours in July and August, so if you're making a special trip for something specific, call ahead.

**June: Riverside Park Festival** features dances, chess tournaments, a bubble-blowing contest, gospel concert, and other entertainment.

**June: Hudson River Rally and Festival** sails the *Clearwater, Sojourner Truth,* and the *Intrepid's* fireboat, plus countless canoes, ferries, and kayaks, performances by Peter Seeger and others, including the Steam Whistle Symphony.

**June: Queens Festival** brings professional entertainment, games, rides, and exhibits to Flushing Meadows—and a crowd of millions to enjoy it all. Flushing Meadows-Corona Park, Queens, tel. 718/886–5454.

**Early to mid-June: Feast of St. Anthony** is celebrated with 10 days of cannelloni and veal and sausage and things parmigiana. Sullivan St. near Houston St., tel. 212/777–2755.

**Mid-June: Puerto Rican Day Parade** marches to Latin rhythms and the most exuberant of crowds. Fifth Ave., between 42nd and 86th Sts., tel. 212/665–1600.

**Early to mid-July: American Crafts Festival** is where spinners spin; weavers weave; and puppeteers, jugglers, and other entertainers keep things lively as hand-crafted goods are "ooh"-ed and "ah"-ed over. Lincoln Center, tel. 212/877–2011.

**Aug.: Tap-O-Mania** at Macy's is, according to the *Guinness Book of World Records,* "the world's largest assembly of people tap dancing the same routine at one time." Because the chorus line fills up Herald Square, it can be held only on a Sunday. 34th St. and Sixth Ave., tel. 212/695–4400.

**Late Aug. to early Sept.: U.S. Open Tennis Championships** are the high point of the local tennis lover's year. National Tennis Center, Flushing Meadows-Corona Park, Queens, tel. 718/271–5100.

**Aug.: Harlem Week** highlights workshops, street carnivalia, dance, rap, jazz, fairs, gospel singing, and other cultural events. Throughout Harlem, tel. 212/427–7200.

**Autumn** The street festival season continues as baseball fans wait with bated breath for the outcome of the year's pennant races. With crowds at the beaches thinning out, it's a great time to enjoy the surf in solitude. Later on, the fall foliage is glorious, particularly in the parks. October marks the beginning of Rockefeller Center ice skating—a first taste of the winter delights to come.

**Mid-Sept.: New York Is Book Country** brings New Yorkers out in droves to enjoy a sunny Sunday and scores of bookstalls and exhibits from major publishers, as well as clowns, balloons, and entertainment. Fifth Ave., between 48th and 57th Sts., tel. 212/984–7616.

**Mid-Sept.: Feast of San Gennaro,** 10 days honoring the patron saint of Naples, is the biggest of the city's Italian street fairs. You'll find plenty of fattening sweets, fried food, two-bit carnival games—and great people-watching. Mulberry St., Little Italy, tel. 212/226–9546.

**Late Sept.–early Oct.: New York Film Festival** is the high point of the local film buff's year. Alice Tully Hall, Lincoln Center, tel. 212/877–1800.

**Early Oct.: Pulaski Day Parade** commemorates Polish hero Casimir Pulaski. Fifth Ave., between 26th and 52nd Sts.

**Late Oct. or early Nov.: New York City Marathon** begins at the Verrazano-Narrows Bridge and loops through all the boroughs. Tel. 212/860–4455.

**Early Nov.:** The **National Horse Show,** the oldest continuing indoor horse show in the world and one of the most prestigious equestrian events anywhere, is full of pomp and pageantry: scarlet riding coats, buff breeches, sparkling horse-drawn vehicles, and more. Madison Square Garden, tel. 212/563–8300.

**Nov.: Virginia Slims Tennis Championships** in mid-month and the **Nabisco Masters Tennis Championships** bring the stars of the tennis world to town. Madison Square Garden, tel. 212/563–8300.

**Nov. 11: Veteran's Day Parade** honors our nation's war heroes. Fifth Ave., between 24th and 39th Sts., tel. 212/267–1998.

**The Holidays**      During the Christmas holidays, many stores that are closed on Sundays through most of the year do a booming Sunday business. In fact, on the two Sundays before Christmas, midtown blocks of Fifth Avenue are closed to vehicular traffic, while crowds of shoppers pause en route to admire the giant Christmas tree at Rockefeller Center—even more magical in life than in photographs. Meanwhile, the Cartier building is wrapped in a big red bow, the center mall up Park Avenue is studded with fir trees twinkling with little white lights, and all New York positively glitters with special events.

The **American Museum of Natural History** decks a wonderful Christmas tree with origami figures, and the adjacent **Hayden Planetarium** has its traditional Christmas star show. Animated displays depicting Yuletide fantasies fill windows of the great Manhattan stores on Fifth Avenue: **Lord & Taylor** at 38th Street, and **Saks** at 50th Street.

The Christmas Spectacular, a musical extravaganza featuring the high-kicking Rockettes, fills the stage at **Radio City Music Hall** in Rockefeller Center (tel. 212/757–3100).

At the **Metropolitan Museum of Art,** exquisite Neapolitan crèche figures ornament the museum's Christmas tree, set against a wonderful medieval choir screen. The *Nutcracker*, performed by the **New York City Ballet** at Lincoln Center's New York State Theater, never fails to dazzle (tel. 212/870–5570).

## Personal and Business Services

The following establishments are all open on Sunday most of the year. Always call ahead, however, since some may close for vacations or holidays or in summer.

**Automotive Services** Manhattan gas stations that are open Sundays, from downtown northward, include the following.

*Gas* **Mobil** (Allen and Division Sts., tel. 212/966–0571).
**Mobil** (Spring St. at 6th Ave., tel. 212/925–6126).
**Amoco** (Broadway at Houston St., tel. 212/473–5924).
**Mobil** (Houston St. at Ave. C, tel. 212/529–9320).
**Gaseteria** (Houston and Lafayette Sts., tel. 212/226–9530).
**Citgo** (Bowery at 3rd St., tel. 212/254–7790).
**Gulf** (10th Ave. at 23rd St., tel. 212/924–1260).
**Gulf** (FDR Dr. at 23rd St., tel. 212/686–4546).
**Mobil** (11th Ave. at 51st St., tel. 212/974–0243).
**Mobil** (York Ave. at 61st St., tel. 212/308–8318).
**Gaseteria** (59th St. at West End Ave., tel. 212/245–9830).

*Car Rentals* Most car-rental outlets at the major airports and throughout the city are open Sundays. Reserve well in advance for summer weekends. The major companies are **Avis** (tel. 800/331–1212), **Budget** (tel. 212/807–8700), **Hertz** (tel. 800/654–3131), and **National** (tel. 800/328–4567).

*Towing and Repairs* The Automobile Club of New York (AAA) provides help to members. To protect other drivers, the City Council sets towing rates for all five boroughs—currently $25 for a hookup plus $1.75 per mile and tolls. The Yellow Pages list dozens of services under "Towing", and "Automobile Repairing and Service," among them:

**A & M Auto Repair** (556 W. 37th St., tel. 212/465–8250).
**Elite Auto Service** (428 E. 75th St., tel. 212/734–5434).
**Express Auto Repairs** (276 7th Ave. at 26th St., tel. 212/242–5982 or 212/242–5811).
**J & S Auto Repair** (456 11th Ave. at 37th St., tel. 212/465–2401).

*Car Wash* Sundays are perfect for a vehicular scrubdown: You can zip over and back with not a traffic jam in sight, and you seldom have to wait, especially early in the day.

**Carzapoppin'** (Broadway at Houston St., tel. 212/673–5115), open 24 hours.
**East Side Car Wash** (92nd St. at 1st Ave., tel. 212/722–2222), open Sundays 7–6.
**Underwest Car Wash** (12th Ave. at 46th St., tel. 212/757–1141), open 24 hours.

**Baby-sitters** The **Babysitters Guild** (60 E. 42nd St., Suite 912, tel. 212/682–0227), in business since 1940, screens sitters rigorously.

**Balloon Bouquets** **Balloon Bouquets of New York** (457 W. 43rd St., tel. 212/265–5252) offers balloon decorations for dinner parties, birthdays, and such—but you have to order on Saturday for a Sunday delivery in Manhattan.

**Beauty Care and Haircuts** **Astor Place Hair Designers** (2 Astor Pl., tel. 212/475–9854) is the place to get a downtown look—or anything else you want. The barbers in this funky spot are happy to oblige, and the fee is nominal: $10 for men, $12 for women. Open Sundays 9–6.

**Entre Nous** (210 E. 34th St., tel. 212/213–2213) does hair, nails, and facials. Open Sundays 11–5.

**International Haircutters** (86th St. at Columbus Ave., tel. 212/769–2792, and 66th St. and Columbus Ave., tel. 212/877–3300) offers haircuts for men, women, and kids. Open Sundays 11–5 (at 86th St.) or noon–5 (at 66th St.).

**Larry Mathews Beauty Salon** (536 Madison Ave. at 54th St., tel. 212/246–6100) does hair cuts, perms and coloring, manicures, pedicures, waxing, and facials. Open Sundays 9–5.

**Mark and Albert** (147 W. 72nd St., tel. 212/787–3023) features unisex and children's cuts, as well as manicures and pedicures. Open Sundays 11:30–5.

**Mr. Edwards Cuts-Are-Here** (1400A 2nd Ave. between 72nd and 73rd St., tel. 212/535–8999) takes care of hair and nails. Open Sundays 10–6.

*For Kids* **Glemby Hair Salon at Macy's** (34th St. at 6th Ave., tel. 212/695–4624) also welcomes adults, but the Sunday cutters are specially trained to handle kids, and they hand out little toys to amuse small fry. Open Sundays 10–5.

**Shooting Star at F.A.O. Schwarz** (767 5th Ave. at 58th St., tel. 212/644–9400) has been masterfully cutting children's hair for generations. Open Sundays noon–5.

**Currency Exchange** **Chequepoint USA** (551 Madison Ave. at 55th St., tel. 212/980–6443) is open Sundays 10–6.

**Delivery** **Jiminy Split Delivery Services** (147 W. 46th St., tel. 212/354–7373) hand-delivers packages anywhere within New York City and the continental United States. Rates include messengers' travel fare (by plane or train), plus delivery expense. Sunday deliveries must be arranged in advance.

**Dry Cleaner** Same-day service you will not find, but you can pick up or drop off your dry cleaning anytime at the automated **Mr. Dry Clean** (92 8th Ave. near 14th St., tel. 212/627–5980). The service takes 24 hours. The machine that logs in and returns your clothes is activated by a credit card.

**Eyeglasses** Repairs can be handled and new eyeglasses made—within the hour in many cases—at the following:

**Cohen's Fashion Optical** (2163A Broadway at 76th St., tel. 212/769–1410; 767 Lexington Ave. at 59th St., tel. 212/751–6652; 117 Orchard St. at Delancey St., tel. 212/674–1986; and 5 Greenwich Ave. at 6th Ave., tel. 212/645–1395), open Sundays noon–5.

**Optical Exchange/New York Soft Lens Center** (373 5th Ave. at 35th St., tel. 212/689–9000), is open Sundays 11–5.

**Sol Moscot, Inc.** (118 Orchard St. at Delancey St., tel. 212/477–3796) is open Sundays 9–5:15.

**Triangle Optical** (95 Delancey St. at Ludlow St., tel. 212/674–3748) is open Sundays 9–5.

**Florists** Korean markets all over the city sell some beautiful flowers and are generally open on Sundays. For full service, usually including delivery, the following will be helpful:

**Anthony & Diane** (314 W. 57th St., tel. 212/581–0304), open Sundays 9–6.

**Danos Floral** (236 E. 86th St., tel. 212/472–2440), open Sundays 9–5.

**Murray Hill Greenery** (557 3rd Ave. at 37th St., tel. 212/679–7243), open Sundays 9–7.

**Primrose Flower Shop** (1225 3rd Ave. at 70th St., tel. 212/744–4595), open Sundays 10–6.

**Rialto** (707 Lexington Ave. at 57th St., tel. 212/688–3234), open 24 hours.

**Simpson & Co.** (1318 2nd Ave., between 69th and 70th Sts., tel. 212/772–6670), open Sundays 10–6.

**Tony's Greenery** (511 3rd Ave. at 34th St., tel. 212/689–9600, and 1200 3rd Ave. at 70th St., tel. 212/439–0040), open Sundays 8–6.

**Windsor Florist** (1118 Lexington Ave. at 78th St., tel. 212/734–4540, and 1382 2nd Ave. at 71st St., tel. 212/734–4521), open Sundays 9–6.

**Housekeepers** **McMaid** (127 E. 59th St., tel. 212/371–5555) can provide bonded help on Sunday if you arrange on Friday or Saturday.

**Limousine Services** **Tel Aviv** (343 E. 21st St., tel. 212/505–0555).

**Carey Limousine** (62–07 Woodside Ave., Woodside, Queens, tel. 212/599–1122).

**Surrey Limousine Service** (41 Crescent St., Long Island City, Queens, tel. 718/937–5700).

**Locksmiths** **Night and Day Locksmith** (1335 Lexington Ave., tel. 212/722–1017) can make all types of keys (including car keys) around the clock.

**Medical** **Dental Emergency Service** (tel. 212/679–3966, 212/679–4172 af-
*Dentists* ter 8 PM) can make referrals in Manhattan.

*Minor Medical* A number of immediate-care facilities and walk-in clinics spe-
*Emergencies* cialize in annoying but not life-threatening problems. Those associated with hospitals are usually entered through the emergency room; all have doctors, nurses, and facilities for X-rays and lab tests, including:

**B-Well Immediate Medical Care** (1483 York Ave. near 79th St., tel. 212/570–2200), open Sundays 10–8.

**Immediate Medical Care of Manhattan** (116 W. 72nd St., tel. 212/496–9620), open Sundays noon–5.

**New York Hospital's Urgent Care Center** (520 E. 70th St., tel. 212/746–0795; 212/746–5050 for the emergency room), open Sundays noon–8.

**Roosevelt Hospital's Walk-In Clinic** (58th St. at 9th Ave., tel. 212/523–6765), open Sundays 11–7.

*Pharmacies* A pharmacist is on duty in each of the following during operating hours. The cost of filling prescriptions can vary widely; you may want to call around.

**Apthorp Pharmacy** (2201 Broadway at 78th St., tel. 212/877–3480), open Sundays 11–8.

**Bigelow Pharmacy** (414 6th Ave., between 8th and 9th Sts., tel. 212/533–2700), open Sundays 8:30–5:30.

**Boghen Pharmacy** (1080 Park Ave. at 89th St., tel. 212/289–5866), open Sundays 10–5.

**Kaufman's Pharmacy** (Lexington Ave. at 50th St., tel. 212/755–2266), open 24 hours.

**Leroy Pharmacy** (342 E. 23rd St., tel. 212/505–1555), open Sundays 11:30–5:30.

**Plaza Pharmacy** (1657 2nd Ave. at 86th St., tel. 212/879–3878), open Sundays 10 AM–midnight.

**Village Apothecary** (346 Bleecker St. at 10th St., tel. 212/807–7756), open Sundays 10–8.

**Windsor Pharmacy** (1419 6th Ave. at 58th St., tel. 212/247–1538), open Sundays 9 AM–11:30 PM.
**Zitomer Pharmacy** (969 Madison Ave., between 75th and 76th Sts., tel. 212/737–5560), open Sundays 10–5.

*Physicians* **Doctors on Call** (tel. 212/737–2333), a 24-hour housecall service, can send doctors to Manhattan or the boroughs.

**Office Services** **Around the Clock Staffing** (235 W. 56th St., tel. 212/245–1750)
*Clerical Help* provides legal proofreaders, word processors, and other clerical help at all hours.
**Dial-A-Secretary** (521 5th Ave., tel. 212/348–9575, and 149 E. 81st St., tel. 212/348–8982) offers clerical help.
**World-Wide Business Centres** (575 Madison Ave., tel. 212/486–1333) also rents office space.

*Computer Stations* These organizations have Macintosh and IBM-compatible work stations for rent by the hour, along with a range of fancy printers.

**Key Word Process** (44 W. 17th St., tel. 212/206–8060), open Sundays noon–5.
**Userfriendly** (128 W. 72nd St., tel. 212/580–4433), open Sundays 10–6.

*Photocopying* Most copy shops have fax machines, and many also offer laser
*and Fax* typesetting, word processing, and other office services. The following are among those open Sundays.

**Chelsea Copy and Printing** (255 W. 23rd St., tel. 212/924–4953), open Sundays 9–5.
**Copy Cats** (968 Lexington Ave. at 70th St., tel. 212/734–6236; 1626 2nd Ave. at 84th St., tel. 212/734–6104), open Sundays noon–8.
**Copy 77 W.** (225 W. 77th St., tel. 212/595–9340), open Sundays 8 AM–11 PM.
**434 Copy Center** (434 6th Ave. near 10th St., tel. 212/674–9724), open Sundays noon–6.
**Kinko's the Copy Center** (24 E. 12th St., tel. 212/924–0802), open 24 hours.
**Mid-City Duplicating** (222 E. 45th St., tel. 212/687–6699), open Sundays 7–5.
**Village Copier** (20 E. 13th St., between Fifth Ave. and University Pl., tel. 212/924–3456), open 24 hours.

**Photographic** **Photographic Unlimited/Dial-A-Darkroom** (17 W. 17th St., tel.
**Services** 212/255–9678) leases a full range of photographic equipment
*Darkroom Rental* and darkroom facilities (for black-and-white and color film development) to amateurs and professionals alike. Open Sundays noon–7.

*Photo Processing,* Most one-hour film-processing outlets also offer passport pho-
*Passport Photos* tos. Pros say that these shops do color print film just as well as custom labs.

**Fromex Photo Systems** (535 3rd Ave. at 36th St., tel. 212/696–4220; 1247 3rd Ave. at 72nd St., tel. 212/288–8897; 1475 3rd Ave. at 83rd St., tel. 212/772–8686; 150 E. 86th St., tel. 212/369–4821; 2041 Broadway at 71st St., tel. 212/580–8181; 2151 Broadway at 76th St., tel. 212/496–2211), open Sundays, generally between noon and 5 PM.

*Photostats* **SMP** (26 E. 22nd St., tel. 212/254–2282), open Sundays 11–6.
**Stat Store** (148 5th Ave., between 19th and 20th Sts., tel. 212/929–0566), open Sundays noon–4.

| | |
|---|---|
| **Picture Framing** | **Chelsea Frames** (194 8th Ave., between 19th and 20th Sts., tel. 212/807–8957), open Sundays noon–5.<br>**Jinpra New York Picture Framing** (1208 Lexington Ave. at 82nd St., tel. 212/988–3903), open Sundays noon–5.<br>**O.J. Art Gallery** (933 Madison Ave. at 74th St., tel. 212/517–2790), open Sundays 11–6. |
| **Post Office** | The main post office (421 8th Ave., between 31st and 33rd Sts., tel. 212/967–8585) provides a full range of postal services 24 hours every day. Stamp vending machines at Grand Central Terminal (450 Lexington Ave., tel. 212/826–4628) never close. |
| **Tailor** | **Rupen's** (17 E. 37th St., tel. 212/685–9113), open Sundays 10–2. |
| **Typing** | **All-Language Services** (545 5th Ave., tel. 212/986–1688) is open around the clock to handle manuscripts in any of 59 languages. |
| **Veterinarians** | **Animal Medical Center** (510 E. 62nd St., tel. 212/838–8100) is a nonprofit clinic open 24 hours; no appointment is necessary. |

## Emergencies, Complaints, and Problems

Dial **911** for police, fire, or ambulance in an emergency (tel. 800/342–4537 for deaf callers). To reach the nearest **police precinct,** call 212/374–5000).

| | |
|---|---|
| **Complaints** | **Better Business Bureau** (tel. 212/533–6200).<br>**Taxi complaints** (tel. 212/382–9301). Be sure to take the driver's name and medallion number.<br>**Sex crimes reports** (tel. 212/267–7273).<br>**Crime victims hotline** (tel. 212/577–7777). |
| **Lost and Found** | **Amtrak** (tel. 212/560–7388 for Penn Station, 212/560–7534 for Grand Central Terminal).<br>**City buses** (tel. 718/625–6200).<br>**Long Island Railroad** (tel. 212/990–8384).<br>**Metro-North** (tel. 212/340–2555).<br>**New Jersey Transit** (tel. 212/560–7388 in New York, 201/642–7518 in Newark, and 201/714–2739 in Hoboken).<br>**PATH trains** (tel. 212/432–1272 or 201/963–2677).<br>**Subways** (tel. 718/625–6200).<br>**Taxi and Limousine Commission** (tel. 212/869–4513). |

# 2    Where to Eat

Given the sheer number of New York restaurants—some 16,000 in all—it would be fair to say that eating is New York's favorite leisure activity. On Sundays this bustling dining scene is a little mellower, a little more relaxed than it is on Saturday, which is the busiest day of the restaurant's week. There's nothing more pleasant than enjoying the sunshine over food or drinks at one of the sidewalk cafés that sprout on the avenues in fair weather. Hundreds of places, particularly in residential neighborhoods, offer your standard brunch—eggs many styles, salads, burgers, and pastas—while others accent such fare with the exotic flavors of various ethnic and regional cuisines. Dinner can be anything from a formal gourmet feast to a homey, comforting supper.

Hotel dining rooms, which used to offer dreary food to captive audiences, currently offer innovative cuisine in splendid, sparkling surroundings. Food is prepared with panache and served on real silver, at tables covered with linens so crisp and snowy you can practically crease them. Hotels also stage the city's most lavish brunches: extravagant all-you-can eat-buffets with dozens of salads, pastas, casseroles, hot vegetables, carved meats, and desserts. Like many brunches in independent restaurants, these meals are served prix fixe, and the price of the meal includes at least one drink.

Live music is another singular Sunday pleasure at New York restaurants. Sometimes, the music is the star; elsewhere it simply creates a festive mood. Usually, there's no extra charge.

The restaurants below were chosen to give a representative picture of the city's offerings—the old and the new, the glitzy and the rustic, the cavernous and the cozily charming. Because restaurants frequently change chefs, dishes, and even decor, specifics are mentioned merely to suggest the house style. In general, the dress policy is casual everywhere on Sundays; if men are required to wear a jacket and tie, however, it is noted in the entry.

Restaurants are listed by neighborhood corresponding to the maps in the back of this book. The neighborhoods are:

Lower Manhattan
TriBeCa
SoHo
Little Italy and Chinatown
Lower East Side
East Village and NoHo
West Village
Gramercy Park and Union Square
Midtown East (from 24th to 49th streets east of Fifth Avenue)
Midtown West (from 24th to 49th streets west of Fifth Avenue)
the East 50s
the West 50s
the East 60s
The Upper East Side
Yorkville (all of the East 80s and 90s except Fifth and Madison avenues)
Lincoln Center
the Upper West Side

the Far Upper West Side (above 96th Street)
Harlem
the Bronx
Brooklyn
Queens
Staten Island

**Reservations**  Often small spots with low prices don't accept reservations. If you hate standing in line, go early or late. Keep in mind, too, that many restaurants that don't accept bookings for two may do so for larger parties. When reservations are advised, a day in advance usually suffices, but for major holidays, popular restaurants may begin taking names weeks ahead of time.

New York City law now stipulates that restaurants with more than 50 seats set aside nonsmoking sections. Make your preference known when you reserve.

**Dining Hours**  The following entries show Sunday hours only; if you're looking for a restaurant on Saturday, be aware that some formal spots that serve brunch and dinner on Sundays do not open until dinnertime on Saturdays, so you may want to call ahead. Most restaurants don't serve breakfast. Those that do begin at 7 or 7:30 AM and offer brunch from 11AM or noon until 3 or 4PM; a few serve a bit earlier or later. Dinner hours on Sunday are customarily from 6 to 10 or 11 PM. Usually there is a gap of an hour or two, during which the kitchen preps for dinner. If you're hungry during this awkward period, have tea, stop at a café for a pastry and a snack, or look around for a casual eatery that serves continuously.

**Prices**  The price categories outlined below are based on dinner prices; lunch and brunch prices are often ⅓ to ½ of those at dinner, and prix-fixe menus offer an even better value, bringing the price of an expensive restaurant into the moderate range or lower. Prix fixe menu availability is noted in the italicized service information following the restaurant description. Note that in many restaurants, waiters recite the day's specials without quoting prices. Don't let them get away with it! If more diners are firmer on this point, the practice may end.

| Category | Dinner entrée | Dinner cost* |
|---|---|---|
| Very Expensive | $18 and over | over $50 |
| Expensive | $14–$21 | $35–$50 |
| Moderate | $10–$18 | $26–$35 |
| Inexpensive | $5–$10 | $25 and under |

*\* per person, including one drink and tip*

The following credit card abbreviations are used: AE, American Express; DC, Diners Club; MC Master Card; V, Visa.

Symbols at the end of an entry signify: CH: Good for children; L: Serves after 11 PM; MU: Live music; O: Outdoor dining; VU: Great view. Look at the end of individual restaurant reviews for additional information.

# Restaurants

## Lower Manhattan

The South Street Seaport, chock-full of charming restaurants that serve adequate food at slightly elevated prices, really gets hopping on Sunday, and on the other side of the island the World Financial Center is opening more and more restaurants, some with stunning sunset views of the Hudson. Despite the Sunday air of quiet elsewhere in the neighborhood, several notable restaurants keep their doors open for business.

**American/International**

**Bridge Café.** The Seaport's only wood-frame building (ca. 1801) charms with its pressed-tin ceiling, white wood-slat walls, and listing linoleum floor. Basic brunch fare is spiced with dishes such as warm scallop salad with citrus vinaigrette; dinners are similarly lively. The eponymous Brooklyn Bridge is practically overhead. *279 Water St. at Dover St., tel. 212/227–3344. Reservations advised. AE, DC, MC, V. Sun. brunch, dinner. Moderate. L*

**Greenhouse Restaurant & Wine Bar.** The breakfast buffet that starts the day at this airy atrium-restaurant full of ficus trees is only a warm-up for the lavish brunch later on, complete with sundae bar and piano-violin duo. *Vista International Hotel, 3 World Trade Center, tel. 212/938–9100. Reservations advised. AE, DC, MC, V. Sun. breakfast (prix fixe), brunch (prix fixe), dinner. Moderate. CH, L, MU*

**Windows on the World.** Like a cruise ship in the sky, this 107th-floor complex of dining rooms is one of New York's grandest settings for Sunday meals. In *The Restaurant*, creamy rose hues frame a 55-mile view with Manhattan rising like a mirage on the north and an eclectic mix of New Yorkers and out-of-town couples and families celebrate over the dazzling Grand Buffet (a mere $22.50). Less formal is the adjacent *Hors d'Oeuvrerie*, good for wild mushroom ravioli and dim sum at brunch and small-portion ethnic delicacies and jazz later on. Oenophiles praise the moderately priced 800-item wine list, and the City Lights Bar pours 112 brands of Scotch and 21 of gin. You can park free in the building. *1 World Trade Center, tel. 212/938–1111. Reservations required for meals. Jackets required; no denims. AE, DC, MC, V. The Restaurant noon–7:30, Hors d'Oeuvrerie brunch noon–3 and tidbits with music 4–9. Moderate. MU, VU*

**American/Casual**

**Ham Heaven.** Sugar-cured Virginia hams star in soups, sandwiches, and omelets at this skylit establishment in an old warehouse. *49 Warren St. between W. Broadway and Church St., tel. 212/513–7224. No reservations. AE. Sun. breakfast, lunch. Inexpensive.*

**Hamburger Harry's.** Mesquite-grilled burgers are served with 17 toppings. *157 Chambers St. near W. Broadway, tel. 212/267–4446. No reservations. AE, DC, MC, V. Sun. lunch, dinner. Inexpensive. CH*

**Italian**

**Ecco.** When this restaurant opened in 1984, limousines gridlocked outside while waiters and well-heeled patrons gridlocked within. It's quieter now, but the old mahogany cabinetry, black-and-white tile floor, and bar bristling with moldings are unchanged, as are the great antipasto buffet, exquisite Napoleons, and terrific veal chops. *124 Chambers St.,* *between W. Broadway and Church St., tel. 212/227–7074. Reservations advised. AE. Sun. dinner (closed Sun. July and Aug.). Very Expensive.*

**Gianni's.** This is the Seaport's spot for people-watching, pasta, and garlic bread with Gorgonzola pesto. *15 Fulton St. at South St. Seaport, tel. 212/608–7300. Reservations not necessary. AE, DC, MC, V. Sun. lunch, dinner. Expensive. L, O*

**Seafood** **Sloppy Louie's.** This Seaport institution has been renovated to comfortable tidiness—and, some say, stripped of the sloppiness that made it wonderful. But its fresh fish, plainly prepared, makes it a viable low-cholesterol option in a world that generally equates brunch with butter and eggs. *92 South St., between Fulton and John Sts., tel. 212/509–9694. Reservations advised. AE, DC, MC, V. Sun. lunch, dinner. Expensive.*

## TriBeCa

All over this area of old warehouses and new galleries, restaurants are sprouting up—many with specific themes or striking decor, and most with modest prices. As more establishments continue to move in, however, the prices may go up. Easy on-street parking is a plus.

**American/ International** **Odeon.** Black banquettes, a terrazzo floor, dark paneling, racks of newspapers, a neon-rimmed clock, and mismatched chairs decorate this art deco former cafeteria. The ambitious kitchen does Sunday proud, with such dishes as smoked salmon and airy buttermilk pancakes at brunch, steak frites and poached skate with vinegar butter and Savoy cabbage at dinner. *145 W. Broadway, between Thomas and Duane Sts., tel. 212/233–0507. Reservations advised. AE, DC, MC, V. Sun. brunch, dinner, supper. Moderate. L*

**American/Casual** **Smoke Stacks Lightnin'.** This dim, antique bistro has roomy tables, a spirited kitchen, and video games that kids adore. *380 Canal St. at W. Broadway, tel. 212/226–0485. Reservations advised. AE, DC, MC, V. Sun. brunch (prix fixe), dinner. Moderate. CH, L*

**American Regional** **Hows Bayou Café.** A neon sign on the ceiling at this funky spot glows over gumbo, chicken-fried steak, and corned beef and grits. Every guest takes home a string of Mardi Gras beads. *355 Greenwich St. at Harrison St., tel. 212/925–5405. No reservations or credit cards. Sun. brunch (prix fixe), dinner. Inexpensive. CH, L*

**French/Continental** **Capsouto Frères.** Though the crowd is chic, the tone is mellow and congenial in this tall-windowed, lofty-ceilinged, brick-walled landmark warehouse. Brunches feature dishes such as poached salmon with herb vinaigrette or cold sliced chicken with oriental sauce, and there's a good selection of single-malt Scotches. *451 Washington St. at Watts St., tel. 212/966–4900. Reservations advised. AE, DC, MC, V. Sun. brunch, lunch, dinner. Expensive. L*

## SoHo

Sunday is SoHo's big day, and every restaurant does a booming business. Restaurants on West Broadway, the main drag, tend to serve adequate food at prices that reflect their prime location. Soaring spaces, architectural presence, and late hours are the rule, and many ethnic cuisines are represented.

**American/International**

**Canal Bar.** This simply decorated spot, the darling of *le tout New York*, serves food that's equally simple but sophisticated enough to please the palates of the glitterati. Owner Brian McNally also had a hand in Café Luxembourg (*see* Lincoln Center, below). *511 Greenwich St. at the corner of Spring St., tel. 212/334–5150. Reservations required. AE, DC, MC, V. Sun. dinner (closed Sun. Aug.). Expensive. L*

**Greene Street Café.** In this lofty brick-walled space full of palm and wicker, jazz musicians entertain all day while the kitchen turns out elaborate fare, such as salmon with three caviars and poached eggs in puff pastry. *101 Greene St., between Prince and Spring Sts., tel. 212/925–2415. Reservations advised. AE, DC, MC, V. Sun. brunch, early dinner. Expensive. MU*

**Berry's.** Thick, extraordinary brioche French toast stars amid dark wood, ornate mirrors, and patterned wallpaper in this longtime favorite. *180 Spring St. at Thompson St., tel. 212/226–4394. Reservations advised. AE, DC, MC, V. Sun. brunch, dinner. Moderate.*

**Cupping Room Café.** Exposed brick, a pot-bellied stove, and an antique bar set the scene in this mellow, skylit spot. Whole-wheat waffles and date-nut bread make breakfasts grand. Go early. *359 W. Broadway, between Broome and Grand Sts., tel. 212/925–2898. No reservations. AE, DC, MC, V. Sun. breakfast, brunch, tea, dinner. Moderate. L*

**Madeline's Restaurant and Pâtisserie.** Miniature muffins at breakfast, creative salads and candlelight later on, a cholesterol-free selection, and classical music on tape make this a good bet any time. *177 Prince St., between Sullivan and Thompson Sts., tel. 212/477–2788. Reservations advised. AE. Sun. breakfast (prix fixe), brunch, dinner. Moderate.*

**SoHo Kitchen.** The city's biggest cruvinet serves 96 different wines by the glass—and 14 champagnes—at this lofty-ceilinged brick-walled charmer next to the Greene Street Café. Pastas and pizza star on the menu. *103 Greene St., between Prince and Spring Sts., tel. 212/925–1866. No reservations. AE, DC, MC, V. Sun. lunch, dinner. Moderate.*

**American/Casual**

**Aggie's.** This funky counterculture coffee shop hops all day, thanks to reasonable prices for sprightly soups and sandwiches. *146 W. Houston St. at MacDougal St., tel. 212/673–8994. No credit cards. Sun. breakfast, lunch. Inexpensive.*

**Ear Inn.** At this artsy hangout, homemade fare has an international accent and the jukebox plays selections from reggae to New Wave. *326 Spring St., between Washington and Greenwich Sts., tel. 212/226–9060. No reservations. AE, DC. Sun. brunch, dinner. Inexpensive. L*

**5 & 10 No Exaggeration.** At this quirky spot, big band music animates Sunday brunches and old silent movies flicker in the background. *77 Greene St., between Spring and Broome Sts., tel. 212/925–7414. Reservations necessary. AE, DC, MC, V. Sun. brunch, dinner. Moderate. CH, MU*

**Jerry's.** The kitchen of this former truckers' hangout (now done up in red and lime-green) explores dishes such as chili-rubbed pork loin and fettuccine with Parmesan, shrimp, and sun-dried tomatoes—at surprisingly easy prices. *101 Prince St., between Greene and Mercer Sts., tel. 212/966–9464. Reservations accepted. AE. Sun. brunch. Moderate.*

**Manhattan Brewing Company.** The beer is made on the

premises—a different brew for each season—and you can dance to oldies and nosh on brisket sandwiches, oysters on the half shell, sweet potato fries, and other homey fare. *40–42 Thompson St., between Sullivan St. and W. Broadway, tel. 212/219–9250. Reservations accepted. AE, DC, MC, V. Sun. lunch, dinner. Inexpensive. L*

**Moondance Diner.** Pin-spot lighting, eclectic taped music, and sparkly vinyl banquettes and counter stools here have true SoHo panache. On Sundays the joint's abuzz, and every seat in the house is taken by diners happily devouring frittatas, eggs rancheros, and fresh fruit pancakes. *80 6th Ave., between Canal and Grand Sts., tel. 212/226–1191. No reservations or credit cards. Sun. breakfast, lunch, dinner. Inexpensive. CH, L*

**Spring Street Natural Restaurant.** Hanging plants, huge windows, and ceiling fans make this a pleasant spot for artists, students, hippies, and Yuppies to while away a Sunday. Join them for garlic-ginger stir-fried vegetables or roast turkey-Jarlsberg sandwiches at lunch or broiled Pacific salmon with tomatoes and basil-lemon butter at dinner. *62 Spring St. at Lafayette St., tel. 212/966–0290. No reservations. AE, DC, MC, V. Sun. brunch, dinner. Inexpensive. CH, L*

**Tennessee Mountain.** Barbecues and thick fried onion rings headline at this skylit, down-home spot. *143 Spring St. at Wooster St., tel. 212/431–3993. Reservations advised. AE, DC, MC, V. Sun. lunch, dinner. Inexpensive.*

**Eastern European**   **Triplet's Roumanian.** This dressed-up version of Sammy's Roumanian (*see* Lower East Side, below) is a rollicking place for chopped liver, potato pancakes, and chops in mammoth portions. A belly dancer, singing waiters and waitresses, and the odd magician keep things wild and crazy. *11–17 Grand St. at 6th Ave., tel. 212/925–9303. Reservations required. AE, DC, MC, V. Sun. dinner. Expensive. CH, MU*

**Ethiopian**   **Abyssinia.** Diners sit on squat three-legged stools and tear off bits of pancakelike bread called *injera* to scoop up hot meat-puree stews, mild or spicy, from a communal platter. *Doro wat* (spicy chicken) and *azefa wot* (lentil puree) test adventurous palates. *35 Grand St. at Thompson St., tel. 212/226–5959. No reservations. AE. Sun. brunch, dinner. Inexpensive. L*

**French**   **Raoul's.** This chic storefront bistro serves satisfying country French dishes—steak au poivre, sweetbreads, fresh fish with light sauces—in a tin-ceilinged barroom, a back dining room, and a plant-filled conservatory out beyond the kitchen. *180 Prince St. near Sullivan St., tel. 212/966–3518. Reservations required. AE, DC, MC, V. Sun. dinner. Very Expensive. L*

**Italian**   **I Tre Merli.** This soaring brick-walled spot pairs some 36 wines, served by the glass, and food with a Genovese accent. *463 W. Broadway, between Houston and Prince Sts., tel. 212/254–8699. Reservations required. AE, DC, MC, V. Sun. lunch, dinner. Expensive. L*

**Mezzogiorno.** At this airy, art-filled trattoria, tall windows let the sun shine on thin-crust pizzas, risotto pancakes, Parmesan-topped polenta, and more. Italian rock music fits with the general Euro-Chic mood. *195 Spring St. at Sullivan St., tel. 212/*

---

**Symbols at the end of an entry signify:** *CH: Good for children; L: Serves after 11 PM; MU: Live music; O: Outdoor dining; VU: Great view.*

*334–2112. Reservations advised. No credit cards. Sun. lunch, dinner. Moderate. L*

**Arturo's.** At this animated antique, the real star is pizza from the brick-lined, coal-fired oven; the savory blistered crust is first-rate. Nighttime jazz is a plus. *106 W. Houston St. at Thompson St., tel. 212/475–9828. No reservations. AE, MC, V. Sun. lunch, dinner. Inexpensive. CH, L, MU*

**Japanese**   **Omen.** Out-of-the-ordinary Japanese fare at this diminutive rustic includes traditional *omen*, a ginger-tangy noodle soup. *113 Thompson St., between Prince and Spring Sts., tel. 212/925–8923. Reservations advised. AE, DC. Sun. dinner. Moderate. L*

**Mexican**   **Cinco de Mayo.** Twenty-foot ceilings, skylights, and mariachi music set the scene for out-of-the-ordinary offerings, such as *budin de tortilla*, a pie of layered tortillas and tangy cheese. *349 W. Broadway, between Broome and Grand Sts., tel. 212/226–5255. Reservations advised. AE, DC, MC, V. Sun. lunch, dinner. Moderate. MU*

---

## Little Italy and Chinatown

Every year the once-thriving area of Little Italy shrinks just a bit as the population of neighboring Chinatown swells. Yet both retain their distinctive ethnic flavors, offering good eating almost across the board. In Chinatown, Sunday is especially busy for dim sum—assorted Chinese dumplings that in many restaurants are served from trolleys from early morning until mid- or late afternoon. If you don't want dim sum, stop in around 7 PM, when the pace is slower. Many Chinese restaurants serve special banquets at Chinese New Year (late January–early February), when Chinatown is packed to the rafters and bursting with firecrackers. Although you never know whether the restaurant that enraptured you on your last visit will repeat the performance, it's hard to get a really bad meal in Chinatown.

Note that many restaurants in these neighborhoods don't accept reservations or credit cards, and many have no liquor license; check before you go.

**Chinese**   **Mandarin Court Restaurant.** Sparkling and stylish with black tables and pastel walls, it's a terrific spot for dim sum. Try turnip cakes with Chinese sausage. *61 Mott St., between Canal and Bayard Sts., tel. 212/608–3838. No reservations. AE, DC, MC, V. Sun. dim sum, dinner. Expensive. L*

**Canton.** With its powder-blue tablecloths and blond wood walls, this Cantonese seafood specialist turns out consistently good food, reflecting owner-chef Larry Leong's interest in French and Italian cuisine. Go before 6 or after 9. *45 Division St., between Market St. and the Bowery, tel. 212/226–4441. Reservations advised. No credit cards. BYOB. Sun. lunch, dinner (closed 2 wks mid-July–mid-Aug.). Moderate.*

**Peking Duck House.** Crisp-skinned Peking duck, which must be ordered ahead elsewhere, is served every day in these notably unprepossessing digs. *22 Mott St. near Bayard St., tel. 212/227–1810. Reservations advised. AE, DC. Sun. lunch, dinner. Moderate.*

**20 Mott Street Restaurant.** Crowds jam this bright multitiered restaurant to enjoy dim sum treats, such as golden fried crab claws or rice-flour dumplings with pork. The Cantonese menu offered later on is encyclopedic. *20 Mott St., between the Bowery and Pell St., tel. 212/964–0380. Reservations advised. AE, MC, V. Sun. dim sum, dinner. Moderate. CH, L*

**Bo Ky.** Half Thai, half *teo-chew* (indigenous to China's Quangdong province), this absolutely plain storefront restaurant offers fiery main-course soups unique to Chinatown. *80 Bayard St., between Mott and Baxter Sts., tel. 212/406–2292. No reservations or credit cards. Sun. breakfast through dinner. Inexpensive.*

**Nice Restaurant.** Well-turned-out in the best Hong Kong style, Nice does well with dim sum and with unusual dishes, such as soy-flavored squab, salt-baked chicken, and roast suckling pig. *35 E. Broadway, between Catherine and Market Sts., tel. 212/406–9776. Reservations advised. AE. Sun. dim sum, dinner. Inexpensive.*

**Phoenix Garden.** The subtleties of the cuisine in this unbeautiful Cantonese favorite in a grimy arcade off the Bowery render the nondecor a nonissue. Enjoy tasty roast squab three ways, salt-roasted chicken, or pepper-and-salt shrimp and end with the milky almond gelatin. *46 Bowery, in the arcade north of Elizabeth St., tel. 212/962–8934. No reservations or credit cards. Sun. lunch, dinner. Inexpensive. CH*

**Wo Hop.** These two locations are New York's source for *congee*, a soupy rice puree chunky with beef, chicken, duck, pork, or seafood. *15 Mott St., between Bowery and Park Row, tel. 212/766–9160, Sun. lunch, dinner; reservations accepted. 17 Mott St., tel. 212/962–8617; no reservations. No credit cards at either. Inexpensive. L*

**Italian** **Benito's II.** One of the few restaurants in Little Italy to accept reservations, this charmer, with exposed brick walls, tile murals, a dark wood ceiling, and small tables neatly covered in white linen, offers substantial fare that's pungently laced with garlic. A guitarist often entertains. *163 Mulberry St., between Broome and Grand Sts., tel. 212/226–9012. Reservations advised. No credit cards. Sun. lunch, dinner. Moderate. MU*

**Grotta Azzurra.** Everyone waits patiently during prime supper hours for the pleasure of descending into the blue grotto and, amid murals and celebrity photos, sampling Neapolitan favorites, such as *zuppa di pesce* (seafood stew) and lobster fra diavolo. *387 Broome St. at Mulberry St., tel. 212/925–8775. No reservations or credit cards. Sun. lunch, dinner (closed Sun. July). Moderate. L*

**Puglia.** This vintage red-sauce specialist is rowdy and crowded; the house entertainer may get guests to sing along, and waiters may dance in the aisles—you never know what to expect. Raw red wine and hefty portions of lasagna, spaghetti, and veal can really hit the spot. *189 Hester St. at Mulberry St., tel. 212/966–6006. No reservations or credit cards. Sun. lunch, dinner (closed Sun. July). Inexpensive. L, MU*

**Vincent's Clam Bar.** Seafood and pasta are doused with the house's famous hot sauce amid old wood beams and big arched windows. *119 Mott St. at Hester St., tel. 212/226–8133. No reservations or credit cards. Sun. lunch, dinner. Inexpensive. L*

---

**Symbols at the end of an entry signify:** *CH: Good for children; L: Serves after 11 PM; MU: Live music; O: Outdoor dining; VU: Great view.*

Vietnamese **Saigon Restaurant.** Barbecued pork balls, shredded pork rolls, and other fare perfumed with chili, coriander, garlic, and lemon grass make for good eating at this comfortable little cellar hideaway facing Columbus Park, behind the Criminal Courts building. *60 Mulberry St. near Bayard St., tel. 212/227–8825. Reservations for 5 or more. AE, DC, MC, V. Sun. lunch, dinner. Inexpensive.*

## Lower East Side

Deli fare and Eastern European cooking, the specialties of this area, are fun to combine with a Sunday shopping blitz of Orchard Street. Glamor you won't get, but the food makes up for it.

Chinese/Kosher **Bernstein-on-Essex.** Manhattan's only kosher-Chinese spot serves a great lean, peppery-smoky pastrami. *135 Essex St., between Delancey and Houston Sts., tel. 212/473–3900. Reservations not necessary. AE, DC, MC, V. Sun. breakfast, lunch, dinner. Moderate. CH, L*

Jewish Dairy **Ratner's Restaurant.** Potato pancakes or pirogen, gefilte fish and kreplach, baked egg barley with creamed mushrooms, borscht, matzo brei, and other Jewish dairy favorites star at this classic deli restaurant, one of the last of its type. The surroundings are no-nonsense, the cuisine so deeply satisfying that handsome brunch spots elsewhere seem prissy by comparison. *138 Delancey St., between Norfolk and Suffolk Sts., tel. 212/677–5588. Reservations not required. No credit cards. Sun. breakfast, lunch, dinner. Inexpensive. CH*

Deli **Katz's Deli.** The sign that exhorts passers-by to "send a salami to your boy in the Army" is a recent addition to this huge Jewish heartburnland founded in 1888. Though the meats are still cured on the premises, some say standards have fallen since the good old days. But crowds still line up, so waiting is always part of the scene, along with the old-hand waiters, the guard-dog doorman, and an aroma that alone will clog your arteries. *205 E. Houston St. at Ludlow St., tel. 212/254–2246. No reservations or credit cards. Sun. breakfast, lunch, dinner. Inexpensive. CH, L*

Eastern European **Sammy's Roumanian.** To call this Jewish steakhouse a "hole in the wall" suggests a charm that does not exist. It's simply a clamorous storefront whose chief distinction is the high decibel level of the entertainment and the gargantuan servings of steaks, chops, and traditional flanken, kreplach, and stuffed cabbage. As food critic Mimi Sheraton observed, the only people who don't go back to Sammy's are those who are tone-deaf to New York. *157 Chrystie St. near Delancey St., tel. 212/673–5526. Reservations advised. AE, DC, MC, V. Sun. dinner. Expensive. MU*

## East Village and NoHo

The adventurous can eat well relatively cheaply in this neighborhood, an old-time Ukrainian stronghold that later became a bastion of punk and is currently in the process of rapid gentrification. Odd and ethnic eateries still abound, however. Every New Yorker has his favorite on Indian Restaurant Row (6th Street between First and Second avenues), and the ubiquitous Polish or Ukrainian coffee shops cheerfully serve delicious meals for the price of entrées uptown.

**Afghan**  **Khyber Pass.** A brick-walled setting with plants and throw pillows set the cordial scene for kebabs, breads, and *aushaks* (lamb-and-scallion-stuffed dumplings). *34 St. Mark's Pl., between 2nd and 3rd Aves., tel. 212/473–0989. Reservations advised. AE. Sun. lunch, dinner. Moderate. L*

**American/Casual**  **NoHo Star.** This bright, festive spot with quirkily mismatched windows, an amazing terrazzo floor, and marble-inlaid mahogany tables regales the neighborhood with French toasts and Irish oatmeals (flavored with hazelnuts and raisins) at brunch, spaghettini with green fennel pesto or shrimp with panblackened string beans later on. *330 Lafayette St. at Bleecker St., tel. 212/925–0070. No reservations. AE, DC, MC, V. Sun. breakfast, brunch, lunch, dinner. Moderate. L*
**DoJo.** This woodsy Japanese-vegetarian restaurant and burger joint is young and amusing—a real scene. *24 St. Mark's Pl., between 2nd and 3rd Aves., tel. 212/674–9821. No reservations or credit cards. Sun. lunch, dinner. Inexpensive. L*
**McSorley's Old Ale House.** At what claims to be the city's oldest bar, old-timers mingle with students. Women were banned here from 1854 to 1970, but today they, too, can enjoy the house ale, pub grub, and the sawdust-on-the-floor atmosphere. *15 E. 7th St., between Second and Third Aves., tel. 212/473–9148. No reservations or credit cards. Sun. all day. Inexpensive. L*

**American Regional**  **Great Jones Street Café.** Small and funky, this is a must if you're in the mood for Cajun martinis (spiked with jalapeños), blackened redfish, a collegial crowd, and a resonant jukebox. *54 Great Jones St. west of the Bowery, tel. 212/674–9304. No reservations or credit cards. Sun. brunch, dinner. Inexpensive. L*

**Deli/Eastern**  **Second Avenue Kosher Delicatessen.** The decor is strictly formi-
**European**  ca, but some rate the place as New York's best deli, next to the Carnegie Deli (*see* West 50s, below), with great gefilte fish, chicken in a pot, and perhaps the city's best pastrami. Go early. *156 2nd Ave. at 10th St., tel. 212/677–0606. No reservations or credit cards. Sun. breakfast, lunch, dinner. Inexpensive. CH, L*
**Teresa's.** One of the area's simple Polish coffee shops, this nook serves great hot soups and potato pancakes that are light, not leaden. *103 1st Ave., between 6th and 7th Sts., tel. 212/228–0604. No reservations or credit cards. BYOB. Sun. breakfast, lunch, dinner. Inexpensive. L*

**Indian**  **Gaylord.** At this polished neighborhood newcomer, prices are higher than on Indian Restaurant Row, but the style is definitely more uptown: an arched ceiling twinkling with lights and a wall full of bright faux windows. The food is refined, particularly the tandooris, and Indian musicians weave a spell. *87 1st Ave. near 5th St., tel. 212/529–7990. Reservations advised. AE, MC, V. Sun. lunch, dinner. Moderate. L, MU*
**Mitali East.** The brunch buffet is a steal at this warm, low-ceilinged Indian standard. *334 E. 6th St., between First and Second Aves., tel. 212/533–2508. Reservations required. AE, MC, V. Sun. brunch (prix fixe), dinner. Inexpensive. L*

---

**Symbols at the end of an entry signify:** *CH: Good for children; L: Serves after 11 PM; MU: Live music; O: Outdoor dining; VU: Great view.*

| | |
|---|---|
| **Italian** *Northern* | **Cucina di Pesce.** Free antipasto and robust pastas and seafoods draw crowds to this rococo downstairs room full of antique mirrors and decorative trinkets. *87 E. 4th St., between Second and Third Aves., tel. 212/260–6800. No reservations or credit cards. Sun. dinner. Inexpensive. L* |
| *Southern* | **Siracusa.** An artsy neighborhood crowd enjoys homemade Sicilian pastas, such as bow ties with fresh artichokes and fava beans or spaghetti with fennel sausage, in this unassuming small dining room. A dozen Italian wines are poured by the glass, and the gelati are terrific. *65 4th Ave., between 9th and 10th St., tel. 212/254–1940. Reservations advised. AE. Sun. dinner (closed Sun. July–Aug.). Expensive.* |
| **Latin** | **Bayamo.** A million-dollar loft with cast-iron columns and a high-tech sound system glorify Cuban-Chinese peasant food like *ropa viejas* (Cuban pot roast). *704 Broadway, between 4th St. and Washington Pl., tel. 212/475–5151. Reservations advised. AE, DC, MC, V. Sun. lunch, dinner. Moderate. CH, L*<br>**11 Café.** This friendly little restaurant has a tropical decor and a tape deck that resonates with sambas. The menu features Venezuelan specialties—garlicky roast pork with hot sauce, shredded beef, goat stew, sautéed sweet plantains. The *arepas* (airy cornmeal fritters) are addictive. *170 2nd Ave. at 11th St., tel. 212/982–4924. No reservations. AE, DC. Sun. noon–midnight. Inexpensive. L* |
| **Vietnamese/ Cambodian** | **Indochine.** The exotic aura of this Asian-colonial dining room features Corinthian columns and walls painted with oversized palm fronds straight from Rousseau. The high noise level is easy to forgive when you tuck into the spring rolls; tamarind-spiked sweet-and-sour shrimp soup; or the minty, lemony, basil-pungent steamed shrimp. *430 Lafayette St., between Astor Pl. and 4th St., tel. 212/505–5111. Reservations required. AE, DC, MC, V. Sun. dinner. Expensive. L* |

## West Village

The West Village is thick with restaurants often tucked in among its town houses on the sometimes baffling maze of quiet little streets. Most are open on Sundays, and late hours are fairly common.

| | |
|---|---|
| **American/Casual** | **Sweet Basil.** Brunch at this brick-and-wood spot with a pressed-tin ceiling features not only top-rated burgers but some of the city's best jazz (there's a music charge from 10 PM to 2 AM). *7th Ave. S, between Grove and Bleecker Sts., tel. 212/242–1785. Reservations required. AE, DC, MC, V. Sun. brunch, dinner. Expensive. L, MU*<br>**Lion's Head.** Regulars remember an aspiring Jessica Lange as the second-prettiest on her shift when she waitressed at this well-known writer's hangout. Blueberry pancakes and thick French toast will start your day off right; stop in mid-afternoon for a draft Guinness and homemade potato chips. *59 Christopher St. near 7th Ave. S, tel. 212/929–0670. Reservations accepted for 3 or more. AE, DC, MC, V. Sun. brunch, dinner. Moderate. L*<br>**Chumley's.** This former speakeasy, still without a sign outside, is seductively cozy for burgers served hearthside. *86 Bedford St., between Barrow and Grove Sts., tel. 212/675–4449. No reservations. AE. Sun. late brunch, dinner. Inexpensive. L*<br>**White Horse Tavern.** A rickety favorite of Dylan Thomas, this |

genial saloon draws a delightfully varied New York crowd. *567 Hudson St. at 11th St., tel. 212/243-9260. No reservations or credit cards. Sun. brunch, dinner. Inexpensive. L, O*

**American/ International**

**Coach House.** For the past four decades, this former coach house has been a patrician, brick-and-paneled-wood dining room embellished with graceful bouquets and crowded with 19th-century paintings. The menu offers equally pleasing fare, including crackly corn sticks, rack of lamb, sparkling bouillabaisse, and midnight-dark black bean soup. Sunday dinner here is a New York tradition. *110 Waverly Pl., between Washington Sq. and 6th Ave., tel. 212/777-0303. Reservations required. AE, DC, MC, V. Sun. dinner. Very Expensive.*

**Gotham Bar & Grill.** On Sunday an elegant assembly of food lovers replaces the partying Saturday crowd in this pale-yellow postmodern dining room. The mood is relaxed, the better to enjoy inventively seasoned, creatively presented fare, such as squab salad, goat cheese ravioli, and sautéed black bass. *12 E. 12th St., between Fifth Ave. and University Pl., tel. 212/620-4020. Reservations required. AE, DC, MC, V. Sun. dinner. Very Expensive.*

**One If By Land, Two If By Sea.** Aaron Burr's former carriage house is perfect for romance, with its velvet settees, flowers, piano music, and fireside bar. But go for drinks—the pricey food falls short. *17 Barrow St., between 7th Ave. and W. 4th St., tel. 212/228-0822. Reservations advised. AE, MC, V. Sun. dinner (closed Sun. July and Aug.). Very Expensive.*

**Vanessa.** A romantic plum-walled establishment with fresh flowers, a turn-of-the-century aura, and a classical guitarist, this is a reasonably priced brunch bet, offering both a buffet and a prix-fixe menu. *289 Bleecker St. near 7th Ave. S, tel. 212/243-4225. Reservations advised. AE, DC, MC, V. Sun. brunch (prix fixe), dinner (prix fixe). Very Expensive. MU*

**Barrow Street Bistro.** Though the dining rooms here are austere, the California cuisine is sunny and bright. Dishes, such as winter vegetable soup chunky with parsnips or corn and potato pancakes with crème fraîche and three caviars, reflect the kitchen's sure hand and inventive approach. Even grills feature creative sauces. *48 Barrow St., between 7th Ave. S and Bedford St., tel. 212/691-6800. Reservations advised. AE, MC, V. Sun. dinner. Expensive.*

**Café Loup.** In its new location, this longtime Village favorite, with photographs and paintings on the walls, is keeping regulars happy with an American-bistro menu of dishes, such as cassoulet and roast duck with green peppercorn. At brunch, eggs supplement substantial luncheon fare like grilled fish and roast veal. *105 W. 13th St., between Sixth and Seventh Aves., tel. 212/255-4746. Reservations advised. AE, DC. Sun. brunch, dinner. Moderate.*

**Garvin's.** Here is a romantic spot for Sunday brunch, high-ceilinged and full of flowers and pink linen, with piano music. *19 Waverly Pl., between Broadway and 5th Ave., tel. 212/473-5261. Reservations advised. AE, DC, MC, V. Sun. brunch (prix fixe), dinner. Moderate. MU*

**Knickerbocker Bar & Grill.** Hung with vintage posters and Hirschfeld drawings, this large room offers some of the best

---

**Symbols at the end of an entry signify:** *CH: Good for children; L: Serves after 11 PM; MU: Live music; O: Outdoor dining; VU: Great view.*

jazz in the city from 9 PM onward. *33 University Pl. at 9th St., tel. 212/228–8490). Reservations required. AE, MC, V. Sun. brunch, dinner. Moderate. L, MU*

**La Bohème.** Restaurant design freethinker Sam Lopata's charming little faux-Provençal bistro has colander-shaded light bulbs, thin-crust pizzas, good steak-frîtes, and first-rate apple tart and roast chicken. *24 Minetta La. near 6th Ave., tel. 212/ 473–6447. Reservations advised. AE. Sun. brunch, lunch, dinner. Moderate.*

**Sazerac House Bar & Grill.** The mood is New Orleans revisited, with an old mahogany bar, vintage wood booths, Sazerac cocktails (a Pernod-zapped bourbon drink), and a menu full of Deep South dishes such as jambalaya. *533 Hudson St. at Charles St., tel. 212/989–0313. Reservations required. AE, DC, MC, V. Sun. brunch, dinner. Moderate. L*

**American Regional**

**Ye Waverly Inn.** Yankee pot roast, Southern fried chicken, and chicken pot pie recall Sunday dinners of 30 years ago in four dark-paneled, low-ceilinged rooms in a 180-year-old town house; two of these have working fireplaces. A guitarist entertains during brunch. *16 Bank St. at Waverly Pl., tel. 212/929–4377. AE, DC, MC, V. Sun. brunch, dinner. Moderate. MU, O*

**Cottonwood Café.** At this Tex-Mex eatery, every meal's a party, with mesquite-smoked ribs, terrific mashed potatoes, and live country and rock-and-roll music. *415 Bleecker St., between Bank and 11th Sts., tel. 212/924–6271. No reservations or credit cards. Sun. brunch, dinner. Inexpensive.*

**Gulf Coast.** A whimsical spirit is at work in this funky self-styled "Playground of the South," so don't be surprised to find a far-out drink menu that lists "jello shots"—cherry jello made with vodka. The Cajun-Creole-Southern menu is full of bread pudding, bourbon-sauced French toast, crawfish and tasso ham omelets, and grits and veal grillades. If you come for dinner, sit upstairs and watch the sunset over the Hudson. *489 West St. at 12th St., tel. 212/206–8790. Reservations advised. No credit cards. Sun. brunch, dinner. Inexpensive. CH, L, VU*

**Manhattan Chili Company.** A serious chili specialist, this restaurant features a backyard garden abloom with fuschias and impatiens. Children like the festooning balloons, and parents appreciate the booster seats. *302 Bleecker St., between 7th Ave. and Grove St., tel. 212/206–7163. Reservations essential for 5 or more. AE, MC, V. Sun. brunch, dinner. Inexpensive. CH, L, O*

**Pink Tea Cup.** In this simple pink café, hung with pictures of Martin Luther King and the Supremes, you can order soul foods such as pork chops, hash, and pigs feet; breakfast grits and biscuits available all day. *42 Grove St. near Bleecker St., tel. 212/807–6755. No reservations or credit cards. BYOB. Sun. all day. Inexpensive. L*

**Belgian**

**Café de Bruxelles.** Hearty French and Belgian dishes—juicy grilled *boudin blanc,* tangy *choucroute de Breugel,* and *waterzooi* fish stew—are the specialties at this lace-curtained brasserie with a zinc-topped bar. The french fries are crisply terrific, and distinctive Belgian beer is available. *118 Greenwich Ave. at 13th St., tel. 212/206–1830. Reservations advised. AE, DC, MC, V. Sun. brunch, dinner (closed 2 weeks in Aug.). Moderate.*

**Cuban**

**Sabor.** At this narrow, tiny restaurant, the fish is fresh, the green sauce hot, and the red sauce hotter; beef dishes, such as *ropa vieja* (shredded pot roast), are aromatic with spices, as good Cuban cooking should be. Service is matter-of-fact. *20 Cornelia St., between W. 4th and Bleecker Sts., tel. 212/243–9579. Reservations advised. AE, MC, V. Sun. dinner. Moderate.*

**French**  **La Tulipe.** This sophisticated little restaurant in a handsome brick town house on a tree-lined street is graced with plum walls; soft lighting; beautiful flowers; and delicate, handsomely presented French fare. The menu changes seasonally; the tiny soft-shell crabs of spring and early summer are superb, as is the brittle-crisp apple tarte. Service ranges from leisurely to lax. *104 W. 13th St., between Sixth and Seventh Aves., tel. 212/691–8860. Reservations required. AE, DC, MC, V. Sun. dinner (prix fixe; closed late Aug.–early Sept.). Very Expensive.*

**Black Sheep.** A country French spot with exposed brick walls and rustic wood tables, this restaurant serves hearty dinners, such as leg of lamb Provençale, but it really shines at brunch. Devise your own omelet, order smoked trout, or sample Amaretto French toast made with nutty whole wheat bread. *344 W. 11th St. at Washington St., tel. 212/ 242–1010. Reservations advised. AE, DC, MC, V (cash only at brunch). Sun. brunch, dinner. Expensive.*

**La Gauloise.** This civilized bistro serves homey roast chicken, rabbit, and rösti to a cadre of regulars. *502 6th Ave., between 12th and 13th Sts., tel. 212/691–1363. Reservations advised. AE, DC, MC, V. Sun. brunch (closed 3 weeks in summer). Expensive.*

**Provence.** Here you'll find lusty, spirited fare, such as *pissaladière* (Provençal pizza), *bourride* (a garlicky fish stew), and *morue St. Tropez* (salt cod sautéed with anchovies, olives, garlic, and tomato). With its yellow walls and bouquets of dried flowers, the restaurant is as pleasant in winter as in summer, when tables are set up in the stone-fountained back garden. *38 MacDougal St. at Prince St., tel. 212/475–7500. Reservations required. AE. Sun. lunch, dinner. Expensive. O*

**Florent.** This unpretentious diner in the meat district offers soul-warming bistro fare around the clock: onion soup gratinée and eggs with kippers or smoked salmon for breakfast; charcuteries, grilled fish, and pot au feu for dinner. It's always busy. *69 Gansevoort St., between Greenwich and Washington Sts., tel. 212/989–5779. Dinner reservations required. No credit cards. Open 24 hrs. Moderate. CH, L*

**Italian**  **Da Silvano.** This old-time Tuscan standby with a sidewalk café ranks among New York's fair-weather pleasures for its setting and its imaginative, if erratic, kitchen. *260 6th Ave., between Houston and Bleecker Sts., tel. 212/982–2343. Reservations required. AE. Sun. dinner. Very Expensive. O*

**Cent'Anni.** This bright, streamlined trattoria with close-together tables has a delicious menu of Florentine dishes such as capelliri with lobster and clams. *50 Carmine St., between Bleecker and Bedford Sts., tel. 212/989–9494. Reservations required. AE. Sun. dinner (closed 3 wks in July). Expensive.*

**Il Cantinori.** It's hard to go wrong in this wonderful dining room with dark beams and white stucco walls, and on occasion—

---

**Symbols at the end of an entry signify:** *CH: Good for children; L: Serves after 11 PM; MU: Live music; O: Outdoor dining; VU: Great view.*

if grilled wild mushrooms are available, for instance—the fare can be sublime. The Tuscan cuisine emphasizes simple combinations of the freshest possible ingredients. The helpful and professional service staff is just one more reason why many rate the establishment New York's best Italian restaurant. *32 E. 10th St., between University Pl. and Broadway, tel. 212/673 –6044. Reservations advised. AE, DC, MC, V. Sun. dinner (closed Sun. July and Aug.). Expensive.*

**Zinno.** Peach-painted brick walls, fresh flowers, flattering lighting, and expertly executed pastas and grills make this spot a pleasure. Terrific jazz is frosting on the cake. *126 W. 13th St., between Sixth and Seventh Aves., tel. 212/924–5182. Reservations required. AE, DC, MC, V. Sun. dinner (closed Sun. July and Aug.). Expensive. MU*

**Cucina Stagionale.** Is terrific food in intimate surroundings at miniscule prices worth waiting in line for? Fans of this "seasonal kitchen" say yes. Go early to avoid the rush for inspired pleasures such as mussels with Pernod or sun-dried tomato and mozzarella salad. *275 Bleecker St., between 6th and 7th Aves., tel. 212/924–2707. No reservations or credit cards. BYOB. Sun. lunch, dinner. Inexpensive.*

**John's of Bleecker Street.** It's hard to find better pizza than you get at this rough-around-the-edges, half-century-old Villager; thin crusts are charred to perfection in the coal-fired brick oven. *278 Bleecker St., between 6th and 7th Aves., tel. 212/243– 1680. No reservations or credit cards. Sun. lunch, dinner. Inexpensive. CH, L, O*

**Mexican**  **Benny's Burritos.** The style at this funky-60s corner café is Cal-Mex: Everything is made without lard, preservatives, microwaves, or MSG. The vast tortillas come in whole wheat and blue corn versions, and tasty rice pudding and flavored flans are made on the premises. Brunch stars salsa fresca omelets, green egg frittatas, and chorizo and scrambled egg tacos. *113 Greenwich Ave. at Jane St., tel. 212/633–9210. No reservations or credit cards. Sun. brunch (prix fixe), dinner. Inexpensive. CH, L*

**Tortilla Flats.** Regulars crowd into this funky café on Sundays for huevos rancheros, soda biscuits, and grits. *767 Washington St. at 12th St., tel. 212/243–1053. No reservations or credit cards. Sun. brunch, dinner (closed Sun. summer). Inexpensive. L*

**Russian**  **Glasnost.** This tiny corner spot is a good bet for a quick bite of blintzes or blini among exuberant folk paintings. *70 Greenwich Ave. near 11th St., tel. 212/691–0998. No reservations or credit cards. Sun. lunch, dinner. Inexpensive. CH*

**Seafood**  **John Clancy's.** Stylish and calm, this elegant town house restaurant was the first in the city to grill fish over mesquite and still does it superbly. It also offers subtle preparations with sauces—one day a pompano with ginger and saffron, another a red snapper with tomatoes, shallots, and olives. Among the terrific desserts, the authentic English trifle is famous. *181 W. 10th St. at 7th Ave. S, tel. 212/242–7350. Reservations required. AE, DC, MC, V. Sun. dinner. Very Expensive.*

**Jane Street Seafood Café.** This reliable fish house offers a huge roster of well-prepared seafood, sometimes grilled and sometimes sauced, perhaps à la Provençale. The crunchy coleslaw, sharpened with celery seeds, is a perfect accompaniment. Brick walls, a wood floor, tin ceilings, and a fireplace make things cozy. Dine early to avoid a wait. *31 8th Ave. at Jane St., tel. 212/243-9237. No reservations. AE, DC, MC, V. Sun. dinner. Expensive.*

**Spanish** **El Rincón de España.** Gazpacho and ham-tinged lentil soup, grilled chorizo sausages, and garlicky mixed shellfish stews are good choices in this stucco-walled neighborhood saloon festooned with bullfight art. A guitarist serenades at dinner. *226 Thompson St., between 3rd and Bleecker Sts., tel. 212/260-4950. Reservations required. AE, DC, MC, V. Sun. lunch, dinner. Moderate. MU*

**Rio Mar.** This bright, tidy Spanish restaurant with a loyal following and terrific seafood stews comes as a surprise in this grimy district of wholesale meat companies. Try the *caldo gallego* (a brew of potatoes, white beans, kale, and meats). *7 9th Ave. at Little W. 12th St., tel. 212/243-9015. Reservations advised. No credit cards. Sun. brunch, lunch, dinner. Moderate. L*

**Vietnamese** **Cuisine de Saigon.** This quiet brownstone restaurant offers shrimp on a sugarcane stalk and other culinary adventures. *154 W. 13th St., between Sixth and Seventh Aves., tel. 212/255-6003. Reservations advised. AE, DC, MC, V. Sun. dinner. Moderate.*

## Gramercy Park and Union Square

Some of Manhattan's glitziest new restaurants have sprouted here alongside a few relics of Old New York. On weeknights, limos stand three-deep as hopeful patrons line up outside; Sundays are a better time for the less club-happy to see what all the excitement is about. A special neighborhood pleasure is outdoor eating on tranquil Irving Place.

**American/Casual** **Friend of a Farmer.** At this countrified little restaurant on Irving Place, you get homey, rustic fare—apple butter and cheddar cheese omelets, buckwheat pancakes with walnuts, and muffins and cinnamon rolls from the restaurant's own talented bakers. *77 Irving Pl., tel. 212/477-2188. No reservations or credit cards. Sun. brunch. Inexpensive. O*

**Hungry Howard's/Island Grill.** Half of this bilevel newcomer offers simple grilled fish in elegant tropical surroundings complete with waterfall; the other is a bustling café that stars boneless grilled chicken breast "burgers." *40 E. 20th St., tel. 212/529-3366. Reservations suggested. AE, DC, MC, V. Sun. brunch, dinner. Moderate.*

**Pete's Tavern.** You come not for the food but for the low-ceilinged antiquity of the spot where O. Henry supposedly penned "The Gift of the Magi." And there's fine sidewalk dining in summer. *129 E. 18th St., tel. 212/473-7676. Reservations advised. AE, DC, MC, V. Sun. brunch, dinner. Moderate. L, O*

**American Regional** **America.** This stadium-sized restaurant has a menu that can please both adult palates and stubbornly unadventurous childish ones. Offerings range from Cajun popcorn and grills to peanut butter-and-marshmallow-whip sandwiches, and most is adequately prepared. *9 E. 18th St., tel. 212/505-2110. Reservations advised. AE, DC, MC, V. Sun. all day. Moderate. CH, L*

**Symbols at the end of an entry signify:** *CH: Good for children; L: Serves after 11 PM; MU: Live music; O: Outdoor dining; VU: Great view.*

**Italian** **Canastel's.** Careful promotion and savvy management made this northern Italian restaurant an instant hit when it opened in 1985; solid cooking and handsome premises, attractively lighted by 800 feet of peach-colored neon, keep it full now that the trend-followers have moved on. *229 Park Ave. S at 19th St., tel. 212/677-9622. Reservations advised. AE, DC, MC, V. Sun. dinner. Expensive. L*

**Giorgio's.** Purple neon on the ceiling may not do wonders for pastas and goat-cheese-topped pizza, but you can't go too far wrong at this glitzy little trattoria. Sandwiches on slabs of Italian bread make a good change of pace in the neighborhood. *245 Park Ave. S at 20th St., tel. 212/460-9100. Reservations suggested. AE, DC, MC, V. Sun. dinner. Moderate.*

**Sal Anthony's.** This town house dining room opened in 1966, long before a pasta palace anchored every other corner, and a loyal cadre has gathered since then, drawn by the deferential service, superior wine list, thick veal chops, and pretty decor: oil paintings on brick walls, huge bouquets, and crisp white cloths on well-spaced tables. *55 Irving Pl., tel. 212/982-9030. Reservations advised. AE, DC, MC, V. Sun. lunch (prix fixe), dinner. Moderate.*

**Tex-Mex** **Café Iguana.** The fake jungle and its 16-foot-long crystal-bead iguana is a sight; a DJ spins records from 9 PM on. Don't expect wonders of the "Vacation Cuisine" and you won't be disappointed. *235 Park Ave. S. at 19th St., tel. 212/529-4770. Reservations advised. AE, DC, MC, V. Sun. brunch, lunch, dinner. Expensive. L*

## Chelsea

As gentrification rapidly transforms this once slightly down-at-the-heels brownstone neighborhood, there's a restaurant mix of pioneer fern bars and glitzy spots in the best postmodern style. A youthful clientele means late hours, but prices are higher than in the East Village.

**American/Casual** **Chelsea Central.** This unpretentious Chelsea institution has a pressed-tin ceiling, a vintage mahogany bar, and a lively menu of dishes, such as pecan-coated baked chicken. *227 10th Ave. near 23rd St., tel. 212/620-0230. Reservations advised. AE, DC, MC, V. Sun. brunch, dinner. Moderate.*

**Harvey's Chelsea Restaurant.** One of the few saloons to survive Prohibition, this one built for Anheuser-Busch in 1889 is full of mahogany and etched glass; good fish and chips, prime rib, and bratwurst and potato salad win hearts. It makes an especially snug refuge on foul days. *108 W. 18th St., tel. 212/243-5644. Reservations advised. No credit cards. Sun. brunch, dinner. Moderate. L*

**Empire Diner.** This stainless steel diner is as au courant as ever, with its eclectic menu, terrific beer selection, and live music from noon to 3 PM. *210 10th Ave. at 22nd St., tel. 212/243-2736. No reservations. AE, MC, V. Open 24 hrs. Moderate. CH, L, MU*

**Lox Around the Clock.** This is the spot for basic bagels, blintzes, borscht, and burgers amid mid-renovation decor—battered plaster and pendant fluorescent tubes. There's a blasting jukebox. *676 6th Ave. at 21st St., tel. 212/691-3535. Open 24 hrs. AE. No reservations. Inexpensive. CH, L*

**American Regional**

**Blue Hen.** Countrified quilts on the walls are in keeping with the menu full of homey American fare, such as flaky-crusted pot pies and chicken and dumplings. Every meal starts out with first-rate corn muffins and buttermilk biscuits. *88 7th Ave. near 15th St., tel. 212/645–3015. No reservations. AE, DC, MC, V. Sun. brunch (prix fixe), dinner. Moderate.*

**Miss Ruby's Café.** Every two weeks this laid-back storefront eatery changes its menu to spotlight a different American regional cuisine—often to very good effect. *135 8th Ave., between 16th and 17th Sts., tel. 212/620–4055. Reservations advised. AE. Sun. brunch, dinner. Moderate.*

**Caribbean**

**Claire.** Amid lattices, greenery, and ceiling fans, you can sample the food of the tropics, including conch chowder, Chelsea's best grilled fish, and terrific Key lime pie. *156 7th Ave., between 19th and 20th Sts., tel. 212/255–1955. Reservations advised for dinner. AE, DC, MC, V. Sun. brunch, dinner. Moderate. L*

**Lola.** Brunchtime gospel singers keep the house rolling and shaking while happy diners down thin, cayenne-peppered onion rings, West Indian shrimp-and-chicken curry with wild rice waffles, and other South American-Caribbean dishes. Amen. *30 W. 22nd St., tel. 212/675–6700. Reservations required. AE. Sun. brunch (seatings at noon and 2:15). Moderate. MU*

**French**

**L'Acajou.** Were it not for the low lighting and the hearty, slightly Germanic Alsatian menu, you'd take this austere little bistro for a coffee shop. A classical guitarist occasionally entertains. *53 W. 19th St., tel. 212/645–1706. Reservations accepted. AE, MC, V. Sun. dinner. Expensive. L*

**Quatorze.** Bistro staples, such as steak-frîtes and chicory with warm bacon vinaigrette, come in hefty portions in this long narrow room hung with giant Fernet Branca posters. Even the yellow menu card looks Parisian. *240 W. 14th St., tel. 212/206–7006. Reservations advised. AE. Sun. dinner. Expensive.*

**La Lunchonette.** This rickety but decidedly stylish boîte, unpromisingly located on an ungentrified corner, offers the rich, soothing cassoulets and rabbit stews of France's Dordogne. An accordionist plays French tunes at dinner. *130 10th Ave. at 18th St., tel. 212/675–0342. Reservations advised. No credit cards. Sun. brunch, Sun. dinner (closed Sun. Aug.). Moderate. MU*

**Italian**

**Twigs.** A sleek little Italian café, all marble and brass, this is a good bet for individual pizzas with well-blistered crusts and toppings such as fennel-perfumed sausage and eggplant. *196 8th Ave. at 20th, tel. 212/633–6735. No reservations. AE, MC, V. Sun. brunch, dinner. Inexpensive. L*

## Midtown East

Though office workers are absent on Sundays, many restaurants in this area are open for business—some all day long and some in the evening. Every hotel has its dining room, too, often quite sumptuous.

**American/ Casual**

**Horn and Hardart.** The last of the automats is fun for children. Cafeteria service is available as well as the coin-op slots. *200 E.*

---

**Symbols at the end of an entry signify:** *CH: Good for children; L: Serves after 11 PM; MU: Live music; O: Outdoor dining; VU: Great view.*

*42nd St., tel. 212/599–1665. No reservations or credit cards. Sun. all day. Moderate. CH*

**American/ International**

**Aurora.** In this dressy restaurant, rosy lamps float overhead like clouds at dawn, the silver is heavy, and the leather-covered chairs are incredibly comfortable. Brunch begins at lunchtime and continues through dinnertime; the chef offers a family-style feast, bringing out pot after pot of homey French food while you luxuriate in those chairs. *60 E. 49th St., tel. 212/692–9292. Reservations advised. AE, MC, DC, V. Open Sun. 1–9 (prix fixe only; closed Sun. summer). Very Expensive.*

**Ambassador Grill.** A striking contemporary space in the UN Plaza Hotel, with deep wine-colored banquettes and artful bouquets, this establishment offers the rich, polished cuisine of Gascony at dinner. Its gala champagne brunch buffet proffers a bounty of international flavors in pastas, phyllos, eggs, salads, roast meats, and more. *1 UN Plaza (44th St. at 1st Ave.), tel. 212/702–5014. Reservations advised. AE, DC, MC, V. Sun. breakfast; brunch, dinner (both prix fixe). Expensive. MU.*

**Courtyard Café.** This comfortable but pleasantly unstuffy Murray Hill newcomer in the Doral Court Hotel offers a changing menu of grills, inventively flavored pastas, and, at brunch, grilled lamb steak and Dungeness crabmeat omelets. The lovely courtyard is open in warm weather, and a harpist plays on occasion. *130 E. 39th St., tel. 212/779–0739. Reservations required. AE, DC, MC, V. Sun. breakfast, brunch (prix fixe), dinner. Expensive. CH, MU, O*

**Park Bistro.** An inviting, gently lit spot with gray walls and red banquettes, this restaurant serves a gutsy Provençal menu of vibrant dishes, such as fresh codfish with tomatoes that have been oven-dried to concentrate their pungency. *414 Park Ave. S at 28th St., tel. 212/689–1360. Reservations required. AE, DC. Sun. dinner. Expensive.*

**Smith & Wollensky.** Boisterous and noisy, this wood-paneled, wood-floored steak house blankets plates with huge slabs of meat; lamb chops, prime rib with crisp hash browns, and pecan-walnut pie are a carnivore's perfect Sunday dinner. Oenophiles go into raptures over the rarefied, well-priced wine list. *201 E. 49th St., tel. 212/753–1530. Reservations advised. Jacket and tie advised. AE, DC, MC, V. Sun. dinner. Expensive. L*

**Sumptuary.** Consistently good northern Italian and southern French fare come in this longtime favorite with a fireplace, a pretty garden, and a view of an old brick church's wonderful stained-glass windows. *400 3rd Ave. near 28th St., tel. 212/889–6056. Reservations advised. AE, MC, V. Sun. dinner. Moderate. O*

**Chinese**

**Chin Chin.** The city's handsomest Chinese restaurant offers a cuisine as streamlined as the contemporary setting: a subdued rust-and-peach front room, hung with turn-of-the-century family photographs of the ancestral Chins, and an airy back room that's all snowy white. The original fare stars dumplings, hot-and-sour and corn-and-crabmeat soups, and tea-smoked duck. *216 E. 49th St., tel. 212/888–4555. Reservations advised. Sun. dinner. AE, DC, MC, V. Moderate. O*

**Fortune Garden Pavilion.** Sundays here produce an intriguing combination: good Chinese food and live jazz. *209 E. 49th St., tel. 212/753–0101. Reservations advised. AE, DC, MC, V. Sun. dinner. Moderate. MU*

**Eastern European** **Christine's.** This simple café, with glass-topped tablecloths and crowded tables, serves crisp potato pancakes, robust soups, superbly fresh egg salad sandwiches on raisin-pumpernickel bread, and other Polish-American fare at amazingly gentle prices. *344 Lexington Ave., between 39th and 40th Sts., tel. 212/ 953–1920. Reservations not required. AE. Sun. lunch, brunch (prix fixe), dinner. Inexpensive.*

**French** **Box Tree.** At this intimate, exquisite town house restaurant, setting, service, and food are refined and elegant to the *n*th degree. *250 E. 49th St., tel. 212/758–8320. Reservations required. AE. Sun. dinner. Very Expensive.*

**Indian** **Akbar.** Arched doorways, dark red carpet, and white walls hung with portraits of princes spin the mood of a Mogul palace courtyard here while a card reader foretells futures. *256 E. 49th St., tel. 212/838–1717. Reservations advised. AE, DC, MC, V. Sun. brunch, lunch, dinner (prix fixe). Expensive.*

**Bukhara.** Foods cooked in the searing tandoor clay oven take the spotlight in this rug-scattered Indian-rustic room. The culinary interest derives from the interplay of sweet, sour, and hot flavorings, such as ginger, lime, mint, coriander, and onion. Start with the huge pizzalike breads, then move on to meats roasted in the tandoor. Every diner gets a huge bib, but no utensils unless requested; you eat with your hands. *148 E. 58th St., tel. 212/838–1811. Reservations advised. AE, DC, MC, V. Sun. brunch, lunch, dinner (prix fixe at all). Moderate. CH*

**Seafood** **Water Club.** The view of Queens that you get from Manhattan's yacht-clubbiest restaurant may not excite, but the waterside location makes brunchtime lobster salad, crabcakes, and grilled salmon a special delight. On a perfect summer day, it's fun to sip an aperitif on the deck and watch fluttering helicopters land at the nearby heliport. *500 E. 30th St., tel. 212/683–3333. Reservations advised. AE, DC, MC, V. Sun. brunch, dinner. Very Expensive.*

**Dock's.** With its high ceilings and raised dining platforms, this giant fish house-saloon is one of the better-looking restaurants in the neighborhood. The brunch is more eggy than you might expect, but a complement of seafare is available. Dinner is all fish—all great. *633 3rd Ave. at 40th St., tel. 212/986–8080. Reservations advised. AE, DC, MC, V. Sun. brunch, dinner. Moderate.*

**Middle Eastern** **Sido Abu Salim.** Dark-wood-paneled walls and white tablecloths topped with glass are a neat setting for excellent *mezze* —appetizers such as *baba ghannouj* (smoky-flavored eggplant puree), hummus, tabbouleh, the mashed-bean croquettes known as felafel, and stuffed grape leaves. Though main courses are available, delights like these are what regulars go for. *81 Lexington Ave. at 26th St., tel. 212/686–2031. Reservations advised at dinner, not accepted at lunch. AE, MC, V. Sun. lunch, dinner. Inexpensive.*

**Russian** **Kavkazian.** This unprepossessing nook stars the borschts, pirozhki, and other hearty fare of Soviet Georgia—and vodka,

---

**Symbols at the end of an entry signify:** *CH: Good for children; L: Serves after 11 PM; MU: Live music; O: Outdoor dining; VU: Great view.*

straight up. *361 E. 49th St., tel. 212/751–0416. Reservations accepted. AE, DC. Sun. lunch, dinner. Moderate.*

**Japanese** **Inagiku.** At the tempura bar of this attractive Waldorf-Astoria restaurant, chefs in tall black mesh hats fry up some of the city's best batter-dipped vegetables and fish. Wind up your meal with a fritterlike *kakiage,* made of leftovers of the preceding courses. *111 E. 49th St., tel. 212/355–0440. Reservations required. AE, DC, MC, V. Sun. dinner. Expensive.*

**For Drinks** **Top of the Tower.** This viewful lounge is one of the city's best-kept secrets, with an open-air terrace that's sheer heaven in summer. *Beekman Tower Hotel, 49th St. and 1st Ave., tel. 212/355–7300. AE, DC, MC, V. Sun. 5–after midnight. VU*

## Midtown West

This neighborhood encompasses the southwestern fringes of Rockefeller Center, the theater district's Restaurant Row, and the area in and around the Manhattan Towers artists' housing complex. In the mix, there are some wonderfully old-fashioned restaurants and unpretentious hangouts, with a certain special New York grittiness and punch. Especially near the theater district, spotting celebrities is practically an everyday event.

**American/Casual** **Landmark Tavern.** A fireplace and potbellied stove warm this Old New York relic with a burnished bar and smoke-darkened pressed-tin ceiling. The terrific brunch features Irish oatmeal pancakes and traditional soda bread. Anglo-Irish dinner fare includes such favorites as shepherd's pie, fish and chips, and a good selection of single-malt Scotches. *626 11th Ave. at 46th St., tel. 212/757–8595. Reservations required. AE, DC, MC, V. Sun. brunch, dinner. Expensive. L*

**Joe Allen.** This Restaurant Row institution, homey with its red-checkered tablecloths, is fun for basic pub fare and late-night noshing. *326 W. 46th St., tel. 212/581–6464. Reservations advised. MC, V. Sun. lunch, dinner. Moderate. L*

**Manhattan Island.** This leisurely greenhouse-restaurant has lively California cuisine, great frozen drinks, an outdoor terrace, and a view of the Manhattan Plaza Health Club's pristine turquoise pool. *482 W. 43rd St., tel. 212/967–0533. Reservations advised. AE, MC, V. Sun. brunch (prix fixe). Moderate. O*

**American/ International** **Red Blazer Too.** Jazz at brunch and Dixieland and big bands at dinner swing amid pale wood, stained glass, and bright murals. *349 W. 46th St., tel. 212/262–3112. Reservations advised. AE, DC, MC, V. Sun. brunch, dinner. Very Expensive. L, MU*

**Algonquin Hotel.** This legendary New York landmark has been attracting the arts-and-letters crowd since the '20s, when Dorothy Parker and her luncheon companions became known as the Algonquin Round Table and made the place famous. Redolent of Old New York, the Rose Room and Edwardian Lounge bustle with conversationalists and people watchers. At brunch, apple pancakes and corned beef hash star, and there's a Sunday supper from 6 PM. *59 W. 44th St., tel. 212/840–6800. Reservations advised. AE, DC, MC, V. Sun. breakfast, brunch, dinner. Expensive.*

**The View.** The city's only revolving restaurant is worth at least one visit in a lifetime. *Marriott Marquis Hotel, 1535 Broadway between 45th and 46th Sts., tel. 212/704–8900. Reservations required. AE, DC, MC, V. Sun. brunch, early dinner (prix fixe only). Expensive. VU*

**B. Smith.** Sunday matinee goers brunch on pecan pancakes and fried whiting and grits with homemade biscuits in a shiny postmodern room punctuated by huge earth-toned urns and gigantic bouquets. At dinner, good grills complement eccentric preparations such as scampi with mango glacé. *771 8th Ave. at 47th St., tel. 212/247–2222. Reservations advised. AE, DC, MC, V. Sun. brunch, dinner. Moderate. MU*

**American Regional** **Carolina.** Here's a good bet for down-home Dixie fare, such as crab cakes, corn pudding, Key lime pie, and bread pudding. *355 W. 46th St., tel. 212/245–0048. Reservations advised. AE, MC, V. Sun. dinner. Very Expensive.*

**Brazilian** **Cabana Carioca.** In this dim, unpromising spot where Portuguese is the lingua franca, the exuberantly flavored Brazilian cooking deserves a visit. *123 W. 45th St., tel. 212/581–8088. Reservations required. AE, DC, MC, V. Sun. lunch, dinner. Inexpensive. L*

**French** **Crêpe Suzette.** Once upon a time, New York had many French restaurants like this one, with a *patronne* who welcomed every diner warmly and a menu of familiar dishes, such as sole amandine, beef bourguignon, and crème caramel. One of the last of the breed, this one endures, refreshingly unchanged, unabashedly old-fashioned, and reassuringly reliable. *363 W. 46th St., tel. 212/581–9717. Dinner reservations required. AE, DC, MC, V. Sun. brunch, early dinner (prix fixe at both; closed Sun. June–Sept.) Expensive.*

**Restaurant Bellevues.** This little French restaurant is a bright spot on one of the bleakest blocks of what used to be called Hell's Kitchen. The 50s-luncheonette decor focuses attention on the food—homey fare that tastes as if it's straight from a Paris neighborhood restaurant. At brunch, that means charcuteries, cheeses, and *boudin noir* with apples and onions; at dinner, there is always curried lamb among the fish and meat specials. *496 9th Ave., between 37th and 38th Sts., tel. 212/967–7850. Reservations advised. No credit cards. Sun. brunch, tea, dinner. Moderate.*

**Le Madeline.** Behind lace curtains, this Theater Row café features an ivy-walled garden and a bistro menu. Try the banana-walnut pancakes at brunch. *403 W. 43rd St., tel. 212/246–2993. Reservations required. AE, MC, V. Sun. brunch, dinner. Moderate. L, O*

**Indian** **Raga.** Antique stringed instruments hang on raw-silk-covered walls in this lovely restaurant full of slender teak pillars. Dinner, the only meal served on Sunday, is the one the kitchen does best: tandoori chicken, flaming vindaloo curries, and lamb chunks sauced with spinach or herbed yogurt. *57 W. 48th St., tel. 212/757–3450. Reservations not necessary. AE, DC, MC, V. Sun. dinner. Moderate.*

**Italian** **Orso.** This bright, casual spot, a sort of Sardi's of the '80s with mauve-and-cream walls and hand-painted Italian china, delivers consistently good celebrity-spotting and consistently tasty fare, from lively pastas and thin-crusted pizzas with vibrant toppings to zesty entrées, such as grilled quail and homemade

**Symbols at the end of an entry signify:** *CH: Good for children; L: Serves after 11 PM; MU: Live music; O: Outdoor dining; VU: Great view.*

sausages. *322 W. 46th, tel. 212/489–7212. Reservations required. MC, V. Sun. all day. Moderate.*

**Japanese** **Sapporo.** The Japanese film *Tampopo* celebrated the quest for perfect noodle soup; this steamy luncheonette is one of the few spots in the city where you can enjoy this delectable broth. *152 W. 49th St., tel. 212/869–8972. Reservations required. No credit cards. Sun. lunch, dinner. Moderate.*

**Peruvian** **Peruvian Restaurant.** In this hole in the wall, complete with plastic plants, the adventurous can sample native specialties, such as beef-and-rice *sancochado* soup, ceviche, mashed potato pies, and terrific tamales. *688 10th Ave. near 49th St., tel. 212/581–5814. No reservations or credit cards. Sun. all day. Inexpensive.*

**Thai** **Siam Grill.** This small, neat restaurant offers fare worth a trip from outside the neighborhood—spicy grills, such as beef *satay* and curry-spiked chicken *gai yang. 585 9th Ave., between 42nd and 43rd Sts., tel. 212/307–1363. Reservations advised. AE, DC, MC, V. Sun. dinner. Inexpensive. L*

## East 50s

This is prime territory for hotel dining rooms and their fabulous, no-holds-barred, all-you-can eat brunches. To the east, along First and Second avenues, simple neighborhood restaurants abound; snug, comfortable, and sedate, these are good for brunch or for a Sunday dinner that's satisfying and not too expensive. A sprinkling of restaurants north of 57th Street near Bloomingdale's caters to shoppers and moviegoers.

**American/Casual** **Billy's.** In this mahogany-paneled bit of Old New York, the menu of honest roasts, chops, and seafood says "home" to a crowd of politicos, personalities, and U.N. leaders. *948 1st Ave., between 52nd and 53rd Sts., tel. 212/753–1870. Reservations required. AE, DC, MC, V. Sun. lunch, dinner. Expensive.*

**Brasserie.** This streamlined New York favorite in the Seagram Building's lower level is still a comfortable place to tuck into simple, slightly French fare, such as steak-frites or chicken breast vinaigrette. The rectangular counter is good for solitary meals. *100 E. 53rd St., tel. 212/751–4840. Reservations accepted. AE, DC, MC, V. Open 24 hrs. Moderate.*

**P. J. Clarke's.** This venerable tile-floored saloon doesn't look much different than it did in the 1944 movie *Lost Weekend.* Sundays are mellow, particularly in midday when sunlight from the south-facing windows gilds the battered paneling and burnished pressed-tin ceiling. Nobody seems to mind that the plain fare is so-so. *915 3rd Ave. at 55th St., tel. 212/759–1650. Reservations advised. AE, DC. Sun. lunch, dinner. Moderate. L*

**Wylie's Ribs & Co.** Here's an essential stop for anyone who loves barbecued ribs and chicken, which are served here by the platterful. *891 1st Ave. at 50th St., tel. 212/751–0700. No reservations. AE, DC, MC, V. Sun. lunch, dinner. Inexpensive. L*

**American/ International** **Brive.** Eccentric chef/owner Robert Pritzker gives free play to outlandish fantasies in this antique-scattered town house with burled-wood paneling and lacquered apricot-colored walls. When he is good, he is very, very good (witness salmon terrine flecked with roe or lobster meringue tart), and when he is bad, his food is weird (as with salmon sauerbraten). Follow your own ideas of what's good and expect transcendent eating. *405 E. 58th St., tel. 212/838–9393. Reservations advised. AE, DC, MC, V. Sun. dinner (closed Sun. 4 weeks in summer). Very Expensive.*

**Edwardian Room.** This stately Plaza Hotel institution, with ornate paneling and coffered wood ceilings, offers large portions of excellent veal chops, orange-perfumed lobster salad over angel hair pasta, and other superior fare. Central Park views from the tall windows make it grand for brunch. *5th Ave. at Central Park South, tel. 212/759–3000. Reservations required at brunch, advised for breakfast and dinner. AE, DC, MC, V. Sun. breakfast, brunch, dinner. Very Expensive.*

**Palm Court.** This lofty roomful of potted palms and gold leaf in the Plaza Hotel serves one of the city's most lavish Sunday brunch buffets, with a pianist to set the mood. *59th St. at Central Park South, tel. 212/546–5350. Reservations essential for brunch, not accepted for tea. AE, DC, MC, V. Sun. brunch, tea. Expensive. MU*

**Deli** **Kaplan's.** The best bet for simple deli in the neighborhood, this spot serves terrific potato pancakes and smoked fish. *59 E. 59th St., tel. 212/755–5959. Reservations not necessary. AE, DC, MC, V. Sun. breakfast, lunch, early dinner. Inexpensive.*

**French** **Adrienne.** Tall arched windows overlooking Fifth Avenue and roomy tables make this Peninsula Hotel dining room a delight. The spread is sumptuous, reflecting the Mediterranean preferences of the kitchen; you might find fresh codfish with whipped potatoes or an olive oil sauce heady with truffles. A harpist entertains. Bistro d'Adrienne, the hotel's more informal room, serves Provençal fare with comparably lusty flavors. *700 55th St. at 5th Ave., tel. 212/903–3918. Reservations advised. AE, DC, MC, V. Adrienne: Sun. breakfast, brunch. Bistro d'Adrienne: Sun. dinner. Very Expensive. MU*

**Prunelle.** This luxurious Sam Lopata–designed restaurant, one of the prettiest in town with its burled maple and exquisite flowers, serves salmon with butter–red wine sauce, veal medallions with lobster sauce, and other fare consistently ranging from good to excellent. *18 E. 54th St., tel. 212/759–6410. Reservations advised. AE, DC, MC, V. Sun. dinner (prix fixe). Very Expensive.*

**Chez Louis.** The new bistro menu offered here by the irrepressible David Liederman—who studied with the brothers Troisgros and then struck it big with David's Cookies—stars one of the city's best roast chickens, served with a crusty potato pie. You can also get baked wild mushrooms, cassoulet, and grilled seafood with flavors as intense as the café's red lacquer walls. Two no-fat dishes are on the menu every day. *1016 2nd Ave., between 53rd and 54th Sts., tel. 212/752–1400. Reservations advised. AE, DC, MC, V. Sun. dinner. Very Expensive.*

**Indian** **Dāwat.** Actress-author Madhur Jaffrey offers a number of her intriguing, innovative preparations at this sophisticated, serene restaurant stylishly decorated in pink and green. Dishes such as eggplant with tamarind sauce or chicken *makhani* aromatic with ginger and coriander are a change from the usual curries. Try the *bhel poori*, an appetizer that explodes with

---

**Symbols at the end of an entry signify:** *CH: Good for children; L: Serves after 11 PM; MU: Live music; O: Outdoor dining; VU: Great view.*

sweet, sour, and hot sensations. *210 E. 58th St., tel. 212/355-7555. Reservations advised. AE, DC, MC, V. Sun. dinner. Moderate.*

**Italian**   **Alfredo's the Original of Rome.** Italian food of a high level of authenticity is served here. The Sunday prix fixe brunch adds good jazz. *153 E. 53rd, tel. 212/371-3367. Reservations required. Jacket and tie advised. AE, DC, MC, V. Sun. brunch, dinner. Expensive. MU*

**Bice.** This chic trattoria offers pastas with a Milanese accent in an Adam Tihany–designed setting of brass, beige, and wood. Very chic. *7 E. 54th St., tel. 212/688-1999. Reservations required. AE, V. Sun. lunch, dinner. Expensive.*

**Trattoria Pino.** A lively, casual pizzeria, this spot serves thin-crusted pies cooked in a wood-fired oven. *981 3rd Ave., between 58th and 59th Sts., tel. 212/759-1220. Reservations not required. AE, DC, MC, V. Sun. lunch, dinner. Inexpensive.*

**Mexican**   **Rosa Mexicano.** Margaritas with pomegranate juice keep the bar packed, while diners in the rosy-stuccoed back room devour tortillas with pork, piquant grills, and tasty guacamole prepared tableside. *1063 1st Ave. at 58th St., tel. 212/753-7407. Reservations advised. AE, DC, MC, V. Sun. buffet lunch, dinner. Moderate. L*

**Zarela.** Gutsy red snapper hash, tuna with *mole* sauce, coconut shrimp, and the trademark chicken Chilaquiles (chicken layered with fried tortillas) will expand your view of Mexican cuisine. At brunch, choose from eggs rancheros on corn tortillas or more complex shrimp with garlic and two chilis, while a Mexican trio serenades. *953 2nd Ave., between 50th and 51st Sts., tel. 212/644-6740. Reservations advised. AE, DC. Sun. brunch, dinner. Moderate. MU*

## West 50s

The West 50s area, home to Rockefeller Center, Carnegie Hall, and Central Park South, also contains some spectacular Italian restaurants, New York's premier caviar purveyor, wonderful little ethnic finds, and a host of hotels that offer fine places for drinks.

**American/Casual**   **Gallagher's.** The West Side's best steak house, this has long been a hangout for sports figures, whose photos hang on the wood-paneled walls. You'll also find unquestionably fine aged prime beef, displayed by the side out front. *228 W. 52nd St., tel. 212/245-5336. Reservations advised. AE, DC, MC, V. Sun. lunch, dinner. Very Expensive. L*

**Mickey Mantle's.** Hash-and-eggs brunches and chicken-fried steak and hickory-smoked ribs at dinner take second place to the World Series footage on video monitors, a bartender who talks batting averages, and appearances by the Bronx Bomber himself. *42 Central Park South, between Fifth and Sixth Aves., tel. 212/688-7777. Reservations advised. AE, DC, MC, V. Sun. brunch, lunch, dinner. Expensive. CH*

**Hard Rock Café.** This cavernous boîte with a Cadillac-fin marquee, a casual menu, and a deafening sound system may be New York's top must-see for preteens. Go between 4 and 6 for the shortest line out front. *221 W. 57th St., tel. 212/489-6565. No reservations. AE, DC, MC, V. Sun. all day. Inexpensive. CH, L*

**American/ International**

**China Grill.** In this jumbo brasserie with black granite walls and bleached-wood floors, the culinary East meets West with a Chinese-California menu featuring such items as quail with crispy noodles and ginger-curry lobster. *60 W. 53rd St., tel. 212/333–7788. Reservations advised. AE, DC, MC, V. Sun. dinner (prix fixe); closed Sun. July–Aug. Very Expensive.*

**Petrossian.** With mink-trimmed banquettes, rosy granite floors, and Erté etched glass, this outpost of the Parisian caviar shop is perhaps Manhattan's most luxurious restaurant. Come for the affordable Sunday brunch and champagne by the glass or splurge for a French dinner with Russian touches. *182 W. 58th St., tel. 212/245–2214. Reservations required. AE, DC, MC, V. Sun. brunch, dinner (prix fixe at both). Very Expensive.*

**Rainbow.** This gala restaurant complex atop the RCA Building in Rockefeller Center stars the two-story-high **Rainbow Room,** a lavish, romantic spot with aubergine silk walls, cast-glass balusters, and silver lamé tablecloths. Choral groups serenade during the splendid brunch; during dinner you can waltz and cha-cha on the revolving dance floor to the music of big oldies and Latin bands. At the **Rainbow Promenade,** a splendidly viewful bar, you can opt for less expensive pleasures: lively little meals served while a classical guitarist entertains. *30 Rockefeller Plaza, tel. 212/632–5100. Rainbow Room reservations essential. Dress code. AE. Sun. brunch (prix fixe), tea, dinner (prix fixe; music, $15 charge). Very Expensive. L, MU, VU*

**Symphony Café.** This newcomer with soft lighting and mahogany walls is a poor man's Le Bernardin, with an appealing menu and accomplished kitchen. Try the roast chicken with mashed potatoes or the mustard-thyme grilled shrimp. *950 8th Ave. at 56th St., tel. 212/397–9595. Reservations advised. AE, DC, MC, V. Sun. brunch (prix fixe), dinner; closed Sun. June–Aug. Expensive. L*

**American Regional**

**American Festival Café.** American regional classics are served here amid folk art and patchwork quilts, light woods and marble. Brunch on roast chicken with Gilroy garlic and lemon thyme, orange-vanilla French toast, or roast beef hash. Dinner features Baltimore crab cakes with homemade potato chips or roast duck with potato pie and rhubarb compote. In summer, light fare is served al fresco on the site of the famous Rockefeller Plaza ice rink. *20 W. 50th St., tel. 212/246–6699. Reservations advised. AE, DC, MC, V. Sun. breakfast, brunch, dinner. Moderate. CH, L, O*

**Deli**

**Carnegie Deli.** Peppery pastrami is served in mile-high sandwiches at this institution, founded in 1934 and immortalized in Woody Allen's *Broadway Danny Rose.* The matzoh ball soup and corned beef give the legendary pastrami a run for its money, too—no wonder there are lines outside the door most of the day. *854 7th Ave., between 54th and 55th Sts., tel. 212/757–2245. No reservations or credit cards. Sun. breakfast, lunch, dinner. Inexpensive. L*

**Stage Deli.** Fans dispute whether the Stage or the Carnegie does a better job. Try both and decide for yourself. *834 7th Ave., between 53rd and 54th Sts., tel. 212/245–7850. No reservations or credit cards. Sun. all day. Inexpensive. L*

---

**Symbols at the end of an entry signify:** *CH: Good for children; L: Serves after 11 PM; MU: Live music; O: Outdoor dining; VU: Great view.*

**French** **Maurice.** Despite the departure of nouvelle cuisine wizard Alain Senderens, the Maurice remains not only one of the city's best hotel dining rooms but one of its best restaurants, period. Accomplished service, roomy tables, and a moderate noise level create the perfect environment for savoring distinctive soups made with wonderful herbs and stocks. Try the signature duck, basted with honey, coriander seed, cumin, saffron, and pepper. *118 W. 57th St., tel. 212/245-7788. Reservations advised. Jacket and tie required. AE, DC, MC, V. Sun. dinner. Very Expensive.*

**La Bonne Soupe.** Red-checked cloths cover wobbly tables at this longtime standby for meals that don't cost a fortune. The savory soups are among the city's tastiest buys, and the Provençal codfish-potato puree known as *brandade,* available in winter, is a delight. *48 W. 55th St., tel. 212/586-7650. Reservations advised. AE. Sun. brunch, lunch, dinner. Inexpensive. L*

**Indian** **Darbár.** Persian carpets hung against dusky rose velvet walls and carved wooden screens create a hushed, elegant setting. The menu features highly refined northern Indian cuisine: tamarind-tangy chick peas and potatoes, moist chicken tandoori, and rice biriyani with lamb, raisins, and spice seeds whose flavor explodes when you bite into them. *44 W. 56th St., tel. 212/432-7227. Reservations advised. AE, DC, MC, V. Sun. lunch, dinner (prix fixe at both). Moderate.*

**Italian** **San Domenico.** The creation of veteran New York restaurateur Tony May earns raves for exquisite Bolognese pastas, seafood, and meats. Favorite dishes include egg-filled ravioli with hazelnut butter and sage, shrimp and beans with Tuscan olive oil, and venison with juniper berries. Designer Adam Tihany's cordovan leather chairs are supremely luxurious. The tasting menu represents excellent value. *240 Central Park South, between Seventh Ave. and Broadway, tel. 212/265-5959. Reservations required. AE, DC, MC, V. Sun. dinner (prix fixe). Very Expensive.*

**Trattoria dell'Arte.** Designer Milton Glaser filled this huge space with giant bas-relief lips and breasts and sepia prints of oversized eyes and noses. Equally diverting are the carefully prepared antipasti and tender pastas exquisitely doused with uncommon sauces. *200 W. 57th St., tel. 212/ 245-9800. Reservations advised. AE, DC, MC, V. Sun. lunch, dinner (prix fixe at both). Expensive. L*

**Russian** **Russian Samovar.** Hearty eggplant dishes and good grills soothe theater folk in this snug, unprepossessing little dining room with long banquettes and well-spaced tables. *256 W. 52nd St., tel. 212/757-0168. Reservations advised. AE, DC, MC, V. Sun. dinner (closed Sun. July-Aug.). Moderate.*

**Russian Tea Room.** In this famed celebrity haunt, oil paintings on deep green walls, red banquettes, and brass samovars create a festive backdrop for brunching on mushrooms à la Russe or blinchiki with cherry preserves and sour cream. Sample the caviars and exotic vodkas, too. *150 W. 57th St., tel. 212/265-0947. Reservations required. Jacket required. AE, DC, MC, V. Sun. brunch, dinner (prix fixe). Very Expensive. L*

**Seafood** **Manhattan Ocean Club.** This attractive pastel dining room excels at preparations, such as mahi-mahi with citrus butter and spaetzle or rare tuna with tomato-mint vinaigrette; the shoestring potatoes are fabulous. The excellent wine list reflects the expertise of Alan Stillman, who also owns Smith & Wollensky. *57 W. 58th St., tel. 212/371–7777. Reservations required. AE, DC, MC, V. Sun. dinner. Very Expensive.*

**Thai**  **Bangkok Cuisine.** Eighth Avenue in the 50s is full of Thai restaurants, but this is among the best. Order a Thai beer, such as Amarit, to accompany steamed fish or crispy *mee krob* noodles. *885 8th Ave., between 52nd and 53rd Sts., tel. 212/581–6370. Reservations advised. AE, DC, MC, V. Sun. dinner. Inexpensive. L*

---

## East 60s

Though many luxury restaurants in the blocks between Fifth and Park avenues close on Sunday, several others serve dinner in quiet surroundings. Farther east, restaurants are busy and brunch is popular, especially in the singles hangouts along First and Third avenues.

**American/Casual**  **Nickels Steak House.** Piano music and a soft pastel color scheme end weekends romantically here; straightforwardly prepared fish, chicken, and chops assure that you don't leave hungry. *227 E. 67th St., tel. 212/794–2331. Reservations advised. AE, DC, MC, V. Sun. dinner. Expensive. L, MU*
**Loeb Boathouse.** Of several places to eat in Central Park, this full-service restaurant is the finest. Take your choice of seating indoors or out. *Central Park near 74th St., tel. 212/517–2233. No reservations. AE, DC, MC, V. Sun. lunch, dinner. Moderate. CH, O*
**Serendipity 3.** This happy mix of ice cream parlor and general store opened in 1954 and has been going strong ever since. Movie goers and models, families and singles come for casseroles, pastas, pizzas, and sandwiches—and the best-ever hot fudge sundaes. *225 E. 60th St., tel. 212/838–3531. Reservations advised. AE, DC, MC, V. Sun. lunch, dinner. Moderate. L*

**American/ International**  **Café Pierre.** Soothing and civilized, with ornate mirrors and cloud murals overhead, this has long been a sumptuous place for breakfast. An updated menu now offers stylish fare at other meals, too—scallop and salmon terrine sauced with watercress, for instance, or lamb with braised endive. *2 E. 61st St., tel. 212/940–8185. Reservations recommended. AE, DC, MC, V. Sun. all day. Very Expensive. L, MU*
**Huberts.** Len Allison and Karen Hubert's new space, designed by Adam Tihany, is spare, dramatic, and as original as the cuisine: classic fare creatively conceived, in dishes such as Roquefort soufflé or rabbit sausage with *mole* sauce. *575 Park Ave. at 63rd St., tel. 212/826–5911. Reservations advised. AE, DC, MC, V. Sun. dinner (prix fixe). Very Expensive.*
**Sign of the Dove.** This softly lit restaurant full of antiques finally has a kitchen to boast about, both for brunchtime scrambled eggs with warmed smoked salmon and for elaborate dinner fare. (Try caramelized bass with crisp leeks and lobster broth.) Skylights keep daytime bright, and pianists play all day. *1110 3rd Ave. at 65th St., tel. 212/861–8080. Reservations advised. AE, DC, MC, V. Sun. brunch, dinner (prix fixe). Very Expensive. L, MU*

---

**Symbols at the end of an entry signify:** *CH: Good for children; L: Serves after 11 PM; MU: Live music; O: Outdoor dining; VU: Great view.*

**Post House.** This long-standing institution, a comfortably masculine spot, serves some of the city's best steaks, chops, and lobsters. *28 E. 63rd St., tel. 212/935–2888. Reservations advised. AE, DC, MC, V. Sun. dinner. Very Expensive.*

**Pembroke Room.** In this creamy-hued Lowell Hotel hideaway, mirrored walls reflect chandeliers, English chintz cascading at the windows, and voluptuous bouquets. Baby chicken and grilled beef highlight the English brunch; order anything from burgers to Beluga at other meals. *28 E. 63rd St., tel. 212/838–1400. Reservations advised. AE, DC, MC, V. Sun. breakfast, brunch, tea. Expensive.*

**American Regional**   **Arizona 206.** Barbecued foie gras with cactus pears and pistachio-crusted rabbit demonstrate in stunning fashion the potential of Southwestern cuisine here. Spicy chili and a fireplace keep diners warm in winter. *206 E. 60th St., tel. 212/838–0440. Reservations required. AE, DC, MC, V. Sun. dinner. Expensive.*

**Chinese**   **David K's.** The man who first brought Szechuan cuisine to New York now offers clear-flavored, low-fat Cantonese fare, such as white seafood soup and whole wheat pancakes rolled around shredded vegetables with Chinese sausage. *1115 3rd Ave. at 65th St., tel. 212/371–9090. Reservations accepted. AE, DC. Sun. lunch, dinner. Moderate.*

**French**   **Le Régence.** This lavish Plaza Athénée Hotel restaurant features light, refined fare. Salmon-and-scallop tart and thin-sliced black bass with caviar-flecked sauce are as opulent as the Louis XV decor. Sunday brunches are positively artful. *37 E. 64th St., tel. 212/606–4647. Reservations advised. Jacket and tie required. AE, DC, MC, V. Sun. breakfast, brunch (prix fixe), dinner. Very Expensive.*

**Le Relais.** Eating takes a back seat to people watching inside this bistro and its summertime outdoor café. Leg of lamb typifies the hearty offerings. *712 Madison Ave., between 63rd and 64th Sts., tel. 212/751–5108. Reservations advised. AE, MC, V. Sun. lunch, dinner. Expensive. O*

**Madame Romaine de Lyon.** This old-timer prepares omelets with a delightfully light touch—in 500 varieties. *29 E. 61st St., tel. 212/758–2422. Reservations accepted for 3 or more. AE, DC, V. Sun. 10:30–3:30 (closed Sun. June–Aug.). Expensive.*

**Italian Northern**   **Alo Alo.** This tall-ceilinged, noisy café, full of whimsical papier-mâché mannequins, is known for its chic menu of sprightly fare such as thin-shaved swordfish and pennette with duck meat. *1030 3rd Ave. at 61st St., tel. 212/838–4343. Reservations advised. AE, DC, MC, V. Sun. brunch, dinner. Expensive. L*

**Primola.** A good-looking European crowd appreciates the lively cooking served in the spare, pale yellow dining room here. Salmon marinated with fennel, grilled quail with polenta, and lamb chops come in giant portions, and the minestrone is fabulous. *1226 2nd Ave., between 64th and 65th, tel. 212/758–1775. Reservations required. AE, MC, V. Sun. dinner. Expensive.*

**Contrapunto.** This casual, bright-white upstairs restaurant focuses on pasta, with 20-odd options ranging from angel hair with clams and dried tomatoes to fettucine with sage and lobster. It's a good bet before or after the movies. *200 E. 60th St., tel. 212/751–8616. No reservations. AE, DC, MC, V. Sun. lunch, dinner. Moderate.*

**Gino's.** Fuschia Scalamandre wallpaper frolicking with zebras is the trademark of this old-fashioned room crowded with regulars, who happily tuck into bluefish oreganato, pasta e fagioli, and ossobuco with risotto. *780 Lexington Ave., between 60th and 61st Sts., tel. 212/758–4466. No reservations or credit cards. Sun. lunch, dinner. Moderate.*

*Southern* **Il Vagabondo.** The happy bustle shows no signs of letting up in this 20-year-old dining room hospitably awash in checkered tablecloths—Manhattan's only restaurant with an indoor boccie court. *351 E. 62nd St., tel. 212/832–9221. No reservations. AE, DC, MC, V. Sun. dinner. Moderate. CH, L*

**Seafood** **John Clancy's East.** With no notable lapse in quality, a fine downtown restaurant (*see* West Village, above) has brought its menu uptown to this oak-paneled space with forest-green suede banquettes. *20 E. 63rd St., tel. 212/752–6666. Reservations required. AE, DC, MC, V. Sun. dinner. Expensive.*

## Upper East Side

There is no shortage of places to stop to eat in this neighborhood before or after an expedition to Central Park or along Museum Mile. Besides the museums' own cafés, which are often quite good, you'll find chic, sleek trendsetting restaurants alternating with warmly welcoming ethnic nooks.

*Afghan* **Pamir.** This tiny, dimly lit eatery, hung with rugs and shawls, is aromatic with the spices of its cuisine, which is a cross between Middle Eastern and Indian. Try the kabobs, meat pastries, and rice palaws, and enjoy the subtlety and sheer foreignness of it all. *1437 2nd Ave. at 75th St., tel. 212/734–3791. Reservations required. MC, V. Sun. dinner. Moderate.*

**American/Casual** **E.A.T.** With Eli Zabar of the gourmet food store dynasty in charge, you're sure to be pleased with the sandwiches, salads, and entrées here, not to mention the superlative hard-crusted breads. Breakfast is the quietest and least expensive time to make the marbled, mirrored scene. *1064 Madison Ave., between 80th and 81st Sts., tel. 212/753–5171. No reservations. AE. Sun. breakfast, lunch, tea, dinner (closed Sun. July–Aug.). Expensive.*

**Shelby.** Skylights make this pine-paneled restaurant an extremely pleasant place to spend a Sunday, as bright sun makes the glazed ochre walls fairly glow. Enjoy the smoked and grilled items, prepared with a slight southern accent. *967 Lexington Ave., between 70th and 71st Sts., tel. 212/988–4624. Reservations advised. AE, MC, V. Sun. brunch, dinner. Expensive.*

**Camelback & Central.** For a romantic, casual dinner, come here. You'll find soft lighting, a Southwestern color scheme, fresh flowers, and a menu with roast duck with port-and-currant sauce and swordfish with anchovy butter. Brunch bus-

---

**Symbols at the end of an entry signify:** *CH: Good for children; L: Serves after 11 PM; MU: Live music; O: Outdoor dining; VU: Great view.*

tles with neighborhood folk and celebrities. *1403 2nd Ave. at 73rd St., tel. 212/249–8380. No brunch reservations; dinner reservations accepted. AE, DC, MC, V. Sun. brunch, dinner (prix fixe at both). Moderate. O*

**Jim McMullen.** This clubby spot draws a well-heeled crowd spanning several generations. Reliable plain fare is served at gentle prices. *1341 3rd Ave., between 76th and 77th Sts., tel. 212/861–4700. No reservations. AE. Sun. brunch, dinner. Moderate.*

**American/ International**

**Carlyle Restaurant.** With its thick carpets, comfortable chairs, and beautiful appointments, the Carlyle Hotel would make an exceptional place for brunch even without its fabulous brunch buffet. The kitchen takes a classic French approach then and at dinner, when hearty chops and rösti join lighter dishes, such as veal medallions with julienned vegetables. *35 E. 76th St., tel. 212/744–1600. Brunch reservations required, lunch, dinner reservations advised. AE, DC, MC, V. Sun. brunch (prix fixe), lunch, dinner. Very Expensive.*

**Metro.** Chef Patrick Clark, who made his name at Café Luxembourg (*see* Lincoln Center, below), now works his magic at this subtly lighted, elegantly paneled, and blessedly quiet restaurant designed by Adam Tihany. Even the roast chicken and modest potato pancakes and homemade sausage are stellar, not to mention more inventive dishes, such as grilled salmon with lentils and bacon. *25 E. 74th St., tel. 212/249–3030. Reservations advised. AE, DC, MC, V. Sun. brunch, dinner. Very Expensive.*

**Lion's Rock.** This town house restaurant is named for the startling red granite boulder that walls the rear of the garden, where tables are set up among the greenery and falling water every summer. Seafood ravioli with ginger and roast duck with currant sauce and wild rice reflect the chef's spirit. At brunch, try trout with lime beurre blanc. *316 E. 77th St., tel. 212/988–3610. Reservations advised. AE, DC, MC, V. Sun. brunch (prix fixe), lunch, dinner (prix fixe). Expensive. L, O*

**Table d'Hôte.** Those who like this sliver of a restaurant rave about its brunches, where eggs reign in many styles: on English muffin with avocado and bacon; on chopped chicory, endive, and radicchio with mustard sauce; or in fried bread pockets with provolone and ham. A barn-red floor, white wainscoting, and antique tables and silverplate create a country-house aura. Occasionally a guitarist wedges himself in to play. *44 E. 92nd St., tel. 212/348–8125. Reservations advised. AE. Sun. brunch (from 10:30), dinner. Expensive. MU, O*

**Adam's Rib.** The focal point of this favorite with a sunny glassed-in sidewalk café is red meat, specifically roast beef. A Caesar salad comes with every entrée, and live music is played from 1 to 3. *1338 1st Ave. at 72nd St., tel. 212/535–2112. Reservations advised. AE, DC, MC, V. Sun. brunch, lunch, dinner. Moderate. MU*

**Ravelled Sleave.** A piano, fireplace, candlelight, beautiful flowers, and a well-balanced, straightforward menu make this a favorite stop on a winter's day. *1387 3rd Ave., between 78th and 79th Sts., tel. 212/628–8814. No reservations at brunch. AE, DC, MC, V. Sun. brunch, dinner. Moderate. MU*

**Chinese**

**Fu's.** Kinetic proprietress Gloria Chu coddles celebrities and regular folk alike, making this gray-walled dining room with a shiny black bar and bright red banquettes a longtime uptown favorite for Chinese food. Low-fat, low-salt specials are highlights of the menu. *1395 2nd Ave., between 72nd and 73rd Sts., tel. 212/517–9670. Reservations advised. AE, DC, MC, V. Sun. lunch, dinner. Moderate. L*

**Eastern European** **Csarda.** Hungarian folk art decorates the walls, and homesick Hungarians enjoy familiar flavors at the tables—homely goulash, schnitzels, roast duck with nockerls or cabbage, and strudels. *1477 2nd Ave., between 77th and 78th Sts., tel. 212/ 472–2892. Reservations advised for 3 or more. AE. Sun. lunch, dinner. Moderate.*

**Vašata.** This folksy Czech restaurant has been serving goulash, schnitzels, and crisp-skinned roast goose since 1952. With its snowy tablecloths and pale yellow walls, it is as neat and fresh as ever. The cuisine is hearty but not heavy, perfectly mated to Pilsner Urquell, the house beer. *339 E. 75th St., tel. 212/988– 7166. Reservations advised. AE, DC, MC, V. Sun. lunch, dinner. Moderate.*

**French** **Bistro du Nord.** Consistently interesting fare—say, salmon with sherry vinaigrette or lotte perfumed with saffron and fennel—keep an Upper East Side set coming back to this stylish Carnegie Hill nook. There's European music on tape and black-and-white photographs by Avedon, Beaton, and Horst on the yellow walls. *1312 Madison Ave. near 93rd St., tel. 212/ 289–0997. Reservations required. AE. Sun. brunch, lunch (prix fixe), dinner. Very Expensive. L*

**Voulez-Vous.** Brunch here ranges far beyond eggs Benedict— try cheese soufflé, spicy sausages with lentils, or *pizze banana*, with mozzarella, banana, cocoa, and cinnamon. Earthy French bistro dishes such as cassoulet and bouillabaise are a homey way to end a blustery Sunday. The mirrored, bouquet-scattered dining room makes an attractive background for the young neighborhood clientele. *1462 1st Ave. at 76th St., tel. 212/249–1776. Reservations required. AE, DC, MC, V. Sun. brunch, dinner (prix fixe at both). Moderate.*

**Italian** **Lusardi's.** This attractive restaurant with mahogany paneling and original posters on pale yellow walls attracts a well-dressed group of regulars for Sunday afternoon dinner—perhaps tortelloni with four cheeses, veal chop stuffed with ham and Fontina, or Cornish hen cooked with a weight on top. *1494 2nd Ave., between 77th and 78th Sts., tel. 212/249–2020. Reservations required. AE, DC, MC, V. Open Sun. 4–11. Very Expensive.*

**Petaluma.** A pastel dining room where Yuppies once grazed on nouvelle California fare now offers grills, thin-crusted pizzas from the brick oven, and pastas *puttanesca* (redolent of olives and capers) and *amatriciana* (with tomato, onions, and pancetta). *1356 1st Ave. at 73rd St., tel. 212/772–8800. Reservations advised. AE, MC, V. Sun. brunch, dinner. Expensive.*

**Ciao Bella.** In this breezy café, a bicycle on the ceiling alludes to the owner's favorite hobby and there's much ado about Bellinis, carpaccio, and tiramisù—or whatever else is hot among local Italophiles. *1311 3rd Ave. at 75th St., tel. 212/288–2555. No reservations or credit cards. Sun. all day. Moderate. L, O*

**Mezzaluna.** Despite the incessant din and wait for tables, many people love this casual, ultra-chic trattoria with a clouds-and-

---

**Symbols at the end of an entry signify:** *CH: Good for children; L: Serves after 11 PM; MU: Live music; O: Outdoor dining; VU: Great view.*

sky motif on the ceiling. Menu highlights include carpaccios, pizzas, and high-powered pastas—ricotta-stuffed pansotti with sage and Parmesan, for example. *1295 3rd Ave., between 74th and 75th St., tel. 212/535–9600. No reservations or credit cards. Sun. all day. Moderate.*

**Maruzzela.** This stucco-and-tiled café is lively for simple pastas and tasty thin-crust pizzas cooked in the wood-burning oven. *1479 1st Ave. at 77th St., tel. 212/988–8877. No reservations or credit cards. Sun. all day. Inexpensive. L*

**Mediterranean** **Island.** On Sundays, a chic young neighborhood clientele settles into comfortable wicker bistro chairs and lingers at the terrazzo tables here over the robust flavors of Provence and Italy. Brunch features frittatas with goat cheese and *pissaladière*, a Provençal onion tart with olives and anchovies. At dinner, gnocchi comes with spicy sausage and grilled rabbit gets zest from mustard and basil. *1305 Madison Ave., between 92nd and 93rd Sts., tel. 212/996–1200. Sun. brunch, dinner. Reservations required. AE. Expensive.*

**Spanish** **Café San Martin.** In this relaxed restaurant, paella comes several ways. At brunch, the menu offers gazpacho and eggs *flamenca* (baked in a clay pan with sausage and peppers). At dinner, a pianist entertains. Either time sample the good Spanish wines. *1458 1st Ave., between 75th and 76th Sts., tel. 212/288–0470. Sun. brunch, dinner. Reservations not necessary. AE, MC, V. Expensive. MU*

**Thai** **Bangkok House.** This comfortable, deep purple favorite offers a long menu of dishes, such as cucumber salad, beef satay, spring rolls, and hot-lemony squid salad. *1485 1st Ave., between 77th and 78th Sts., tel. 212/249–5700. Sun. dinner. Reservations advised. AE, MC, V. Inexpensive.*

**Turkish** **Uskudar.** Stews, sautés, and grills at this mellow, pastel nook full of native crafts provide authentic tastes and aromas. *1405 2nd Ave., between 73rd and 74th Sts., tel. 212/ 988–2641. Sun. lunch, dinner. Reservations advised. AE. Sun. dinner. Moderate. L*

## Yorkville

Once New York's Little Germany, Little Hungary, and Little Czechoslovakia, this area is worth visiting these days for a couple of dozen excellent—and expensive—Italian restaurants. There's a cluster of other attractive little restaurants as well.

**American** **Ruby's River Road Café.** Young and lively, this restaurant
**Regional** stages a Sunday brunch with extravagant drinks and taped music that's like a quick trip to New Orleans. *1754 2nd Ave., between 91st and 92nd Sts., tel. 212/348–2328. Reservations not required. AE, MC, V. Sun. brunch (except July–Aug.), dinner. Moderate.*

**Belgian** **Flamand.** Tie-back curtains and deep pink walls hung with posters set a cozy scene for bright Belgian specialties prepared with an imaginative hand. Braising in Belgian beers gives rabbit, veal, and chicken livers extra zest; a salad of dandelion greens with bacon makes a good beginning. *349 E. 86th St., tel. 212/722–4610. Reservations accepted. AE, DC, MC, V. Sun. dinner. Expensive.*

**Chinese** **Pig Heaven.** Don't be put off by the pink pig balloons, dancing-pig mural, and other piggy accoutrements. The terrific Cantonese fare here emphasizes pork, from the scallion-pancake dim sum to the heavenly roast suckling pig, though there are nonporcine options as well. *1540 2nd Ave., between 80th and 81st Sts., tel. 212/744–4887. Reservations advised. AE, DC. Sun. brunch, dinner. Moderate. CH*

**Eastern European** **Mocca Hungarian Restaurant.** Robust Hungarian food and wines make this café convivial. Savor hearty goulashes and the preserve-filled crêpes called *palacsinta*—you won't be hungry again for hours. *1588 2nd Ave., between 82nd and 83rd Sts., tel. 212/734–6470. Reservations advised. No credit cards. Sun. lunch (prix fixe), dinner. Inexpensive.*

**French** **Le Boeuf à la Mode.** This bistro with etched-glass partitions and white tablecloths pleases a conservative crowd with classics such as duck à l'orange and chateaubriand. Roomy and pleasant, it's a spot to linger in. *539 E. 81st St., tel. 212/249–1473. Reservations advised. AE, DC, MC, V. Sun. dinner (prix fixe). Expensive.*

**Le Refuge.** Romantic decor and consistently good renditions of lamb chops with rosemary and pistachio-stuffed veal make this a favorite of a dressed-up East Side group. *166 E. 82nd St., tel. 212/861–4505. Reservations advised. No credit cards. Sun. lunch, dinner. Expensive.*

**Italian Northern** **Primavera.** Pampering service and a polished setting keep the rich and famous coming back here. Specialties include roast marinated kid, succulent and sweeter than lamb, and fresh fruit carved into fanciful shapes for dessert. *1578 1st Ave. at 82nd, tel. 212/861–8608. Reservations required. AE, DC, MC, V. Sun. dinner. Very Expensive.*

**Sistina.** East Siders line up at this genial café full of blond wood and white linen. Animated Romeo-waiters describe the esoteric fare from the untranslated Italian menu: "Fantastico!" they exclaim. The spaghetti *alla carbonara* is authentic, but when white truffles are on the menu, don't pass them up. *1555 2nd Ave., between 80th and 81st Sts., tel. 212/861–7660. Reservations required. AE. Sun. dinner (closed Sun. July–Aug.). Very Expensive.*

**Paola's.** In this romantic, dollhouse-sized charmer, little mirrors on the walls show off a flotsam of bric-à-brac and allow a genteel crowd to preen surreptitiously over pastas, soups, and grills. *347 E. 85th St., tel. 212/794–1890. Reservations required. AE. Sun. dinner. Expensive.*

**Elaine's.** Go early Sunday evening and you'll be seated speedily and treated well; order the double veal chop and you'll relish your dinner. Linger until 9 and you may spot a celebrity basking in the proprietress's warmth. *1703 2nd Ave., between 88th and 89th Sts., tel. 212/534–8103. Reservations accepted. AE, MC, V. Sun. dinner. Expensive. L*

**Divino.** Good pastas and herb-aromatic grills cost a shade less here than elsewhere in the neighborhood. *1556 2nd Ave., between 80th and 81st Sts., tel. 212/861–1096. Reservations required. AE, DC, MC, V. Sun. dinner. Moderate.*

**Due.** It's mobbed and modern, with an airy, geometric design

**Symbols at the end of an entry signify:** *CH: Good for children; L: Serves after 11 PM; MU: Live music; O: Outdoor dining; VU: Great view.*

by architect Charles Gwathmey. The menu spotlights focaccia, which are inch-thick pocketless pitas with pizzalike toppings. *1396 3rd Ave., between 79th and 80th Sts., tel. 212/772–3331. Reservations required. No credit cards. Sun. lunch, dinner. Moderate. L*

**Il Giorno.** Such a solid little Italian eatery stands out in this neighborhood for its modest prices. *1600 3rd Ave. at 90th St., tel. 212/348–1600. Reservations advised. AE, DC, MC, V. Sun. brunch (prix fixe), dinner. Inexpensive. L*

*Southern* **Azzurro.** This friendly storefront café, with a star-scattered blue ceiling, offers beautiful renditions of unusual Sicilian dishes: bucatini tossed with sardines and fennel or penne with roasted eggplant and tomato. It can be noisy, but diners love the happy hubbub. *1625 2nd Ave. at 84th St., tel. 212/517–7068. Reservations required. AE, DC. Sun. dinner. Expensive.*

**Middle Eastern** **Anatolia.** This postmodern exotic, with faux stone columns and crinkle-glazed pastel walls, offers quail in vine leaves, lamb shanks with lemon sauce, and other bright fare. The *mezze* (hors d'oeuvres) are a meal in themselves. *1422 3rd Ave., between 80th and 81st Sts., tel. 212/517–6262. Reservations advised. AE, DC, MC, V. Sun. dinner (closed Sun. July–Aug.). Moderate.*

**Istanbul Cuisine.** This crowded nook, a reliable if less original alternative to Anatolia, offers its tasty fare at a bargain price. *303 E. 80th St., tel. 212/744–6903. Reservations not required. No credit cards. Sun. dinner. Inexpensive.*

*Seafood* **Wilkinson's Seafood Café.** This peach-hued, softly lit fish house offers innovative lobster, scallop, and shrimp ravioli; red snapper poached with sake; and grills. Meat eaters can savor the good strip steak with fries. *1573 York Ave., between 83rd and 84th Sts., tel. 212/535–5454. Reservations advised. AE, DC, MC, V. Sun. dinner (closed Sun. Aug.). Very Expensive.*

## Lincoln Center

"Yuppieterias" have been sprouting like crazy along Columbus Avenue and on adjacent side streets in the past few years—in fine weather there must be more seats outdoors per block here than on any other avenue in the city. The experience is often more memorable than the food.

**American/ International** **Andiamo!** This glitzy high-ceilinged café has a menu as interesting as the premises, thanks to specials, such as Maine lobster with sweet pepper butter and fettucine in dill-salmon cream sauce. No smoking is allowed. To get here, follow the corridor alongside the inexpensive Café Bel Canto. *1991 Broadway at 67th St., tel. 212/362–3315. Reservations advised. AE, MC, V. Sun. dinner. Very Expensive.*

**Café des Artistes.** Howard Chandler Christy's lush murals of nudes would draw crowds to this romantic West Side institution even if the food were not as good as it is. The interesting Sunday brunch features fine main dishes, such as smoked salmon Benedict with tarragon hollandaise. At dinner, don't miss the dessert sampler. *1 W. 67th St., tel. 212/877–3500. Reservations required. AE, DC, MC, V. Sun. brunch, dinner. Very Expensive. L*

**Tavern on the Green.** This sumptuous Central Park fantasy now offers a bright new chef's contemporary cuisine, with dishes such as duck breast with apples, walnuts, corn, and green beans at brunch and sea scallops with Chinese cabbage at dinner. The Chestnut Room is cozy, the chandelier-hung Crystal Room sparkles, and the terrace delights in pleasant weather. *Central Park West at 67th St., tel. 212/873-3200. Reservations required. Jacket advised. AE, DC, MC, V. Sun. brunch, dinner. Very Expensive. O*

**Café Luxembourg.** In this hip local favorite, a sophisticated, good-natured staff offers well-honed brasserie standbys salted with nouvelle American ideas. The setting is pure Paris bistro, the buzzing crowd pure New York. *200 W. 70th St., tel. 212/873-7411. Reservations required. AE, DC, MC, V. Sun. brunch, dinner. Expensive. L*

**Cameos.** A piano-bass duo makes beautiful music to brunch by in this elegant, vaguely Art Deco newcomer. The innovative kitchen crosses French and Japanese flavors to good effect. Heavenly crab cakes are a must at brunch. *169 Columbus Ave., between 67th and 68th Sts., tel. 212/874-2280. Reservations advised. AE, DC, MC, V. Sun. brunch (prix fixe), dinner. Expensive. MU*

**The Saloon.** This cavernous saloon, with some waiters on skates, is conveniently opposite Lincoln Center. The menu is inventive but immense; stick to simpler dishes and you'll call it a find. *1920 Broadway at 64th St., tel. 212/874-1500. Reservations not required. AE, MC, V. Sun. brunch, lunch, dinner. Moderate. CH, L*

**Chinese** **Shun Lee Café.** This sleek black-and-white spot is the area's dim sum darling, offering fare such as drunken chicken and eggplant chips. The menu ranges from the ridiculous to the sublime. *43 W. 65th St., tel. 212/769-3888. Reservations advised. AE, DC, MC, V. Sun. brunch, dinner. Moderate.*

**French** **La Boîte en Bois.** At this tiny restaurant, decorated in rustic country-French style, you can dine on monkfish in saffron sauce or green peppercorns and zesty fish soup. The food generally reveals cooks of a high order at work—not often true in this area. *75 E. 68th St., tel. 212/874-2705. Reservations advised. No credit cards. Sun. dinner. Expensive.*

**Italian** **Sfuzzi.** Fanciful faux-Pompeii decor sets the scene for the eponymous fun food: savory, clear-flavored pasta dishes, grilled fish and chops, and pizzas. Try the frozen Sfuzzis, which mix sparkling wine, peach schnapps, peach puree, and ice. *58 W. 65th St., tel. 212/873-3700. Reservations preferred. AE, DC, MC, V. Sun. brunch, dinner. Expensive.*

**Fiorello's Roman Café.** This bustling restaurant across from Lincoln Center offers outdoor seating and cozy, comfortable tables inside. Specialties include thin-crusted individual pizzas and he-man veal chops. *1900 Broadway, between 63rd and 64th Sts., tel. 212/595-5330. Reservations advised. AE, DC, MC, V. Sun. lunch, dinner. Moderate. O, CH.*

**Japanese** **Lenge.** This local landmark offers diverting Japanese fare, including the hearty *nabe*, (noodle soups). *200 Columbus Ave. at 69th St., tel. 212/799-9188. Reservations advised. AE, DC. Sun. lunch, dinner. Inexpensive.*

**Symbols at the end of an entry signify:** *CH: Good for children; L: Serves after 11 PM; MU: Live music; O: Outdoor dining; VU: Great view.*

**Mexican/**
**Southwestern**

**Santa Fe.** The desert-sunset color scheme is sophisticated, fish dishes have real zest, and the margaritas rate kudos. What's for brunch? Try Southwestern omelets and enchiladas suizas. *72 W. 69th St., tel. 212/724–0822. Reservations advised; not required at brunch. AE, MC, V. Sun. brunch (prix fixe), lunch, dinner. Expensive. L*

## Upper West Side

There are so many restaurants here that you wonder whether the local folk ever eat in. Many are the kind of ordinary spots that you pop into only because they're there, but a few stand out for prices, ambience, or honest-to-goodness good food.

**American/Casual**

**Amsterdam's.** The real focus of this occasionally cacophonous brick-walled café is its rotisserie, which turns out mouth-watering grilled chicken. You can also get pastas, salads, and, in the afternoons, sandwiches. *428 Amsterdam Ave., between 80th and 81st Sts., tel. 212/874–1377. Reservations not required. AE, DC, MC, V. Sun. lunch, dinner. Moderate. CH, L*

**Good Enough to Eat.** Displays of baskets, quilts, and farm tools make this nook feel like Vermont. The homey fare includes apple pancakes and pecan waffles, chicken grills and vegetable melts, and meat loaf and chicken pot pie. *483 Amsterdam Ave., between 83rd and 84th Sts., tel. 212/496–0163. Reservations advised. No credit cards. Sun. breakfast (from 9), brunch, tea, dinner. Moderate.*

**Museum Café.** This sunny café has spent the past 15 years serving its own versions of whatever's most fashionable on the New York food scene. At present, it's something-for-everyone American regional-Chinese-Mexican-Italian. *366 Columbus Ave. at 77th St., tel. 212/799–0150. Dinner reservations accepted. AE, MC, V. Sun. brunch, dinner. Moderate. L*

**Popover Café.** This once-tiny eatery, built around an airy puff of eggs and flour, has expanded yet again, to the delight of New Yorkers and Europeans who come to enjoy the eponymous popovers' accompaniments: soups, sandwiches, salads, and omelets. Try the cappuccino eggs, cooked to fluffiness in the shell by steam from the espresso maker. *551 Amsterdam Ave. at 87th St., tel. 212/595–8555. No reservations. AE. Sun. brunch (from 10), dinner. Moderate.*

**All State Café.** This low-ceilinged, brick-walled old-timer has a good jukebox, rickety chairs, and '60s charm. You'll find good fish, poultry, and pastas at very pleasant prices. *250 W. 72nd St., tel. 212/874–1883. No reservations or credit cards. Sun. brunch, dinner. Inexpensive. L*

**Sarabeth's Kitchen.** This beige-and-peach tea room beguiles the brunch set with pumpkin waffles, apple-cinnamon French toast, and green-and-white eggs—scrambled with scallions and cream cheese. *423 Amsterdam Ave., between 80th and 81st Sts., tel. 212/496–6280. No reservations. AE, DC, MC, V. Sun. breakfast and brunch (from 9). Inexpensive.*

**American/**
**International**

**AROC–A Restaurant on Columbus.** In this quiet, lofty-ceilinged newcomer, many menu offerings may sound odd (grilled sushi tuna with miso-butter sauce, for example), but the kitchen usually comes through. The low-calorie, low-sodium, low-cholesterol offerings are commendable. *Live music for brunchtime is in the works. 384 Columbus Ave., between 78th and 79th Sts., tel. 212/799–9100. Reservations advised.*

*AE, DC, MC, V. Sun. brunch, dinner (prix fixe at both). Moderate.*

**Boulevard.** A lively mural sets the tone with stylized taxicabs and street scenes. Brunchtime's eclectic offerings range from Cajun sausage on English muffin to egg foo young; dinner features sprightly grills, pastas, and house-smoked meats. Kids enjoy doodling on the tables' butcher-paper coverings. *2398 Broadway at 88th St., tel. 212/874–7400. Reservations advised. AE, DC, MC, V. Sun. brunch, lunch, dinner. Moderate. CH, L, O*

**Goodbye Columbus.** This country-French spot with lace-curtained French windows draws an eclectic crowd with its modestly priced brunch and suave dinner entrées, such as black linguine with shrimp or chicken breast stuffed with goat cheese. *718 Amsterdam Ave., between 95th and 96th Sts., tel. 212/222–1222. No reservations. AE, MC, V. Sun. brunch, lunch, dinner. Moderate.*

**Julia.** The mystery is why this mellow, pretty restaurant is known only to its coterie of regulars. Good grills, fine pastas, and fresh fish are prepared with restrained creativity, and service is very pleasant. *226 W. 79th St., tel. 212/787–1511. Reservations accepted. AE, DC, MC, V. Sun. brunch (prix fixe), dinner. Moderate.*

**West Side Storey.** Roomy booths indoors and a crowd of sidewalk tables invite lingering here. West Siders arrive early to tuck into brunch's offbeat nova-and-vegetables Benedict and apple-walnut pancakes and grilled tuna Niçoise and Thai-spiced chicken *gai yang* later on. *700 Columbus Ave. at 95th St., tel. 212/749–1900. No credit cards or reservations. Sun. breakfast, brunch, lunch, dinner. Moderate. O*

**American Regional**  **Sidewalkers.** At New York's only Maryland crab house, you drink beer while pounding and picking away at spiced blue crabs in a huge dining room full of paper-covered tables. *12 W. 72nd St., tel. 212/799–6070. Reservations advised. AE, DC, MC, V. Sun. dinner. Moderate.*

**Dallas BBQ.** Here is the West Side's best source for onion rings and barbecue. *27 W. 72nd St., tel. 212/873–2004. No reservations. AE, DC, MC, V. Sun. lunch, dinner. Inexpensive. L*

**Yellow Rose Café.** This tiny café, with a Lone Star State motif, wows locals with eggs in flour tortillas and green-chili-and-sour-cream omelets at breakfast; with cubed-meat chili, chicken fried steak, and supreme mashed potatoes at dinner; and with great biscuits and corn bread all the time. *450 Amsterdam Ave., between 81st and 82nd Sts., tel. 212/595–8760. No reservations. AE, DC, MC, V. Sun. brunch (from 10), dinner. Inexpensive.*

**Ethiopian**  **Blue Nile.** This cousin of SoHo's Abyssinia (*see* above) is slightly less funky, delightfully quiet, and a reward for the adventurous. *103 W. 77th St., tel. 212/580–3232. Reservations not required. AE. Sun. lunch, dinner. Inexpensive.*

**French**  **Poiret.** This minimalist French bistro, home of one of the neighborhood's more ambitious kitchens, tempts a chic crowd with sophisticated fare all day long—whiting meunière and omelets with chanterelles at brunch, beef carbonnade and roast chicken

---

**Symbols at the end of an entry signify:** *CH: Good for children; L: Serves after 11 PM; MU: Live music; O: Outdoor dining; VU: Great view.*

at dinner. It can be noisy when it's busy. *474 Columbus Ave.,
between 82nd and 83rd Sts., tel. 212/724–6880. Reservations
required. AE, MC, V. Sun. brunch, dinner. Expensive. L*

**Italian**   **Baci.** In this welcoming storefront spot, a raked-glass ceiling
and terrazzo-topped tables add up to a supremely stylish setting. The food is gutsy Sicilian fare, such as penne with
eggplant and bucatini with sardines and pine nuts. *412 Amsterdam Ave., between 79th and 80th Sts., tel. 212/496–1550. No
reservations or credit cards. Sun. brunch (prix fixe), lunch,
dinner. Moderate. L*
**Cavaliere.** A rosy hearthside main room, glassed-in garden,
and skylit back room are pleasant spots for crisp lemon-
perfumed zucchini fries with sesame seeds and duck breast
with corn pancakes and wild mushrooms. Dishes are devised by
consultant-chef Anne Rosenzweig, of Arcadia. *108 W. 73rd St.,
tel. 212/799–8282. Reservations advised. AE, DC, MC, V. Sun.
all day. Moderate. L*
**Caffè Bernini.** Marble tabletops on ornate cast-iron bases lend
style here, but it's the old-fashioned pasta menu with
pregentrification prices that lures the clientele, mostly West
Side intelligentsia. *250 W. 77th St., tel. 212/496–6674. No reservations or credit cards. Sun. dinner. Inexpensive.*
**Genoa.** Why the line outside this hole-in-the-wall? The hours
are short (5:30–9:30 on Sunday), the prices rock bottom, and
the fare tasty old favorites, such as spaghetti carbonara or
puttanesca. *271 Amsterdam Ave., between 72nd and 73rd Sts.,
tel. 212/787–1094. No reservations. AE, MC, V. Sun. dinner.
Inexpensive.*

**Japanese**   **Fujiyama Mama.** The high-tech decor here features a row of
white-slipcover-draped chairs up front; a DJ is crammed into a
rear corner. The menu's highlight is the deep-fried ice cream
flambé—when it's served for a birthday, it comes with a spar-
kler. *467 Columbus Ave., between 82nd and 83rd Sts., tel. 212/
769–1144. Reservations advised. AE. Sun. dinner. Moderate.*
**Bon 75.** Daily, monthly, and seasonal specials supplement the
menu at this unassuming black-and-gray restaurant. The extensive appetizer list lets you create a meal Japanese-style,
with several tasty small-portion dishes. Broiled fish is good,
too. *2140 Broadway at 75th St., tel. 212/724–1414. Reservations advised. AE, MC, V. Sun. brunch, dinner. Inexpensive.*

**Latin-Chinese**   **La Caridad.** Formica dominates the decor in this favorite of savvy cabbies, where the prices are low and the atmosphere is
warm. Specialties include the Cuban pot roast known as *ropa
vieja*, garlicky squid fried rice, and banana egg foo young. *2199
Broadway at 78th St., tel. 212/874–2780. No credit cards or reservations. BYOB. Sun. lunch, dinner. Inexpensive.*

**Seafood**   **Coastal.** Silkily fresh seafood is poached or broiled to order
here and served with pear mango salsa, hollandaise, beurre
blanc, and other sauces amid hyperenlarged nautical charts
and huge multipaned windows. The very good California
whites poured by the glass help you tolerate the busy roar. *300
Amsterdam Ave. at 74th St., tel. 212/769–3988. Reservations
for 4 or more. AE. Sun. brunch, dinner. Moderate.*
**Dock's Oyster Bar and Seafood Grill.** The long bar and black-
and-white tiled floors are relics of the old West Side, but this
fish house is au courant, with its changing menu of grills,
stews, and sautéed dishes. On Sundays, try scrambled eggs
with nova or smoked fish. *2427 Broadway, between 89th and*

*90th Sts., tel. 212/724–5588. Reservations advised. AE, DC, MC, V. Sun. brunch, dinner. Moderate.*

**Spanish** **Alcala.** The archetypal grazing food, Spanish tapas, are the specialty of this softly lit, brick-walled restaurant. After sampling such treats as cumin-spiked chick peas and seafood bits vinaigrette, you could stay to enjoy an entrée, perhaps a paella or peppery grouper. Oenophiles call the Spanish wine selection among New York's best. *349 Amsterdam Ave., between 76th and 77th Sts., tel. 212/769–9600. Reservations not required. AE, DC, MC, V. Sun. dinner. Moderate.*

## Far Upper West Side

The neighborhood from 96th Street north to Columbia University, rapidly gentrifying, is thick with Chinese restaurants, a few of them noteworthy. The local hot spots are well worth a visit, and inexpensive eating abounds.

**Caribbean** **Bahama Mama.** For hipsters, islanders, and regular neighborhood folk, this place sets a tropical mood with a reggae and calypso sound track, scattered paper fruits and birds, and a pink-yellow-green-and-blue color scheme. The menu offers exotic dishes, such as the okra-and-corn bread concoction known as *coo-coo* at brunch and Jamaican jerk chicken, curried goat, and flying fish for dinner. A steel drummer plays all afternoon. *2628 Broadway, between 99th and 100th Sts., tel. 212/866–7760. Reservations advised. AE. Sun. brunch (prix fixe), dinner. Moderate. MU*

**Chinese** **Hunan Balcony.** Decor is standard—chrome, glass, blond wood, hanging plants—and the extensive menu virtually the same as that of most non-Chinatown Szechuan/Hunan spots. The difference here is reliably careful preparation: crisply steamed vegetables, non-greasy sauces, and no stinting on the meat or fish. Cold noodles with sesame sauce are a spicy-hot treat. *2596 Broadway at 98th St., tel. 212/865–0400. Reservations not required. AE, DC, MC, V. Sun. lunch, dinner. Inexpensive. L.*

**Italian** **V&T Restaurant.** The substantial-crusted pizza comes with an array of toppings as old-fashioned as the oilcloth on the tables. A Columbia students' hangout since 1945, it's handily opposite St. John the Divine. *1024 Amsterdam Ave., between 110th and 111th Sts., tel. 212/663–1708. Reservations accepted. No credit cards. Sun. all day. Inexpensive. L*

## Harlem

**Soul Food** **Sylvia's Soul Food Restaurant.** People come from all over the city to feast in this Harlem legend. For years it has been serving zesty collard greens, black-eyed peas, candied sweet potatoes, and gritty homemade cornbread with terrific pork chops, smothered chicken, tender braised short ribs, and pecan pie. *329 Lenox Ave. near 126th St., tel. 212/996–0660. Reservations required. No credit cards. Open Sun. 1–7. Inexpensive.*

**Symbols at the end of an entry signify:** *CH: Good for children; L: Serves after 11 PM; MU: Live music; O: Outdoor dining; VU: Great view.*

## The Bronx

Arthur Avenue in the Belmont section is like an old-fashioned Italian Restaurant Row; it will change your ideas about the Bronx forever.

**Italian** **Amerigo's.** This half-century-old restaurant feeds hungry diners in two dining rooms, one casual and one formally filled with Italian sculpture. You'll find anchovy-sauced fried mozzarella, gnocchi with a verdant pesto, prime steaks and chops, first-class osso buco, and sublime pork chops with vinegar peppers. All this comes in huge portions—at fair prices. *3587 E. Tremont Ave., between Sullivan Pl. and Lafayette St., Throgs Neck, tel. 212/792–3600. Reservations required. Jacket advised in main dining room. AE, DC, MC, V. Sun. lunch, dinner. Expensive.*

**Dominick's.** It's always crowded at this 30-year-old pasta house where platters of spaghetti come saturated with freshly made sauce to down with crusty bread and rough red wine. Everyone sits at long communal tables to feast on shrimp, calamari in red sauce, and fettuccine with bacon-mushroom cream sauce. There is no menu, and waiters keep the running tabs in their heads. The draw is simply honest fare at honest prices. *2335 Arthur Ave., tel. 212/ 733–2807. No reservations or credit cards. Sun. lunch, dinner. Inexpensive.*

## Brooklyn

Brooklyn restaurants reflect the tastes both of its deeply rooted ethnic populations and of the newcomers to its gentrifying neighborhoods. Montague Street in Brooklyn Heights; Fifth Avenue in Park Slope; and Court Street in Cobble Hill, south of Atlantic Avenue, are full of tiny little restaurants that serve casual American fare with international accents in quaint surroundings. Flatbush Avenue is an outpost of Jamaica, while Brighton Beach, down by Coney Island and the Aquarium, is full of boisterous Russian restaurants.

**American/** **River Café.** From this elegantly unassuming barge-restaurant
**International** in the shadow of the Brooklyn Bridge, Manhattan seems close enough to touch, and you can enjoy quail breasts stuffed with foie gras or roast squab with risotto as boats chug briskly by. The presentations are exquisite—a parfait may come with a lacy dome of chocolate and a chocolate butterfly on top. Whether you go for a festive brunch, with the sun sparkling on water, or for dinner or drinks with music and the glittering after-dark view, it's a wonderful spot. *1 Water St., tel. 718/522–5200. Reservations required. Jacket and tie advised. AE, DC, MC, V. Sun. brunch, dinner. Very Expensive. L, MU, O, VU*

**Nightfalls.** This stunning postmodern restaurant—all gray, salmon, and peach, with a 36-foot-wide waterfall—comes as a surprise in Bay Ridge, which most New Yorkers know best as John Travolta's home town in *Saturday Night Fever.* Beer-battered coconut shrimp and pecan-coated chicken breast with raspberry mustard sauce typify the kitchen's regional American approach. A pianist plays at brunch. *7612 3rd Ave., between 76th and 77th Sts., Bay Ridge, tel. 718/748–8700. Reservations advised. AE, DC, MC, V. Sun. brunch (prix fixe), dinner. Expensive. MU, O, VU*

**Parker's Lighthouse.** The management offers you a newspaper, gratis, and serves homemade breads at an all-you-can-eat brunch buffet along with omelets, salads, and grills. The stunning Manhattan view makes this one of the city's best-kept restaurant secrets. *1 Main St. at Fulton Landing, tel. 718/237–1555. Reservations advised. AE, DC, MC, V. Sun. brunch (prix fixe), dinner. Expensive. VU*

**Aunt Sonia.** This cozy little restaurant has a pressed-tin ceiling, black-and-white tile floor, a vintage bar, and formica tables. It offers creditable fare, such as blackened shrimp with dirty rice and bacon-spiked braised chicken with cornmeal dumplings. *1123 8th Ave. at 12th St., Park Slope, tel. 718/965–9526. Reservations necessary. MC, V. Sun. brunch, dinner. Moderate. L*

**De'Vine Restaurant & Wine Bar.** No fewer than 45 wines are poured by the glass at this brick-walled eatery with black-tile-topped tables and rosy low lighting. The quirky cuisine ranges from Italy to Thailand, depending on the chef's whim. *396 7th Ave., between 12th and 13th Sts., Park Slope, tel. 718/499–9861. Reservations advised. DC, MC, V. Sun. brunch (prix fixe), dinner. Closed 2 weeks. Aug. Moderate.*

**American Regional**

**Gage & Tollner.** Brooklyn's only interior landmark restaurant boasts gas-fueled chandeliers, red wallpaper, burnished paneling, etched mirrors, and creaky waiters in short black jackets and long white aprons. The menu offers steaks, chops, grills, chowders, clam bellies, and almost every kind of oyster and clam you can name. *372 Fulton St., between Boerum Pl. and Smith St., tel. 718/875–5181. Reservations advised. AE, DC, MC, V. Sun. brunch, dinner (prix fixe at both). Moderate.*

**Italian**

**Monte's Venetian Room.** At this amiable old-timer with antique murals, scarlet banquettes, and snowy tablecloths, waiters bring fried zucchini and garlic bread before they bring the enormous menu of reliable Neapolitan fare. Go for straightforward pasta dishes, filet mignon, or shrimp with tomato, olives, and garlic. *451 Carroll St., between 3rd Ave. and Nevins St., tel. 718/624–8984. Reservations advised. AE, DC, MC, V. Sun. all day. Very Expensive.*

**Tommaso.** The traditional fare here includes stuffed squid on linguini and rabbit with cornmeal; wine lovers come for the vast selection of wines at prices that haven't been seen in stores for a decade. Regulars pile in for their big meal of the day, and an Italian singer performs all afternoon. *1464 86th St., between 14th and 15th Aves., tel. 718/236–9883. Reservations advised. AE, DC, MC, V. Sun. lunch, dinner. Moderate. MU*

**Middle Eastern**

**Moroccan Star.** This simple, neat nook stands out for its lamb steaks, chicken pie with spices and garlic, and robust lamb stew with almonds, prunes, and carrots. *205 Atlantic Ave., tel. 718/643–0800. Reservations accepted. AE, MC, V. Sun. lunch, dinner. BYOB. Inexpensive.*

**Russian**

**Odessa.** This Brighton Beach Russian nightclub-restaurant is like a Las Vegas revue, an Italian wedding, a glitzy bar mitzvah, and a trip to Moscow all rolled into one. Waiters deliver platterfuls of fare, such as stuffed cabbage and apple-and-celery Russian salad. *1113 Brighton Beach Ave., Brighton Beach, tel. 718/332–3223. Reservations not required. AE, DC, MC, V. Sun. dinner. Moderate. MU*

---

**Symbols at the end of an entry signify:** *CH: Good for children; L: Serves after 11 PM; MU: Live music; O: Outdoor dining; VU: Great view.*

**Steak**　**Peter Luger.** Giant aged tenderloins and extra-thick lamb chops are the attractions at this bit of culinary Old New York, an austere dining room full of oak wainscoting and beer-hall tables. Save room for pecan pie, served with a whopping bowl of whipped cream. *178 Broadway, tel. 718/387-7400. Reservations advised. No credit cards. Sun. lunch, dinner. Very Expensive.*

## Queens

This sprawling borough is full of ethnic neighborhoods, each with a complement of restaurants where robust flavors can be enjoyed for a song. Roosevelt Avenue, in the shadow of the elevated train, shows off food from Argentina, Colombia, Cuba, and the Philippines. Elmhurst is full of Thai spots, Flushing is home to New York's second-largest Chinese community, and in Astoria, Greek restaurants line the streets.

**American/**　**Water's Edge.** The psychological distance between this roman-
**International**　tic spot and Manhattan keeps many New Yorkers from discovering its sublime view of the city skyline. The food lives up to the setting, too; try the consistently fresh seafood or grilled quail with chestnut ravioli. A shuttle sails regularly from 23rd Street, Manhattan, in summer. *44th Dr. at East River, Long Island City, tel. 718/482-0033. Reservations advised. AE, DC, MC, V. Sun. brunch (prix fixe), dinner. Very Expensive. O, VU*

**German**　**Chalet Alpina.** An accordionist strolls, and waitresses in embroidered blouses serve draft Spaten and Dortmunder beers, robust schnitzels, and bacon-infused potato salad. *98-35 Metropolitan Ave. at 70th Ave., Forest Hills, tel. 718/793-3774. Reservations advised. AE, MC, V. Sun. lunch, early dinner. Moderate. MU*

**Greek**　**Roumeli Taverna.** This winning outpost of Greece, its vine-entwined stucco walls twinkling with lights, serves consistently good grape leaves, grilled fish, and roast lamb. *33-04 Broadway, Astoria, tel. 718/278-7533. Reservations advised. AE. Sun. lunch, dinner. Moderate. L*

**Latin**　**La Fusta.** Parrillada—huge Argentine mixed grills barbecued tableside—are the specialty at this neighborhood favorite with riding crops ("la fusta" in Spanish) on the walls. Start with the garlicky meat dumplings and end with caramelized milk flan. *80-32 Baxter Ave., Elmhurst, tel. 718/429-8222. No reservations or credit cards. Sun. 2-11. Moderate.*
**Cali Viejo.** Stop in at this simple spot for tamales or *envueltos de maíz* (honey-sweet fritters). *84-24 Roosevelt Ave., Jackson Heights, tel. 718/424-2755. No reservations. AE. Sun. lunch, dinner. Inexpensive.*

**Thai**　**Jai Ya Thai.** This basic diner's Thai food is about as authentic as you can get this side of Bangkok. *81-11 Broadway, between 74th St. and Queens Blvd., tel. 718/651-1330. Reservations dinner only. AE, DC, MC, V. Sun. lunch, dinner. Inexpensive.*

## Staten Island

**French**　**La Fosse Aux Loups.** When you ferry to Staten Island, this little French restaurant is a good bet, just a couple of minutes' walk from the ferry. *11 Schuyler St., tel. 718/442–9111. No reservations. AE, MC, V. Sun. dinner. Moderate.*

**Italian**  **Basilio Inn.** This old-timer, in a mid-19th-century stable, has a boccie court, grape arbor, and charm aplenty. Its homey chicken scarpariello and red snapper Livornese are worth the trip. *2 and 6 Galesville Court, tel. 718/447–9292. Reservations advised. AE. Sun. 1–8. Inexpensive.*

# Ice Cream, Pastries, Coffee, and Tea

**Downtown**  **Minter's Ice Cream Kitchen.** Premium ice cream in flavors like Kahlua and cream is served with mix-ins. *3rd floor, Pier 17, South St. Seaport, tel. 212/608–2037. Sun. 10–10. No credit cards.*

**Minter's Fun Food and Drink.** Choose among six kinds of chocolate chip cookies and exotic drinks such as chocolate martinis. *4 World Financial Center, 2200 Vesey St., near the West Side Hgwy., tel. 212/945–4455. Sun. noon–8. AE, MC, V.*

**SoHo**  **Dean & DeLuca.** Espresso or cappucino are served among the tea kettles. *560 Broadway at Prince St., tel. 212/431–1691. Sun. 10–6. AE, MC, V.*

**Dimitri's.** You'll find Ben & Jerry's ice cream here in a gray-and-white café. *156 Spring St. at W. Broadway, tel. 212/334–9239. Sun. 10 AM–11 PM. No credit cards.*

**Madeline's Restaurant and Pâtisserie.** This restaurant-café is pleasant for lemonade or espresso and beignets, madeleines, and bittersweet fudge brownies. *177 Prince St., between Sullivan and Thompson Sts., tel. 212/477–2788. Sun. 9:30 AM–11 PM. AE.*

**Chinatown and**  **Caffè Roma.** This authentic old Italian coffee house features
**Little Italy**  marble-topped tables and a long pastry case. *385 Broome St. at Mulberry St., tel. 212/226–8413. Sun. 8 AM–midnight. No credit cards.*

**Chinatown Ice Cream Factory.** Head here when you're in the mood for green tea, coconut, or red bean ice cream. *65 Bayard St. near Mott St., tel. 212/608–4170. Sun. 11–11. No credit cards.*

**Ferrara.** This New York institution remains a pleasure for espresso, dessert, and people watching. *195 Grand St. at Mulberry St., tel. 212/226–6150. Sun. 7:30 AM–midnight. No credit cards.*

**East Village**  **De Robertis Pastry Shop.** This mosaic-tiled coffeehouse has been around forever—and looks it. Try *biscotti* (the hard, dunkable Italian cookies). *161 1st Ave. at 10th St., tel. 212/674–7137. Sun. 9:30AM–midnight. No credit cards.*

**Gelateria Siracusa.** Here you can get real Italian gelati in flavors such as hazelnut and ricotta. *65 4th Ave., between 9th and 10th Sts., tel. 212/254–1940. Sun. 5–11. No credit cards.*

**Gem Spa.** One of the first places in New York to serve egg creams, it still pours some of the best. *131 2nd Ave. at St. Mark's Pl. Open 24 hrs. No credit cards.*

**Symbols at the end of an entry signify:** *CH: Good for children; L: Serves after 11 PM; MU: Live music; O: Outdoor dining; VU: Great view.*

**Pravinie Gourmet Ice Cream.** Fancy ice cream comes in 35 flavors here. *27 St. Mark's Pl., between 2nd and 3rd Aves., tel. 212/673–5948. Sun. noon–midnight. No credit cards.*

**West Village** **Caffè Dante.** This convivial spot serves superlative espresso. *79–81 MacDougal St., between Houston and Bleecker Sts., tel. 212/982–5275. Sun. 10 AM–3 AM. No credit cards.*

**Caffè Reggio.** A smoke-darkened, vintage-1927 room holds a huge, fanciful espresso machine and lots of old Italian art. *119 MacDougal St., between W. 3rd St. and Bleecker St., tel. 212/475–9557. Sun. 10 AM–2 AM. No credit cards.*

**Caffè Vivaldi.** This neighborhood spot is a pleasant place to soak up Greenwich Village atmosphere any time. In summer, its quiet side street makes for peaceful sidewalk-sitting. *32 Jones St. at Bleecker St., tel. 212/691–7538. Sun. 10 AM–1 AM. No credit cards.*

**Danal.** A good tea is served at this comfortable charmer. *90 E. 10th St., between 3rd and 4th Aves., tel. 212/982–6930. Sun. 11:30–5:30. AE, MC, V.*

**Pappa's Place.** This modern, white-and-pink ice cream parlor has a vast candy counter sure to delight youngsters. *510 6th Ave. at 13th St., tel. 212/924–3799. Sun. 10:30 AM–12:30 AM. AE, MC, V.*

**Pravinie Gourmet Ice Cream.** Thirty-five exotic flavors of ice cream are available here. *193 Bleecker St., between 6th Ave. and MacDougal St., tel. 212/475–1968. Sun. noon–midnight. No credit cards.*

**West 50s** **Rumpelmayer's.** A pricey ice cream parlor that's generally a hit with kids, it also serves a peerless egg salad sandwich with chopped olives. *50 Central Park South, between Fifth and Sixth Aves., tel. 212/755–5800. Sun. 7 AM–midnight. AE, DC, MC, V.*

**East 50s** **Gold Room.** A harpist sets the mood in this grand and gilt spot for scones with cream and tea. *Helmsley Palace Hotel, 455 Madison Ave. between 50th and 51st Sts., tel. 212/888–7000. Sun. tea 2–5. AE, DC, MC, V.*

**Palm Court.** The quintessential afternoon tea is served here, complete with potted palms, oodles of chintz, and a violin-piano duo. *Plaza Hotel, 5th Ave. at Central Park South, tel. 212/759–3000. Sun. tea 4–6. AE, DC, MC, V.*

**East 60s** **Mayfair Lounge.** This cream-and-gold spot puts on a truly splendid tea, with seven aromatic brews, delicious little finger sandwiches, pastries, and ice creams. *Mayfair Regent Hotel, 610 Park Ave. at 65th St., tel. 212/288–0800. Sun. tea 3–5:30. AE, DC, MC, V.*

**Pembroke Room.** This Lowell Hotel hideaway makes an oh-so-English setting for tasty teas. *28 E. 63rd St., tel. 212/838–1400. Sun. tea 3:30–6:30, reservations advised. AE, DC, MC, V.*

**Serendipity.** At this peerless ice cream parlor, try the frozen hot chocolate, made with 14 blends of imported cocoa and chocolate, or the huge hot fudge sundaes. *225 E. 60th St., tel. 212/838–3531. Sun. 11:30 AM–midnight, reservations advised. AE, DC, MC, V.*

**Swensen's.** It's simpler than Serendipity, quicker, and a better bet when you're with youngsters with unsophisticated palates. *1246 2nd Ave., between 65th and 66th Sts., tel. 212/879–8686. Sun. 10 AM–midnight. AE.*

**Upper West Side**  **Zabar's.** This awkward, uncomfortable corner storefront happens to be *the* spot for coffee and pastries in the neighborhood. *2241 Broadway at 81st St., tel. 212/874–5400. No credit cards. Sun. 8:30 AM–6 PM.*

**Steve's Ice Cream.** In this cone shop, premium ice cream is kneaded to softness so that broken-up Oreo cookies, sprinkles, and other tidbits can be mixed in to order. *286 Columbus Ave. at 74th St., tel. 212/496–1325. Sun. noon–midnight. No credit cards.*

**Upper East Side**  **Le Glacier.** Madison Avenue's frozen dessert heaven attracts dieters as well as premium ice cream freaks. *1022A Madison Ave. at 79th St., tel. 212/772–3870. Sun. noon–11. No credit cards.*

**Le Salon.** This formal, very pretty green-and-white room off the Stanhope Hotel's lobby serves an elegant tea. *5th Ave. at 81st St., tel. 212/288–5800. Sun. tea 2–5:30. AE, DC, MC, V.*

**Sant' Ambroeus.** This brass-and-marbled outpost of the Milan gelateria/pasticceria tempts with incredibly opulent sweets. *1000 Madison Ave. near 77th St., tel. 212/570–2211. Sun. 10:30 AM–6. AE, DC, MC, V.*

**Yorkville**  **Agora Boutique and Ice Cream Parlor.** A real turn-of-the-century ice cream parlor, full of mahogany, stained glass, and onyx, offers a menu of light, eclectic fare and gooey ice cream confections. Changes are in the offing at press time; call before you make your plans. *1550 3rd Ave. at 87th St., tel. 212/860–3425. Sun. noon–7 PM. AE, DC, MC, V.*

**Kleine Konditorei.** This old-time Yorkville restaurant invites mid-afternoon lingering over Sacher torte and steaming black Viennese coffee. *234 E. 86th St., tel. 212/737–7130. Sun. 10 AM –midnight. AE, DC.*

**Little Nell's Tea Room.** Imagine a rosy brick-walled English village tea room transported to New York and you've got the picture. *343 E. 85th St., tel. 212/772–2046. Sun. tea 2–5. AE, DC, MC, V.*

# Sports Bars

Watching the playoffs at the neighborhood local bar is a way of life across America, but New Yorkers enjoy a variation on this theme: a group of new sports bars where meat and potatoes are served within viewing range of multiple large television screens.

**Entourage Sports** (1571 2nd Ave., between 81st & 82nd Sts., tel. 212/535–3700) has four screens; the biggest is four feet.

**Sporting Club** (99 Hudson St. at Franklin St., tel. 212/219–0900) attracts a heavily male crowd that jams the bleachers, mezzanine, and tables to watch the action on nine screens; the biggest is 20 feet across.

**Sports** (2182 Broadway at 77th St., tel. 212/874–7208), a huge no-nonsense bar, provides stadiumlike bleachers and many oversized screens. The largest is 13 feet across. Eight different programs may be shown at once.

Other spots show sports on a more limited basis. Possibilities

---

**Symbols at the end of an entry signify:** *CH: Good for children; L: Serves after 11 PM; MU: Live music; O: Outdoor dining; VU: Great view.*

include **Mickey Mantle's** (*see* above; 42 Central Park South, tel. 212/688–7777), a baseball-mad spread with 10 screens; **Runyons** (932 2nd Ave., between 49th and 50th Sts., tel. 212/759–7800); and **Rusty's** (1271 3rd Ave. at 73rd St., tel. 212/861–4518), owned by former Met Rusty Staub.

# 3 Sightseeing

With workaday crowds gone, weekends become the time to see the city from a fresh perspective. Circle around it, get an overview from up high or from down below, or explore a new neighborhood. There are as many ways to see the city as there are means of locomotion and vantage points.

# Views

New York is grander and more expansive from on high than it seems from street level. There are small buildings and tall ones, bits of green, cars like flashing beetles, and water all around. On a clear afternoon, when the sun glints on the sea or flashes on a million panes of glass, or at sunset as the building facades turn first to gold and then to rose, there's no finer spectacle. Though Sundays are busy, lines for the elevators to observation decks are not usually a problem. In summer, however, it's a good idea to go early or late—the most beautiful times of day in any case.

### Rooftop Panoramas

Some people prefer the view from the **Empire State Building.** Measuring 1,454 feet high, this limestone, granite, and stainless steel tower designed by Shreve, Lamb & Harmon is no longer the world's tallest building, as it was when it debuted in 1931. But the view from its observation decks on the 86th and 102nd floors still gives a sense of New York's huge scope: Central Park, the George Washington Bridge, and the Bronx to the north; Queens and the ocean to the east; New Jersey to the west; and, to the south, the skinny twin towers of the World Trade Center. A strong-walled open-air terrace around the deck on the 102nd floor offers views of up to 80 miles on a clear day. *350 5th Ave. at 34th St., tel. 212/736–3100. Admission: $3.50 adults, $1.75 children 5–12 and senior citizens. Open Sun. 9:30 AM–midnight.*

From its perch on the southern tip of the island, the **World Trade Center** offers a watery view that emphasizes New York's importance as a port. Directly below is New York Bay; the mighty Hudson lies just to the west. To the north, midtown's skyscrapers rise like Emerald City from the jumble of low rises in the Village and SoHo. Inch up to the floor-to-ceiling windows; the view straight down the side of the building is dizzying. Take the escalator to the Rooftop Promenade, the world's highest outdoor observation platform. When it's open, it's just you, the breezes, the birds, and the occasional helicopter or private airplane, many of which are flying *below* your feet. You may also want to combine the view with a meal at Windows on the World (*see* Chapter 2). *2 World Trade Center, tel. 212/466–7397 or 212/466–7377 for recorded information. Admission: $3.50 adults, $1.75 children 6–12 and senior citizens. Open Sun. 9:30–9:30 (mid-June–mid-Sept., to 11:30 PM).*

### Other Views

The lawns of Staten Island's **Alice Austen House** (*see* Historical Treasures in Chapter 4) sweep down to the harbor, practically at the base of the Verrazano-Narrows Bridge, and the views of both are wonderful.

The bar at the **Beekman Tower Hotel** (3 Mitchell Pl., tel. 212/ 355–7300) offers a pleasant view from its terrace, which wraps around the hotel.

The **Soldiers' and Sailors' Memorial Arch** in Brooklyn's Grand Army Plaza, open on Sundays only, has fine views of Prospect Park, south Brooklyn, and lower Manhattan.

At **Green-Wood Cemetery's** high point, the views of the Manhattan skyline are framed in trees (*see* Cemeteries in Chapter 6).

**River Café,** nestled at the Brooklyn base of the Brooklyn Bridge, offers a water-level look at the East River bridges, the Statue of Liberty, and all those skyscrapers. Go for a meal or just a drink at the bar on the terrace (*see* Chapter 2).

The tower at **Riverside Church** (122nd St. and Riverside Dr., tel. 212/222–5900) is a mere 21 stories high—not much in the pantheon of New York panoramas. But from here, the Hudson is practically at your feet, along with views of the George Washington Bridge a couple of miles uptown and the crenellated Palisades of New Jersey to the west. An elevator leads to the 20th floor. Walk the last flight up on a twisty staircase that winds among the 74 bells of the world's largest carillon. *Admission: $1; open Sun. 12:30–4.*

The tennis court at the **Turtle Bay Tennis Club** (UN Plaza Hotel, 44th St. and 1st Ave., tel. 212/355–3400) has a fine city view (*see* Chapter 6).

At Riverdale's **Wave Hill,** the expansive Hudson River views are framed by some of the city's most exuberant plantings of perennials, especially glorious in midsummer (*see* Chapter 6).

# Great Walks

While the country-weekend contingent flees the city for state park and forest trails on weekends, their urban counterparts—dedicated walkers—know that there's no day like a Sunday for hoofing it up and down the city streets. Do as they do. Step into your best walking shoes, choose any avenue or street, and follow it from one end to the other or from river to river, observing how the neighborhoods shade gradually into each other. Or hike across one of the city's 2,098 bridges for a fresh look at scenery that usually speeds by in a blur.

### George Washington Bridge

The famous architect Le Corbusier called the George Washington Bridge "the most beautiful bridge in the world. Made of cables and steel beams, it gleams in the sky like a reversed arch . . . the only seat of grace in the disordered city . . ." It's an apt description, as anyone who ever walks across it will discover. Not many people do; joggers are the most frequent travelers. And it's a little scary because the bridge is more than 200 feet above the water level and the only thing that separates walkers from water is a steel railing on either walkway. From one end of the 3,500-foot span to the other, this bridge offers the best of all possible views up and down the river.

## Brooklyn Bridge

This 1,595½-foot East River crossing, designed by John Augustus Roebling is both airy and monumental. Its great towers and cables form an elegant frame for city and river, with the Williamsburg and Manhattan bridges to the north. Sometimes the river sparkles like a sea of diamonds or the whole surface is splashed with whitecaps; sometimes it's like cold steel. It's almost always windy, so take a hat or scarf.

Although the bridge was acclaimed as the Eighth Wonder of the World when it was completed in 1883, Brooklynites and New Yorkers were skeptical that a span so long and airy could really be sound. The year after it opened, P. T. Barnum took 21 elephants across to prove the point.

Since the fanfare of the bridge's centennial celebration in 1983, it has been lovingly tended. The filigree of cables, long a cold battleship gray, has been repainted in the original warm pale brown. The bicycle/pedestrian path that runs down the middle—raised for better viewing—is now surfaced with smooth wood planks, and the stairways that once punctuated this route have been removed. The vehicular roadway has been paved, thereby eliminating the high whine that car tires used to make as they rolled across the metal grates. At the south end, stop for a bite at a restaurant in Brooklyn Heights, itself a charmer full of brownstones as stately as any on Washington Square (*see* Explorable Neighborhoods, below). On the Manhattan end, stroll a bit farther downtown to South Street Seaport for some window-shopping and snacking.

## Brooklyn Heights Esplanade

When the Brooklyn–Queens Expressway was built, it was placed below grade between Middagh Street and Atlantic Avenue and covered by a cantilevered roof. In this one stroke, the already handsome and architecturally distinguished Brooklyn Heights acquired a wide ⅓-mile–long river-edge promenade that remains one of the few spots for New Yorkers to enjoy the waterfront. Honey locust trees, shrubs, ornamental lampposts, and a delicate iron railing frame a view of spiky masts, short redbrick buildings, and a great mass of glittering skyscrapers in the backdrop. Take a picnic and linger to enjoy this panorama of the Seaport and Lower Manhattan to the accompaniment of bird songs and tugboats' braying. Manhattan, as close as it is, seems very far away.

## 42nd Street

The geographical midpoint of the island is still the "naughty, bawdy, gawdy, sporty" spot "where the underworld can meet the elite," as Al Dubin and Harry Warren described it in their 1932 song. A stroll from river to river, west to east, shows off Manhattan's extremes as do few other city thoroughfares.

Between Ninth and Tenth avenues is **Manhattan Plaza**, subsidized housing for artists. Across the street, **Theatre Row** and its Off-Broadway playhouses mark the first steps in the revitalization of this end of the street. Between Eighth and Ninth avenues are **Holy Cross Roman Catholic Church**, the Hell's Kitchen base for Father Duffy (of Duffy Square), and **Port Au-**

thority **Bus Terminal,** the world's largest. The seediness of the block between Eighth and Seventh avenues almost conceals the fact that there are wonderful sights to see here. But the astute observer will note the fine architecture above the gaudy theater marquees on both sides of the street. Several of these are distinguished enough to have been proposed for landmark status. The **New Amsterdam** (214 W. 42nd St.), once considered the country's most opulent theater, is already landmarked inside and out. **Times Square,** where Seventh Avenue crosses Broadway, was once the focal point of the carriage dealers' district, the Longacre. It was renamed when the *New York Times* moved to the building on the triangle between 42nd Street, Broadway, and Seventh Avenue (its New Year's Eve opening in 1904, celebrated with fireworks, inaugurated a city tradition). The building's early Beaux Arts style has been obscured by concrete and a so-called Motogram, which flashes headlines in some 15,000 light bulbs.

The **Graduate Center** of the City University of New York, between Fifth and Sixth avenues, redone in 1970, was built in 1912; its third-floor Aeolian Hall hosted the premiere of George Gershwin's *Rhapsody in Blue.* The **New York Public Library's** central research facility, on Fifth Avenue, is equaled in its Beaux Arts splendor only by **Grand Central Terminal** at Vanderbilt Avenue, a short block and a half farther east (*see* Architecture below). The ultracontemporary **Philip Morris Building,** across the street from the terminal, houses a branch of the Whitney Museum of American Art, and the sculpture court is open on Sundays. The Art Deco **Chanin Building** at Lexington Avenue is embellished with bas reliefs, and it's just catty-corner from the **Chrysler Building,** one of the most splendid of the city's skyscrapers from its radiator-cap ornaments and stainless steel spire to the African marble lobby and its muraled ceiling. Continuing east are the city's last **Automat,** which is open on Sundays (*see* Chapter 2); the Art Deco **Daily News Building,** whose lobby contains the world's largest interior globe; and the greenhouselike **Ford Foundation Building** at 43rd Street, generally acknowledged to be one of the most elegant modern office buildings in the city. Just beyond that is the **Tudor City** apartment complex, designed in the mid-1920s as a self-contained city. The **United Nations,** along the East River, has gardens and fine views.

## Fifth Avenue

Grand prewar apartment buildings, fabulous mansions, swank hotels, museums, and exclusive shops line Fifth Avenue between the Metropolitan Museum of Art at 81st Street and the Empire State Building. The impression is of one great long parade of New York City's wealth, past and present. Residential buildings opposite Central Park feature marble columns and voluted capitals, delicate wrought-iron railings and doorways, French windows and leaded panes, elaborate cornices, porticoes, balconies, entablatures, and roof balustrades; they cost fortunes to build (as they now do to purchase). Particularly splendid are the François I mansion at 79th Street, now the **Ukrainian Institute of America;** the Duke mansion at 78th Street, now part of **New York University;** the **Frick Collection** at 70th Street, Henry Clay Frick's former home; and the **Metropolitan Club** at 60th Street, which McKim, Mead & White designed for J. P. Morgan and his cronies, who couldn't get into existing private clubs. Just off the avenue on the side streets there are others—most notably the former **Charles Scribner** residence at 9 East 66th Street and coal magnate **Edward Berwind's** house at 2 East 64th Street (now co-op apartments). Grand mansions like these used to inhabit Fifth Avenue farther south as well—the current **Cartier Building** at 52nd Street was among these stately structures.

Below **St. Patrick's Cathedral** and **Rockefeller Center,** itself a small city worth an hour or two, the avenue changes. There's a procession of airline offices and luggage, lace, and electronics stores where going-out-of-business sales are a way of life; you'll also find a clutch of smaller, not so pricey shops that don't look like much. But in their gracious Beaux Arts and Gothic Revival styles, what's overhead speaks eloquent volumes to those who bother to look up—as is often true around New York. Passing the **New York Public Library** and **Lord & Taylor** the avenue leads to the **Empire State Building,** where visitors can collect their thoughts about it all from a loftier perspective.

# Architecture

There's only one way to appreciate a great building: Look it up and down, admire its proportions, and notice its detailing—the hood-ornament decorations on the Chrysler Building, for instance, or the constellation-studded ceiling in Grand Central.

### Great Buildings

**AT&T Building** (1984). The Philip Johnson/John Burgee–designed headquarters building, nicknamed "the Chippendale skyscraper" for its broken keyhole pediment, is one of a kind. A stroll around the base of the building makes it seem even larger, even grander. The lobby's statue, "The Spirit of Communication," by Evelyn Longworth, is a stroke of gold. *550 Madison Ave., between 55th and 56th Sts.*

**Chrysler Building** (1930). William Van Alen's streamlined tour de force, with its crown-shaped illumination at the top, is a New York icon. The stainless-steel frills, a decorative band emblazoned with cars, and the varied stonework reveal the magnitude of the architect's accomplishment. The 480 fluorescent tubes on the tower were finally added a few years ago; apparently, technology of the '30s wasn't up to Van Alen's designs for the illumination, and his plans had been scrapped. *405 Lexington Ave. at 42nd St.*

**City Hall** (1811). One of the city's architectural treasures, City Hall was designed by Joseph François Mangin and John McComb, Jr., in the French Renaissance and Federal styles. The rear elevation was originally brownstoned to cut costs—at the time it was built, the architects believed that nobody important would ever live north of City Hall. The glorious rotunda inside is closed on Sunday. *City Hall Park, between Broadway and Park Row.*

**Federal Hall** (1834–42). George Washington took the oath of office on the site of this Manhattan Parthenon, designed by Town & Davis and built of Westchester marble around the foundations of a previous city hall. Walk to the top of the steps, to the base of the Doric columns near the John Quincy Adams Ward statue of Washington, and admire the view. *28 Wall St. at Nassau St.*

**Grand Central** (1903–13). In railroad parlance, Grand Central is not a *station*—that is, a stop on the way to somewhere else—but a *terminal*, the end of the line. Its grand proportions, the airiness created by its immense windows, and a ceiling resplendent with the constellations of the zodiac make this one of the city's truly great spaces.

This Warren & Wetmore masterpiece offers two special experiences. Behind the window at the terminal's west end, which is really a sandwich of two windows, you can walk along cast-glass sidewalk-bridges accessible via the stairway to the right of the bar near Vanderbilt Avenue. And just outside the entrance to the Oyster Bar, a whisper into one corner of the Guastavino tile vaulting will be heard perfectly in the opposite corner. *42nd St. at Vanderbilt Ave., between Park and Madison Aves.*

**Radio City Music Hall** (1932). The home of the Rockettes and one of the showpieces of Rockefeller Center was threatened with demolition a few years ago, and it took the work of dedicated preservationists to stay the wrecker's ball. This is a grandiose space, with three cantilevered mezzanines, a soaring four-story lobby, and a shimmering gold curtain—all three tons of it. *6th Ave. at 50th St., tel. 212/632–4041. 1-hr backstage tours daily, $6.*

**Rockefeller Center** (1932–40). On 22 acres of prime Manhattan real estate, this is a city in its own right, with the Channel Gardens, the Lower Plaza, the sleek 850-foot RCA Building, and, all around, mid-rise buildings such as the former Time & Life Building at 1 Rockefeller Plaza and the Associated Press Building. The gray limestone structures are at once modern and timeless, and the sculptures and plaques communicate a romantic view of capitalism, the city, and the workplace. Terrific sculpture, including Paul Manship's colossal *Prometheus* and Isamu Noguchi's 10-ton stainless steel panel *News*, are the grace notes. *47th–50th Sts., between 5th and 6th Aves.*

**Seagram Building** (1958). This great structure, designed by Mies van der Rohe, looks as modern as the day it was built. The proportions and detailing, exuding calm and stability, set it apart from its imitators; the expansive plaza was a fresh idea when the building went up. *375 Park Ave., between 52nd and 53rd Sts.*

**Woolworth Building** (1913). Architect Cass Gilbert's imposing tower for dime-store king F. W. Woolworth was known as the "Cathedral of Commerce" when it was built (and paid for with $13.5 million cash). This gothic-style skyscraper, the world's tallest building when it opened, is embellished with bas reliefs representing the continents on the second story and a Noah's ark of gargoyles outside the 26th, 49th, and 51st floors. *233 Broadway, between Barclay St. and Park Pl.*

## Lobbies

Some of the city's most palatial architecture can be seen in the lobbies of its office buildings. Mirrors and gilt, ceilings painted with clouds, glossy marble, Beaux Arts and rococo: it's all there, and no two are quite alike. Although most lobbies are officially closed on Sundays, the guards on duty specifically to admit weekend workers often accommodate sightseers.

**Chrysler Building** (1930). The lobby is practically paved in African marble with touches of chrome, and the Art Deco motifs are as abundant inside as out (*see* Great Buildings, above).

**Film Center Building** (1929). Mosaics in gold and other colors fill the lobby with light and texture—part Art Deco, part Islamic. *630 9th Ave., between 44th and 45th Sts.*

**Fred F. French Building** (1927). The headquarters of the Tudor City apartment complex's designer and builder is ornate and beautifully preserved. Brass, gilt, and marble all gleam under a coffered ceiling. *551 5th Ave. at 45th St.*

**General Electric Building** (1931). It's an Art Deco palace, all tan marble and stainless steel—recently renovated from stem to stern. *570 Lexington Ave., at 51st St.*

**Helmsley Building** (1929). The interior of Warren & Wetmore's former New York Central Building is another study in gleaming splendor. The elevators have clouds on the ceilings. *230 Park Ave., between 45th and 46th Sts.*

**New York County Courthouse** (1926). Footsteps echo and voices reverberate in the central lobby of this hexagonal structure, fronted by a Corinthian portico, although jurors who come on weekdays see a plainer side of the building—the utilitarian courtrooms and the labyrinthine corridors and stairways. *60 Centre St., between Pearl and Worth Sts. in Foley Sq.*

**110–115 Broadway,** recently renovated, is all white marble and leaded glass, with a sculpted and painted ceiling.

**127 John St.,** at Water St. (1969), offers the 20th-century counterpart to these elaborate details: neon. A tunnel full of it makes designer Rudolph de Harak's lobby as playful as the others are grand.

**Surrogate's Court/Hall of Records** (1899–1911). Impressing the small citizen with the power of government was what public architecture was all about at the turn of the century, and it shows in the extremely grand entry space of this building. *31 Chambers St., between Centre and Elk Sts.*

**Woolworth Building** (1913). This structure is even more lavish inside than outside, with jewel-like mosaics, lacy wrought-iron cornices covered with pure gold leaf, three-story high arches, and fanciful sculptures: Mr. Woolworth counting his dimes, the renting agent closing a deal, the architect cradling a model of the building. The helpful guards usually proffer the building brochure; if they don't, ask for one (*see* Great Buildings, above).

## Atriums

The late 20th-century answer to yesteryear's lobbies, these public spaces are generously scaled, lushly landscaped, handsomely designed, and climate controlled, which makes them especially appealing when it's too cold or hot outdoors. Many of Manhattan's best atriums are open on Sundays from morning to evening. Some have small snack stands where coffee and pastries are available.

**Chemcourt** displays a bronze statue of a businessman hailing a cab to welcome visitors to this three-story glass house where terraced pools and 50 types of flowers and plants, provided and tended by New York Botanical Garden horticulturalists, create a bit of the tropics in New York. *277 Park Ave. at 47th St.*

**Citicorp Center** boasts "The Market," a personable public space inside the distinctive slant-topped aluminum-clad tower, with three levels of shops and restaurants, many of which are open on Sundays. Tables in the center are comfortable for reading and resting, and there are occasional free concerts. *53rd St., between 3rd and Lexington Aves., tel. 212/559–2330 for recorded information.*

**IBM Garden Plaza's** graceful bamboo plants nearly brush the lofty ceiling of this wonderful greenhouse-atrium. *Madison Ave., between 55th and 56th Sts.*

**Olympic Tower,** containing offices, shops, and apartments, is sheathed in an unrevealing black glass skin, so the pleasant interior space comes as a surprise. Trees, benches, and a waterwall with a reflecting pool set the scene. *5th Ave. at 52nd St.*

**Park Avenue Plaza** offers green glass and marble, a waterfall, and banks of flowers in this exceptionally pleasant spot. *52nd–53rd Sts. off Park Ave.*

**Trump Tower** shops are closed on Sundays—at least as of press time—but the rose marble, shiny brass, and soothing 80-foot waterfall provide a pleasant spot to rest weary feet on a Fifth Avenue tour. *5th Ave. at 56th St.*

**Winter Garden's** indoor park is as big as the Grand Central concourse, except that its army of 90-foot-tall Washingtonia robusta palms make it gloriously green. Perpetually sheltered from the rain by its barrel-shaped glass roof, it's one of the newest and best of the city's atriums. Concerts and other entertainments fill the calendar on many a Sunday (*see* Chapter 7). *200 Liberty St. at West St.*

# Explorable Neighborhoods

People come from all over the tristate area to sample the cultural, culinary, and commercial pleasures of Sundays on the Upper West Side, SoHo, and Greenwich Village. But the city certainly does not begin and end with these neighborhoods. There are other city treasures just a subway ride away, neighborhoods that for most people are just names in the real estate section of the Sunday *Times*. There may be a small museum, a restaurant, or shop worth exploring. Or you may find an endless block of perfect brownstones shaded by fine old trees. Possibly you'll discover an exotic cultural enclave that makes you feel a world away from your home ground.

## Manhattan

**Ladies' Mile** The gaslight era's premier shopping and entertainment district (Broadway from 8th to 23rd Sts. and 6th Ave. from 14th to 23rd Sts.) was where Benjamin Altman, Aaron Arnold, James Mansell Constable, Paul J. Bonwit and Edmund D. Teller, Samuel Lord and George Washington Taylor, and others built dry-goods stores into retail institutions that changed the face of American merchandising. In real-estate parlance, some of this area is now known as Sofi (short for *so*uth of *Fl*at*i*ron), in reference to Daniel Burnham's 1902 wedge-shaped office tower at 23rd Street and Fifth Avenue. Photographers, architecture firms, publishing houses, and advertising agencies moving into the area's lofts and once-decrepit office buildings are making it the focus of the city's first commercially driven gentrification.

**Marble Hill**  The Harlem River at the northern tip of the island hasn't always flowed as it does now. In 1859, to cut the distance between the East River and the Hudson, the loop that the river used to make was filled in. A new, more direct waterway was dredged out, thereby severing Marble Hill, south of the old arc, from Manhattan. Though it officially remained part of the borough, Marble Hill has had an air of separateness ever since.

The old Victorian villas were never spit-and-polished into gentrification, and the mood is quiet and small-town. **St. Stephen's Methodist Episcopal Church** (122 W. 69th St.), an arresting Shingle-style structure, is the major landmark along the twisting lanes. It's pleasant just to ramble and admire the towers and turrets and verandas of the old homes.

**Harlem**  Well-to-do Germans, Irish, Jews, and Italians came in successive waves to the ornate, late 19th-century apartment houses and brownstones of Harlem, once a quiet country village. The black population of the Tenderloin District in the West 30s, dislocated by the construction of Macy's, Penn Station, and other buildings in the neighborhood, also began to settle here during the 1920s. An important influence on many aspects of American culture, Harlem has many faces, and the one that visitors see on Sunday is very different from the Harlem of Saturday night. It still boasts abundant architectural treasures, and it warrants a visit by anyone with any interest at all in New York's history.

Turn-of-the-century churches endure. Among them: the **First Corinthian Baptist Church**, formerly the Regent Theatre (7th Ave. at 116th St.); wildly eclectic **St. Thomas the Apostle Church** (160 W. 118th St.); **St. Martin's Episcopal Church,** a massive Romanesque structure with the city's second-largest carillon (18 W. 122nd St.); and the **Metropolitan Baptist Church** (151 W. 128th St.). **St. Philip's Church** (204 W. 134th St.) was designed by Vertner W. Tandy, the first registered black architect in New York State. And gothic **Abyssinian Baptist Church** (132 W. 138th St.) is where the charismatic Adam Clayton Powell, Jr., once preached. Fine residential buildings include numerous row houses dating to the late 19th century along 130th Street between Lenox and Seventh avenues, at 136th and 137th streets between Seventh and Eighth avenues, at 26-46 Edgecombe Avenue between 136th and 137th streets, and 321 W. 136th Street between Edgecombe and Eighth avenues. The late 19th-century King Model Houses of the St. Nicholas Historic District are now better known as **Strivers' Row** (roughly 138th to 139th Sts. between 7th and 8th Aves.). Most celebrated is the **Apollo Theatre** (253 W. 125th St.), where, since 1914, audiences have applauded great performers from Bessie Smith and Billie Holiday to Dinah Washington, Duke Ellington, Count Basie, and Aretha Franklin.

**Lower Manhattan**  Some of the best small corners of the city are down here, set against some of its biggest buildings. The streets, by turns narrow and wide, are reminiscent of those the early settlers remembered from the medieval quarters of their European homelands. Each turn reveals a different perspective on the buildings along its route. There is some wonderful public art here, along with enough terrific old buildings to make this area a sort of museum without walls. There are some outstanding new skyscrapers as well.

Start at the **World Financial Center** on the west or at **South Street Seaport** on the east and work your way from river to river. Some sights to see: **Castle Clinton** in **Battery Park** and the out-of-the-ordinary lobby of the **Broad Financial Center** (33 Whitehall St.); the imposing **Federal Hall National Memorial,** closed on Sunday but still interesting outside (Nassau St. at Wall St.); **Trinity Church** (Broadway at Wall St.; *see* Chapter 6); and **Fraunces Tavern** (54 Pearl St. at Broad St.; *see* Chapter 4). Stroll down **Water Street,** which was entirely under water when Trinity Parish was chartered in 1697 (successive generations added landfill, first as far as Front Street, then to South Street). Inland, at **City Hall Park,** the Horace Greeley and Benjamin Franklin statues across Park Row (formerly Newspaper Row) recall the area's days as the city's publishing center— home of the *New York World, Sun, Tribune, Recorder, Evening Post, American,* and other papers. Also bordering the park are the Georgian-Renaissance **City Hall,** and the great **Woolworth Building** (*see* Architecture, above). The **Municipal Building** is only slightly less grand (Chambers St. at Centre St.), and **Foley Square** impresses with its flotilla of courthouses, including the hexagonal **New York County Courthouse** and **U.S. Courthouse** with their columned porticoes.

**East Village and NoHo** The East Village is probably the island's most colorful neighborhood. Here, holdouts from the 1960s coexist with a deeply entrenched Eastern European community. Artists, punks, and account executives move freely between the Polish and Ukrainian coffee shops and the latest trendy pasta bar. Galleries, offbeat shops, and a wander down St. Mark's Place, one of the East Village's major thoroughfares, provide diversion.

In **Astor Place,** the northern tip of the triangle that's more recently been known as NoHo, four of the colonnaded town houses that were home to the fashionable Astors, Vanderbilts, and Delanos can still be found across the boulevard from the New York Shakespeare Festival's Public Theater. Many a speaker made history in the basement of **Cooper Union,** the country's oldest building framed with steel beams. (Here, in 1860, Abraham Lincoln made the "Right Makes Right" speech that catapulted him into the White House.) **St. Mark's-in-the-Bowery Church** and the **Old Merchant's House** (*see* Historical Treasures in Chapter 4) are both in the area, as is the city's only building by the Chicago architect Louis Sullivan, Frank Lloyd Wright's teacher—the **Bayard Building** at 65 Bleecker Street between Crosby St. and Broadway. **Stuyvesant Street, East 10th Street,** and **East 11th Street** are worth exploring for their pretty Federal houses. Tack east and west between avenues A and D, for a look at the tenements and brownstones, shops, and sights.

## The Bronx

The Bronx as depicted in the film *Fort Apache: The Bronx* and Tom Wolfe's novel *Bonfire of the Vanities* is not the only Bronx. Yet visitors to the borough today can only imagine the setting as it was early in the 19th century—green, rural, and tranquil. First settled in colonial times, it has seen wave upon wave of immigrants since the 1840s—first the Irish, many of whom built the Croton Aqueduct (for about 75¢ a day); then the Germans, Italians, Jews, blacks, Hispanics, Albanians, and Cambodians. The landscape is hillier than Manhattan's, and its geological base, a kind of ancient rock known as Fordham gneiss, gives it a completely different character than Manhattan, where the substrata is mica schist.

**Belmont** The colorful food markets in **Belmont,** as the thoroughly Italian neighborhood around **Arthur Avenue** is known, are more or less shuttered tight on Sundays. But the restaurants do a booming business, and after dinner it's pleasant to explore the almost surrealistically tidy streets full of shops and small apartment buildings.

**City Island** Located just south of the Westchester County line, off the coast of Pelham Bay Park and Orchard Beach (to which it's connected by bridge), this 230-acre landfall feels more like a New England fishing village than New York City. The home of a saltworks in 1830, it became a center for oystering and later, yacht building. August Belmont once envisioned the island as a race course, and many developers are itching to get at the place. But it remains what it's been for years—a lively, somewhat funky place for dining out and the principal destination for passionate sailors and would-be sailors.

Stroll down **City Island Avenue,** the main drag, and enjoy the festive Sunday spirit, the salt tang in the air, the little nautical museum, yacht clubs, and the handful of old homes and appropriately nautical new condos, all shipshape. (The shingle-sided house at 21 Tiel Street was featured in director Sidney Lumet's 1962 film version of Eugene O'Neill's *Long Day's Journey into Night*). Gulls wheel and cry, and off in the distance, Manhattan's skyscrapers appear like a mirage.

**Riverdale** Seen from the Henry Hudson Parkway, this area north of 240th Street, from Broadway to the Hudson River, looks to be all high-rise apartment buildings of no particular distinction. But a Sunday drive along its winding roads, after exiting the parkway on Kappock Street, reveals a treasure house of architectural feats and fantasies, both antique and modern: neo-Georgian and Stick style, contemporary and English Tudor. The Hudson River and the dramatic Palisades form a backdrop to these former summer homes of millionaires, erected in the early 20th century. For quintessential Riverdale scenery, meander along **Palisade Avenue, Sycamore Avenue** north of 252nd Street, and **Independence Avenue** from 248th to 254th streets. Of the estates, **Wave Hill** is open to the public. The mansion is handsome and the gardens are superlative, the lawns graced with giant elms and maples (*see* Chapter 6). Drive past other estates, including **Alderbrook,** circa 1880, where the artist Elie Nadelman once lived (4715 Independence Ave. near 248th St.). John F. Kennedy attended **Riverdale Country School** on Fieldston Road, the main thoroughfare of **Fieldston,** where charming English cottages date from the '20s.

## Brooklyn

The neighborly spirit in the air here, nearly absent in Manhattan even on Sunday, makes Brooklyn seem almost like a small town grown up. It also feels greener than most of Manhattan and more varied.

**Brooklyn Heights** Over the Brooklyn Bridge and just south of the up-and-coming Fulton Ferry landing area, Brooklyn Heights has long been one of the city's most civilized neighborhoods. It's not surprising that the Landmarks Preservation Commission designated it a historic district before any other neighborhood in the city.

**Montague Street,** the east–west commercial thoroughfare, sets the tone. It's vibrant; lively; but, above all, neighborly and low-key—a place where the stoops are tall and photocopied hand-bills flutter on lampposts. Shops ensconced in row houses purvey the necessities of Yuppie life (coffee beans, imported cheeses, hardware, books, and stylish clothing), and restaurants do a lively brunch business.

On other streets, stately brownstones prevail, with stoops of stone or curled wrought-iron railings and high windows. Many streets bear the names of fruits and trees, the legacy of a certain influential Miss Middagh, who despised the practice of honoring city fathers by emblazoning their surnames on street signs. **Willow Street,** between Clark and Pierrepont streets, is pretty and architecturally varied, with bay windows, turrets, towers, and terra-cotta; **Columbia Heights,** where Norman Mailer lives, is particularly graceful. And note the landmarks: At **2–3 Pierrepont Street,** mid-19th-century brownstone palaces were used in John Huston's film *Prizzi's Honor;* the **Plymouth Church** is where preacher Henry Ward Beecher once auctioned off a nine-year-old girl to dramatize the evils of slavery; the Romanesque Revival **Our Lady of Lebanon Roman Catholic Church** (113 Remsen St.) shows off doors salvaged from the wrecked liner *Normandie;* and the Gothic Revival **Grace Church** (254 Hicks St.), shaded by an 80-foot elm, presides over **Grace Court** and **Grace Alley,** a mews full of restored carriage houses. Scores of creative people have called the Heights home, including W. H. Auden, Benjamin Britten, Hart Crane, Richard Wright, Gypsy Rose Lee, Truman Capote, Walt Whitman, Thomas Wolfe, and Arthur Miller.

**Cobble Hill and Carroll Gardens** This charming brownstone district, more varied and less formal than the Heights, was farming country in the 17th century and became a strategic point in the Revolutionary War. Bounded by Atlantic Avenue on the north, Degraw Street on the south, Hicks Street on the west, and Court Street on the east, it filled with comfortable row houses in the 19th century. Germans and Italians swelled the population before World War I, and Syrians and Lebanese came just afterwards. The neighborhood was stable for years, well kept by first- and second-generation residents. More recently, young families have moved in, and the New York City Landmarks Commission has declared 22 blocks of the area the Cobble Hill Historic District. **Clinton Street,** which runs right down the center of it all, makes for very pleasant strolling, with its varied Victorian houses and stoops with stone or wrought-iron balustrades. Landmarks include **197 Amity St.,** where Jennie Jerome, Winston Churchill's mother, was born; **40 Verandah Place,** where the novelist Thomas Wolfe once lived; and the **Workingmen's Cottages** and adjoining **Tower and Home Apartments** (near Warren, Baltic, and Hicks Sts.), a group of cottages and apartments put up by the philanthropist Alfred Tredway White in 1879. The nearby **Christ Church and the Holy Family** Episcopal church (Kane St. at Strong Pl.) was one of several churches designed by the architect Richard Upjohn, who also did Manhattan's

Trinity Church. In fact, all **Kane Street** is attractive, with its Italianate row houses, fine wrought-iron work, and other touches.

**Carroll Gardens,** which adjoins Cobble Hill to the south, is a deeply Italian neighborhood, where octogenarians play bocce in the park and congregate on corners. Many of the row houses have little front yards, and the scene has scarcely changed since the turn of the century on streets like **First Place, Carroll Street,** and **President Street.** The **Cammereri Brothers Bakery** (502 Henry St.) is where Nicholas Cage labored over a hot oven in the 1987 film *Moonstruck.*

**Park Slope** This area, bounded by Flatbush Avenue and Prospect Park on the east and Fifth or Sixth Avenue on the west, St. Mark's Place on the north, and 15th Street on the south, eventually became Brooklyn's Gold Coast; it was designated a historic district in 1973. Yet it was largely farmland until the Brooklyn Bridge connected Brooklyn to Manhattan, and thus its architecture is late Victorian, characterized by excess and elaboration. Along Prospect Park West, each house is more heavily embellished than its neighbor, with bay windows, stained glass, and other accoutrements of Italianate, Gothic Revival, Romanesque Revival, Queen Anne, and other styles. The gateway to Park Slope is **Grand Army Plaza,** an oval of roadways radiating from the 80-foot-high **Soldiers' and Sailors' Memorial Arch;** the commercial center of the area is lively **Seventh Avenue.** But the real character of the Slope is best seen on its side streets, particularly those south of Grand Army Plaza between Eighth Avenue and Prospect Park West. **Carroll Street** is the site of work by some of the city's best architects. **Montgomery Place,** with most of its houses designed by C. P. H. Gilbert, is known as the "block beautiful"; there's hardly a street in the city with forms so strong and textures so rich. The **Henry Carlton Hulbert Mansion** and the **William Childs Mansion** near Montgomery Place bristle with Flemish brickwork and gargoyles. Another exceptional building is the old **Montauk Club,** a Venetian Gothic palazzo at the intersection of Lincoln Place and Eighth Avenue. The Park Slope skyline is spiked by splendid churches. **Augustine's Roman Catholic Church** at Sterling Place and Sixth Avenue is like a cantata in mottled sandstone, brick, copper, and marble, with a jubilant chorus of gargoyles and statues. Mosaics, paintings, and stained-glass windows complete the effect.

## Roosevelt Island

The tram ride over and back, arching high above the East River, is the spectacular beginning of a pleasant visit to this 600-foot-wide sliver of land, once known as Welfare Island. Some of it is old: an 18th-century farmhouse, a 19th-century chapel, and a Gothic-style ruin. But more is new: apartment towers, waterfront promenades, and other facilities—all strictly 1980s-vintage, master-planned by architects Philip Johnson and John Burgee. Still, except for the sound of helicopters taking off and landing on the east side of Manhattan and the buzz of motorized craft in the river, it's exquisitely quiet. There's a supermarket on the island and a deli on the main street where picnic fixings are available. Automobiles reach the island via Queens; you can also get there via the Q subway.

## Queens

The second most populous of the five boroughs, Queens is the largest in land area, with 114.7 square miles representing almost a third of the city. It did not become a part of New York City until 1898 and it remained relatively rural for years afterward. Residents still identify with their villages, and most New Yorkers are familiar with their names—Astoria, Sunnyside, Woodside, Rego Park, Fresh Meadows, and Howard Beach, to list just a few.

**Astoria** In this vital ethnic neighborhood, extending between Ditmars Boulevard and Broadway and 21st and Steinway streets, Greek is more commonly spoken than is English. Pastry shops (*xaxaroplasteion*) and coffee houses (*kaffenion*) send their heady fragrances into the streets, and there are Greek restaurants and nightclubs galore. The heart of it all is the Greek Orthodox Church of **St. Demitrios** (30–11 30th Dr.), a sprawling yellow brick building with a red tile roof and the largest congregation of the sect outside Greece. The monumentally columned **Kaufman Astoria Studios** (34–12 36th St.) have come to life again to film movies and, next door, the **American Museum of the Moving Image** (*see* Chapter 4) has begun welcoming visitors.

**Flushing** Once an enclave of rambling white clapboard and Shingle-style late 19th-century homes, this historic community took off haphazardly after the completion of the Bronx–Whitestone Bridge and the 1939–40 New York World's Fair. Now a modern mishmash of new buildings and less-than-distinguished older structures, it is also an Asian boomtown. You'll find the local patois sharp and often incomprehensible to an English speaker; the shop signs are in Chinese, and the food markets are as exotic as those in Korea, Hong Kong, or Taiwan. Along with the usual complement of synagogues and churches, there are many temples of Asian religions tucked away on the side streets.

If you're looking for historic landmarks, visit **Bowne House,** built in 1661 (37–01 Bowne St.), between 37th and 38th Aves., and the shingle-sided, hip-roofed **Friends' Meeting House** (137–16 Northern Blvd. between Main and Union Sts.), built in 1694, which makes it the oldest house of worship in the city in continuous use. Not far away is the surprising **Waldheim** residential neighborhood, a few small-town Victorian blocks north of the **Queens Botanical Garden** and southwest of Parsons Boulevard and Franklin Avenue.

**Forest Hills Gardens** It's not an English village, but it may be the next best thing, just a short subway ride from Manhattan. Just off Queens Boulevard, between Flushing Meadows-Corona Park and Forest Hills Park, you'll find curving little thoroughfares with names such as Deepdene Place and Goodwood Road, Seasongood Road and Beechknoll Place, lined with row houses of brick and slate with occasional towers, turrets, and half-timbering. Frederick Law Olmsted, Jr., landscaped the area for the Russell Sage Foundation, which created Forest Hills Gardens with the intention of relocating low-income families here. Before long, however, the well-to-do claimed it for themselves, and it has been that way ever since—snug and smug. Cover the main commercial center—"the village," as **Austin Street** is known—pass by the old **Forest Hills Stadium,** the first site of the U.S. Open, and then move south to **Kew Gardens,** a pre–World War I development south of Union Turnpike. Its streets, with their British-sounding names, are full of wonderful stucco houses roofed in Spanish tiles.

**Long Island City**  This community across the 59th Street Bridge (or the Queensboro Bridge, depending on your perspective) is the latest district to attract artists with its low rents and big spaces. The community has an energy all its own; its beauty is of the practical, stark sort, with the midtown skyline a glorious backdrop. In the **Hunters Point Historic District,** well-kept row houses, constructed of tough Westchester stone, retain their original stoops and cornices; an oversize metal sculpture—Daniel Sinclair's "Bigger Bird"—in the center of the small park at 21st Street proclaims the artistic spirit of the local residents. By comparison, **Vernon Boulevard,** particularly around its intersection with **Jackson Avenue,** is an incongruous mix of shingled homes, butcher shops, diners, and art galleries cowering beneath the four-barreled stacks of the behemoth Pennsylvania Railroad generating plant. **Silvercup Studios,** west of Vernon at the intersection of 21st Street and 43rd Avenue, has 14 soundstages; *Compromising Positions, Broadway Danny Rose,* and other films and music videos were shot here. **Court House Square,** at 21st Street and 45th Avenue, is overshadowed by I. M. Pei's greenish 48-story **Citicorp Building.** It's the largest building in Queens and it may permanently change the character of this low-key, rarely visited neighborhood.

**Sunnyside Gardens**  Representing urban planning at its most successful, Sunnyside Gardens is a pretty and still vital area of two-story homes and common gardens crossed by footpaths and leading to neat parks. Envisioned by architects and thinkers, such as Clarence Stein, Henry Wright, and Lewis Mumford, it was built in 1924 to provide housing for the middle class. During the Depression, Eleanor Roosevelt led protest marches to discourage marshals from evicting its out-of-work residents. It's located between 43rd and 48th streets and Barnett and Skillman avenues.

### Staten Island

Most off-islanders who ride the ferry return on the same boat, without ever setting foot on the 13.9-by-7.5-mile island where Joan Baez was born, Aaron Burr died, and Ichabod Crane is buried. Yet it's an excellent place to spend an exploring Sunday. Take in a concert or visit one of the local museums; then, with a good street map in hand, stroll around a little. And have fun getting lost—an almost inevitable prospect because Staten Island's streets are hard to follow.

Good routes to explore are along the North Shore, home of the **Snug Harbor Cultural Center** and the **Staten Island Institute of Arts and Sciences,** and along the East Shore, where you'll find the **Alice Austen House** (*see* Chapter 4). The center of the island is verdant with parks and wildlife refuges, thanks to the Greenbelt system, and beaches edge the island's coastline (*see* Chapter 6).

**Hamilton Park**  Just a blip on the map, this corner of Staten Island is nonetheless impressive for its cluster of stuccoed Italianate villas trimmed in gingerbread and its huge Shingle-style "cottages" put up just before and just after the Civil War. Streets to explore—all a little more than a mile from the ferry terminal—

are **Harvard Avenue, Pendleton Place, Prospect Avenue, Lafayette Street,** and **Ellicott Place.** The Tudoresque **110 and 120 Longfellow Avenue** was Casa Corleone in Francis Ford Coppola's 1971 movie *The Godfather;* the wedding scene was shot in the garden at 120.

**Todt Hill**  At 409 feet, this is the tallest of Staten Island's hills and the loftiest point along the Atlantic seaboard south of Maine. It's also the island's most prestigious residential neighborhood, particularly the area between **Flagg Place** and **Todt Hill Road,** just south of the **Richmond County Country Club.** On and off this thoroughfare there are handsome homes, modern and antique, including works by the highly respected architects Ernest Flagg (d. 1947) and Robert A. M. Stern. One of the prettiest spots is the 80-acre **Moravian Cemetery,** adjoining the **High Rock Conservation Center** (*see* Chapter 6).

# Small Spaces, Secret Places

These cul-de-sacs, mews, exceptional blocks, and special streets are like neighborhoods in miniature; intimate and charming, they show off city living at its best. Each is a notable feature of its own corner of New York, a high point in a visit there.

## Manhattan

**Beekman Place** is one of the abodes of Manhattan's quiet money. Its houses, in English Tudor, French Renaissance, and Georgian styles, have been home to songwriter Irving Berlin and socialite Mary Astor, among others. On a bluff above the East River, it's tucked away between 51st Street and Mitchell Place (as 49th Street is known east of First Avenue).

**Grove Court,** a half dozen three-story Federal redbrick town houses built in the 1850s around a Greenwich Village courtyard, inspired O. Henry's short story *The Last Leaf.* Peek through its entrance gate, between 10 and 12 Grove Street.

**Henderson Place,** a group of three-story vine-entwined redbrick town houses in Queen Anne style, was built in 1881. It's somehow even more charming for its position alongside a mammoth apartment building, between 86th and 87th streets off East End Avenue.

**Hudson View Gardens,** a cluster of vine-covered Gothic-style apartment buildings from the 1920s, is private property, but occasional visitors do enter to admire the exuberantly gardened interior and catch one of the romantic panoramas that gave the complex its name. It's in Washington Heights, at 116 Pinehurst Avenue between 183rd and 185th streets.

**MacDougal Alley,** a Greenwich Village alcove blocked off by an iron fence, is lined with houses built in the 1830s as stables for the mansions of Washington Square North. Artists took over the horses' quarters in the 1920s. Among its past residents: painter Jackson Pollock, actor John Carradine, buffalo-nickel designer James Earle Fraser, and arts patroness Gertrude Vanderbilt Whitney. From West 8th Street, go south on MacDougal Street and look to your left.

**Milligan Place** is another Village charmer—a triangular courtyard with a trio of brick houses. Enter on the west side of Sixth Avenue, around the corner from Patchin Place (*see* below).

**Mott Street** in Chinatown is narrow, curving, and jammed with stores selling roots and herbs, rice bowls, cheap wind-up toys, and paper parasols.

**Patchin Place,** lined by 10 tan brick three-story town houses dating from the 19th century, was once the home of the poet e. e. cummings. You'll find it off West 10th Street in Greenwich Village, just north of the Jefferson Market Courthouse.

**Pomander Walk,** two rows of Tudoresque town houses facing each other across a common walkway, was inspired by the sets for a play by the same name and intended for the use of stage folk. Actress Madeline Carroll lived here, as did Humphrey Bogart, Lillian and Dorothy Gish, and Rosalind Russell. Look for it on the Upper West Side, between 94th and 95th streets, West End Avenue, and Broadway.

**Riverview Terrace,** a cobblestoned East Side nook, is visible through its iron gates on Sutton Square. To get there, walk north on Sutton Place to Sutton Square and then turn right and left again.

**St. Luke's Place,** shaded by a canopy of lacy-leafed gingko trees, is one of the prettiest Village streets. The city's colorful mayor, James J. Walker, lived at No. 6. It's actually Leroy Street, which changes its name between Hudson Street and Seventh Avenue.

**Sniffen Court,** a well-kept midtown mews with 10 diminutive Romanesque Revival town houses, is on the south side of 36th Street between Third and Lexington avenues.

**Washington Mews,** MacDougal Alley's shady, cobblestoned cousin, is now mainly staff housing for New York University. It's hard to believe that a spot like this, where Betsy Ross or Abigail Adams might descend from their carriages at any moment, could exist in today's New York. You'll find it just south of 8th Street between Fifth Avenue and University Place.

## Brooklyn

**Grace Court Alley,** a Brooklyn Heights mews east of Hicks Street, near Grace Church, is where residents of Remsen and Joralemon streets' mansions once kept their carriages. The iron hay cranes are now used for hanging plants. West of Hicks Street is **Grace Court.**

**Hunts Lane** is almost more like London than London. You'll find this Brooklyn Heights mews full of window boxes just across Henry Street from Grace Court Alley.

# Tours

Although it's fun to discover the city on your own, serendipitously, it can also be rewarding to explore more methodically. You may want to take one of the dozens of sightseeing tours that form on street corners and piers all over the city every Sunday or pick up one of the handful of printed tours published by various organizations, both public and private.

## Guided Tours

**From the Water** The everyday spectacle of Manhattan's rivers and harbors is larger than life. Blue skies and a bright sun can make even New

York's tired waters dazzling. The air is tangy, and a fresh breeze blows in memories of the clipper ships and transatlantic liners that once made Manhattan the greatest port in the world.

*Sailing* **The Pioneer,** a 102-foot two-masted schooner built in 1885 to carry cargo along the Delaware River, sails regularly for two or three hours at a time in season. If the spirit moves you, you can help the crew raise her sails—or even take the helm. *South St. Seaport, tel. 212/669–9417 weekdays. Reserve 14 days before a sail. Fare: $15 for 2 hrs; $22 for 3 hrs; $10 and $16, respectively, for children 12 and under. Cruises May–Sept., Sun. noon and 3 (also at 6 beginning mid-June).*

**The Petrel,** New York's fastest yawl, was built for the Bermuda Cup races in 1938. Resplendent in teak and mahogany, she cruises the harbor as well, boarding as many as 40 passengers. *Battery Park, tel. 212/825–1976. Fare: $18 except for early departure, $14 adults, $8 senior citizens and children under 13. Cruises Apr.–Oct., Sun. 1–2:30, 3–5, and 5:30–7:30.*

*Motor Cruises* **Circle Line.** More than 40 million passengers have steamed around Manhattan on the eight 165-foot Circle Line yachts since the three-hour cruises were inaugurated in 1945. No other tour gives visitors such a terrific sense of Manhattan as an island. The 35-mile trip takes in such sights as the Little Red Lighthouse, the Palisades, Spuyten Duyvil, Grant's Tomb, Harlem, the *Intrepid*, the Javits Center, and, of course, the Statue of Liberty—never so fine as when seen from close up. The company's **Harbor Lights** cruises take in the sunset and Manhattan's lighted skyline. Basic snack foods plus beer and soft drinks are sold on board. *Pier 83, 12th Ave. at 42nd St., tel. 212/563–3200. No reservations necessary. Fare: $15 adults, $13.50 senior citizens, $7.50 children under 12. Sails every 45 min Mar.–Nov., 9:30–4:15; June–Sept., 9:30–7.*

**Seaport Line.** The sidewheeler *Andrew Fletcher* and the *DeWitt Clinton*, a re-creation of a turn-of-the-century steamboat, pull out of their South Street Seaport piers several times every Sunday. *Pier 16, South St. Seaport, tel. 212/406–3434. Fare: $12 adults, $10 students and senior citizens, $6 children under 13. 90-min cruises hourly Apr.–Sept., Sun. 11–5.*

**Staten Island ferry.** It still costs only two bits, and even if you've ridden it before, a new crop of sailing ships, a cluster of new buildings on shore, or a blazing sunset can completely transform the experience. Complete the round-trip right away for an hour of fine views and fresh air, or stay on Staten Island for awhile. *Staten Island Ferry Terminal near Battery Park, tel. 212/806–6940. Fare: 25¢. Around the clock year-round.*

**Walking Tours** The following organizations regularly sponsor special tours. Write in advance for a brochure or call to find out what's on when you want to go and make reservations if necessary. Or watch for announcements in *New York* magazine's Cue listings. Meeting places vary from tour to tour, so be sure of the rendezvous point. Fees range from $5 up to about $35.

**Adventure on a Shoestring** takes in oddball corners of the city—perhaps Hell's Kitchen, Yorkville, Chelsea, Murray Hill, Roosevelt Island, or other areas. Its motto is "exploring the world within our reach . . . within our means." *300 W. 53rd St., New York 10019, tel. 212/265–2663.*

**Art Deco Society of New York** explores the Art Deco aspects of Central Park South, the East and West 50s, 42nd Street, and other locations. *90 West St., Suite 1400, New York 10006, tel. 212/385-2744.*

**Broadway Excursions,** led by Alfred Pommer, cover landmark buildings and outdoor sculpture. *Box 69, New York 10029, tel. 212/348-3854. Apr.–Dec., Sun. at 1.*

**The Brooklyn Historical Society** offers walking tours several times a month. *128 Pierrepont St., Brooklyn 11201, tel. 718/ 624-0890.*

**Historywalks with Joyce Gold,** offered intermittently on Sundays throughout the year, take in Ladies' Mile or old Dutch New York. Gold, a local historian, has also written a couple of very good miniguides to these areas. *141 W. 17th St., New York 10011, tel. 212/242-5762.*

**Landmark Tours** focus on the architecture and history of neighborhoods, from midtown to Union Square and the Village. Two tours, led by guides with master's degrees in political science and urban history studies, are offered most summer Sundays. *151 1st Ave., Suite 189, New York 10003, tel. 212/979-5263.*

**Lower East Side Tenement Museum's Peddler's Pack** tours, offered most Sundays at noon, are led by costumed actors, who, in the roles of members of a real family, tell tour participants about their lives as they stroll through their neighborhood. *97 Orchard St., between Delancey and Broome Sts., New York 10002, tel. 212/431-0233.*

**Michael Levin,** an urban historian, leads tours of TriBeCa, SoHo, and other areas. *Tel. 212/924-7187, Apr.–July and Sept.–Nov.*

**Municipal Art Society,** one of New York's principal preservation groups, offers tours focusing on architecture, history, and urban planning intermittently throughout the summer. *457 Madison Ave., New York 10022, tel. 212/935-3960.*

**Museum of the City of New York Walking Tours** take architecture as a vehicle for understanding the social and political history of New York neighborhoods, ranging from Park Slope to Tompkins Square. *1220 5th Ave., New York 10029, tel. 212/ 534-1672. Four tours each Sun. in spring and fall.*

**New York City Department of Parks & Recreation's Urban Rangers** lead dozens of guided Sunday strolls all over the city. *1234 5th Ave., Room 111, New York 10029, tel. 212/860-1353.*

**New York Walk-Abouts** cover the Lower East Side, Roosevelt Island, Greenwich Village, New York's Gold Coast, Brooklyn Heights, and many other destinations. *30 Rockefeller Plaza, New York 10112, tel. 212/582-2015 weekdays, 914/834-5388 weekends and nights. Tours available regularly Mar.–July and Sept.–Nov.*

**New-York Walks** take a historic and architectural approach to neighborhoods all over the city. *New-York Historical Society, Public Programs, 170 Central Park West, New York 10024, tel. 212/873-3400. About 6 Sun. a year.*

**92nd Street Y** sponsors one of the city's richest and most varied arrays of walking tours. You might stop at sites that inspired Antoine de Saint-Exupéry to write *The Little Prince* or revisit Tammany haunts or famous New York disaster sites. Tours are sometimes led by well-known local figures, such as New York–born writer Kate Simon. *1395 Lexington Ave., New York 10128, tel. 212/415-5600 or 212/996-1100. Offered every Sun. year-round.*

**Prospect Park Environmental Center** offers Brooklyn tours most Sundays year-round. *Tennis House, Prospect Park, Brooklyn 11215, tel. 718/788-8549.*

**River to River Downtown Walking Tours,** led by a chatty retired schoolteacher named Ruth Alscher-Green, cover lower Manhattan, specifically the area around Battery Park City. *375 South End Ave., Suite 19U, New York 10280, tel. 212/321–2823.*

**Sidewalks of New York** concentrates on what's lively and colorful about the neighborhoods visited—murder sites, speakeasies, celebrity hangouts, haunted houses, movie locations, and good gossip. Guides are licensed by New York's Department of Consumer Affairs. *33 Alan Terr., Suite 2, Jersey City, NJ 07306, tel. 212/517–0201. At least 1 tour every Sun.*

**South Street Seaport Walks** show off the adjacent unrestored district, which looks the way the entire area did before the current boom. *207 Water St., New York 10038, tel. 212/669–9416. Offered on the hour many Sun. 10–6.*

**Tours of Jewish New York City** explore the Lower East Side, Colonial Jewish New York, and Brooklyn's Chassidic neighborhood of Williamsburg. Brussels-born Oscar Israelowitz, an architect and photographer, leads. *Box 228, Brooklyn 11229, tel. 718/951–7072. Offered intermittently.*

**Walk of the Town** customizes walks for small groups on special themes—literary New York, for instance. Gather a group of like-minded friends, and proprietor Marvin Gelfand will work out an itinerary. *280 Riverside Dr., New York 10025, tel. 212/ 222–5343.*

**Victorian Society** covers manifestations of the late 19th century as seen in Brooklyn and Manhattan. *217 E. 85th St., Suite 296, New York 10028, tel. 718/369–6004. Offered intermittently.*

**Theme Tours** These tours cover specific territories in small buses and vans.

**Art Tours of Manhattan** provides tours of museums, studios, and galleries with private guides—mainly Ph.Ds. *76 Library Pl., Princeton, NJ 08540, tel. 609/921–2647.*

**Doorway to Design** specializes in tours for groups but can also custom-tailor an itinerary for an individual or very small group when time is available. A Sunday shopping spree covering the best of the Lower East Side discount shops is one option, or take in tapestry, jewelry, and ceramics studios in Manhattan and Brooklyn. *1441 Broadway, Suite 33, New York 10018, tel. 212/221–1111 or 718/339–1542.*

**Harlem** **Harlem Spirituals** concentrates on traditional black music, as sung by parishioners at Sunday morning services. *1457 Broadway, Suite 1008, New York 10036, tel. 212/302–2594.*

**Harlem Your Way!** has regular Sunday walking tours, gospel music tours, and tours that focus on antiques, galleries, or soul food. *129 W. 130th St., New York 10027, tel. 212/690–1687.*

**New York Big Apple Tours** has three-hour Sunday gospel tours year-round. *203 E. 94th St., New York 10128, tel. 212/691–7866.*

**Harlem Renaissance Tours** has Sunday gospel tours; community residents are guides. *18 E. 105th St., New York 10025, tel. 212/722–9534. Available June–Nov.*

**Brooklyn** **Louis Singer,** once described as the Virgil of Brooklyn, is a gutsy embodiment of all that's New York. A former newspaper deliveryman, he has been exploring his city since the late 1930s and he's an encyclopedia of trivia about everything from Bay Ridge's glacial moraine to where to find the perfect half-sour pickle. *130 St. Edwards St., Brooklyn 11201, tel. 718/875–9084.*

**Personalized Tours**  **Manhattan Passport** (236 E. 47th St., New York 10017, tel. 212/ 832–9010) offers custom tours and provides knowledgeable guides for sightseeing, shopping, and gallery hopping.

**Citywide Bus Tours**  A variety of tours, ranging in length from two hours to 8½ hours, are available from **Gray Line** (900 8th Ave., New York 10019, tel. 212/397–2600), **Manhattan Sightseeing Tours** (150 W. 49th St., New York 10019, tel. 212/869–5005), and **Short Line Tours** (166 W. 46th St., New York 10036, tel. 212/354– 5122).

**Helicopter Tours**  A tour by the city's main helicopter sightseeing outfit, **Island Helicopter Sightseeing,** is definitely an eye-opening experience. Five different tours are available, each longer (and more expensive) than the one before. The longest lasts 40 minutes and zips all the way down to Coney Island. *Departures from heliport at 34th St. and East River, tel. 212/683–4575 for recorded information. Fares: $30–$139, depending on the tour. Operates Apr.–Dec., Sun. 9–9; Jan.–Mar., 9–6.*

## Self-Guided Tours

**On Tape**  **Pathfinder Productions** has 90-minute cassettes covering midtown, lower Manhattan, the Village, Chinatown to SoHo, and Fifth Avenue's Millionaire's Mile. *Box 3426, Noroton, CT 06820, tel. 203/854–0880. $10.95 per tour plus $1.50 postage.*
**Talk-A-Walk** has four cassette-recorded walking tours through lower Manhattan: "Gotham's Markets," "Gotham's Expanding Waistline," "The Power Structure," and "Across the Brooklyn Bridge." Each tape covers history, culture, architecture, legends, and lore. *Sound Publishers, 30 Waterside Plaza, Suite 10D, New York 10010–26301, tel. 212/686–0356. $9.95 per cassette.*

**In Print**  These guide books and pamphlets may be somewhat hard to find. **Urban Center Books** (457 Madison Ave. at 51st St. in the Helmsley Palace Hotel, tel. 212/935–3595), always open on Sundays, carries many of them. Also check **New York Bound Bookstore** at 50 Rockefeller Center (lobby of the Associated Press building, tel. 212/245–8503), although it isn't open Sundays.

*Citywide*  The *AIA Guide to New York City,* by Elliot Willensky and Norval White ($21.95, Harcourt Brace Jovanovich), is an architectural encyclopedia of the five boroughs. Each borough is covered neighborhood by neighborhood, landmark by landmark; these are listed as they would be encountered on a walking or driving tour. Everyone who loves New York should own this fabulous book.
*Guide to the Metropolis,* by Gerard Wolfe ($14.95, McGraw-Hill Paperbacks), covers 14 neighborhoods in Manhattan, five in Brooklyn, and one in Queens. It notes New York City landmarks and buildings on the National Register of Historic Places and includes fascinating photographs of the neighborhoods as they used to be.

*Lower Manhattan*  *From Windmills to the World Trade Center,* by Joyce Gold, covers the area from Trinity Church to the Seaport via 45 sites, both familiar and unfamiliar, ($4.95 plus $1.25 postage from Old Warren Road Press, 141 W. 17th St., New York 10011, tel. 212/242–5762, or in bookstores).
*Heritage Trail* explores from Foley Square to the South Street

Seaport via 17 sites (free from Port Authority, Public Services, 1 World Trade Center, New York 10048, tel. 212/466–4170).

*Juror's Guide to Lower Manhattan,* a Municipal Arts Society publication, is full of tours beginning and ending at Foley Square ($2.50 at Urban Center Books).

*Map and Guide to Lower Manhattan: From Shoreline to Skyline* is a map-brochure covering nine districts and their highlights (free from Port Authority, *see* above).

*Where They Lit Up New York,* a Con Edison publication, is devoted to historic sites in the area of Thomas Edison's first commercial generating station on Pearl Street (free from ConEd at 4 Irving Pl., Suite 1625–S, New York 10003, tel. 212/460–6905).

SoHo    *A Walking Tour of Cast Iron Architecture in SoHo,* by Margot Gayle and Robin Lynn, explores the elegantly ornamented buildings on the National Register in this historic district ($3 from Friends of Cast Iron Architecture, 235 E. 87th St., Room 6C, New York 10128, tel. 212/369–6004).

Lower East Side    *The Lower East Side* details shops and historic sites, synagogues, and settlement houses ($1 from the Lower East Side Businessmen's Association, 88 Rivington St., New York 10002, tel. 212/995–9170).

Greenwich Village    *A Walking Tour of the Village,* by Maggie Kenyon, discusses architecture, politics, and culture ($2.50 from the author, Box 798, Village Station, New York 10014).

*From Trout Stream to Bohemia,* by Joyce Gold, gives background on famous Villagers, churches, taverns, and such ($4.95 plus $1.25 postage from Old Warren Road Press, 141 W. 17th St., New York 10011, tel. 212/242–5762, or in bookstores).

*Greenwich Village: A Brief Architectural and Historical Guide,* a New York University booklet, offers two walking tours to major points of interest ($2 from NYU Book Centers, 18 Washington Pl., New York 10003, tel. 212/998–4674).

Sofi    *End of the Road for Ladies' Mile,* by Margaret Moore, details the splendid buildings in the area that was the city's most fashionable shopping district in the Gilded Age ($5 from US Design, 853 Broadway, Room 1605, New York 10003, tel. 212/505–1454).

Midtown    *42nd Street: River to River,* by Gerard Wolfe, spends 42 pages describing the area from Theater Row to the United Nations (free from 42nd Street E.T.C., c/o Lalli Associates, 124 W. 24th St., New York 10011, tel. 212/206–8816).

Harlem    *Harlem Today,* by A. Peter Bailey, covers five historic districts and their landmarks and cultural facilities ($4.95 plus $1.75 postage from Gumbs & Thomas, 2067 Broadway, Suite 45, New York 10023, or at the gift shop at the Cathedral of St. John the Divine, Amsterdam Ave. and 112th St.).

Brooklyn    **10 Walking Tours,** a map of Brooklyn neighborhoods, pinpoints landmarks, parks, shops, and cultural institutions. They are described in greater detail in the accompanying *Brooklyn Neighborhood Book* (book $4, map free, from Fund for the Borough of Brooklyn, 16 Court St., Suite 900, Brooklyn 11241, tel. 718/855–7882).

Queens    *Flushing Freedom Mile Historic Tour* covers nearly two dozen historic sites on and off Northern Boulevard (50¢ from the

Queens Historical Society, 143–35 37th Ave., Flushing 11354, tel. 718/939–0647).

*Staten Island* **Staten Island Walking Tours** takes in wonderful Italianate and Gothic Revival buildings, churches, and homes in six neighborhoods ($6.95 by mail or $5 in person from the Richmondtown Restoration, 441 Clarke Ave., Staten Island 10306, tel. 718/351–1611).

## Sightseeing from City Buses

The slow pace of city buses, so aggravating on busy weekdays, is just right for taking in the scenery on a leisurely Sunday. Riding from one end of the route to the other not only provides a glimpse of a succession of neighborhoods, but gives an overview of how they all fit together. Getting a seat is almost never a problem on Sundays, and the cost is only the price of a token.

Two routes are particularly good for this:

The **M-10** rolls down Central Park West to Columbus Circle, sails down Seventh Avenue to Varick Street and West Broadway, curls around up Church and Hudson streets, then heads straight up Eighth Avenue all the way to 159th Street. Along the route are the American Museum of Natural History at 81st Street; a string of ornate old apartment buildings, including the Beresford at 81st Street and the gabled Dakota at 72nd Street; Times Square; low-key Chelsea; and the World Trade Center. You can start anywhere along Central Park West and make a complete loop.

The **M5** meanders up and down curving, slightly hilly Riverside Drive, with the Hudson River a constant presence to the west and miles of fine prewar apartment houses on the other side. **Grant's Tomb** is at 122nd Street, the **Soldiers' and Sailors' Monument** at 89th Street. The bus crosses 72nd Street, turns south on Broadway, heads east on 57th Street, and then goes straight south on Fifth Avenue, passing **Tiffany's, St. Patrick's Cathedral, Rockefeller Center, Lord & Taylor** and **B. Altman** department stores, and the **Flatiron Building.** Turning across Eighth Street and then down Broadway, the bus rolls finally to Houston and SoHo. If you stay on the bus, you ride up Sixth Avenue, where there's a whole different scene: the **Flower District, Macy's** department store, **Bryant Park,** and modern office towers.

## Horse-Drawn Carriage Rides

These rides are certainly not for tourists only. Whether the air is frosty and crisp or soft and warm, it's extremely pleasant to lean back, watch the scenery slip by, and listen to the clip-clop-clip-clop of horses' hoofs on pavement.

Catch one of these cabs on 59th Street near the Plaza Hotel, at the southeast corner of the park. The cost is city-regulated at $34 for the first half hour, $10 for each quarter-hour after that; the fare is calculated by time, not per passenger.

# Best Bets for Children

Transportation and tall buildings are two of the most exciting things about sightseeing in New York for children. Just riding in a taxicab or bus can be a thrill; so is the subway (especially the first car of the train, with its view of the tunnels and track). The city's helicopters, horse-drawn carriages, sailboats, and ferryboats are also child-pleasers. Try the tram ride to Roosevelt Island, too, or the Circle Line boat trip around Manhattan, which takes in the Little Red Lighthouse, known to youngsters all over America from Hildegarde Hoyt Swift's book, *The Little Red Lighthouse and the Great Gray Bridge.*

A trip to the top of one of New York's viewing platforms is another must. Should you do the Empire State Building or the World Trade Center? In deciding, consider the view you want and proximity to other sites. On its lower level, the **Empire State Building** boasts an exhibit devoted to esoteric facts and figures from "Guiness World of Records Exhibit Hall" columns, and it's a quick cab ride from there to the aircraft carrier *Intrepid.* The **World Trade Center's** view of the harbor and its scattering of big ships gets raves, as does the rest of Lower Manhattan, which also offers the **South Street Seaport, Fraunces Tavern,** the **Brooklyn Bridge,** and more. The **Woolworth Building,** also in the area, is like every child's fantasy of a fairy-tale palace, with its gold-mosaic lobby and ornate stonework. It's also one of the few landmarks of the New York architectural scene that will delight children of almost any age. Another appealing landmark is **Grand Central Terminal**—kids love its constellation-studded ceiling, glass-paved footbridges, and whispering gallery.

For preteens, the **East Village** is the essential scene to make. And everybody enjoys City Island, with is sea breezes and marinas full of boats of all sizes.

# 4 Museums and the Visual Arts

Renoir and Rembrandt, Madame Jumel and Samuel Fraunces are the perfect companions for a leisurely afternoon that begins with croissants and café au lait in SoHo and ends in one of New York's 150-odd museums. Saturday and Sunday are the city's biggest museum days: Some exhibit spaces that are closed at other times of the week are open on weekends, and those that are open almost daily bustle with special programs— lectures, concerts, films, tours.

Always call ahead to check opening times, for many museums close on Sundays during summer or when holidays fall on a Sunday. Admission fees are given below; however, these are usually waived for members, babies, and toddlers, and students can show IDs to qualify for reduced rates. Special rates for children ordinarily prevail only when they are accompanied by a parent or guardian.

While items listed in the descriptions below indicate the scope of each museum's collections, note that they may not be on display at the time of your visit. With traveling exhibits, special shows, and the need to rotate works from collections too vast to display all at once, New York's museums offer a continually changing panoply of delights.

# Art Museums

How long has it been since you looked at Claude Monet's *Water Lilies* or Vincent Van Gogh's *Starry Night* or Henri Matisse's *Red Studio?* Or called on Auguste Rodin's *Balzac*, Pierre-Auguste Renoir's *Madame Charpentier and Her Children*, or Jan Vermeer's *Young Woman with a Water Jug?* Or stopped in to see Rembrandt's *Aristotle with a Bust of Homer* or Egypt's Queen Hatshepsut? Their worlds of color and form are as invigorating as any eight hours in the countryside, as inspiring as a morning in church. To see these works or their peers, you need not travel far—just head for the Museum of Modern Art, the Metropolitan Museum of Art, or the city's other bastions of the muses, great and small.

### Megamuseums

New York City's megamuseums are really more like several museums under one roof, with a huge variety of collections ranging from Egyptiana to European painting, sculpture, and decorative arts. They are usually humming on Sundays, with crowds spilling over into the gift shops and nearby restaurants.

**Metropolitan Museum** There isn't another museum in the city with so much that's so wonderful: 2,000 European paintings, 3,000 European drawings, an equal number of American paintings and statues, 4,000 medieval objects and a comparable group of musical instruments, a million prints, as well as decorative arts and quite a lot more. Temporary exhibitions are mounted with great regularity, and items go in and out of storage constantly, for even with its 32 acres of floor space, only a quarter of what the Met actually owns is on view at any given time.

To get the most from this embarrassment of riches, take in just a bit on each visit. Attend a special program or make a beeline for one gallery that interests you. And allow a little extra time en route to discover something new and unexpected.

*Highlights*   The **American wing** (first, second, and third floors) centered on the Astor Court, is green, cool, and restful regardless of the day of the week, regardless of the weather outside. The 20 room settings never seem too crowded, and there are wonderful paintings as well.

**Arms and armor** (first floor) has handsomely wrought artifacts that children often find entertaining.

The **Egyptian wing** (first floor) is full of bas reliefs, sculptures, and artifacts covering nearly four millennia. The Temple of Dendur is one of the focal points of this area.

**Medieval art** (first floor) is especially noteworthy for its cavernous sculpture hall. Built to resemble a church, it feels cool and quiet no matter how busy the day. The wrought-iron choir screen is splendid.

**Primitive art** (first floor, in the Michael C. Rockefeller Wing), with 7,000 sculptures, ritual objects, and everyday artifacts, spans 3,000 years of the history of Africa, the Americas, and the Pacific Islands.

**Greek and Roman art** (first and second floors) has dazzling displays of gold and silver tableware and ceremonial vessels counterpointing a collection of Grecian urns.

**Lehman Pavilion** (first and second floors), a group of seven period rooms, shows off superb 18th-century French furniture, as well as Flemish, Italian, and French paintings, drawings, and tapestries.

The **Dutch galleries** (second floor) have works by Jan Vermeer, Frans Hals, Gerard Ter Borch, and others to restore the soul; there are 33 Rembrandts.

**Musical instruments** (second floor) is a wonderful spot for music lovers. Pick up an Acoustiguide on your way into the museum, and you can hear how exquisite craftsmanship translates to sound.

**19th-century paintings and sculpture** (second floor, Rockefeller Wing, in André Meyer Galleries) is one of the glories of New York. Painting after world-famous painting by Jean-Baptiste Camille Corot, Jean-François Millet, Joseph Turner, Auguste Rodin, Pierre-Auguste Renoir, Camille Pissaro, Vincent Van Gogh, Paul Cézanne, and others can be seen in all their luminous color.

**European sculpture and decorative arts** (to be housed in a new five-story south wing in 1990) will display much that has been in storage for years.

*Sunday Programs*   Lectures, films, and panel discussions take place almost hourly in the Grace Rainey Rogers and Uris Center auditoriums on topics as diverse as the collections. There are also special programs for families.

*Facilities*   The **Museum Dining Room** serves brunch on Sunday (tel. 212/535–7710 for reservations).

A parking **garage** on the premises makes the Met a good bet for rainy days.

*5th Ave. and 82nd St., tel. 212/535–7710; 212/570–3932 for special programs; or 212/570–3711 for recorded tours. Suggested contribution: $5 adults, $2.50 students and senior citizens, children under 12 free. Open Sun. 9:30–5:15.*

**Brooklyn Museum**   In any other city, this vigorous institution, housed in a turn-of-the-century Beaux Arts monument by McKim, Mead & White, would be the art enthusiast's first destination rather than his

fifth or sixth. Many of those who do make the trip come for its
blockbuster exhibitions: Akhenaten and Nefertiti, artist Judy
Chicago's feminist *Dinner Party*, or Andrew Wyeth's *Helga*
pictures. But its own encyclopedic collections—2 million items
running the gamut from plastic-and-metal Elsa Schiaparelli
jewelry to Brooklyn Dodgers uniforms to Winslow Homer
watercolors—are of international caliber. New additions to the
building, by architects Arata Isozaki and James Stewart
Polshek, should make things even better. Moreover, it's all
next door to the glorious Brooklyn Botanic Garden and Prospect Park.

*Highlights*   **Grand Lobby installations** (first floor) feature work created
specifically for this grandiose space by contemporary artists.
**Asian art** (second floor) ranges from Afghanistan to Qajar via
China, the Islamic world, and India.
**The Egyptian galleries** (third floor), guarded by massive Assyr-
ian wall sculptures, contain incredible treasures from ancient
Egypt's tombs and royal cities from the Predynastic period
(4000–3000 BC) to the Muslim conquest (7th century AD). Besides
mummies in glorious sarcophagi, you'll see jewelry; pots; tools;
solemn statues of queens, kings, cats, and dogs; and small pre-
cious objects in bright blue faïence, alabaster, black basalt,
limestone, or carved ivory.
**Period rooms** (fourth floor) include 21 parlors, sitting rooms,
and dining rooms from plantation mansions and New England
cottages from 1675 to 1830. Viewing the Jan Martense Schenck
House, the oldest, is like stepping into a painting by a Dutch
master; the somber, exotic Moorish Room from John D.
Rockefeller's town house is a tycoon's Alhambra. Costume gal-
leries and decorative arts complement the period rooms.
**Old Masters and French impressionists** (fifth floor) focus on such
names as Frans Hals, Joshua Reynolds, Claude Monet, Edgar
Degas, Camille Pissaro, Mary Cassatt, Henri Toulouse-
Lautrec, and others.
**American collection** (fifth floor) chronicles American art from
its origins to the present. With paintings by John Singleton
Copley, John Singer Sargent, Albert Bierstadt, John Lafarge,
Rockwell Kent, John Sloan, Thomas Eakins, and others, the
collection rivals the Met's.
**Iris and Gerald Cantor Gallery** (fifth floor) showcases 58 sculptures by Auguste Rodin, including works relating to *The Gates
of Hell*, *The Burghers of Calais*, and *Balzac*.
**Frieda Schiff Warburg Memorial Sculpture Garden** (behind the
building) is studded with architectural artifacts rescued from
the elaborately ornamented buildings built in the 19th century
and demolished in the 20th: theatrical masks; cherubs; lions;
scrolls; capitals; Medusas; and columns in bronze, copper, limestone, brownstone, terra-cotta, and other materials. Look for
the lamppost from Coney Island's now-defunct Steeplechase
Park (circa 1897), the white goddess that once cradled the Penn
Station clock, a butterfly with a face like Puck's, and a huge
ram's head in ivy.

*Sunday Programs*   Making art captivating for children is the business of the
"What's Up" Sunday gallery explorations (at 2 PM) and Raiders
of the Fine Arts multiweek courses—Boisterous Books, Sculpture Speaks, Paper Possibilities. For adults, there are movie
matinees and gallery talks on pre-Columbian art, Asian lacquer,
and many other subjects.

*200 Eastern Pkwy., Brooklyn, tel. 718/638–5000. Admission:*
*$3 adults, $1.50 students, $1 senior citizens, children under 12*
*free. Open Sun. 10–5. Parking on premises.*

## Other Major Museums

At the **Frick Collection,** a small but exquisite set of Rembrandts, Holbeins, Vermeers, Fragonards, and Bouchers is
beautifully set off by industrialist Henry Clay Frick's splendid
Beaux Arts mansion. You don't have to be an art historian to
appreciate the Frick—everything simply glows. The neoclassic
garden court with its burbling fountain, Ionic columns, stone
benches, and ivy is the oasis within this oasis. *1 E. 70th St., tel.*
*212/288–0700. Admission: $3. Children under 6 not admitted,*
*under 16 must be accompanied by adult. Open Sun. 10–6.*

At the **Guggenheim Museum,** the architecture is as important
as the art. The building, a Frank Lloyd Wright creation that
opened the year its architect died, still looks modern; the interior, with its four-level, quarter-mile-long spiral ramp, is one
of the great public spaces in the city, beautifully light drenched
from 92 feet up with a huge six-lobed skylight. Copper magnate Solomon Guggenheim's collection, the core of the
museum, is particularly strong in the works of Paul Klee and,
to a lesser extent, of Marc Chagall, Robert Delaunay, and
Fernand Léger. Pablo Picasso and others are represented in
the Thannhauser Wing. Sundays are crowded but still pleasant; a museum expansion will increase available space. Free
gallery talks are conducted at 2:30 by graduate students in art
history. A pleasant café serves light fare. *1071 5th Ave. at 89th*
*St., tel. 212/360–3500 or 212/360–3513 for recorded exhibition*
*information. Admission: $4.50 adults, $2.50 students and sen-*
*ior citizens, children under 7 free. Open Sun. 11–4:45.*

**The J. Pierpont Morgan Library,** housed in tycoon J. P.
Morgan's lavish Renaissance-style palazzo, displays his collection of books, manuscripts, incunabula, and works of art on
paper, one of the country's finest. You'll see a real Gutenberg
Bible, along with manuscripts and letters from Honoré de Balzac, Lord Byron, Charles Dickens, John Keats, Albrecht
Dürer, and others; changing exhibitions add further pleasures.
And the West Room's extravagantly carved 16-century ceiling,
the library's fine hardwood cabinets, and the marble, tapestries, and Italian furniture throughout the library are eloquent
testament to what it must have been like to be wealthy at the
turn of the century. *29 E. 36th St., tel. 212/685–0008 or 212/685–*
*0610 for recorded information. Suggested contribution: $3.*
*Open Sun. 1–5.*

The **Museum of Modern Art,** founded a few days after the Crash
of '29, addresses itself to the history and the present status of
contemporary art. Cesar Pelli's revamping a few years ago
added lots of gray stone, gray wood, and white paint—and
plenty of light and air—so the museum never feels too crowded,
even at its Sunday busiest. Paintings represent nearly every
movement in modern art: Bauhaus, Pop, Minimalism, De Stijl,
abstract expressionism, Impressionism, Dadaism, surrealism,
Cubism, and others; and the collection includes celebrated
works such as Claude Monet's *Water Lilies,* Vincent Van Gogh's
*Starry Night,* Henri Rousseau's *Sleeping Gypsy,* Pablo
Picasso's *Les Demoiselles d'Avignon* and *Three Musicians,* and

Andrew Wyeth's *Christina's World*. Photographs by Dorothea Lange, Henri Cartier-Bresson, and other greats are always wonderful, as are the architectural models and objects of design such as the Bell-47D1 suspended above the escalator. The Sculpture Garden offers peaceful moments, and the film department, with its huge library of prints, most screened nowhere else, is an oasis as well as a treasure. (*See* Movies in Chapter 7.) Even the restaurants are pleasant. *11 W. 53rd St., tel. 212/708–9480 for recorded information; 212/708–9490 for film schedules; or 212/247–1230 for the disabled. Admission: $6 adults, $3.50 students, $3 senior citizens, children under 16 free. Open Sun. 11–6.*

Gertrude Vanderbilt Whitney founded the **Whitney Museum of American Art** in 1930 with the idea of celebrating the work of artists while they were still alive. The result is one of Manhattan's most dynamic institutions, a veritable textbook of the nation's artistic output. Mrs. Whitney's own collection is the nucleus of the permanent collection of some 8,000 20th-century paintings, sculpture, and works on paper by such artists as George Bellows, Thomas Hart Benton, Stuart Davis, William de Kooning, Alex Katz, Ellsworth Kelly, Roy Lichtenstein, Georgia O'Keeffe, Maurice B. Prendergast, Jackson Pollock, Mark Rothko, John Sloan, and Frank Stella. In addition, there are always lively special exhibitions: the Shakers' elegantly simple furniture, Grant Wood's provocative drawings, Red Grooms's huge sculpto-pictoramas, Walt Kuhn's carnival portraits, to name a few recent entries. The Biennial invitational exhibition, surveying the previous two years on the art scene, is always exciting and provocative. And the granite-clad Marcel Breuer building (1966) is a work of art in its own right. Weekend gallery talks are at 2 and 3:30. You can get refreshments in the museum restaurant and, in summer, in the outdoor sculpture court. *945 Madison Ave. at 75th St., tel. 212/570–3676, 212/570–0537 for film schedules, or 212/570–3652 for gallery talks. Admission: $4.50 adults, $2.50 senior citizens, students and children under 12 free. Open Sun. noon–6.*

## Small Surprises

**The Bronx Museum of the Arts,** housed since 1982 in a former synagogue, was founded in 1972. Intriguing exhibitions here show off new American art, particularly works by Bronx-based artists. The building stands on the Grand Concourse, a great boulevard lined with mid-rise Art Deco buildings. *1040 Grand Concourse, the Bronx, tel. 212/681–6000. Admission: $2 adults, children under 13 free. Open Sun. 11–4:30.*

The **National Academy of Design,** modeled on Europe's great art academies, has asked every new associate member to contribute a self-portrait since it was founded in 1825 by Samuel F. B. Morse, Thomas Cole, and Rembrandt Peale; it now has the country's largest collection of American portraits. Sculpture, prints, and other paintings are also featured, and exhibitions range from fantasy furniture to landscapes. *1083 5th Ave. between 89th and 90th Sts., tel. 212/369–4880. Admission: $2.50 adults, $2 students and senior citizens. Open Sun. noon–5.*

**Snug Harbor Cultural Center,** a onetime sailors' retirement home on Staten Island, is the site of the city's largest collection of Greek Revival buildings. Together with other equally charming late 19th- and early 20th-century structures, these are home to the Newhouse Gallery, the Staten Island Children's Museum, an art school, the Staten Island Botanical Garden, and Veteran's Memorial Hall. The special events program is fast making Snug Harbor a city treasure. *914 Richmond Terr., Livingston, Staten Island, tel. 718/448–2500. Admission free. Open Sun. 10–dusk; tours at 2 PM.*

**The Studio Museum in Harlem** exhibits black art, photography, sculpture, and artifacts from Africa, the Caribbean, and the Americas in this lively and sophisticated small institution founded in the late 1960s. Don't miss the long-planned T. F. Bing Sculpture Garden, if it has been completed by the time you visit. *144 W. 125th St., tel. 212/864–4500. Admission: $2 adults, $1 children under 13. Open Sun. 1–6.*

## Specialty Museums

In New York, there's a museum for nearly every medium, nearly every artistic point of view, and nearly every era in the arts.

**American Craft Museum.** The monumental spiral staircase at the heart of this undertaking of the American Crafts Council is itself worth seeing. Even more intriguing are the exhibitions— devoted to the oeuvre of furniture maker George Nakashima, for example, or showcasing the confectioner's art with chocolate café tables, marzipan seafood platters, and a Statue of Liberty in jellybeans. You never know what you'll find. *40 W. 53rd St., tel. 212/956–6047. Admission: $3.50 adults, $1.50 students and senior citizens, children under 12 free. Open Sun. 10–5.*

**American Museum of the Moving Image.** Situated on the Astoria Studios site, in the building where Paramount Pictures once produced silents and talkies starring the likes of Rudolph Valentino, Gloria Swanson, and Claudette Colbert, this newcomer to the city's cultural scene is the first public museum in the country devoted solely to the history of the movies and film production, promotion, and exhibition. It attends to aesthetics like an art museum, interprets its material like a history museum, and emphasizes technology like a science center. Static and interactive displays explore what goes on behind the scenes—the work of directors, actors, set directors, makeup artists, and other industry specialists—and show off selections from the 60,000-item collection of cameras, projectors, costumes, scenery, production logs, studio business documents, lobby cards, licensed artifacts, and much more. On Sundays there are two or three screenings in the 195-seat main theater; meanwhile, old serials from *Captain America* to *Tigerman* play in the smaller screening/conference rooms, the shag-rug-and-vinyl-sofa "TV Lounge," and in the "Tut's Fever" theater, a work of art in its own right, in which artists Red Grooms and Lysiane Luong pay witty homage to neo-Egyptian picture palaces of the 1920s. Sunday is the busiest day—and a pleasant time to savor an increasingly colorful neighborhood (*see* Explorable Neighborhoods in Chapter 1). The surrounding studio complex—the only movie studio on the National Register of Historic Places—is once again a film-making center; *Brighton Beach Memoirs, Radio Days,* and *The Verdict* were all made here. *35th Ave. at 36th St., Astoria, Queens, tel. 718/ 784–4520. Admission: $5 (includes screenings; small extra fees for celebrity appearances). Open Sun. 11–6.*

**Cloisters.** The Metropolitan Museum's upper Manhattan

branch for medieval art occupies a cool, silent building that could be set centuries ago in France, Germany, or Spain. Once called the crowning achievement in American museology, the museum, which incorporates elements of five medieval cloisters, is spectacularly situated overlooking the Hudson River, at the high point of Fort Tryon Park. (John D. Rockefeller, Jr., who donated the 4-acre site, also purchased 700 acres of New Jersey's Palisades to protect the view.) The collection of medieval European art, the country's best, includes icons and chalices, tapestries and altarpieces, paintings and polychromed wood sculptures, illuminated manuscripts and works in stained glass, metal, enamel, and ivory. The formal gardens (*see* Gardens in Chapter 6) are exquisite. From fall through spring, there are special concerts of medieval and Renaissance music. Sundays, which draw a more diverse crowd than weekdays, are busiest in spring, when the gardens come into bloom, and less crowded in cold months, except during December when there are concerts. If you want to see a quieter side of the Cloisters, come in the morning. *Fort Tryon Park, tel. 212/923–3700. Admission: $5 adults, $2.50 students and senior citizens. Open Nov.–Feb., Sun. 9:30–4:45; Mar.–Oct., Sun. 9:30–5:15.*

**Cooper-Hewitt Museum.** The permanent collection at this delightful institution—founded in 1897 by three granddaughters of 19th-century inventor-philanthropist Peter Cooper, and since 1976 the Smithsonian's National Museum of Design—are equaled only by those at the Victoria and Albert in London and the Musée des Arts Décoratifs in Paris. Some 167,000 objects represent 3,000 years of design: ceramics, woodwork, furniture, glass, porcelain, and textiles ranging from fine lace to tapestries, not to mention some 30,000 drawings and prints, and enchanting miscellany—bird cages, valentines, pressed flowers, and even Christmas tree ornaments. All these are displayed selectively, in special shows addressing aspects of design. The museum's home, the landmark neo-Georgian 1901 Andrew Carnegie mansion, is full of wonderful old oak paneling, coffered ceilings, and parquet floors. The Conservatory, which bubbles out on the east end of the house, is one of the loveliest gardens in the city. Tours of the mansion are offered every other Sunday at 1 and 2:30. *2 E. 91st St., tel. 212/860–6868. Admission: $3 adults, $1.50 students and senior citizens, children under 12 free. Open Sun. noon–5.*

**International Center of Photography.** Housed in another splendid early 20th-century neo-Georgian town house, this focal point of the American photographic community displays works by photographers from around the world, emerging talents and masters, from the earliest days to the present. It was founded in 1974 by Cornell Capa, brother of the famous photographer Robert Capa. The permanent collection includes 10,000 prints from greats such as Eugene Smith, Diane Arbus, Eugene Atget, Edward Weston, and Alfred Steiglitz; ICP also mounts terrific temporary shows. *1130 5th Ave. at 94th St., tel. 212/860–1777. Admission: $3 adults, $1.50 students. Open Sun. 11–6.*

**Museum of American Folk Art.** This institution, founded in 1961, recently moved into new space near Lincoln Center, and work is progressing on a permanent building on West 53rd Street, where it started out. For the moment, the Lincoln Center space is excitement enough with its quartet of well-lighted galleries, displaying such objects as a nine-foot Indian chief weather vane, carousel animals, a Stars-and-Stripes quilt, trade signs, decoys, rag dolls, cigar store figurines, and more. *2 Lincoln Sq. (Columbus Ave. between 65th and 66th Sts.), tel. 212/977-7298. Admission free. Open Sun. 9-9.*

**Museum of Holography.** Holograms re-create real objects with a difference—the holographic object, made using a technique developed in 1947 and enhanced with the development of the laser in 1962, has no solidity. Since its founding in 1976, this museum has been a center for understanding and advancing the medium. Now the world's foremost exhibitor of these ghostly presences, it focuses on science as well as art. Some displays are from the museum's collection of holograms, the world's largest; and there are always special exhibitions as well. The museum is sometimes crowded on Sundays; the best time to come is at opening. *11 Mercer St., between Grand and Canal Sts., tel. 212/925-0581. Admission: $3 adults, $2.75 students, $1.75 children under 12 and senior citizens. Open Sun. 11-6.*

**New Museum of Contemporary Art.** This maze of rooms and galleries may be hosting a temporary exhibition of the French artist Christian Boltanski's tin drawers and vitrines containing his childhood possessions, or you might see the work of Malcolm McLaren, the Svengali of punk, or any number of other exuberantly original works. Eclectic is the watchword. At Weekend Dialogues, museum docents conduct informal discussions with interested visitors. Sunday is busy but seldom daunting. *583 Broadway, between Houston and Prince Sts., tel. 212/219-1222 or 212/219-1355 for recorded information. Admission: $2.50 adults; $1.50 artists, students, and senior citizens; children under 12 free. Open Sun. noon-6.*

**Nicholas Roerich Museum.** The eponymous Russian artist enjoyed a varied career that included archaeological excavations, Asian journeys over antique caravan routes, and set design for Diaghilev's *Prince Igor* and Stravinsky's *Rite of Spring.* His paintings of the Himalayas—serene presences in rich colors, grand and majestic, vast and isolated, and unquestionably awe inspiring—are the focal point of the work displayed in the museum's mansion home (circa 1898), designed by Clarence True. The frequent Sunday concerts are usually, but not always, at 5 and sometimes, but not always, classical. The museum is small; some think it weird. You won't have to fight crowds to enjoy the special tranquility here. *319 W. 107th St., tel. 212/864-7752. Admission free. Open Sun. 2-5.*

## World Cultures

The institutions listed below showcase the art of specific countries or cultures. A Sunday stroll through their galleries can be a trip around the world, to the far Pacific or the heart of Africa.

**Asia Society.** John D. Rockefeller III's considerable Asian art collection, one of the great ones in the field, is the backdrop for changing exhibits in a stunning modern building. *725 Park Ave. at 70th St., tel. 212/288-6400. Admission: $2 adults, $1 students and senior citizens. Open Sun. noon-5.*

**Center for African Art.** The traditional art of Africa has been beautifully displayed since 1984 in this duo of town houses. Three times annually the center draws on the storerooms of the world's great museums to mount special exhibitions—works from a single institution or an important collector, or topical shows focusing on single objects such as the gourd, or single subjects such as Africa and the Renaissance. There are ceremonial masks, ritual items, utilitarian objects, and musical instruments in ivory, shells, wood, gold, skins, and fibers. *54 E. 68th St., tel. 212/861–1200. Admission: $2.50 adults, $1.50 senior citizens and children. Open Sun. noon–5.*

**Chinatown Project.** A former elementary school, in use from 1893 to 1976, now houses a gallery where you can browse through changing exhibitions—for example, a German's antique photographs of San Francisco's Chinatown. The focus is on the heritage of New York's Chinese community of 100,000 people. Walking tours illuminating the area may eventually become available on Sundays; reserve in advance. *70 Mulberry St. at Bayard St., 2nd floor, tel. 212/619–4785. Admission free. Open Sun. noon–5.*

**El Museo del Barrio.** The country's only museum dedicated to Puerto Rico's culture—and one of the most important institutions of Latin American arts—exhibits dozens of hand-carved Santos de Palo (saints). Special exhibitions may showcase works by folk artists living in New York or replicate studios of craftsmen from Caribbean states. Concerts are occasionally held on Sundays. *1230 5th Ave., between 104th and 105th Sts., tel. 212/831–7272. Admission: $2 adults, $1 students and senior citizens, children under 12 free. Open Sun. 11–5.*

**Hispanic Society of America.** Visiting the main court here, done in Spanish Renaissance–style terra-cotta, is like taking a quick trip to the Alhambra. Subtly hued hand-painted tiles, carved wood screens and statues, elaborately worked gold and silver, original opera scores, ivories, textiles, and wrought-iron pieces are the backdrop for magnificent paintings by such artists as Diego Velásquez, El Greco, and José Ribera. Francisco de Goya's *Duchess of Alba* and the room full of murals by 20th-century realist Joaquín de Sorolla y Bastida are among the best known. Thousands of manuscripts and books make this also a superb center for research on Spanish and Portuguese history, art, and literature. But it is an appealing place for casual visitors as well—and practically unknown (visited by only 10,000 people a year). No more than 50 visitors are permitted inside the building at any one time, so it's always quiet and is even more pleasant on Sundays. Audubon Terrace, where the Hispanic Society is located, contains several other museums in the same Spanish Renaissance style, among them the Museum of the American Indian, below. *613 W. 155th St., tel. 212/926–2234. Admission free; Acoustiguides with 45-min tours 50¢ for one person, 75¢ for two. Open Sun. 1–4.*

**Jacques Marchais Center of Tibetan Art.** There is a heady Oriental air to this institution in the Staten Island hills. The square stone buildings have the feeling of temples; the gardens are studies in tranquility with a lotus pond, terraces, and view of lower New York Bay; and the collection is this hemisphere's largest private grouping of Tibetan art. You can admire exquisite metalwork, the many inscrutable manifestations of Buddha and Hindu deities, a temple altar surrounded by prayer wheels and lamps where priests once burned yak butter. There are also Sunday lectures, demonstrations, and recitals in the serene main gallery. A harvest festival is held every year in October. *338 Lighthouse Ave., near Richmond Rd., Richmondtown, Staten Island, tel. 718/987–3478. Admission: $2.50 adults, $2 senior citizens, $1 children under 12. Open Apr.–Nov., Sun. 1–5.*

**Japan Society.** Three times a year, for periods ranging from three weeks to three months, this institution, in a spare

Japanese-style building, mounts special exhibitions dealing with aspects of Japanese life and culture, some familiar to Americans and some not. Subjects include textiles—fireman's coats, horse blankets, and less familiar clothing; sculpted objects in wood and lacquer; impressionist-style paintings created by Japanese artists living in Japan; three-dimensional paper dolls; and Kabuki theater objects. Artisans occasionally demonstrate highlighted crafts; a pool and a small bridge enhance the atmosphere of serenity. *333 E. 47th St., tel. 212/832–1155. Admission: $2.50. Open Sun. 10–5 only during special exhibitions.*

**Jewish Museum.** This institution, the largest in the Western Hemisphere dedicated to preserving and interpreting Jewish culture, has an appeal that transcends religion, for it concentrates not just on art and artifacts but on the society—and the individuals—who produced or used them. Special history- and issue-oriented exhibitions may deal with topics such as art and Jewish life in Italy, the Golem legend, or Jewish journalism in America; the permanent collection contains more than 14,000 works of art and artifacts covering four millennia of Jewish history. There are workshops and demonstrations at the Activity Center; the museum also hosts parties for holidays, minitours, lectures, panel discussions, and films, often on topics related to current exhibitions. *1109 5th Ave. at 92nd St., tel. 212/860–1888 for recorded information or 212/860–1863 for special programs. Admission: $4 adults, $2 students, children 6–16, and senior citizens (includes Activity Center admission). Open Sun. 11–6, Activity Center 2–4.*

**Museum of the American Indian.** Current plans are for this institution—the world's largest museum devoted to the subject—to move to Washington, DC, as part of the Smithsonian Institution, with a satellite gallery in downtown New York at the U.S. Customs House. As long as the status quo prevails, however, these premises are a good spot to be on Sunday—away from the crowds in the better-known museums and among the memories of Cherokee, Eskimo, Navajo, and other great civilizations of North America, Central America, and the West Indies. Studying displays of baskets, bead and quill work, costumes, carvings, peyote paraphernalia, ritual objects, tomahawks, and wampum, anyone whose ideas of "Indians" have been shaped by Westerns will learn something new. The objects go on and on for three floors, and the sheer quantity is all the more impressive for the fact that it was amassed by a single man, George Gustav Heye. *Broadway at 155th St., tel. 212/283–2420. Admission: $3 adults, $2 students and senior citizens, children under 8 free. Open Sun. 1–5.*

**Ukrainian Museum.** Located in the midst of a still-thriving Ukrainian community, this newcomer to the New York museum scene, founded in 1976, collects, preserves, displays, and interprets the culture of this southwestern corner of the Soviet Union through paintings, drawings, and watercolors by Ukrainian artists living here and abroad, as well as photographs focusing on Ukrainian immigration, costumes, textiles, coins, kilims, decorative ceramics, brass and silver jewelry, and 900 brilliantly colored Easter eggs. Weekend courses, held in winter and spring, give visitors the chance to try their hand at Ukrainian embroidery, bake traditional Ukrainian Easter breads, and make *gerdany* (bead necklaces) and *pyansky* (Easter eggs). Parking lots along Third and Fourth avenues are less crowded on weekends, and there's plenty of free parking along side streets. *203 2nd Ave., between 12th and 13th Sts., tel. 212/228–0110. Admission: $1 adults, 50¢ students and senior citizens, children under 6 free. Open Sun. 1–5.*

**Yeshiva University Museum.** Housed in the Yeshiva University library, the collection and the special exhibits on topics ranging from Jewish weddings to Shtetl customs emphasize Jewish life throughout history. Synagogue models illustrate architectural manifestations of Judaism in different cultures. *2520 Amsterdam Ave., between 185th and 186th Sts., tel. 212/960–5390. Admission: $3 adults, $1.50 children under 16 and senior citizens. Open Sun. noon–6.*

# Galleries

Since most of New York's 400 art galleries are open Tuesday through Saturday, working New Yorkers have always done their gallery going on the first day of the weekend. But just as many newer galleries in the city are breaking artistic trails, so they are abandoning the usual Sunday closing.

*The New Yorker, 7 Days,* and the *Village Voice* describe galleries by neighborhood; *New York* magazine's "Cue" listings classify first by solo and group shows and then by neighborhood, with special attention to photography and performance art. The *New York Times* runs gallery ads on a regular basis.

*Art in America/New York: Galleries and Museums,* published 10 times a year by Brant Art Publications, Inc. (980 Madison Ave., New York 10021, tel. 212/734–9797), lists galleries and the artists they're showing. Photography gets special coverage in the bimonthly ***Photography in New York*** (Box 20351, Park West Station, New York 10025, tel. 212/787–0401; $2.95 per issue or $15 annual subscription); gallery and museum exhibitions are listed by neighborhood, and there are listings of private dealers, an auction preview, and a calendar of workshops, lectures, gallery talks, and other programs.

# Contemporary Public Art

Manhattan's first piece of public sculpture—a gilded lead statue of George III—was melted down for bullets in 1776. And that was it on the outdoor sculpture front, more or less, until 1876, when city fathers and special-interest groups went on a statue-building spree that lasted some four decades and left monumental images of local heroes and important events uptown and down. There's the Augustus Saint-Gaudens statue of **General Sherman** (1900) astride his horse, led by a triumphant Victory, at Fifth Avenue and 59th Street; Lee Lawrie's titanic bronze **Atlas** (1937), who holds the world on his shoulders at the Fifth Avenue entrance to Rockefeller Center's International Building, and Paul Manship's larger-than-life golden **Prometheus** (1934), glistening at the west end of Rockefeller Center's lower plaza. And, of course, there's the city's great gift from France, the **Statue of Liberty,** by Frédéric-Auguste Bartholdi.

In more modern times, developers have been erecting mammoth sculptures on the plazas at the base of their towers, turning New York into a gigantic open-air gallery of contemporary sculpture. It's open around the clock and can be seen at its best on Sunday, when the work week population has cleared away.

Most of these new sculptures, listed below with their sculptors, dates, and locations, are within walking distance of each other in several neighborhoods.

*Downtown*  **Double Check** (J. Seward Johnson, 1982), one of a handful of realistic bronze businessmen positioned here and there around the city, is dressed in real clothing. *1 Liberty Plaza, between Broadway and Church St.*

**Five in One** (Tony Rosenthal, 1971), consists of five large interlocking circles. *Police Headquarters Plaza, behind the Municipal Building at Chambers and Centre Sts.*

**Four Trees** (Jean Dubuffet, 1972), a fanciful group of white-painted structures with black decoration, looks like papier-mâché but is really epoxy-painted fiberglass over aluminum. *1 Chase Manhattan Plaza, between Pine, William, Nassau, and Liberty Sts.*

**The Immigrants** (Luis Sanguino, 1973) is a group of men and women placed in front of Castle Clinton, which was once an immigration station. *Battery Park.*

**New York Vietnam Veterans Memorial** (Peter Wormser and William Fellows, 1984–85), is a wallful of glass blocks etched with the excerpts of some 83 letters to and from soldiers and their loved ones at home. Measuring 69 feet long and 16 feet high, it's one of the most moving of the city's monuments. *Near 55 Water St., between Coenties Slip and Broad St.*

**The Red Cube** (Isamu Noguchi, 1967), stands 18 feet high and tilted onto its corner. *Marine Midland Plaza, 140 Broadway.*

**Shadows and Flags** (Louise Nevelson, 1977), a cluster of seven black-painted steel shapes, occupies a triangle of land with black stone benches for sitting, a dozen trees, and a trio of lamps that children compare to lollipops. *Louise Nevelson Plaza, near William St. at Maiden La.*

**Three Red Wings** (Alexander Calder, 1970–71), is a bright red stabile, 25 feet high, though you'll have to position yourself carefully to spot it above the overpass. *7 World Trade Center.*

**The Upper Room** (Ned Smyth, 1984–87), a cast concrete Egypto-Roman gazebo minus the roof, stands 75 feet long and 20 feet wide, with columns 40 feet high. *Albany St. at the Esplanade, Battery Park City.*

*Greenwich Village*  **Alamo** (Tony Rosenthal, 1966–67), a black cube 10 feet high, is balanced on a corner on a traffic island. *Astor Pl., 8th and Lafayette Sts.*

**Bust of Sylvette** (Pablo Picasso, 1968) depicts a monumental girl with a ponytail in sandblasted basalt and concrete. *505 La Guardia Pl., near Mercer St.*

*East 20s and 30s*  **The Child** (Edwina Sandys, 1979) shows parents in profile caught while cradling their progeny; sculpted in marble by the granddaughter of Sir Winston Churchill, it is 16 feet high. *United Nations International School, 24–50 East River Dr., between 24th and 25th Sts.*

**Mitochondria** (John Rhoden, 1972–75), a bronze representation of the DNA molecule, almost seems to move. *Bellevue Hospital lawn, east of 1st Ave., between 26th and 27th Sts.*

**Triad** (Irving Marantz, 1969) is a bronze that alludes to Picasso's *Three Musicians* or perhaps to the three brothers, realtors, who commissioned the piece. *475 Park Ave. at 32nd St.*

*Midtown*  **Continuum** (José de Rivera, 1956) is a sculpture of two abstract leaping figures in highly polished stainless steel. *711 3rd Ave., between 44th and 45th Sts.*

**Cubed Curve** (William Crovello, 1972) is a 12-by-8-foot bent *S*, painted blue. *Time & Life Building, 1271 6th Ave. at 50th St.*

**Peace Form One** (Daniel Larue Johnson, 1972–80), a 50-foot stainless steel needle, memorializes Ralph J. Bunche. The sculptor was his friend. *Ralph Bunche Park, opposite the UN at 1st Ave. and 43rd St.*

**Performance Machine** (Lowell Jones, 1986) consists of fat, giant-size, chain-link fragments that rotate, break, and entwine almost imperceptibly via power supplied by a solar-powered motor. *245 Park Ave. at 47th St.*

**Single Form** (Barbara Hepworth, 1964), a 21-foot bronze slab, pierced near the top by a single round hole, stands at the center of a circular pool. *UN, 1st Ave. at 46th St., near the Secretariat building.*

**Sun Triangle** (Athelstan Spilhaus, 1973) is a polished steel triangle in the grasp of a post. The designer is also a meteorologist, and the piece represents the relative positions of the sun and earth at the solstices. Note the maps embedded in the plaza paving and the reflecting pool with its nine "planets." *McGraw-Hill Building plaza, 6th Ave., between 48th and 49th Sts.*

**Taxi!** (J. Seward Johnson, Jr., 1983) is one of the city's troop of lifelike bronze businessmen. *Chemical Bank, Park Ave. and 48th St.*

*West 30s and 40s*  **42nd Street Ballroom** (George Rhoads, 1983), an 8-foot cube, is a fun assemblage of chimes, whistles, and metal pinballs. *North wing, Port Authority terminal, 8th Ave. at 42nd St.*

***The Garment Worker*** (Judith Weller, 1984) celebrates the workers of one of the city's greatest industries in a lifelike bronze. Some two dozen companies in the area funded the work. *555 7th Ave., between 39th and 40th Sts.*

**Golda Meir** (Beatrice Goldfine, 1980), is a portrait in bronze of Israel's fourth prime minister. *1411 Broadway near 39th St.*

**Neon for 42nd Street** (Stephen Antonakos, 1979–81) consists of four red and blue neon circle-segments arching and diving around each other against a blue wall along Theater Row. *440 W. 42nd St., between 9th and 10th Aves.*

*Lincoln Center*  **Le Guichet** (Alexander Calder, 1963) shows claws dragging an airplane tail in black painted steel. *In front of the Library of the Performing Arts, Lincoln Center, Broadway at 65th St.*

**Martin Luther King, Jr., Memorial** (William Tarr, 1973), a 28-foot black steel cube, punctuates the edge of the plaza at the junior high school named for the civil rights leader. *122 Amsterdam Ave. at 66th St.*

**Reclining Figure** (Henry Moore, 1965), monumental bathers in the abstract, is made of 30 feet of bronze. *In the reflecting pool fronting the Vivian Beaumont Theater, Lincoln Center, Broadway at 65th St.*

**Richard Tucker** (Milton Hebald, 1979), a bronze bust, was commissioned by the famous singer's widow. *Richard Tucker Park, at Broadway, Columbus Ave., and 66th St.*

**Three Times Three Interplay** (Yaacov Agam, 1971), has three movable 32-foot zigzags in polished stainless steel. *On the raised plaza outside the Juilliard School, near Broadway on 65th St.*

*Upper East Side* **The Castle** (Priscilla Kapel, 1970), a welded steel construction, is part dollhouse and part birdhouse. *985 5th Ave. at 79th St.*

**Embrace** (Herbert Feuerlicht, 1973), is a pair of extremely simple shapes in red-painted steel, almost geometric, but aptly named. *425 E. 61st St., between 1st and York Aves.*

**Kryeti-Aekyad #2** and **Eaphae-Aekyad #2** (Douglas Abdell, 1979) are angular squiggles in black-painted steel. *John Jay Park, York Ave. at 76th St.*

**Night Presence IV** (Louise Nevelson, 1972) is a monument full of giant squiggles and posts in steel painted black. *Park Ave. at 92nd St.*

**Tau** (Tony Smith, 1965–80) a giant, bent letter *T*. *Hunter College, 68th St. and Lexington Ave.*

**Unidentified Object** (Isamu Noguchi, 1979) is a freeform basalt monolith. *Adjoining Metropolitan Museum of Art, 5th Ave. and 80th St.*

*Queens* **Socrates Sculpture Park** has 4.2 acres of large, abstract artwork that first appear to be an urban hallucination, and then take shape to reveal some two dozen sculptures by artists from all over the world, such as Di Suvero, Sonfist, and Stakiewicz. *31–27 Vernon Blvd., between 31st Dr. and Broadway, Long Island City, tel. 718/956–1819. Admission free. Open Sun. 9–8.*

# Historical Treasures

Rushing from here to there and back in your weekday life, it's easy to forget that New York is one of the most historic cities in the nation. But if you look, the evidence is all around: the brick warehouse reflected in the glass-walled skyscraper, the bronze plaque on the side of an apartment tower, the great mansion that no amount of money could replicate today. Sunday is a perfect time for visiting the institutions that preserve and disseminate knowledge about the people and events that shaped the city's past.

### Museums

**American Numismatic Society.** Founded in 1858, this institution showcases one of the world's foremost collections of coins and medals. Among the million objects, you might see a bronze medal of Marchese Leonello d'Este designed by Pisanello (1397–1455), a dinar from 7th-century Damascus, or a $2 note issued by the Paterson, New Jersey, Cataract City Bank. *Broadway at 155th St., tel. 212/234–3130. Open Sun. 1–4.*

**Boathouse.** Jacopo Sansovino's Library of St. Mark in Venice inspired this terra-cotta building on the meandering Lullwater in Brooklyn's Prospect Park, but it had definitely seen better days until restoration got under way in 1984. A million dollars later, it's sparkling. Its graceful steps, below a row of arched windows and illuminated by reproductions of its original 1,500-pound dolphin lamps, make a fine place to contemplate the lake and Olmsted's great park beyond. Inside there are exhibits of Brooklyn art and history. *East Lake Dr. at Lincoln Rd., Prospect Park, Brooklyn, tel. 718/287–3474. Admission free. Open Sun. 11–6.*

**City Island Historical Nautical Museum.** First-time visitors to this pleasant corner of the Bronx are often curious about how the island came to be as quaint as it is. This little museum, as quirky and intimate as any small-town historical society, gives the story from pre-Colonial days to the present, with flags, model ships, artifacts, and paintings. Sunday is the only day of the week it's open. *190 Fordham St., City Island, the Bronx, tel. 212/885–2531. Admission free. Open Sun. 2–4.*

**Ellis Island.** From 1892 to 1954, some 12 million immigrants took their first steps on U.S. soil on this 27½-acre island in New York harbor. Now, after many years of restoration, Ellis Island is to reopen as an immigration museum (or may have already by the time you read this). The cavernous Great Hall, where the immigrants were registered, has amazing tiled arches by Rafael Guastavino. White-tiled dormitory rooms overlook this grand space; the Railroad Ticket Office at the back of the main building houses exhibits on the "Peopling of America," recounting 400 years of immigration history, and "Forced Migration," focusing on the slave trade. The many-columned baggage room, now replastered, is an orientation area. The old kitchen and laundry building has been stabilized, rather than restored, so that you can see what the whole place looked like just a few years ago. If your ancestors arrived here, the visit is especially meaningful. *Ferries leave from Castle Clinton in Battery Park, Manhattan. Ellis Island, tel. 212/264–8711 or 212/269–5755 for ferry schedules. Fares not set at press time. Projected Sun. hours: 8:30–5.*

**Harbor Defense Museum.** A wedge-shape caponier, the best-preserved part of Brooklyn's original Fort Hamilton, houses a range of exhibits about the miscellaneous weaponry that has defended the city since the fort was built in the early 19th century. Youngsters go for the Howitzers and other artillery; adults like strolling along the cannon walk; and everyone enjoys the occasional reenactments, band concerts, and paratroop jumps. (Most interiors are not open to the public). *Fort Hamilton Reservation, 101st St. and Fort Hamilton Pkwy., Brooklyn, tel. 718/630–4349. Admission free. Open Sun. 1–5.*

**Intrepid Sea-Air-Space Museum.** The spiffy modern marquee and ticket booth in front of the USS *Intrepid* send up the red flag of caution: "Tourist attraction!" you may say to yourself, and drive on. Think again. The 150,000-square-foot veteran of World War II, Vietnam, and NASA recovery missions is stuffed with artifacts, exhibits, and movies of surprisingly general interest. Beginning with the impressive film that explains just what an aircraft carrier is all about, the exhibits sweep you along from battle to battle, war to war, era to era, and hero to hero. Narrow-bodied, needle-nosed fighter planes from several eras fill the windswept deck; some 70 historic planes, rockets, capsules, satellites, and mock-ups are scattered around the ship, whose deck alone is as big as many a city park. Children have a field day. *Intrepid Sq., Pier 86, 12th Ave. and 46th St., tel. 212/245–0072. Admission: $4.75 adults, $4 senior citizens, $2.50 children 7–13. Open Sun. 10–5 (ticket booth closes at 4).*

**Museum of the City of New York.** The neo-Georgian redbrick building, which seems like an oversize New York mansion, is actually home to one of the most pleasant museums in the city (and the first in the country dedicated to portraying the history of a single metropolis). Begin at the top with John D. Rockefeller's bedroom—heavy, dark, romantic, faintly oriental, and exquisitely detailed as only the late 19th century could make it. Then work your way down. En route, don't miss the antique mechanical banks and the fanciful and elaborate dollhouses. Also beloved by regulars are the Port of the New World Marine Gallery, with exhibits related to the sea; the Volunteer

Fire Gallery, with antique fire engines; the costumes; decorative arts pieces; paintings and sculpture; theater materials; and prints and photographs. Sundays tend to be crowded with families. *1220 5th Ave. at 103rd St. tel. 212/534-1676 or 212/534 -1034 for current programs. Suggested contribution: $3 adults, $1.50 students and senior citizens, $1 children under 12, $5 families. Open Sun. 1-5.*

**New-York Historical Society.** The city's oldest museum preserves images of New York before skyscrapers. Hudson River School paintings, William H. Beard's *The Bulls and Bears in the Market*—a herd of animals charging through this narrow, curved thoroughfare—and the original watercolors from John James Audubon's *Birds of America* are highlights among the prints and paintings. The country's largest display of Tiffany stained-glass lamps is here as well, along with Victorian silver, antique dolls and toys, and whimsical objets d'art. Sundays have traditionally been a special time. One summer the museum screened old films set in Manhattan, "Murder, Mystery, and Mayhem"; another year, walking tours explored the changing streetscapes. *170 Central Park West, between 76th and 77th Sts., tel. 212/873-3400. Admission: $2 adults, $1.50 senior citizens, $1 children under 12. Open Sun. 10-5.*

**Queens Museum.** The star here is the Panorama of the City of New York, an amazing creation that Parks Commissioner Robert Moses conceived for the 1964 World's Fair. It takes up 9,000 square feet, and every detail in every borough is there, right down to the planes taking off at La Guardia Airport. New buildings are added as they go up, to keep the vision current. *New York City Building, Flushing Meadows-Corona Park, Flushing, Queens, tel. 718/592-5555. Admission: $2 adults, $1 students and senior citizens, children under 5 free. Open Sun. noon-5:30.*

**Richmondtown Restoration.** A modest hamlet in the late 17th century, the Staten Island county seat 50 years later, and a major civic center during the Industrial Revolution, the village of Richmond faded from the public eye after the island became a part of New York City in 1898. But this oblivion meant the salvation of some wonderful structures—the oldest surviving elementary school in the country (circa 1695), the Queen Anne-style New Dorp Railroad Station (circa 1850), and 25 other historic buildings representing architectural styles ranging from Greek Revival to Victorian. Restoration has been going on since 1939, and today, on 100 acres in Staten Island's Greenbelt, 15 of the historic structures are open to the public. Inside, craftspeople demonstrate the customs and trades of old Richmondtown: carpentry, ceramics, furniture making, saddle making, quilting, basket weaving, tinsmithing, and printing. Museum exhibits show off Staten Island history. Children enjoy the antique dolls, toys, and small-scale furniture on exhibit in the Bennett House. Special events, an integral part of the presentation, usually take place on Sundays. *441 Clarke Ave., La Tourette Park, Staten Island, tel. 718/351-1611. Admission: $4 adults, $2.50 students and senior citizens, children under 6 free. Open Sun. 1-5.*

## South Street Seaport

One of the busiest places in the city on Sundays, it's all too easy to forget that the Seaport offers more than a terrific opportunity to drop a couple of hundred bucks on gizmos and gadgets. It's also a museum—a cobblestone complex of small galleries and exhibit buildings that tell the story of the days when South Street really was the Street of Ships. While the Fulton Fish Market, founded in 1922, stabilized the area after years of decline, preservationists prevailed in establishing the South Street Seaport Historic District and South Street Seaport Museum. Following hard upon this was a large-scale development project by the Rouse Company that brought the area to the state in which you find it today—as bustling as in its heyday but with a different sort of commerce. The museum's historic structures, galleries, and activities are a fine counterpoint to the shopping.

Among the attractions are several ships moored at Pier 16, including *Peking,* a 347-foot four-masted bark built in 1911 and the second-largest sailing ship in existence; *Wavertree,* a 293½-foot full-rigged ship currently being restored to continue her sailing career; and *Ambrose,* a 135-foot steel lightship that guided vessels coming into New York harbor until 1963. At the *Children's Center* (165 John St.), your youngsters can watch a 15-minute film of sailors battling a storm off Cape Horn six decades ago and then participate in various workshops. **Bowne & Co.** (211 Water St.) is an old print shop, where several vintage presses use antique type to print notepads, invitations, and other items to order.

At the **Boat Building Shop** (Burling Slip), craftsmen construct replicas of historic vessels while others whittle away on ship models, figureheads, and other carvings at the **Maritime Crafts Center** (head of Pier 15, under the *Wavertree* bowsprit). In the **A. A. Low Building** (171 John St.), **Visitors' Center** (207 Water St.), and **Museum Gallery** (213 Water St.), there are changing exhibitions of paintings, photographs, models, and tools from the museum's collections. The *Seaport Experience* (210 Front St., tel. 212/608–7888) is a multimedia show with 104 projectors, one 45-foot screen and 31 auxiliary screens, a 33-speaker quintaphonic sound system, and 150 special effects from fog to fire to fireworks. (Admission: $4.25 adults, $4 senior citizens, $3.25 children under 12; family rates available. Sunday shows hourly on the half hour 10:30–6:30.) *South Street Seaport Museum ticket sales at Visitors' Center near Titanic Memorial Tower at Fulton and Water Sts. and on Pier 16 at the Pilothouse; tel. 212/669–9424 for recorded information. Admission: $5 adults, $4 senior citizens, $2 children 4–13 (includes all the above attractions unless additional fees are noted). Open Oct.–May, Sun. 10–5; May–Oct., Sun. 10–6.*

## Statue of Liberty

For tristate residents, this great monument, modeled after the sculptor's mother, is almost a cliché—the thing you take out-of-towners to see. But France's gift to America, officially entitled *Liberty Enlightening the World,* retains the power to impress even the most jaded New Yorker. From close up, she seems even taller than her 151 feet, with her position atop an 89-foot pedestal, which itself rests on the 65-foot-high star-shaped ramparts of the old Fort Wood. If you arrive early enough, before the crowds, you may be able to get to the top without undue waiting. First take the elevator to the viewing platform atop the pedestal (for terrific views over the harbor) and from there, trek up (12 stories and 171 steps) through the statue's body to the crown for even better views. With the wind whipping at your face, the harbor humming with boats and ships, and the torch shining over it all from 305 feet up, it's easy to experience the kind of patriotic feelings that inspired the statue in the first place. *Ferries leave from Castle Clinton in Battery Park. Liberty Island, New York Bay, tel. 212/363–3227 for the statue, 212/363–8832 for the museum, or 212/269–5755 for ferry schedules. Statue admission free. Ferry: $3.25 adults, $1.50 children under 12. Open Sun. 9–5.*

## Restored Houses

*Manhattan*   **Abigail Adams Smith House.** This former carriage house, built of rugged Manhattan schist in the shadow of the Queensboro Bridge, is the only historic home in midtown Manhattan. The museum is open on Sunday—the only weekend day that it welcomes visitors—and it offers special programs on the second Sunday of every month. The nine rooms have Greek Revival detailing and furniture in the Federal and Empire styles. The 18th-century-style gardens were planted by the Colonial Dames of America, who own the house. Abigail Adams Smith was the second U.S. president's daughter and the sixth president's sister. *421 E. 61st St., tel. 212/838–6878. Admission: $2 adults, $1 students and senior citizens, children under 12 free. Open Sept.–May, Sun. 1–5.*

**Dyckman House.** Here at Manhattan's northernmost tip, the modest home that William Dyckman built in 1785, the borough's last remaining Dutch Colonial farmhouse, stands as solid as ever, with its gambrel roof, front and back porches, and walls of fieldstone and white clapboard. Inside, it's pleasantly cool and dim, the rooms low-ceilinged, simple, and are furnished with period pieces. The old cellar kitchen is the liveliest room of a house that is snug rather than splendid. Outside there are lilacs, honeysuckles, and a black cherry tree that have been around since the house was the focal point of Dyckman's farm. *4881 Broadway at 204th St., tel. 212/304–9422. Suggested contribution: $1. Open Sun. 11–noon and 1–4.*

**Fraunces Tavern Museum.** Tucked away above the Old New York restaurant of the same name, this rewarding little museum is a best-guess reconstruction of the tavern once owned by George Washington's West Indian steward, Samuel Fraunces. Exhibits include a fragment of Washington's false teeth, and there are good special exhibitions. Concerts, crafts workshops, lectures, theatrical performances, or walking tours with an early American theme take place almost every Sunday. *54 Pearl St. at the corner of Broad St., tel. 212/425–1778. Admission: $2.50 adults; $1 students, senior citizens, and children under 12. Open Oct.–May, Sun. noon–5.*

**Hamilton Grange.** Alexander Hamilton, the man President John Adams called "the most restless, impatient, artful, indefatigable, and unprincipled intriguer in the United States," lived in this cream-painted frame house only two years before being killed in a duel with Aaron Burr. Now under the care of the National Park Service, which administers the property, it may eventually be restored. In the meantime, the old parlors display furniture, costumes, and early American money—Hamilton was the first secretary of the treasury—and there are occasional Sunday concerts, lectures, films, plays, and other programs. *287 Convent Ave., between 141st and 142nd Sts., tel. 212/283-5154. Admission free. Open Sun. 9-5.*

**Lower East Side Tenement Museum.** At this new Lower East Side institution, housed in an authentic tenement building, you can see an exhibit of photographs about tenement life. There are two special programs, both on Sundays. In an hour-long play, "Family Matters: An Immigrant Memoir," characters tell you about their lives and their world—Hester Street, the synagogue and yeshiva, and that greatest of all luxuries, the public baths. Walking tours explore the streets where immigrants haggled over eggs and argued about politics. *197 Orchard St., between Delancey and Broome Sts., tel. 212/431-0233. General admission free. Tours: $12 adults, $11 senior citizens, $6 students; Sun. at noon. "Family Matters": $10 adults, $9 senior citizens, $5 students; Sun. at 2.*

**Morris-Jumel Mansion.** The knoll known as Mount Morris, the site of this columned Palladian house, is Manhattan's highest elevation and once had a view up to Westchester, over to New Jersey, and down to the tip of Manhattan. The view exists no longer, but the historical color makes up for it. Renovated over the years, this mansion—which was built by an English loyalist, bought by a French merchant, and inherited by his wife (who was in her later years briefly married to Aaron Burr)—is now a splendid structure, a place where time warp takes over and the 18th century prevails. The two-story portico, a Greek Revival structure erected before Greek Revival swept America, sets a gracious tone consistent with the furnishings. The hand-painted Chinese wallpaper and mahogany Chippendale mirrors with gilt phoenix finials in the octagonal drawing room stand out. There's also a bed that once belonged to Napoleon. Abutting the mansion is the **Jumel Terrace Historic District** (between 160th and 162nd Sts. and Edgecombe and St. Nicholas Aves.), where some 50 late 19th-century row houses in limestone, brownstone, clapboard, and brick line up along Jumel Terrace and Sylvan Terrace, among other streets. *1765 Jumel Terr. at 160th St. near St. Nicholas Ave., in Roger Morris Park, tel. 212/923-8008. Admission: $2 adults, $1 students and senior citizens, children under 12 free. Open Sun. 10-4.*

**Old Merchant's House.** On any other day of the week, you can admire only the exterior of this extraordinarily solid redbrick 1832 town house—the only historic house in the city with its original furniture. On Sundays, you can go inside. Guides escort visitors through one floor at a time, showing off the period pieces in the Greek Revival parlors, Rococo Revival bedrooms, and plain-jane servants' rooms; they open the closets stuffed with antique clothing and wrinkled old gloves and point out the bed in which the last surviving family member, Gertrude, was born, slept every night of her life, and died. *29 E. 4th St., between Lafayette St. and Broadway, tel. 212/777-1089. Admission: $2 adults, $1 students and senior citizens, children under 13 free. Open Sun. 1-4.*

**Theodore Roosevelt Birthplace.** The actual birthplace of the 26th president was demolished in 1916, but this reconstruction, dating from 1923, holds a good deal of the furniture original to the house, re-creating the environment of prosperous polish in which the man who gave his name to the Teddy bear spent his first 14 years. The cut-glass prisms of the parlor chandelier glitter as they did when they delighted the young TR; the library is full of the tables, bookcases, overstuffed chairs, and lavish silk hangings that TR associated with "gloomy respectability"; and the dining room chairs have horsehair coverings that "scratched the bare legs," as TR later recalled. *28 E. 20th St., tel. 212/260–1616. Admission: $1 adults; senior citizens and children under 17 free. Open Sun. 9–5, with tours until 3:30.*

*The Bronx* **Bartow-Pell Mansion Museum.** This tranquil spot in Pelham Bay Park, one of the last of the summer houses that old New Yorkers built on Long Island Sound, is only a mile from a snarl of Bronx highways. Yet with its perimeter border of woods and marshes and its fine formal gardens, carriage house, and stable, the mansion feels very much the country estate it was in 1842, when Robert Bartow built the 10-room gray stone Greek Revival structure on 200 acres. An allée of chestnut trees, a path lined with rhododendrons, a lily pond, an herb garden, and lawns show off the presiding horticultural talents of the International Garden Club, headquartered here. *Shore Rd., Pelham Bay Park, tel. 212/885–1461. Admission: $2 adults; children under 12 free. Open Sun. noon–4.*

**Poe Cottage** is not only the last home of American poet, novelist, and storyteller Edgar Allan Poe and his wife, Virginia, but the last remaining house of what used to be the village of Fordham. With its sparkling white clapboards and forest-green trim, it's incongruously tiny and countrified amid the anonymous high rises of the Grand Concourse, a once-stately boulevard lined with some of the city's most splendid Art Deco buildings. A slide show tells the story of the author's life here from 1846 to 1849. *Poe Park, 2460 Grand Concourse, tel. 212/ 881–8900. Admission: $1 adults, children under 13 free. Open Sun. 1–5.*

**Valentine-Varian House.** This two-story Georgian-vernacular structure (1758), the second-oldest house in the borough, is a relic of the days when most of the Bronx was farmland and carriages lumbered along the Boston Post Road nearby. It's a good place to get a feel for the history of the Bronx from the time of the Indians and the Dutch through the Revolutionary War. Changing exhibitions document historical high points in two rooms; others are furnished as they might have been in the 18th century. *3266 Bainbridge Ave. at E. 208th St., tel. 212/881– 8900. Admission: $1. Open Sun. 1–5.*

**Van Cortlandt Mansion.** Occupying a beautiful valley in the city's third-largest park, this three-story fieldstone mansion built by Frederick Van Cortlandt in 1748, is an airy, comfortable home, with high ceilings, wide-planked floors, many fireplaces, a central hallway, and an abundance of Dutch and English furniture dating from the 18th and 19th centuries. Windows look out over the flower gardens to the marshes beyond, and there are herb gardens and fine old trees on the property. While the museum is being renovated, it is open only by appointment; the completion date was not set at press time. *Broadway and 242nd St. in Van Cortlandt Park, tel. 212/543– 3344. Suggested contribution: $2. Usually open Sun. noon– 4:30.*

*Brooklyn* **Brooklyn Historical Society.** The history of the borough across the river, once a city in its own right, is well documented in the library of this institution, housed in a wonderful old mansion designed by George B. Post. The balconied library, decorated with stained glass and carved wood, is a city landmark; a renovation will provide more room for temporary exhibits on Brooklyn life and times and for displaying items from the permanent collection, including the kitchen from the *Honeymooners* TV series, bats and balls used by the Brooklyn Dodgers, and trick mirrors from a Coney Island museum of the 1920s. Frequent Sunday tours and lectures delve more deeply into aspects of the borough's present and past. *128 Pierrepont St. at Clinton St., Brooklyn Heights, tel. 718/624-0890. Admission: $2 adults, $1 children. Open Sun. noon-4:45.*

**Lefferts Homestead.** One of Brooklyn's last Dutch colonial farmhouses, this home was built by Peter Lefferts between 1777 and 1783 and presented to the city by his descendants in 1918. With its sloping eaves, high gambrel roof, rag rugs, colonnaded porches, carved woodwork, and split front door, it's a handsome structure. Perhaps the most entertaining aspect of a visit here is the chance to watch craftspeople shearing sheep, spinning flax, quilting, tape-weaving, casting pewter, caning chairs, coopering, making shoes, dipping candles, and tending an herb and vegetable garden. Changing exhibits explore local Dutch-American farm life, and there are occasional seasonal events, such as cider-making parties, games days, and Halloween hoopla. Sunday is the busiest day of the week here; it's a good idea to come early for a quieter visit. *Flatbush Ave. and Empire Blvd., Prospect Park, tel. 718/965-6505. Admission free. Open Sun. 10-4.*

**Pieter Claesen Wyckoff House Museum.** The first structure to be named a city landmark and one of the oldest homes in the city (circa 1652), this modest house is furnished to reflect the Dutch heritage of its owner, an early American Horatio Alger who came to the New World as an indentured servant and went on to become one of the wealthiest citizens of the area. His descendants lived here until 1902 among furnishings much like those on display—an old Dutch wood cupboard, a spinning wheel, cooking tools, and 17th-century blue-and-white Dutch fireplace tiles. Crafts demonstrations recall long-gone farming days in Brooklyn. In spring, thousands of daffodils and tulips bloom on the home's 1½ acres. *Clarendon Rd. at Ralph Ave., tel. 718/629-5400. Admission: $1 adults, 50¢ children and senior citizens. Open Sun. 10-3.*

Queens **Bowne House.** The borough's oldest house, a 1661 saltbox, has pegged floors, old beams, and fine furniture that date from the days when Quakers held their meetings here and when John Bowne stood up against the persecutions of then-governor Peter Stuyvesant. Inside you'll see a bedroom in which William Penn once slept, along with a great deal of furniture handed down through the nine generations of Bownes who owned the house after their ancestor's death. *37-01 Bowne St., Flushing, tel. 718/359-0528. Admission: $2 adults, 50¢ children under 13. Open Sun. 2:30-4:30.*

**King Manor.** This stately 10-room white clapboard home, with a Greek Revival portico and fluted Doric columns, was owned by the same family from the time it was built in 1733 until it came into the city's hands in 1896. Nursery, library, dining rooms, bedrooms, and parlors—the focus of a $1.4 million renovation—are chockablock with family furnishings and memorabilia: a sleigh bed, Franklin clock, samplers, portraits, dolls, even an antique dollhouse. In the summer, kitchen exhibits document the life and times of Rufus King, for whom the home is named. *150th St. and Jamaica Ave., Jamaica, tel. 718/523-1653. Admission by contribution. Closed for restoration*

*at press time, the house may have reopened by the time you
read this; call for hours.*

**Kingsland House.** This 2½-story home of a wealthy 18th-
century Quaker named Benjamin Doughty stands today only
because history-minded supporters arranged for it to be moved
to its present site on property that once belonged to the Flushing nurseryman Samuel Parsons. Immense and serene, the
now-landmarked Weeping Beech Tree, the oldest in America,
which Parsons's son brought from Belgium as a cutting in a
flowerpot, is one of the attractions of a visit to the house; the
other is a group of modest exhibits of local interest—lace, note-
books, eyeglasses, portraits, and more. *143–35 37th Ave.,
Flushing, tel. 718/929–0647. Admission: $1 adults, 25¢ chil-
dren under 12. Open Sun. 2:30–4:30.*

**Quaker Meeting House.** A familiar sight on a busy street, this is
the city's oldest continuously used meeting house; the spare,
quiet interior is on view only one day a month—a Sunday.
There's a tiny cemetery in back. *137–16 Northern Blvd.,
Flushing., tel. 718/358–9636. Admission free. Open 2–4 the
first Sun. of every month.*

**Queens County Farm Museum.** From the 17th through the 18th
centuries, farming was a way of life in Queens. This museum, in
a spreading old house acquired by the city in 1981 and subse-
quently restored, recalls that era. The property's 53 acres
yield apples and herbs, tomatoes and squash. Ducks and lambs
roam the grounds, and you can buy fresh produce and baked
goods at the occasional old-fashioned county fairs. Any other
time, when the sun streams through the lace-and-muslin curtains onto yellow pine floorboards, it's easy to forget what
century you're in. *73–50 Little Neck Pkwy., Floral Park, tel.
718/347–FARM. Admission free. Open Sun. noon–5; house
tours on the half hour.*

*Staten Island* **Alice Austen House Museum and Park.** By the time the photographer Alice Austen died in a nursing home in 1952, most of the
world had forgotten about her—something that no one who vis-
its her home on the Narrows not far from the ferry will ever do.
Her Victorian cottage, with its steeply peaked dormer windows, flourishes of gingerbread trim, gardens, breathtaking
view of the sea and the Verrazano Narrows, and lush turf
sweeping to the shore, is a charming place, and it still looks
bright and neat from its $1 million restoration in 1985. Some of
the rooms re-create the house as it was when Austen lived
there—the parlor is full of Victorian furniture, for instance—
and you can also see exhibits of her photographs, which
document rural Staten Island life at the turn of the century. *2
Hylan Blvd., tel. 718/816–4506. Suggested contribution: $2.
Open Sun. noon–5.*

**The Conference House.** The 226-acre Conference House Park is
right on the water at the point where the Raritan River meets
the Arthur Kill and flows into the Atlantic. The fieldstone man-
or's considerable historical importance derives from a dramatic
meeting that took place here two months after the signing of
the Declaration of Independence, at which a contingent of
Americans, including Benjamin Franklin, refused a British
peace offer, the terms of which demanded that the Colonies return to British control. The rest is history. The house's
furnishings, including a sea chest that belonged to the family
who built the house in the 17th century, look quite simple today, but were considered luxurious at the time. On the grounds

are beautiful rose and herb gardens, the focus of an annual herb festival. *7455 Hylan Blvd., tel. 718/984-2086. Admission: $1 adults, 50¢ children under 12. Open Mar.-Dec., Sun. 1-4.*

**Garibaldi Meucci Museum.** The mid-19th-century Italian hero Giueseppi Garibaldi, known for unifying Italy, spent an enforced exile before his victories here in the home of his friend, Antonio Meucci, a native of Florence who developed a working model of the telephone long before Alexander Graham Bell. Five small rooms of exhibits honor the house's two occupants and provide a glimpse into an odd corner of New York's past. Tape tours of the museum are available, and on Sundays, screenings explore the works of Italian artists and filmmakers, sometimes in Italian with English subtitles. The museum is owned and operated by the Sons of Italy in America. *420 Tomkins Ave., tel. 718/442-1608. Admission free (including tape tours). Open Sun. 1-5.*

# Science and Technology Museums

New York has long been home to one of the world's great museums of natural history, but in the past few years, it has also gained a handful of museums devoted to the how and why of everyday phenomena. Nowadays, when you wonder why spinach is good for you, why a cake rises, or why some buildings stand up and others fall down, you can check out the lively hands-on exhibits at institutions all over the city.

*Manhattan*   **American Museum of Natural History.** Sundays are busy at this beloved institution, but with over 35 million artifacts and specimens in 40 halls and galleries, there's something to interest everyone, and more than enough room to absorb the scrambling hordes of excited kids and tolerant parents. The museum, still on the cutting edge of research in its fields, is a giant encompassing a whole world of anthropology and natural history: stegosaurus and tyrannosaurus and their descendants; a 1,300-year-old giant sequoia tree; Aztecs and Incas, Eskimos and Plains Indians, with their teepees, totems, and temples; a herd of stuffed wild elephants and a diving whale 94 feet long; the Star of India sapphire and the largest meteorite ever retrieved. Free museum highlights tours provide a good overview for first-timers. Except in July and August, weekend programs examine world cultures several times daily, and there are additional performances, films, lectures, and other special programs on Sunday. Films on the Naturemax Theater's 40-feet-high and 66-feet-wide screen take your breath away, whether the footage explores the Grand Canyon or the magic of flight. *Central Park West and 79th St., tel. 212/769-5000 or 212/769-5315 for Leonhardt People Center events. Suggested contribution: $3.50 adults and $1.50 children to the museum, $3.50 adults and $1.75 children for Naturemax Theater tickets. Open Sun. 10-5:45.* Adjacent is the **Hayden Planetarium,** which has thematic shows several times a day on Sunday. *81st St. near Central Park West, tel. 212/769-5920. Admission: $3.75 adults, $2.75 students and senior citizens, $2 children under 13. Shows Sun. at 1, 2, 3, and 4 (also at 5 Oct.-June).*

**InfoQuest Center.** Welcome to the Information Age. AT&T, the company whose name is practically synonymous with high-tech, has stuffed this good-size space in its world headquarters building with eight floors of exhibits for museum goers young and old. Adults who use computers but don't know how they work can learn about the making of a microchip. Teens can make their own rock videos. Younger kids can command a robot and find out more about computers from a slick-looking auto-Maton named Gor-Don. There's something to intrigue everyone, just enough for a bit of Sunday afternoon scientific diversion. *550 Madison Ave., between 55th and 56th Sts., tel. 212/605–5555. Admission free. Open Sun. 10–6.*

Queens **New York Hall of Science.** This museum, stuffed with hands-on exhibits, is all about scientific fundamentals—with an emphasis on the "fun." Here you can pedal an airplane propeller into motion, control a windmill, make yourself disappear on TV, build an arched bridge that will hold your weight, watch atoms collide, and create shadows on a glowing wall. Specially trained college students lead weekend workshops and answer questions in languages ranging from Ga and Hindi to Spanish and French. There are special festivals and events all the time— "Science Halloween," "Amazing 3-D Holidays," "Bubblemania," "Super Small Science Month," and so on. This is a New York experience that's not to be missed. *47–01 111th St., Flushing Meadows-Corona Park, tel. 718/699–0005. Suggested contribution: $2.50 adults, $1.50 children under 17 and senior citizens. Open Sun. 10–5.*

Staten Island **Staten Island Institute of Arts and Sciences.** The oldest of Staten Island's cultural institutions encompasses not just art, history, or natural science, but all three. This wonderful community resource introduces children to textiles, American paintings and prints, European silver and decorative arts, entymology, birds, seashells, geology, and lots of other exhibits that make the museum fairly burst at the seams. The galleries are rarely crowded here, but Sundays are lively with families and small groups, who come for the regular programs, special exhibitions, or the film series. The Children's Day Fair has a different theme each year, most recently, "The World According to Puppets." *A 5-min walk from the Staten Island Ferry at 75 Stuyvesant Pl., tel. 718/727–1135. Admission free ($2 for films). Open Sun. 1–5.*

# Best Bets for Children

There are children's sections in the major museums—most notably the **Junior Museum** at the **Metropolitan Museum of Art** and the **Discovery Room** at the **American Museum of Natural History.** Other museums offer special programs for kids or families; among them are the **Brooklyn Museum,** the **Jewish Museum,** and the **Museum of the City of New York,** home of wonderful dollhouses and antique toys. At the **Whitney Museum of American Art,** children like the Calder Circus and the film that goes along with it. The **Intrepid Sea-Air-Space Museum, InfoQuest Center,** the **New York Hall of Science,** and the **Staten Island Institute of Arts and Sciences** are hits as well.

In addition, New York has its complement of so-called children's museums—but truly they are places that even adults without offspring can enjoy, since they illuminate familiar phenomena in novel and striking ways. These are definitely places that take fun seriously.

**Aunt Len's Doll and Toy Museum.** "Aunt Len," as Mrs. Lenon Hoyte is known, has collected dolls for her entire adult life. She has thousands from all eras, in cloth and bisque, from Europe and America, dating from the 1850s. *6 Hamilton Terr. at 141st St., tel. 212/926–4172. Admission: $2 adults, $1 children under 14. Open by appointment.*

**Brooklyn Children's Museum.** People from all over the borough bring their small fry to this active spot where neon-resplendent "people tubes" funnel visitors through the museum's four levels, each of which demonstrates some facet of the world—for example, weights and measures or music. Shrieks of delight prove just how effective it all is. In one area, youngsters use their five senses to understand unfamiliar objects; in another, they play a walking piano or other instruments; and in still another, they meet Doctor Dimension and build things with tubes, compare sizes and weights of familiar objects, and more. In the Early Learners Area, children under six have access to an adventure platform, building blocks, and other activities. It's a little out of the way, but parking is easy. *145 Brooklyn Ave., Crown Heights, Brooklyn, tel. 718/735–4400. Suggested contribution: $2. Open Sun. 10–5.*

**Children's Museum of Manhattan.** Designed for toddlers through age seven, this lively institution—now in a spiffy new home—offers interactive exhibits organized around common childhood experiences. Kids can paint, make collages, try on costumes, pet animals, and generally stay amused for hours on end. *212 W. 83rd St., tel. 212/721–1223. Admission: $4. Open 10–5.*

**Staten Island Children's Museum.** The former maintenance building at what is now the Snug Harbor Cultural Center (*see* Art Museums, above) is stuffed with interactive displays, and on Sundays the place is a hive of activity, with kids swarming and buzzing around each exhibit. These have included "Building Buildings" (by an architect), "What if you couldn't . . . ?" (to illuminate what it's like to be disabled), "It's News to Me" (exploring the media), and "Tales in Tall Trees" (about storytelling). *1000 Richmond Terr., Snug Harbor Cultural Center, Staten Island, tel. 718/273–2060. Admission: $2, children under 3 free. Open Sun. 11–5.*

# 5 Shopping

Once upon a time, Sunday was reserved for church and family, and the only place in town to shop for sheets and shoes, party dresses, and a new winter coat was on the Lower East Side. Nowadays, other shopping neighborhoods are also keeping hours on weekends, so that shopping can provide some of the best entertainment in town. Not only can you browse in the small boutiques and fine specialty shops uptown and down, but you can also go on a spree in the flagship stores of the city's great emporiums.

## Shopping Hours

The following Manhattan stores, which usually do a full day of business on Saturday, are generally open on Sunday from noon to 5. Some shops open an hour or two earlier or later, while others, mainly at South Street Seaport, close as late as 8 PM. On the Lower East Side, where businesses are closed on the Jewish Sabbath (Saturday), stores may open as early as 8:30 and close as late as 9 on Sunday—so shopping fanatics can get in a full nine hours of shopping. When a holiday falls on a Sunday, it's wise to call ahead.

## Shopping Neighborhoods

Some of the best of the city's shopping areas keep Sunday hours, and each has a special assortment of shops and a distinctive clientele. Several stores below are also in the listings.

**South Street Seaport** The Seaport's shops, which are all open on Sunday, are located along the cobbled, pedestrians-only extension to Fulton Street; in the Fulton Market building, the original site of the city's fish market; and on the three levels of Pier 17. The merchandise is strictly upscale; you can shop at **Ann Taylor** and **Laura Ashley** for women's clothing, **Brookstone** for fancy hardware, **Coach** for handbags, **Caswell-Massey** for fragrances, and **Sharper Image** for high-tech gimmickry. **J. Crew**, the mail-order catalogue house, chose the Seaport as the location for its first retail outlet. There are also some wonderful smaller stores, notably the **Strand** bookstore, whose used volumes overflow into sidewalk bins; **Mariposa** for butterflies; and **Hats in the Belfry** for every kind of reasonably priced hat.

**World Financial Center** This area, at the tip of Manhattan at Battery Park City, is shaping up as a shopping destination to reckon with on any day of the week, thanks to stores such as **Ann Taylor** and **Barneys New York** for clothing, **Caswell-Massey,** for fancy soaps and toiletries, and the **Gallery of History** for prints and documents. **Godiva Chocolatier** sells chocolates, **Il Papiro** offers hand-marbled Italian paper products, **State of the Art** has home and office accessories, and **CD Street** aspires to be the ultimate compact disc store.

**Lower East Side** Once home to millions of Russian and Eastern European Jewish immigrants, this area has long been New Yorkers' bargain beat. The center of it all—narrow, unprepossessing Orchard Street, which the *New York Times* once called the nation's oldest shopping center still in business—can be nearly impassable on a fine day. Lower East Side merchandise ranges from kitschy to elegant, and service is brisk and businesslike. An influx of Israeli merchants has made things perhaps not quite as friendly as they used to be. But schmoozing was never Orchard

Street's raison d'être anyway, particularly on Sunday, the busiest day of the week. Start at Houston Street, walk down one side of Orchard Street as far as Canal Street, and then walk back up. Essential stops include **Fine & Klein** for handbags and leather goods (between Delancey and Rivington Sts.), **Forman's** for women's clothing (between Grand and Broome Sts.), and **Lace-Up Shoes** (at Delancey St.). Grand Street (off Orchard St., south of Delancey St.) is chockablock with linens, towels, and other household items.

**SoHo**  On West Broadway, SoHo's main drag, and on Wooster, Greene, Mercer, Prince, Spring, Broome, and Grand Streets, major art galleries alternate with chic clothing stores, such as **La Rue des Rêves** (Spring St. at Wooster St.) and **Victoria Falls** (West Broadway between Houston and Prince Sts.). Other well-known stops include decorative-items specialist **Wolfman-Gold & Good Company** and Southwest-themed **Zona** (Greene St. between Spring and Prince Sts.), gourmet food emporium **Dean & DeLuca** (Broadway at Prince St.), and **D. F. Sanders** (West Broadway between Spring and Broome Sts.), home of sleek, stunningly contemporary gifts. Antique shops include **Artery** (100 Wooster St.) for Art Deco, **Elan** (341 Lafayette St.), and **Peter-Roberts** (134 Spring St.) for arts and crafts.

**Columbus Avenue**  From Lincoln Center north, this boulevard mixes brunch, museums, and Central Park with some of the city's most popular shopping in a cluster of stores that are mostly modern in design and upscale (if not strictly top of the line). You can buy clothing ranging from preppy (**Vermont Classic** at 74th St., for women, and **Frank Stella Ltd.** at 81st St., for men) to high funk (**Betsey Johnson** between 71st and 72nd Sts.), to high style (**Charivari** at 72nd St.), and to European-Japanese (**Parachute** at 75th St.). The neighborhood is a good source for showy costume jewelry (particularly **Ylang Ylang** between 75th and 76th Sts. and **Mishon Mishon** at 80th St.). One of the city's biggest flea markets brings crowds to the schoolyard of I.S. 44 (between 76th and 77th Sts.); you can browse for hours. Children (and adults) will enjoy **The Last Wound-Up** (near 74th St.), **Mythology** (between 77th and 78th Sts.), and **Penny Whistle Toys** (near 81st St.).

**Other Options**  
*Fifth Avenue*  The boulevard that is home to some of the biggest names in New York retailing is not usually a Sunday destination. But window shopping can be a delight, and a surprising number of stores are open for business. You might start with brunch in Rockefeller Center, admire St. Patrick's Cathedral, and head north, ending up at 58th Street at **Bergdorf Goodman** or at **F.A.O. Schwarz.** Or start with **Lord & Taylor** (at 38th St.) and stroll northward. Most stores are open on the Sundays preceding Christmas.

*57th Street*  This thoroughfare offers all kinds of goodies: outrageous games at the **Compleat Strategist** (between 8th and 9th Aves.), silks and brocades at **Paron** (between 5th and 6th Aves.), records and books at **Rizzoli** (between 5th and 6th Aves.), high-tech gizmos at **The Sharper Image** (between 5th and 6th Aves.), and high-style women's clothing at **Henri Bendel** (between 5th and 6th Aves.). Eastward on 57th Street, there's some of the city's best window-shopping, plus lingerie at **Victoria's Secret** (between Park and Madison Aves.) and stylish accessories for the home at the flagship **D. F. Sanders** (just west of Lexington

Ave.). From there, it's tempting to end up at **Bloomingdale's**, just two blocks north.

*Herald Square* The huge **Macy's** department store at 34th Street and Sixth Avenue anchors this intersection; across 34th Street, the former E. J. Korvette—the original Saks & Company—has been splendidly renovated into the multilevel **Herald Center**, containing some 70 glittering shops; it's a good place to head in bad weather. While business has been quiet at Herald Center, another atrium-mall opened recently, just next door, to the south on Sixth Avenue. It is anchored by **A&S**, the first major department store to open in Manhattan in more than two decades.

*Madison Avenue* If you begin at the northern end of the avenue, you can buy toiletries and potpourri at **Crabtree & Evelyn** or bestsellers at the **Corner Bookstore** (both at 93rd St.); toys at **Penny Whistle** (between 91st and 92nd Sts.); folk art at **America's Heritage Folk Heritage Gallery** (between 79th and 80th Sts.); books and children's clothing, respectively, at **Books & Company** and **Chocolate Soup** (between 74th and 75th Sts.); the most luxurious T-shirts at **Cashmere-Cashmere** (between 69th and 70th Sts.); quilts and country items at **The Gazebo** (at 61st St.); and wonderful shoes at **Cole-Haan** (at 61st St.). Below 57th Street, look for the latest writing on architecture at **Urban Center Books** (at 51st St.), and books about distant shores at **The Complete Traveller** (at 35th St.).

## Manhattan Department Stores

**Alexander's.** This store has a dual personality: half Polyester Paradise, half bastion of discounted high style. *Lexington Ave., between 58th and 59th Sts., tel. 212/593–0880. Open Sun. noon–5.*

**A&S.** A 300,000-square-foot branch of Abraham & Straus, which has offered good value in the other four boroughs for years, is the anchor tenant of the new A&S Plaza, which opened in late summer 1989 in the former flagship Gimbel's store. *33rd St. and 6th Ave., tel. 212/594–8500. Open Sun. 10–6.*

**Barneys New York.** Founded by Barney Pressman as a discount outlet for men's clothing some 60 years ago, Barneys is one of the city's retail trendsetters. Its huge selection of menswear ranges from made-to-measure and European and American couture to mass-market natural-shoulder suits. The women's duplex, in an adjacent group of brownstones, is a showcase of current women's fashion. The Chelsea Passage area can be counted on for the most distinctive and unusual handmade and antique linens, cachepots, and accessories for the home. *7th Ave. at 17th St., tel. 212/929–9000; branch at 2 World Financial Center, upper level, tel. 212/945–1600. Open Labor Day– Memorial Day, Sun. noon–6 at both locations.*

**Bloomingdale's.** The main floor is a stupefying maze of black walls, low ceilings, and mirrors. But once you reach the elevators, the going gets easier. The selection of everything from clothing and housewares to tabletop furnishings and gourmet gadgetry is peerless. The store is notable for the designer rooms on the fifth floor, with state-of-the-art home furnishings, and for exotic special promotions featuring manufactured items and handicrafts of a single country or region. *1000 3rd Ave. at 59th St., tel. 212/355–5900. Open Sun. noon–6.*

**Bonwit Teller.** Four well-polished floors make this attractive store exceedingly manageable, and it's especially pleasant on

Sundays. The distinctive violet-strewn shopping bags are still as pretty as ever. *4 E. 57th St., tel. 212/593–3333. Open Sun. noon–5.*

**Henri Bendel.** Bought recently by The Limited, this longtime trendsetter still offers savvy buying, stylish displays, and a sophisticated first floor notable for its Street of Shops and Gilded Cage. *10 W. 57th St., tel. 212/247–1100. Open Labor Day–Memorial Day, Sun. noon–5.*

**Lord & Taylor.** This store can be relied upon for the wearable, the fashionable, and the classic in clothes and accessories, primarily for women. It's refined, well stocked, never overwhelming—and the favorite store of many busy New York women. *424 5th Ave., between 37th and 38th Sts., tel. 212/391–3344. Open Sun. noon–6.*

**Macy's.** This miracle on 34th Street is more than the largest retail store in America and one of the biggest on earth. Over the past 15 years, it has grown chic enough to rival Bloomingdale's in the style department. Yet while the merchandise represents practically every Manhattan trend, there's something reassuringly traditional about the place, with its beige travertine columns touched with bands of brass and escalators with wide wood grooves. Estate Jewelry, hidden away on the mezzanine, is a pleasure if you like antique baubles, bangles, and beads. And if you need cooking equipment, The Cellar is one of the city's best bets. *Herald Sq., Broadway at 34th St., tel. 212/695–4400. Open Sun. 10–6.*

## Specialty Shops

**Antiques**
*Antique Mall*

**Manhattan Art & Antiques Center** (1050 2nd Ave., between 55th and 56th Sts., tel. 212/355–4400). More than 100 dealers, including some of the city's most amusing, are crammed into the three floors. The level of quality is not, as a rule, up to that of Madison Avenue's, but then neither are the prices. Shops such as **Funchies, Bunkers, Gaks & Gleeks** offer antique quilts, jewelry, Judaica, paisley shawls, prayer rugs, netsuke, samovars, scientifica, toy soldiers, and much more.

*American and English*

**America's Folk Heritage Gallery** (1044 Madison Ave., tel.212/628–7280). Jay Johnson occupies a unique place among American folk art dealers; he also stocks reproductions and contemporary craft.

**Cynthia Beneduce** (388 Bleecker St., between Perry and 11th Sts., tel. 212/645–5037). Wit and good design predominate in this shop's stock of painted furniture and American folk art; you'll find hooked rugs and quilts, primitive paintings, and unusual 20th-century furniture.

**David A. Schorsch** (30 E. 76th St., Suite 11A, tel. 212/439–6100). New York's only specialist in Shaker furniture and accessories also offers folk art with unusual painted decoration.

**Leigh Keno American Furniture** (19 E. 74th St., 4th floor, tel. 212/734–2381). Before he was 30, Leigh Keno set a new auction record in the American antiques field by paying $2.75 million for a hairy-paw-foot Philadelphia wing chair. He has a good eye and an interesting inventory, including some affordable pieces. The shop is open alternate Sundays, so call ahead.

**Peter-Roberts Antiques** (134 Spring St., between Wooster and Greene Sts., tel. 212/226–4777). The American Arts and Crafts movement is featured here in furniture and accessories.

**Steve Miller American Folk Art** (17 E. 96th St., tel. 212/348–

5219). The author of *The Art of the Weathervane*, this premier American folk art dealer believes in buying for quality, not quantity; his personal collection numbers just over a dozen pieces, though he's been collecting for almost 30 years.

**Wendover's Ltd. of England** (6 W. 20th St., tel. 212/924–6066). This shop features one of the country's largest selections of antique English pine.

**Wooster Gallery** (86 Wooster St., between Spring and Broome Sts., tel. 212/219–2190). The 20th-century furniture display here is sleek, beautifully designed, and classic rather than trendy.

*Architectural*   **Lost City Arts** (339 Bleecker St., between Christopher and W. 10th Sts., tel. 212/645–8311, and 275 Lafayette St., between Houston and Prince Sts., tel. 212/941–8025). Taking home a little bit of New York City can be fun, whether it's a gate, a grille, or an urn.

*Clocks and Watches*   **Clock Hutt** (1050 2nd Ave., between 55th and 56th Sts., tel. 212/759–2395). A family business for over two decades, Clock Hutt shows off New York's largest assemblage of European and American clocks from the 18th and 19th centuries.

*Eclectic*   **Amethyst** (32 E. 7th St., between Second and Third Aves., tel. 212/979–9458). This store features Victorian and Art Nouveau pins and brooches, antique kimonos, glassware, china, and vintage garb.

**Chelsea Mews** (148 9th Ave., between 19th and 20th Sts., tel. 212/807–1223). The home furnishings sold here range from American primitive (a Pennsylvania blanket chest) to haute French (a Louis XV center table).

**Hudson House** (555 Hudson St. near Perry St., tel. 212/645–0353). The armoires, secretary desks, dressers, mirrors, and crystal on display here date from the 18th to the mid-20th centuries.

**Warburtons Ltd.** (37 W. 26th St., tel. 212/532–5810). This shop features a moderately priced collection of furniture and accessories for the home in all materials except glass.

*Fun Stuff*   **Back Pages Antiques** (125 Greene St., between Prince and Houston Sts., tel. 212/460–5998). The spot to remember when you simply must have an antique jukebox or slot machine.

*Metals*   **Brass Antique Shoppe** (32 Allen St., between Canal and Hester Sts., tel. 212/925–6660). Candlesticks, chandeliers, andirons, teapots, and all manner of other objects in brass, sterling, and copper fill the shelves and teeter on the tables in this old shop on the Lower East Side.

**Eastern Silver** (54 Canal St., between Orchard and Allen Sts., 2nd floor, tel. 212/226–5708). This shop has a pirate's chest of silver, both secular and ceremonial.

*Antiques Shows*   The several major shows in Manhattan are busy on Sundays, including the prestigious **Winter Antiques Show,** held in mid- to late January at the Seventh Regiment Armory on Park Avenue at 67th Street. This show is, without question, one of the best in the country for 17th- and 18th-century decorative arts. On the last day, prices may come down a notch or two on items that the dealer doesn't want to cart home. Traditionally there are also good shows in the same location in March and April; a new display of the cream of international dealers debuted in fall 1989. Other fine shows occur at the piers on the Hudson River, among them the **Triple Pier Expo** in February and the **Quilt Festival** in

April. Watch the papers or call weekdays for calendars from frequent fair sponsors: **Sanford L. Smith & Associates, Ltd.** (152 2nd Ave., New York 10003, tel. 212/777–5218), **Stella Show Management** (294 Harrington Ave., Closter, NJ 07624, tel. 201/768–2773), and **Wendy Antique Shows** (Westchester Enterprises, Inc., Box 707, Rye, NY 10580, tel. 914/698–3442).

**Apothecary and Fragrance Shops**    **Caswell-Massey** (South St. Seaport, tel. 212/608–5401; 2 World Financial Center, upper level, tel. 212/945–2630). This is the place to come for sweet-smelling soaps, powders, perfumes, creams, sachets, and oils.

**Crabtree & Evelyn** (2768 Broadway, between 106th and 107th Sts., tel. 212/663–4717; 322 Columbus Ave. at 75th St., tel. 212/787–4409; 1310 Madison Ave. at 93rd St., tel. 212/289–3923; and 153 E. 53rd St., Citicorp Ctr., tel. 212/308–6164). The pastel boxes for sale here, delicately inscribed with flowers and fruits and filled with sweetly scented toiletries, make fine presents for friends or yourself.

**Art Supplies**    **Charrette** (215 Lexington Ave. at 33rd St., tel. 212/683–8822) is the ultimate store for drafting supplies and other essentials for architects, engineers, and graphic designers.

**Pearl Paint** (308 Canal St., between Church St. and Broadway, tel. 212/431–7932). On the five floors of this huge store, you'll find supplies for painting, silkscreen, drawing, and more.

**Bicycles**    **Gene's Bike Shop** (242 E. 79th St., tel. 212/249–9218). The biggest mountain bike seller in New York also has a custom racing department; unclaimed repair bikes are often available at very good prices.

**Bonsai**    **Bonsai Designs** (855 Lexington Ave., between 64th and 65th Sts., tel. 212/570–9160). The East's principal producer and retailer of the diminutive trees.

**Books**    **Barnes & Noble** (105 5th Ave. at 18th St., tel. 212/807–0099).
*General Interest*    This store, with a stock of 3 million, is a reliable source for books on almost any topic. Medicine, business, engineering, and computers are just a few of the subjects covered in depth; the Sale Annex, across the street, cuts prices on selected fiction, nonfiction, children's books, and more.

**Books & Company** (939 Madison Ave., between 74th and 75th Sts., tel. 212/737–1450). The comfy leather sofa on the second floor, with its view of Madison Avenue down below, is an invitation to browse and linger. The store often carries more obscure literary works in hardcover.

**Brentano's** (597 5th Ave. at 48th St., tel. 212/826–2450). Taking over the old Scribner's—an airy, vaulted landmark bookstore with an elegant iron-and-glass facade—this upscale member of the Waldenbooks chain preserved the same scene inside: shelves crammed with wonderful books, fiction and nonfiction, light and serious.

**Burlington Bookshop** (1082 Madison Ave., between 81st and 82nd St., tel. 212/288–7465). This shop's personable staff handpicks a stock of hardcovers and paperbacks to suit the well-read neighborhood trade.

**Coliseum Books** (1771 Broadway at 57th St., tel. 212/757–6139). This bookstore has all the atmosphere of a supermarket, but the range of titles is extensive and interesting, with remainders alongside best-sellers and scholarly works. The staff, aided by a computerized inventory, can quickly tell you what's in stock and where to find it.

**Corner Bookstore** (1313 Madison Ave. at 93rd St., tel. 212/831–3554). This small neighborhood bookstore has an intelligent, well-conceived selection.

**Doubleday Book Shop** (724 5th Ave. at 57th St., tel. 212/397–0550; 673 5th Ave. at 53rd St., tel. 212/223–6550; 777 3rd Ave. at 49th St., tel. 212/888–5590; 1 Citicorp Ctr. at 53rd St., tel. 212/223–3301). A glass elevator ascends through the three floors of the main store on Fifth Avenue near 57th Street, which stocks a wide selection from the parent publishing house and others.

**Endicott Booksellers** (450 Columbus Ave., between 81st and 82nd Sts., tel. 212/787–6300). On an avenue of frivolity, this old-fashioned bookstore in a renovated tenement offers a distinguished selection. Best-selling writers are represented, for the benefit of those who want a good vacation read, but so are lesser-known poets and novelists. Fine cookbooks, travel books, and art books are also available.

**Rizzoli** (31 W. 57th St., tel. 212/759–2424; branches at 454 West Broadway, between Houston and Prince Sts., tel. 212/674–1616; and World Financial Center, Winter Garden west of the World Trade Center, tel. 212/385–1400). An elegant marble entrance, oak paneling, chandeliers, and classical music accompany a stock of records, international periodicals, and books on art, architecture, dance, design, foreign languages, and travel for which the store is famous.

**Shakespeare & Company** (2259 Broadway at 81st St., tel. 212/580–7800; 716 Broadway at Washington Pl., tel. 212/529–1330). The large stock here includes a representative selection of what's happening in publishing today. The travel section is good, and hard-to-find periodicals are available. The store opens earlier (at 10 AM) and closes later (11 PM downtown and 12:30 AM uptown) than most other Manhattan bookstores.

*Architecture* **Urban Center Books** (457 Madison Ave. at 51st St., tel. 212/935–3595). Art, architecture, and preservation topics are the specialty of the extensive collection on sale here; high ceilings, parquet floors, and tall Georgian windows are additional pleasures of this shop.

*Biography* **Biography Bookshop** (400 Bleecker St. at 11th St., tel. 212/807–8655). This tidy, well-organized bookstore stocks all manner of biographical material, including diaries and letters, from both major and minor publishers here and abroad.

*Mystery/Suspense* **Foul Play** (10 8th Ave., between 12th and Bank Sts., tel. 212/675–5115; 1465 2nd Ave., between 76th and 77th Sts., tel. 212/517–3222). Whodunits are the specialty in these black-and-red shops with salespeople who can help you find just the mystery you want.

*Occult* **Samuel Weiser** (132 E. 24th St., tel. 212/777–6363). The English and foreign-language titles here range from esoteric treatises on out-of-body experiences to alchemy and the chakras. The crowd is as colorful as ever, with students of the supernatural, palm readers, and mediums.

*Photography* **Photographer's Place** (133 Mercer St., between Prince and Spring Sts., tel. 212/431–9358). This shop is an inspiration to amateur and professional picture-takers with its fine selection of current and out-of-print books devoted to great photographers. The International Center of Photography bookstore (*see* Museum Shops, below) is also good.

**Science Fiction** **Science Fiction Shop** (56 8th Ave., between 14th and Horatio Sts., tel. 212/741–0270). The only store in the city devoted to science fiction carries current and out-of-print titles.

**Theater/Film** **Applause Theatre Books** (211 W. 71st St., tel. 212/496–7511). Scripts, collections of reviews, biographies, and how-to books for the actor are among the works cramming the shelves of this roomy store devoted to the dramatic arts. For the best in film publications and screenplays, try **Applause Cinema Books** (100 W. 67th St., tel. 212/787–8858).

**Drama Book Shop** (723 7th Ave., between 48th and 49th Sts., tel. 212/944–0595). A comprehensive collection of scripts, scores, libretti, and theater crafts can be found at this shop established by the New York Drama League in 1921.

**Travel** **Complete Traveller Bookstore** (199 Madison Ave. at 35th St., tel. 212/685–9007). The stock at this travel guidebook shop includes current titles and a few old and used books.

**Used Books** **Strand** (828 Broadway at 12th St., tel. 212/473–1452). Eight miles of shelves house a million-plus books at this biggest of Manhattan's used-book stores. Among them are antiquarian books, fiction, nonfiction, how-to, history, and all kinds of other books. A small branch of this store is located at South Street Seaport.

**Cameras/ Electronics/ Appliances** **47th Street Photo** (67 W. 47th St., 115 W. 45th St., 121 W. 45th St., and 116 Nassau St.; tel. 212/398–1410). Cameras and lenses, computers, televisions, radios, and other electronic items are all for sale here. Prices are reasonable to low, the selection is good, and there's plenty of local color—many of the salesmen are Hasidim. The place opens at 10, when shopping is more leisurely.

**Uncle Steve's** (343 Canal St. at Church St., tel. 212/226–4010; 216 W. 72nd St., tel. 212/874–3317). This store has a reputation for being less accommodating to browsers intent on researching a product, but the prices are often reasonable for televisions, radios, VCRs, and other electronics. The Canal Street store, in an old warehouse, lacks amenities. You'll have to pay cash, and there's no delivery.

**Willoughby's** (110 W. 32nd St., tel. 212/564–1600). Calling itself the world's largest camera store, Willoughby's rates high among both amateur and professional photographers for its service and selection of cameras and related equipment.

**Computer Software** **Software Etc.** (101 5th Ave. at 18th St., tel. 212/727–3280). This shop boasts that it has the city's largest software selection. New Age music calms the excitement inspired in computer freaks by the sight of all those boxes, manuals, and irresistible gadgets. Several computers are set up to demonstrate, and salespeople are knowledgeable about everything on sale.

**Fabric** **Paron Fabrics** (60 W. 57th St., tel. 212/247–6451). Bolts of silk, wool, cotton, linen, and all manner of blends are available here. At **Paron II** (56 W. 57th St. between Fifth and Sixth Aves.,), remnants of comparable fabrics are discounted by around half. But don't wait until late afternoon to shop because closing time is 3 PM.

**Food** **Balducci's** (424 6th Ave. at 9th St., tel. 212/673–2600). In this **Gourmet Markets** former mom-and-pop shop, now one of the city's finest gourmet emporiums, food is displayed like art: mounds of baby carrots nudging scallions alongside frilly lettuce leaves and feathery dill. You'll also find some of the city's best meats, fishes, cheeses, chocolates, imported cookies, exotic pastas, vinegars, oils, crackers, and prepared foods.

**Dean & Deluca** (560 Broadway at Prince St., tel. 212/431–1691). This huge SoHo trendsetter, newly renovated to bright-white splendor, has an encyclopedic selection, ranging from the most exotic salad oils and herb vinegars to cookies, crackers, chocolate, jams, 30 kinds of coffee, and more. The austere cheese counter is the place to find everything from Spanish Manchego to West Virginia goat cheese.

**Fairway** (2127 Broadway at 74th St., tel. 212/595–1888). Produce overflowing from the bins inside and out is the main attraction. You can always get fresh herbs, arugula that usually looks healthy and crisp, Jerusalem artichokes, and other hard-to-find vegetables. It's the kind of place you can count on to have blood oranges, fresh chanterelles, and black and white truffles in season. The cheeses are excellent, and the countermen are accommodating. The coffee is even better than at Zabar's.

**Kam-Man** (200 Canal St., between Mott and Mulberry Sts., tel. 212/571–0330). The city's premier Chinese market, Kam-Man is the best place to find bizarre dried foods, mushroom soy sauce, and all the other unusual items required for serious Chinese cooking. The staccato sound of Chinese being spoken and the mysterious smells are like an instant trip to Asia.

**The Silver Palate** (274 Columbus Ave., between 72nd and 73rd Sts., tel. 212/799–6340). If you know the cookbooks and the prepared products under this name, you'll want to look in on this miniscule shop to see the complete selection of sauces, relishes, oils, vinegars, preserves, and such. This is also a good spot to stop for fixings for an elegant picnic in Central Park, a long block away.

**Zabar's** (2245 Broadway at 80th St., tel. 212/787–2000). Visit here not so much to snap up everything in sight—Zabar's now sells by mail order, too—as to enjoy the atmosphere of one of New York's favorite feeding troughs, which is at its liveliest on Sunday. As you're exploring the possibilities among the jams and jellies from a dozen makers and several countries or checking out the barrels of coffees or the wonderful array of teas, keep an eye peeled for celebrities—perhaps Bernadette Peters or the villainness on your favorite soap opera. Dried herbs and spices, dried fruits, chocolates, crackers, oils and vinegars, and assorted bottled foods are on the main floor, along with a fragrant jumble of fresh breads and the cheese, meat, and smoked-fish counters. Upstairs is one of New York's biggest selection of kitchenware. Take a number at the counter of your choice, then do your browsing, rather than the other way around.

*Bagels and Bialys* **Gem Bagels** (203 E. Houston St., between Orchard and Ludlow Sts., tel. 212/505–7590). Bagels are the specialty here, and you can watch how they're made.

**H&H Bagel** (2239 Broadway at 80th St., tel. 212/595–8000). This shop offers bagels in a dozen types, including sourdough, whole wheat, and raisin. Mobbed from 10 to 1.

**Kossar's Bialystoker Bakery** (367 Grand St. at Essex St., tel. 212/674–9747). Flat and chewy bialys are featured here.

*Breads* **A. Zito and Sons** (259 Bleecker St., between Sixth and Seventh Aves., tel. 212/929–6139). The shop's Riviera toast is recommended, and its Italian whole wheat bread—crunchy on the outside and soft on the inside—goes to most of the good restaurants in town.

**D&G Bakery** (45 Spring St., between Mulberry and Mott Sts., tel. 212/226–6688). Robustly wheat-flavored peasant loaves with chewy, crackly crusts are the specialty here.

**E.A.T.** (1064 Madison Ave., between 80th and 81st Sts., tel. 212/772–0022). This store sells some of the best sourdough loaves, rolls, and baguettes you'll ever sink your teeth into, along with wonderful raisin-walnut and whole-grain breads. Expensive, but the absolute best.

**Moishe's** (181 E. Houston St., between Allen and Orchard Sts., tel. 212/475–9624). Old-fashioned Russian pumpernickel and other Old Country treats are sold here.

*British* **Myers of Keswick** (634 Hudson St., between Jane and Horatio Sts., tel. 212/691–4194). This store's stock is all British, including treacle, trifle, toffee, and kidney pie.

*Cheese* **Ben's Cheese** (181 E. Houston St., between Allen and Orchard Sts., tel. 212/254–8290). This store's farmer's cheese becomes transcendent when stuffed with strawberries or raisins or almonds and pistachios.

**DiPalo Dairy Stores** (206 Grand St. near Mott St., tel. 212/226–1033). Come here for heavenly Asiagos and Parmigiano Reggianos, homemade mozzarella, and other Italian specialties.

**East Village Cheese** (34 3rd Ave. near 9th St., tel. 477–2601). This shop's low prices on specials are hard to beat.

**Joe's Dairy** (156 Sullivan St., between W. Houston and Prince Sts., tel. 212/677–8780). The fresh mozzarella here, perhaps the most perfect in town, comes plain, smoked, and salted.

*Chocolate and* **Economy Candy** (108 Rivington St., between Essex and Lud-
*Candy* low Sts., tel. 212/254–1531). Nuts, dried fruit, and even gummy bears come by the barrel here, and everything is just gorgeous.

**Elk Candy Company** (240 E. 86th St., tel. 212/650–1177). This Upper East Side shop is a marzipan fantasy and a chocoholic's sweet dream.

**Godiva Chocolatier** (701 5th Ave., between 54th and 55th Sts., tel. 212/593–2845; Madison Ave. at 67th St., tel. 212/249–9444). The store's big attractions are the cleverly molded chocolates (in shapes such as scallops, oysters, and lions) and the embossed gold boxes.

**Li-Lac Chocolates** (120 Christopher St., between Bleecker and Hudson Sts., tel. 212/242–7374). This unpretentious little shop, the Village's best source for sweets for more than 60 years, features an assortment of delights: truffles, fudge, pralines, chocolate-covered apricots, coconut patties, and chocolate drops.

*Caviar* **Petrossian** (182 W. 58th St., tel. 212/245–2217). At this beautiful restaurant, the shop sells superb beluga, sevruga, and osetra caviar imported directly from Russia.

*Coffee* **McNulty's Tea & Coffee Company** (109 Christopher St., between Bleecker and Hudson Sts., tel. 212/242–5351). The antique wood paneling of this tiny, aromatic shop says "Old New York"; the barrels of beans say Timor, Java, New Guinea. Fine teas are also available.

**Porto Rico Importing Company** (201 Bleecker St., between Sixth Ave. and MacDougal St., tel. 212/477–5421). This dark, old-fashioned shop has been providing Italian espressos and other coffees to local residents since 1907.

*Fresh Fish* **Citarella** (2135 Broadway at 75th St., tel. 212/874–0383). Many New Yorkers consider this shop the best fish market in town. The countermen will pack your purchase on ice on request to keep it fresh until you get home.

*Pastries* **Little Pie Company** (424 W. 43rd St., tel. 212/736–4780). This shop offers more apple goodies than you ever dreamed possible, from apple butter and jelly to apple walnut pie and muffins.

**Miss Grimble** (65th St. and 1st Ave., tel. 212/628–5800). One of the city's tops for cheesecake and pecan pie, Miss Grimble has irresistible tortes with their rich flavors of orange, rum, or coconut.

**My Most Favorite Dessert Company** (1165 Madison Ave. near 78th St., tel. 212/517–5222). The premises, complete with an upstairs café, are spiffy and modern, while the cookies, strudels, cakes, and fruit tarts are delectable.

**Pâtisserie Lanciani** (271 W. 4th St., between Perry and 11th Sts., tel. 212/929–0739). The former chief pastry chef at the Plaza Hotel now turns out exceptional confections for this shop and **Madeline's**, a sister shop that offers sit-down as well as carry-out (177 Prince St., between Thompson and Sullivan Sts., tel. 212/477–2788).

**William Greenberg Jr. Desserts** (1377 3rd Ave., between 78th and 79th Sts., tel. 212/535–7118; 2781 Broadway, between 77th and 78th Sts., 212/945–5426). The superlative cakes and pastries featured here are especially beautiful when they're decorated to order.

*Pickles* **Essex Pickles** (35 Essex St., between Grand and Hester Sts., tel. 212/254–4477). Watermelon rinds, cucumbers, peppers, and much more are pickled here and sold straight from the barrel.

*Spices and Herbs* **Aphrodisia** (282 Bleecker St., between Sixth and Seventh Aves., tel. 212/989–6440). The aroma in the air at this good-size shop is part cardamom, part chamomile, part rose petals, part basil; the 700 herbs and spices in glass jars shelved from floor to ceiling include African yohimbé, Oriental fo-ti-seng, clover blossoms, and, yes, plain basil.

**Kalustyan** (123 Lexington Ave., between 28th and 29th Sts., tel. 212/685–3451). This shop features barrels, jars, and sacks of strange and curious Indian and Middle Eastern spices and items such as sugar-dusted jellies, pomegranate nectar, rose water, and fenugreek.

**Pete's Spices** (174 1st Ave., between 10th and 11th Sts., tel. 212/254–8773). Restaurants and ethnic cooks are the chief patrons of this jam-packed store, which offers just about every obscure ingredient from the West Indies and South America to Europe and elsewhere. Medicinal herbs are also available.

**Fun and Whimsy** **Mythology** (370 Columbus Ave., between 77th and 78th Sts., tel. 212/874–0774). This store stocks a fanciful collection of art books, antique toys, greeting cards, Japanese robots, voodoo dolls, games, and more.

**Star Magic** (743 Broadway, between 8th St. and Astor Pl., tel. 212/228–7770; 275 Amsterdam Ave. at 73rd St., tel. 212/769–2020; 1256 Lexington Ave., between 84th and 85th Sts., tel. 212/988–0300). Astronomy and New Age meet here in a cosmic swirl of kaleidoscopes, crystals, stars, spaceships, and other gadgets—all to the accompaniment of hypnotic electronic music.

**Think Big!** (390 West Broadway, between Broome and Spring Sts., tel. 212/925–7300). This amusing store stocks huge replicas of various ordinary objects, such as crayons and toothbrushes that are five feet tall.

**Tropical Island Traders** (170 5th Ave. at 22nd St., tel. 212/627–0808). Macadamia nuts? Shells glued to magnets for refrigerator doors? Batik sarongs from Java? This is the place to come if you're yearning to buy something with a tropical theme.

**Games**   **Compleat Strategist** (320 W. 57th St., tel. 212/582–1272), Sci-fi, fantasy, mystery, military strategy, adventure, and many other games are sold here.

**Game Show** (474 6th Ave., between 11th and 12th Sts., tel. 212/633–6328). Computer games are well represented here.

**Village Chess Shop** (230 Thompson St., between Bleecker and 3rd Sts., tel. 212/475–9580). You'll find chessboards and pieces in ivory, wood, stone, pewter, brass, onyx, and marble—not to mention a crowd of chess fanatics who spend hours playing here.

**Gifts**   **A Show of Hands** (531 Amsterdam Ave., between 85th and 86th Sts., tel. 212/787–1174). This crafts cooperative, a longtime Upper West Sider, displays wonderful handblown glass candlesticks and goblets, handhewn boxes, metal work, and much more.

**Avventura** (463 Amsterdam Ave., between 82nd and 83rd Sts., tel. 212/769–2150). Italian design is revealed here in all its streamlined beauty in vases, dinnerware, glasses, and accessories for home and tabletop.

**Maxilla and Mandible, Ltd.** (453 Columbus Ave., between 81st and 82nd Sts., tel. 212/724–6173). A huge selection of antlers, horns, skulls, skeletons, butterflies, seashells, and more, from $1 up.

**Simon Pearce** (385 Bleecker St., between Perry and W. 11th Sts., tel. 212/924–1142). This Irish-born glassblower made his fame in his native land before moving to Vermont. Now his handsome rugged mugs, tumblers, goblets, and tankards are available here.

**Home Furnishings**   **ABC Carpet** (888 Broadway at 19th St., tel. 212/473–3000). This large store offers rugs and carpets, as well as linens, bath items, and furniture.
*Carpets/Rugs*

**Central Carpet** (426 Columbus Ave. at 81st St., tel. 212/787–8813). This West Side fixture features discounted dhurries, hooked and contemporary rugs, Belgian-made orientals, new Chinese rugs, and more.

**Einstein Moomjy** (150 E. 58th St., tel. 212/758–0900). This is one of New York's major sources for carpets, with a stock of broadlooms, one-of-a-kinds created by artists, dhurries and orientals, and just about every other kind of rug.

*China*   Try **Lanac Sales** (73 Canal St. at Allen St., tel. 212/226–8925) and **Goldman's** (315 Grand St. at Allen St., tel. 212/226–1423) for discounts on major brands.

*Culinary Items*   **Broadway Panhandler** (520 Broadway near Spring St., tel. 212/966–3434) is one of the city's premier pot shops.

**Cathay Hardware Corporation** (49 Mott St., 1½ blocks south of Canal St., tel. 212/962–6648). The store specializes in Chinese products.

**Williams-Sonoma** (20 E. 60th St., tel. 212/980–5155). The retail outlet of the famous mail-order catalogue house has stylish cooking equipment, tabletop items, and knickknacks.

*Decorative Objects* **Archetype Gallery** (411 E. 9th St., between First Ave. and Ave. A, tel. 212/529–5880). This shop offers a quirky collection of essentials designed by artists for the home.

**Aris Mixon & Company** (381 Amsterdam Ave., between 78th and 79th Sts., tel. 212/724–6904). The intrigue here is in the mix of the newly manufactured, the handmade, and the antique.

**Clodagh Ross & Williams** (122 St. Mark's Pl., between First Ave. and Ave. A, tel. 212/505–1774). This furniture and accessory store carries items on the cutting edge—say, a lacquered-wood snake candle holder, a fold-up plasticized-paper vase, or a jagged, handpainted wood box.

**Conran's** (2-8 Astor Pl., between Broadway and Lafayette St., tel. 212/505–1515; 160 E. 53rd St., tel. 212/371–2225; 2248 Broadway at 81st St., tel. 212/873–9250). The glasses, dishes, linens, and decorative items on display can furnish a sleek, contemporary urban apartment at a reasonable cost.

**Dapy** (230 Columbus Ave. near 70th St., tel. 212/877–4710; 431 West Broadway, between Prince and Spring Sts., tel. 212/925–5082). This is the place for plastic fun stuff in the latest designs.

**D. F. Sanders** (386 West Broadway, between Spring and Broome Sts., tel. 212/925–9040; 952 Madison Ave., between 75th and 76th Sts., tel. 212/879–6161; 127 E. 57th St., tel. 212/753–2121). Come here to purchase trendy postmodern, and beautifully designed items destined to become classics.

**Dot Zero** (165 5th Ave. at 22nd St., tel. 212/533–8322). The spirit of this little store is high-tech and playful. Along with the ultracontemporary aluminum serving dishes, lamps, and black rubber placemats, you'll also find whimsical desk items.

**Folklorica** (89 5th Ave., between 16th and 17th Sts., tel. 212/255–2525). The specialty here is ethnic handicrafts, such as baskets, weavings, traditional implements, and musical instruments.

**Gear** (110 7th Ave. at 17th St., tel. 212/929–2622). Wall-coverings, yard goods, linens, tableware, and other goodies, displayed on the bleached pine tables and stripped antique hutches at this decorating and gift emporium, make for a mix that's part Conran's, part Laura Ashley, part Marimekko.

**Gracious Home** (1217 and 1220 3rd Ave., between 70th and 71st Sts., tel. 212/517–6300). This may be the ultimate New York housewares store. Your basic ironing board and Rubbermaid dish drainer can be found here, as well as upscale, design-conscious products.

**Howard Kaplan's French Country Store** (35 E. 10th St., between Broadway and University Pl., tel. 212/529–1200). The French country look is the emphasis here—in ceramics, kitchen and bath items, fabrics, wallpaper, and even the occasional bird cage.

**Katagiri** (224 E. 59th St., tel. 212/755–3566). This small shop is the city's best source for housewares and food from Japan.

**Wolfman-Gold & Good Company** (116 Greene St., between Prince and Spring Sts., tel. 212/431–1888). Half antique and half contemporary in spirit, this chic SoHo shop is all white, with touches of blond wood and wicker. Tableware is the focus.

**Zona** (97 Greene St., between Prince and Spring Sts., tel. 212/925–6750). This airy, high-ceilinged store remains SoHo's bastion of the Southwestern look, with New Age music, solieri bells, terra-cotta, woven wall hangings, and expensive furniture, all artfully displayed.

*Dried Flowers* **Sura Kayla** (484 Broome St. at Wooster St., tel. 212/941–8757). Dried flowers become an art here, as they're displayed in the elegantly arched windows of the talented proprietress's SoHo corner shop.

*Fabrics* **Harry Zarin's Factory Warehouse** (72 Allen St., between Grand and Broome Sts., tel. 212/226–3492). Over 3 million yards of fabrics at good prices are offered here along with custom slipcovers and window treatments.
**Home Textiles** (132-A Spring St., between Greene and Wooster Sts., 2nd floor, tel. 212/431–0411). This sunny loft of a store has the city's biggest selection of bolts of fabric designed specifically for home furnishings.

*Furniture/Bedding* **Americana West** (120 Wooster St., between Prince and Spring Sts., tel. 212/966–WEST). You can find Southwestern-style furnishings for every room of the house here, with carved items, skulls, and other touches to complete the look.
**Arise** (57 Greene St., between Spring and Broome Sts., tel. 212/ 925–0310; 1296 3rd Ave. at 74th St., tel. 212/988–7274; 265 W. 72nd St., tel. 212/496–8410). This store has a full range of futons in a variety of well-crafted constructions, along with covers and frames.
**Castro Convertibles** (43 W. 23rd St., tel. 212/255–7000). This old standby has sofabeds in spades.
**Charles P. Rogers** (899 1st Ave., between 50th and 51st Sts., tel. 212/935–6900). High-quality brass beds in traditional and contemporary styles are sold here.
**Door Store** (1 Park Ave. at 33rd St., tel. 212/679–9700; 1201 3rd Ave., between 69th and 70th Sts., tel. 212/772–1110; 123 W. 17th St., tel. 212/627–1515; 130 Cedar St. at the corner of Washington St., tel. 212/267–1250). The specialty here is contemporary well-crafted furniture at affordable prices.
**Giles & Co.** (444 Columbus Ave., between 81st and 82nd Sts., tel. 212/362–5330). Try this place for the very latest furnishings for the postmodern apartment.
**Leather Center** (44 E. 32nd St., tel. 212/696–4100). About two dozen European-style leather sofas are featured here.
**Maurice Villency** (200 Madison Ave. at 35th St., tel. 212/725–4840). This store stocks expensive contemporary furniture, including upholstered leather pieces.
**New York Furniture Center** (41 E. 31st St., tel. 212/679–8866). Furniture by Hickory Chair, Kittinger, and other manufacturers is sold here at discounted prices.
**Paradigm International** (48 W. 21st St., 3rd floor, tel. 212/807–0024). Come here for Bauhaus classic furnishings made to original specifications in steel and bronze.
**Preferred Seating** (873 Broadway at 19th St., tel. 212/674–6200). This shop has a wide selection of sofas and chairs in all styles.

*Lighting* **Just Shades** (21 Spring St. at Elizabeth St., tel. 212/966–2757). You have a choice here of 5,000 lampshades in dozens of different styles, and you can also custom order.
**Thunder and Light** (171 Bowery at Delancey St., tel. 212/219–0180). This shop specializes in high-tech lighting, including sleek Italian designs, and knockoffs at moderate prices.

**Linens**  **Ad Hoc Softwares** (410 West Broadway at Spring St., tel. 212/925–2652). This cheerful shop features unusual European sheets, India-print duvet and pillow covers, contemporary shower curtains, thick towels, and accessories for the home and bath.

**Descamps** (454 Columbus Ave. at 82nd St., tel. 212/874–8690). The French-made cotton bed linens, towels, and robes here come in attractive colors and subtle patterns, from the bold and geometric to impressionistic florals.

**Handblock** (487 Columbus Ave., between 83rd and 84th Sts., tel. 212/799–4342). Table linens handprinted in India and coverlets in bright colors and pastels are this shop's specialties.

**Paint/Wallpaper/**  Two home decorating stores can fulfill almost all your needs:
**Blinds**  **Janovic/Plaza** (1150 3rd Ave. at 67th St., tel. 212/772–1400; 159 W. 72nd St., tel. 212/595–2500; 215 7th Ave. at 22nd St., tel. 212/645–5454; 161 6th Ave. at Spring St., tel. 212/627–1100) and **Pintchik** (Broadway at 92nd St., tel. 212/769–1440; 3rd Ave. at 87th St., tel. 212/289–6300; 3rd Ave. at 22nd St., tel. 212/777–3030), which also stocks a few other household necessities, such as shower curtains and closet accessories.

**Luggage**  **A. Altman** (135 Orchard St., between Delancey and Rivington Sts., tel. 212/254–7275). This shop discounts many major brands in current models.

**Innovation Luggage** (10 E. 34th St., tel. 212/684–8288; 300 E. 42nd St., tel. 212/599–2998; 1755 Broadway, between 56th and 57th Sts., tel. 212/582–2044). You'll find a good selection here of moderately priced Pullmans, totes, garment bags, and briefcases.

**Memorabilia**  **The Ballet Shop** (1887 Broadway, between 62nd and 63rd Sts., tel. 212/581–7990). Near Lincoln Center, this store carries programs, books, posters, videos, autographs, and T-shirts for the balletomane.

**Gallery of History** (Palm Grove, Winter Garden, World Financial Center, tel. 212/945–1000). Original historical documents, including handwritten items by everyone from George Washington to Mark Twain, are framed for display and sale.

**Jerry Ohlinger's Movie Material Store** (242 W. 14th St., tel. 212/989–0869). This shop specializes in posters and photos related to motion pictures from the Roaring '20s to the present, including black-and-white stills.

**Menswear**  Because New York is home to investment bankers, corporate lawyers, international businessmen, movie moguls, architects, and writers, its male population demands a variety of fashion styles. In addition to **Barneys, Bloomingdale's,** and **Macy's,** a number of specialty stores are important stops.

**Camouflage** (141 8th Ave. at 17th St., tel. 212/741–9118). The look here is updated classic, as designed by Perry Ellis, Ronaldus Shamask, Jeffrey Banks, and Alexander Julian.

**Frank Stella Ltd.** (440 Columbus Ave. at 81st St., tel. 212/877–5566; 1382 6th Ave., between 56th and 57th Sts., tel. 212/757–2295). This shop offers classic business clothing and casual wear in subtle variations for conservative types.

**Mano à Mano** (580 Broadway, between Houston and Prince Sts., tel. 212/219–9602). SoHo chic prevails here.

**Peter Elliot** (1383 3rd Ave. at 79th St., tel. 212/570–2300). This shop features classic clothing and accessories, including some outstanding jackets, sweaters, and ties made to the store's specifications.

**Saint Laurie, Ltd.** (897 Broadway, between 19th and 20th Sts., tel. 212/473–0100). This family-owned business sells suits manufactured on the premises, using natural fabrics and old-fashioned tailoring; styles range from the boxy and natural shoulder to the streamlined and Italian influenced. While prices may be lower here than for comparable garments elsewhere, they are not inexpensive, yet the fabrics are lovely, and a fairly decent size range is represented. Private label shirts and ties are a recent addition.

**Tommy Hilfiger** (284 Columbus Ave., between 73rd and 74th Sts., tel. 212/769–4910). The look is casual-preppie in this small, brightly lit shop with shelves all the way to the ceiling.

*Discounts* **BFO** (149 5th Ave. at 21st St., 6th floor, tel. 212/254–0059). Come here for silk designer ties, dress shirts, suits from Italy and America, sport jackets, and coats priced as much as 60% below retail.

**Eisenberg and Eisenberg** (85 5th Ave. at 16th St., tel. 212/627–1290). This dependable store has been offering bargains on classic clothing since 1898.

**Harry Rothman** (200 Park Ave. S at 17th St., tel. 212/777–7400). This store aims at a youthful market; the suits by some of the big names in men's clothing are as good as the premises.

**Moe Ginsburg** (162 5th Ave. at 21st St., tel. 212/242–3482). A stock of suits, shoes, shirts, sweaters, coats, and accessories make this one-stop shopping for the man who hates to pay retail.

**Syms** (45 Park Pl., between Church St. and Broadway, tel. 212/791–1199). The longer an item is in the store, the lower its price. Shoppers must hunt for the bargains among the seven floors of pipe racks and pay by cash or check, unless they have a house credit card. But the payoff is designer clothing at prices that are either good, great, or fabulous. Forget the unbeautiful surroundings.

*Shoes* **Cole-Haan** (667 Madison Ave. at 61st St., tel. 212/421–8440). Beautifully made shoes for men and women are displayed here.

**To Boot** (256 Columbus Ave., between 71st and 72nd Sts., tel. 212/724–8249). Western boots, hiking boots, ankle boots, dress boots, and even slippers helped this store make its name; tie shoes and loafers for a more fashionable business look are recent additions.

*Vintage* **Duke's** (57 Grand St. at West Broadway, tel. 212/966–2946). This shop offers gently worn British clothing and accessories from Savile Row and Bond Street, including everything you need for the sporting life of another age: plus fours, cricket sweaters, tweeds, business suits, even walking sticks.

**Papers/Postcards** **80 Papers** (510 Broome St., between W. Broadway and Thompson St., tel. 212/431–7720). The specialty at this charming little shop is handmade paper for wrapping presents and writing notes.

**Il Papiro** (Palm Grove, Winter Garden, World Financial Center, tel. 212/385–1688). Marbleized paper made in Italy and things made from it—address books, pencils, portfolio cases, and such—are offered here.

**Untitled** (159 Prince St. at W. Broadway, tel. 212/982–2088). Thousands of greeting cards and postcards, many bearing images of classic and contemporary works of art, are neatly organized in this well-stocked shop founded by a former photographer and book collector. A branch, **Untitled II** (680 Broadway, between 2nd and 3rd Sts., tel. 212/982–1145), also carries an offbeat selection of art books and magazines.

**Posters**  **Posteramerica** (138 W. 18th St., tel. 212/206–0499). Exploring the graphic qualities of posters made in this country and abroad from late Victorian times to the mid-20th century, this shop—the oldest in the country devoted to this field—is located in a renovated carriage house. The movies, travel abroad, and the two World Wars are a few of the poster themes.

**Poster Originals** (158 Spring St. near W. Broadway, tel. 212/226–7720). Among the hundreds of items here is an outstanding selection of art posters.

**Records/CDs**  **Tower Records** (692 Broadway at 4th St., tel. 212/505–1500).
*General*  This huge emporium has four floors of records, cassettes, and CDs devoted to all kinds of music—rock, reggae, jazz, New Age, movie soundtracks, classical, and more. It's a true New York scene, with a bustling (mostly young) crowd during the weekend. The Upper West Side branch (1965 Broadway at 66th St., tel. 212/799–2500) is convenient to Lincoln Center.

*Rarities*  **Bleecker Bob's Golden Oldies** (118 W. 3rd St., between MacDougal and Sixth Ave., tel. 212/475–9677). This Greenwich Village store, which started out as an oldies specialist, now covers punk, new wave, progressive rock, reggae, R&B, and electronic sounds. It's open Sundays until 1 AM.

**Footlight Records** (113 E. 12th St., between Third and Fourth Aves., tel. 212/533–1572). The out-of-print and hard-to-find titles here cover Broadway and film music, big band, jazz, imports, rock and roll, and country—even very obscure recordings.

**Gryphon Record Shop** (251 W. 72nd St., 2nd floor, tel. 212/874–1588). This store offers some 40,000 out-of-print and rare LPs, with a focus on classical titles, but also including jazz, Broadway, and movie music.

**Sporting Goods/**  **Gilda Marx** (1416 3rd Ave., between 80th and 81st Sts., tel. 212/
**Athletic Wear**  879–4810). This shop carries a very good selection of exercise wear.

**Hudson's** (97 3rd Ave., between 12th and 13th Sts., tel. 212/473–0981). New York's answer to L. L. Bean, Hudson's is a premier source for clothing and equipment for rugged outdoor activities.

**H. Kauffman and Sons** (139 E. 24th St., tel. 212/684–6060). This has long been known as one of the world's top equestrian supply shops.

**Paragon** (867 Broadway at 18th St., tel. 212/255–8036). On its three floors, Paragon carries an in-depth selection of almost every type of equipment an athlete may want, with the clothing and footwear to match.

**Peck & Chase Shoes** (163 Orchard St., between Rivington and Stanton Sts., tel. 212/674–8860). Name-brand running shoes are discounted here.

**Peck & Goodie** (919 8th Ave., between 54th and 55th Sts., tel. 212/246–6123) regularly supplies Holiday on Ice and renowned skaters JoJo Starbuck and Dorothy Hamill with blades, boots, and brackets. The highest quality equipment is available.

**Sailways Manhattan** (859 Broadway at 17th St., tel. 212/727–8850). The specialty here is gear for surfing and windsurfing.

**SoHo Skateboards** (80 Varick St., between Grand and Watts

Sts. tel. 212/925–7868). This shop sells skateboards and skateboard clothing in the latest, hottest styles.

**Tents & Trails** (21 Park Pl., between Broadway and Church St., tel. 212/227–1760). A huge variety of serious camping equipment is available here on seven floors, the stuff you may want to take if you're planning an expedition to the jungles or Antarctica.

**Sunglasses** **Shades of the Village** (167 7th Ave. S at Perry St., tel. 212/255–7767). The 1,200 styles of sunglasses sold here encompass Vuarnets and Nikons, RayBans and Guccis, gold-plateds and pure plastics from America and abroad, in a whole range of prices.

**Women's Wear** **Ann Taylor** (2017 Broadway at 69th St., tel. 212/873–7344; 25
*Classic Looks* Fulton St. on the corner of Water St., tel. 212/608–5600; 2 World Financial Center, upper level, tel. 212/945–1991). These stores provide what the well-dressed young woman needs for work and play.

*Discount* **Bolton's** (225 E. 57th St., tel. 212/755–2527; 27 W. 57th St., tel. 212/935–4431; 1180 Madison Ave., between 86th and 87th Sts., tel. 212/722–4419; 2251 Broadway at 81st St., tel. 212/873–8545; 53 W. 23rd St., tel. 212/924–6860; 4 E. 34th St., tel. 212/684–3750; 1191–93 3rd Ave. at 69th St., tel. 212/628–7553; 19 E. 8th St., between Fifth Ave. and University Pl., tel. 212/475–9547). Moderately priced wardrobe basics are discounted by about a third at this chain, and sales drop prices even further.
**Daffy's** (111 5th Ave., at 18th St., tel. 212/529–4477). The wares here mix the cheap, priced cheaper, and the pricey, marked way down.
**Fine & Klein** (119 Orchard St., between Delancey and Rivington Sts., tel. 212/674–6720). A large selection of handbags, domestic and imported, are sold at reasonable prices here.
**Forman's** (82 Orchard St., between Delancey and Broome Sts., tel. 212/228–2500). This attractive store discounts moderately priced clothing by Vittadini, Jones New York, Calvin Klein, Belle France, and others.
**Loehmann's** (236th St. and Broadway, the Bronx, tel. 212/543–6420). The flagship store of this premier off-price outlet is an institution among shopaholics.
**Ms., Miss or Mrs.** (462 7th Ave., between 35th and 36th Sts., 3rd floor, tel. 212/736–0557). Canny shoppers know this fixture of the garment center for its 30% to 60% discounts.
**S&W** (165 W. 26th St., tel. 212/924–6656). Cheap it is not. But 40% off the latest by Natori, Dior, and others adds up to value that matches the selection. Other locations nearby stock furs, lingerie, and accessories.

*Ethnic Looks* **Putumayo** (856 Lexington Ave., between 64th and 65th Sts., tel. 212/734–3111; 339 Columbus Ave., between 76th and 77th Sts., tel. 212/595–3441; 147 Spring St., between W. Broadway and Wooster Sts., tel. 212/966–4458). There's cool cotton clothing here, much of it crinkly, easy to pack, and made in tropical countries.

*Lingerie* **Joovay** (436 West Broadway, between Prince and Spring Sts., tel. 212/431–6386). Real silk bias-cut tap pants and teddies in naughty blacks, scarlets, and pastels set the scene in this sumptuous SoHo nook.
**Victoria's Secret** (34 E. 57th St., tel. 212/758–5592). Undies and

loungewear are appealing and affordable at this luxurious shop.

*Romantics* **Laura Ashley** (398 Columbus Ave. at 79th St., tel. 212/496–5110; 4 Fulton St. across from Pier 17 and the Fulton Market, tel. 212/809–3556). The hallmark is old-fashioned frocks in the English manner, complete with straw boaters in season.

**Victoria Falls** (451 West Broadway, between Prince and Houston Sts., tel. 212/254–2433). The clothing here is antique or made just yesterday. Suits, lingerie, jewelry, sweaters, and blouses are demure and old-fashioned in cut and color.

*Shoes* **Billy Martin's** (812 Madison Ave. at 68th St., tel. 212/861–3100). Boots in unusual styles and materials attract the glitterati to this Upper East Side shop.

**Ecco** (324 Columbus Ave., between 75th and 76th Sts., tel. 212/799–5229; 94 7th Ave., between 15th and 16th Sts., tel. 212/675–5180; 111 Thompson St., between Spring and Prince Sts., tel. 212/925–8010). Here moderate prices prevail for a good range of colors and styles, including classic pumps and fun shoes.

**Kenneth Cole** (353 Columbus Ave., between 76th and 77th Sts., tel. 212/873–2061). The snazzy shoes featured here run the gamut from dressy to very casual.

**Maraolo** (782 Lexington Ave., between 60th and 61st Sts., tel. 212/832–8182). The good selection of classic heels, flats, and casual shoes from European makers in a variety of colors make this a reliable source for wardrobe basics.

**Perry Ellis Shoes** (1136 Madison Ave., between 84th and 85th Sts., tel. 212/570–9311). The understated elegance of the store reflects that of the soft, classic, comfortable shoes.

**Peter Fox** (105 Thompson St., between Prince and Spring Sts., tel. 212/431–7426 and 212/431–6359; 378 Amsterdam Ave. at 77th St., tel. 212/874–6399). This English maker offers a timeless look for women with a distinctive sense of what looks good: plain pumps with outlandishly contoured heels, lace-up boots, and period styles with ruffles and bows.

**Ritz** (14 W. 8th St., between Fifth and Sixth Aves., tel. 212/228–4137). This shop carries the most up-to-date styles in colors from subdued to sizzling.

*Sweaters* **Bomba de Clercq** (100 Thompson St., between Spring and Prince Sts., 212/226–2484). This Rome-based store is a wonderland of cotton, cashmere, silk, and wool women's sweaters in subtle but clear hues.

**Cashmere-Cashmere** (840 Madison Ave., between 69th and 70th Sts., tel. 212/988–5252). Supersoft sweaters are displayed among cherrywood furnishings. You'll even find cashmere T-shirts, and, for fun, a ruffle-edged knit cashmere cape.

**Stewart Ross** (745 Madison Ave., between 65th and 66th Sts., tel. 212/744–3870; 150 Spring St., between Wooster St. and W. Broadway, tel. 212/966–1024; 105 W. 72nd St., tel. 212/362–9620). The specialty here is fine English sweaters of cotton or wool.

*Trendsetters* **Barneys Women's Store** (106 7th Ave., between 16th and 17th Sts., tel. 212/929–9000). The Women's Store, formerly a duplex atop Barneys Men's Store, now occupies its own lavish annex. The high prices make it seem more like a museum of fashion and lifestyle than a merchandise emporium, but private-label clothing by Basco put many items within reach of smaller spenders.

**Betsey Johnson** (130 Thompson St., between Houston and Prince Sts., tel. 212/420–0169). Having made her name in the '60s, Betsey Johnson is back, showing young New Yorkers how much fun dressing up can be with frills, ruffles, wild patterns, and Day-Glo colors.

**Charivari** (2315 Broadway, between 83rd and 84th Sts., tel. 212/873–1424. Since Selma Weiser founded this store on the Upper West Side, her eagle eye for the up-and-coming and avant-garde have been well known. Fans come from all over the city for her Byblos, Katherine Hamnetts, Yohji Yamamotos, and other fine designer pieces. The branches, too, take a high-style, if somewhat pricey, approach: **Charivari Sport** (201 W. 79th St., tel. 212/799–8650); **Charivari Workshop** (441 Columbus Ave. at 81st St., tel. 212/496–8700), which shows avant-garde Japanese designs, in blacks, grays, whites, and brights; **Charivari 72** (257 Columbus Ave. at 72nd St., tel. 212/787–7272); and **Charivari 57** (18 W. 57th St., tel. 212/333–4040).

**Comme des Garçons** (116 Wooster St., between Prince and Spring Sts., tel. 212/219–0660). A blank white architectural premises with many asymmetrical cuts, housing the clothing of designer Rei Kawakubo.

**Emporio Armani** (110 5th Ave., between 16th and 17th Sts., tel. 212/727–3240). The big-name Italian designer displays a casual line in his large store with 17-foot ceilings and arched windows and doors.

**Parachute** (121 Wooster St., between Prince and Spring Sts., tel. 212/925–8630; 309 Columbus Ave., between 74th and 75th Sts., tel. 212/799–1444). The color scheme and the premises are minimalist in the best SoHo fashion, with baggy and unisex styles, complemented by tight skirts.

**Patricia Field** (10 E. 8th St., between Fifth Ave. and University Pl., tel. 212/254–1699). This store collects the essence of the downtown look.

**La Rue des Rêves** (139 Spring St. on the corner of Wooster St., tel. 212/226–6736). Stylish clothing for stylish women who like either an elegant, understated look or Tina Turner styles is found here.

*Vintage* **Alice Underground** (380 Columbus Ave. at 78th St., tel. 212/724–6682; 481 Broadway, between Grand and Broome Sts., tel. 212/431–9067). Cable knits, shetlands, petticoats, and other stuff from the '40s and '50s are sold here.

**Harriet Love** (412 West Broadway near Spring St., tel. 212/966–2280). The proprietress presents a selection of garments in excellent condition—together with the little handbags you'll need to accompany them.

**Screaming Mimi's** (495 Columbus Ave. at 84th St., tel. 212/362–3158). This Upper West Side fixture has added a children's line, but the black bustiers, vintage clothing, and funky styles on which it built its reputation among fashion editors are as audacious as ever.

*Young and Hip* **Canal Jean** (504 Broadway, between Spring and Broome Sts., tel. 212/226–1130). Dyed cotton knits and other casual funk fill this popular, cavernous store.

**Fiorucci** (125 E. 59th St., tel. 212/751–5638). This wild and whimsical Italian fashion house, high-tech by design, is the place to buy your rubber shoes, rhinestoned sneakers, plastic dresses, and more.

**Reminiscence** (74 5th Ave., between 13th and 14th Sts., tel.

212/243–2292). The theme is strictly '50s and '60s, in vintage and casual new clothing; the window displays are always fun.

**Trash and Vaudeville** (4 St. Mark's Pl., between Second and Third Aves., tel. 212/777–1727). Black, white, and electric colors create the look upstairs and down. Most of the clothing is for teenagers and older, but for with-it babies, you may find a miniature chartreuse swimsuit or all-black rompers.

## Museum Shops

With only a few exceptions, you don't need to pay museum admission to enter the following shops.

**American Museum of Natural History** (Central Park West at 79th St., tel. 212/769–5000). The spacious premises show off a collection of dinosaur models, crystals, handicrafts, nature books, and more.

**Asia Society** (725 Park Ave. at 70th St., tel. 212/288–6400). The selection here includes unusual toys, jewelry, and accessories.

**Cathedral Church of St. John the Divine** (Amsterdam Ave. at 112th St., tel. 212/222–7200). Unique to the spacious shop are handcut stone pieces made by artisans currently renovating the cathedral; the stock also includes books, toys, and cards.

**Cooper-Hewitt Museum** (2 E. 91st St., tel. 212/860–6878). Most items on display relate to the season or to current exhibits, so there's always something new.

**Hayden Planetarium Shop** (81st St. near Central Park West, tel. 212/769–5910). Astronaut ice cream, holograms, mobiles, and other space-related gifts are offered here.

**International Center of Photography** (1130 5th Ave. at 94th St., tel. 212/860–1777). Browse here for excellent publications, posters, and postcards related to photography.

**Metropolitan Museum of Art** (5th Ave. at 82nd St., tel. 212/879–5500). Art lovers will appreciate the fine reproductions and the large selection of books.

**Museum of American Folk Art** (62 W. 50th St., tel. 212/247–5611; Columbus Ave., between 65th and 66th Sts., tel. 212/496–2966). The store carries model villages, clever cards, handwovens, wood apples, and other pieces in the folk art tradition.

**Museum of the City of New York** (5th Ave. at 103rd St., tel. 212/534–1672). A careful selection of books on the city, plus reproductions and old-fashioned toys are available.

**Museum of Modern Art** (11 W. 53rd St., tel. 212/708–9700). The stock features posters, books, reproductions from the collection, and objects for the home.

**New-York Historical Society** (170 Central Park West at 77th St., tel. 212/873–3400). The shop carries dozens of reproductions and other attractive things with an antique look.

**J. Pierpont Morgan Library** (29 E. 36th St., tel. 212/685–0008). The well-chosen selection includes handsome desk items, Old Master reproduction drawings, facsimile editions of books and musical scores, and Morgan's own smoky-flavored tea.

**Studio Museum of Harlem** (144 W. 125th St., tel. 212/864–4500). The handicrafts on sale from Africa and black America range from trendy (Lucite pins) to magnificent (baskets from Botswana) to fun (dolls in 19th-century calico).

**Whitney Museum of American Art Store Next Door** (943 Madison Ave. at 75th St., tel. 212/606–0200). Black ceilinged and track lighted, this small shop offers intriguing handmade objects, baskets, ceramics, wood boxes, and more.

## Flea Markets

There's no telling what you'll find at the flea markets in black-topped school playgrounds and grungy parking lots. The season generally runs from March or April to November or December.

**Annex Antiques Fair and Flea Market** (6th Ave., between 25th and 26th Sts., tel. 212/243–5343). Antiques are the specialty here: both knickknacks and furniture. Some dealers come from as far afield as Pennsylvania to take their bite of the Big Apple, and local designers and dealers come to buy what they'll later mark up.

**Canal Market** (370 Canal St., tel. 718/693–8142). This popular flea market has items on the junkier side from the '50s, '60s, and '70s, including records, shoes, and sometimes costume jewelry.

**Tower Market** (Broadway, between W. 4th and Great Jones Sts., tel. 718/273–8702). The people doing the selling here are often those who created the goods—arty T-shirts, old clothes, jewelry, leather, and handknits—in short, almost anything required to put together a hip downtown outfit.

**I.S. 44 Market** (Columbus Ave., between 76th and 77th Sts., tel. 212/316–1088). An intermediate school playground is jammed with 300 dealers. The draw is costume jewelry, vintage bric-a-brac, old and new clothes, and a farmer's market.

# Best Bets for Children

Books   **Books of Wonder** (464 Hudson St. at Barrow St., tel. 212/645–8006; 132 7th Ave. at 18th St., tel. 212/989–3270). These cheerful stores offer an excellent stock of new and antique children's books for all reading levels, mainly in hardcover versions. Oziana old and new is a specialty.

**Eeyore's Books for Children** (2212 Broadway, between 78th and 79th Sts., tel. 212/362–0634; 25 E. 83rd St., tel. 212/988–3404). Children will enjoy the large selection here, as well as the weekend story hours for the under-six set and occasional appearances by authors.

Clothing   **Bébé Thompson** (98 Thompson St., between Spring and Prince Sts., tel. 212/925–1122). Downtown style is evident here: There's plenty of black and white, batiks, jungle prints, and Lurex among the embroidered treasures.

**Boy Oh Boy!** (18 E. 17th St., tel. 212/463–8250). Flap Doodles, Gotcha, and Surf Fetish take the pain out of shopping with (or for) boys, sizes 2–20.

**Chocolate Soup** (946 Madison Ave., between 74th and 75th Sts., tel. 212/861–2210). This shop offers handcrafted one-of-a-kinds, imports for infants to sixth-graders, and Danish schoolbags.

**Greenstone and Cie** (442 Columbus Ave., between 81st and 82nd Sts., tel. 212/580–4322). West Side kids of Yuppies get outfitted here from a large selection of children's wear.

**Morris Brothers** (2322 Broadway, between 84th and 85th Sts., tel. 212/724–9000). Parents can find just about everything they need for children, from stretchies and Snuglis for infants to hip clothing for teens at prices ranging from the modest to the pricey.

**Toys**  **Big City Kite Co.** (1201 Lexington Ave., between 81st and 82nd Sts., tel. 212/472–2623). Kites flutter from the ceiling of this shop devoted to the magic of flight. The selection here is hard to match in this city or elsewhere.

**Enchanted Forest** (85 Mercer St., between Spring and Broome Sts., tel. 212/925–6677). This shop goes to the heart of bewitchment via its handmade toys and stuffed animals, kaleidoscopes, folk toys, and books of mythology and fairy tales—all of which add up to pure magic.

**F.A.O. Schwarz** (767 5th Ave. at 58th St., tel. 212/644–9400). You will be hooked on this sprawling two-level children's store from the minute you walk through the door and one of the costumed staff members—a donkey, clown, cave woman, or mad scientist—extends a welcome. In front of you is a wonderful mechanical clock with many dials and dingbats, and beyond that, all the stuffed animals in the world, dolls great and small, things to build with (including blocks by the pound), things to play dress-up with, computer things, games, toy cars (including a multithousand-dollar Ferrari), and much more.

**Forbidden Planet** (821 Broadway at 12th St., tel. 212/473–1576; 227 E. 59th St., tel. 212/751–4386). This large funky store, an institution for sci-fi buffs that started out in London, features monster masks; space-age toys; racks of new, old, and reprint comic books (in Japanese and French as well as English); and shelves full of books, games, and posters.

**The Last Wound-Up** (290 Columbus Ave., between 73rd and 74th Sts., tel. 212/787–3388; 889 Broadway at 19th St., tel. 212/529–4197; Pier 17, South St. Seaport, tel. 212/393–1128). "Don't Postpone Joy" is a motto of this store, where people of all ages are encouraged to give free rein to their whimsy by playing with a clever selection of wind-up toys priced at around $2.50 or $3.50 each.

**Penny Whistle Toys** (132 Spring St., between Wooster and Greene Sts., tel. 212/925–2088; 448 Columbus Ave., between 81st and 82nd Sts., tel. 212/873–9090; 1283 Madison Ave., between 91st and 92nd Sts., tel. 212/369–3868). Meredith Brokaw, the wife of TV anchor Tom Brokaw, has developed an intriguing selection of high-quality toys here.

**Second Childhood** (283 Bleecker St., between Sixth and Seventh Aves., tel. 212/989–6140). Old toys from your own childhood and your parents' fill the cases in this small shop. It may not be the biggest collection of toy soldiers, tin trains, and old dolls in the city, but it's splendid enough to make many a grandmother wax nostalgic. Check out the tiny Tin Lizzies, the Big Little books, old-fashioned banks, and other baubles. The shop is not always open on Sunday; be sure to call ahead if you're making a special trip. *See* also Fun and Fantasy, above.

# 6 Sports, Games, and the Urban Outdoors

New Yorkers keep their noses to the grindstone on weekdays but they set aside weekends for R&R. In city parks—24,600 acres of parkland and playgrounds, malls and squares now in the midst of the most ambitious rebuilding program since the Great Depression—people hike and bird-watch, body-surf and windsurf, fly kites and toss Frisbees, bat baseballs and kick soccer balls, stroll, and picnic. Indoors, the competitive spirit flourishes at pool halls and backgammon, bridge, and chess clubs. Those who prefer to leave the gamesmanship to someone else, of course, can always stand on the sidelines and cheer as some of the biggest names in pro sports make New York City their competitive arena.

# The Urban Outdoors

There are no spotted cows and weathered barns in New York's "country," and where there are forests, they are hemmed in by highways. But New York's parks and woodlands constitute the largest urban forest in the nation, nevertheless. A recent project by the parks department's Natural Resources Group recorded more than 750 different native species of plants and animals here, including the American chestnut tree, the endangered peregrine falcon, the sharp-shinned hawk, and the white-tailed deer. Besides great works of landscape architecture, such as Central Park and Prospect Park, there are preserves more numerous than you might imagine, where nature follows its own path in salt marshes, scrubby areas, and forests.

### Beaches

With or without bikinis and sun screen, New York–area beaches are among the city's greatest year-round pleasures. State-of-the-art machinery that gives new meaning to the word "beach-combing" has been introduced to prevent debris from spoiling the sand as it had in past summers, although it's still a good idea to call about swimming conditions before you leave home. All city beaches are guarded, and entry to most, including the 15 miles under Parks & Recreation department supervision, is free. If you go by car, however, you probably will have to pay for parking.

*Long Island* **Jones Beach** (tel. 516/785–1600) is one of the world's great manmade beaches. Built in 1929 by the famous parks commissioner Robert Moses on the site of a much more unprepossessing strand, it is 6½ miles long and extremely wide, so even on Sundays you can claim a patch of solitude and sun of your own if you walk far enough. The Long Island Railroad runs regular trips to the beach in summer, going to Freeport by train and by bus from there.

**Fire Island,** a 3½-mile-long sliver of sand just south of Long Island proper, offers beaches at **Robert Moses State Park** (tel. 516/669–0449), on the western end of the island, and at **Smith Point County Park.** Another 1,400 acres of Fire Island constitute the **Fire Island National Seashore.** Fire Island is accessible by a train and boat combination (tel. 718/454–LIRR or 516/794–LIRR).

*New Jersey* **Sandy Hook** (tel. 201/872–0115), now part of the Gateway National Recreation Area, is the home of the oldest operating lighthouse in the country and the site of a series of forts that protected shipping channels in colonial days. The area today is much better known for its 7 miles of beaches, with terrific swimming and surf fishing. Dunes behind the strand shelter a holly forest that has no equal on the Eastern Seaboard.

*Brooklyn* **Brighton Beach,** located in the Russian enclave known as "Odessa by the Sea," has an Old World atmosphere; even the pushcart foods have an ethnic flavor.

**Coney Island,** once a sandy island that the Dutch named "Konijn Eiland" for its rabbit population, attracts millions every year, as it has ever since the 1830s. While this isn't the beach you want if you're looking for a great nature experience, there's nothing quite like it for New York summer atmosphere: fried clams, skateboards, girls and boys necking under the boardwalk, and old men staring out to sea. It's home to the New York Aquarium, as well as one of the city's most unusual designated landmarks—the Cyclone roller coaster, a ride that offers two minutes of heart-stopping rolls and plunges. And you're just 3½ miles away by boardwalk from Brighton Beach.

**Manhattan Beach,** though less than half a mile long, is one of the nicest city beaches for sunning and swimming. It's located just east of Brighton Beach off Oriental Boulevard.

*Bronx* **Orchard Beach** (tel. 212/885–2275), on Long Island Sound, a grand mile-long sandy arc created in 1934 by the ubiquitous Robert Moses, is sometimes known as "the Riviera of the Bronx," attracting as many as 32,000 people on a scorching summer day. The borough's large Hispanic population gives the place a decidedly Latin beat, but every section has its own style—some attract the elderly, some divorced women, and others are known as "Hollywood" or "Little Puerto Rico."

*Queens* **Jacob Riis Park** (tel. 718/474–4600), part of the Gateway National Recreation Area just west of Rockaway Park, was named for the Danish photographer who documented the lives of so many recent immigrants. A somewhat rickety boardwalk stretches a full mile along the Atlantic surf, and facilities include softball fields, paddleball and shuffleboard courts, and pitch-and-putt golf courses. In winter, the huge parking lot is a favored destination for model airplane flyers, and the beach is given over to anglers, bird-watchers, and stalwart members of the Polar Bear Club, who prefer their swimming when the water's icy.

**The Rockaways** (tel. 718/318–4000), 7½ miles of Atlantic strand, is the nation's largest municipal beach and the site of some of the city's best surf. Originally a weekend resort for a rowdy Irish contingent and Tammany politicians, it was once known as the "Irish Saratoga."

*Staten Island* The entire southeast shore of the island is Atlantic Ocean beach, much of it part of either the New York City park system or the Gateway National Recreation Area. Terrific surf beaches are at **Wolfe's Pond Park** (tel. 718/984–8266) and **Great Kills Park,** a quiet place frequented by locals. The **Franklin D. Roosevelt Boardwalk** leads from Miller Field, part of the Gateway National Recreation Area (tel. 718/351–8700), along the ocean to Fort Wadsworth, under the Verrazano-Narrows Bridge, via Oakwood Beach, New Dorp Beach, Midland Beach, and South Beach—all popular, guarded strands.

**Parks and Woodlands**

Many New Yorkers would be surprised to learn that a full 13% of the city is parkland. A handful of nature centers access short, marked trails where you can see nature at its best.

**Central Park** Created by Frederick Law Olmsted and Calvert Vaux beginning in 1858, this magnificent 840-acre park is unexpectedly full of natural splendors, considering its early 19th-century condition as a vile and barren bog full of oozy slime, polluted creeks, slaughterhouses, and bone-boiling works. Central Park was named a National Historic Landmark in 1965, and the nonprofit Central Park Conservancy, founded in 1980, has raised millions of dollars to improve the park's physical upkeep dramatically. The staff of gardeners—amounting to two in 1979—has been increased to more than 100.

On Sundays, whatever the season, everyone turns out to make merry in the park. Salsa groups quick-step. Boom boxes reverberate. Folk dancers clap and circle. Roller skaters twirl and bop around Wollman Rink or along park roads and promenades. Joggers huff and puff up the hills, while bicyclists whiz past in a blur of clicking gears. Some of the city's best sports facilities are here: baseball and softball fields, basketball courts, a lake for rowing, courts for lawn bowling, bridle paths for riding, and 26 courts for tennis (*see* Sports and Recreation, below).

Various park tours are offered by the Urban Park Rangers (tel. 212/397–3091) and the Department of Parks & Recreation (tel. 212/397–3156). For general information, call 212/397–3081.

*Where to Explore* Your strolls through the park might take you to the following landmarks, described from south to north.

**The Pond** (near Scholars' Gate at 59th St. and 5th Ave.) is a picturesque little body of water dominated by Overlook Rock, a massive outcropping of mica schist streaked with silver, pink, black, and red.
**Central Park Zoo** (*see* Zoos, below).
**Delacorte Musical Clock** (near the zoo) chimes on the half hour with an outburst of performing monkeys, bears, and other bronze figures twirling to taped nursery song chimes.
**The Dairy** (mid-park at 65th St.), originally a working dairy, now holds the delightful park information center.
**Friedsam Memorial Carousel** (mid-park at 65th St.) has been a favorite destination for generations of kids. This 1903 antique has 58 colorful hand-carved horses.
**Sheep Meadow** (mid-park above 65th St.), the largest stretch of grass in Manhattan, has turf so thick and lush that it's hard to believe it had become a dust bowl until its restoration a few years ago. The chain link fence around the perimeter preserves the grass. Sheep grazed here until 1934; they were sheltered for the night across the drive in the structure that is now the Tavern on the Green (*see* Chapter 2).
**The Mall** (just east of the Sheep Meadow), the park's formal promenade, is shaded by one of the nation's last great stands of American elms. Impressive statues of 19th-century men of letters preside over the paved pathways.
**Bethesda Terrace and Bethesda Fountain** (mid-park at 72nd St.), at the northern end of the Mall, feature a magnificent stone staircase; wonderful willows, rhododendrons, and cherry trees; and a formal pool with Emma Stebbins's fine late 19th-

century statue *Angel of the Waters*, at the center, surrounded by cherubs representing the Victorian virtues of Purity, Health, Peace, and Temperance. The terrace overlooks the lake to the north.

**Conservatory Water** (east side of the park just above 72nd St.), the park's model boat pond, may be better known to youngsters as the site of the thrilling boat race in E. B. White's *Stuart Little*. Nearby are statues of Hans Christian Andersen and Alice in Wonderland—the latter worn shiny smooth by clambering children.

**Cherry Hill Concourse** (west of Bethesda Fountain) is a loop-ended drive once used as a turnaround for carriages. It's splendid in spring when the wispy blossoms of the cherry trees frill the hilltop.

**Strawberry Fields** (at W. 72nd St. entrance) covers 2½ acres landscaped with funds from Yoko Ono in memory of her husband John Lennon. The famous former Beatle was killed in front of the building in which they lived, the Dakota, just across Central Park West. A black-and-white mosaic medallion inlaid in the path reads simply "IMAGINE."

**The Ramble** (mid-park north of the lake), 30 acres of shrubby, brushy woods, marks a transition to the less formal, more rustic northern part of the park. Bird-watchers congregate here year-round; some 259 of the 600 regularly occurring species in North America have been sighted here. Despite its woodsy appearance, the Ramble was one of the most carefully planned parts of the park, right down to its "mountain torrent" and its "cave." Among the trees here are cucumber magnolias, shagbark hickorys, Kentucky coffee trees, white oaks, and black locusts.

**Belvedere Castle** (mid-park at 79th St.), a fairy-tale stone structure, perches on one of the highest points of the park, Vista Rock, towering over turtle pond. There are splendid views from its terraces and turrets. The castle is the park's Urban Park Rangers headquarters and an observation station for the U.S. Weather Bureau.

**The Great Lawn** (mid-park between 81st and 84th Sts.), an immense meadow that was once a reservoir, now holds baseball diamonds and playing fields that do double duty as the park's principal venue for concerts. Up to 800,000 gathered here for the New York Philharmonic extravaganza during Liberty Weekend in 1976.

**The Reservoir** (mid-park between 84th and 96th Sts.) is 106 serene acres of water ringed by a chain-link fence and a running path that offers glorious views of green against a backdrop of stately old apartment buildings, turned pink and gold in sunsets. In late fall, Canada geese and ducks speckle the water and call at each other above the distant hum of traffic.

**Conservatory Garden** (*see* Gardens, below).

**Riverside Park**  This 324-acre strip of green along Manhattan's western edge, created by Frederick Law Olmsted from 1873 to 1910, may not offer Central and Prospect parks' natural breadth and variety, but it does have one thing they do not: the Hudson River. Riverside Park's wonderful promenades offer watery panoramas and terrific sunsets, and it's even more dazzling in spring when the cherry trees are a pale pink froth. Riverside Park doesn't draw people from outside its neighborhood with much frequency, so Sundays here remain somewhat relaxed and tranquil compared to Central Park. And community groups currently working to stir up interest in maintaining Riverside Park, as the Central Park Conservancy did in the city's flagship park, have made a difference.

*Where to Explore*   Statues and monuments along Riverside Drive include the Joan of Arc Memorial at 93rd Street, the Fireman's Memorial at 100th Street, the Franz Sigel statue at 106th Street, the Samuel Tilden statue at 112th Street, and the Louis Kossuth Monument at 113th Street. Other landmarks you'll encounter in the park, from south to north, include these:

**The Boat Basin** (at 79th Street) is where a few hundred New Yorkers live in houseboats ranging from funky to sleek.

**The Rotunda** (at the 79th St. underpass) occupies a wonderful circular space punctuated by a fountain, flanked by stairways leading down from the road, and edged on another side by a colonnade and viewing platform over the Boat Basin. The acoustics are excellent, and when professional performing groups are not scheduled—currently there are jazz concerts on summer Sundays—street musicians may hold forth.

**Hudson River Promenade** (from 72nd St. to 96th St.) runs both at water level and in the park above, where you get a loftier view.

**Mt. Tom** (at 83rd St.) is a boulder where a 19th-century neighborhood resident, Edgar Allan Poe, often climbed to ponder the passing river scene.

**Soldiers' and Sailors' Monument** (at 89th St.), an imposing columned Civil War memorial fashioned after Athens's monument to Lysicrates, was designed by architect Paul E. M. Duboy, whose other works include the Ansonia apartment building (Broadway at 72nd St.).

**91st Street Community Garden** (at 91st St.), where local residents cultivate perennials for all to admire, keeps a fabulous couple of blocks blooming. It's especially beautiful in July and August. Volunteer weeders are welcome on weekends; just speak to anyone who's working.

**Bird Sanctuary** (114th to 122nd Sts.) has been planted with berry bushes by the New York Audubon Society as shelter for small birds.

**Grant's Tomb** (Riverside Dr. at 122nd St.) was copied after Mausoleus's tomb in Turkey, a 4th century BC structure that was one of the Seven Wonders of the Ancient World. President Ulysses S. Grant and his wife lie in black marble sarcophagi beneath the soaring rotunda. This formal classical monument stands in fascinating contrast to the gaudily colorful 1960s-era mosaic benches that flank its terrace.

**Grave of an Amiable Child** (at 123rd St.) occupies a peaceful fenced area adjacent to Grant's Tomb and a few steps down. A five-year-old named St. Clair Pollack fell from this point in 1797; the grave has remained here despite Robert Moses and the march of progress.

**Manhattan's**   **Carl Schurz Park,** which runs between 82nd and 90th streets on
**Other Parks**   the eastern edge of Manhattan, is the backyard of Gracie Mansion, the official mayoral residence. Situated on the East River, the park has fine views of Queens and the bridges, and it's a low-key place, perhaps because it's a bit out of the way.

North of Riverside Park but connected to it is peaceful 62-acre **Fort Tryon Park,** which surrounds the Cloisters (*see* Chapter 4) and offers more wonderful views of the Hudson River. The central plaza honors a Revolutionary War heroine named Margaret Corbin.

**High Bridge Park,** on the other side of the island from Fort Tryon, is all forested terraces and rocky ledges, with fine views across the East River to the towers of the Bronx.

Above Dyckman Street, **Inwood Hill Park** covers 196 acres of incredibly quiet hill-climbing woods laced with hidden paths.

The 12-acre **Peace Garden** at the United Nations provides a lovely lookout over the East River. Lawns edged with hedges and ivy, punctuated with statues presented by many nations, are crisscrossed by paths for strolling, while near the General Assembly Building, the Rose Garden—a gift of the All-America Rose Selections group—shows off some of the country's most beautiful flowers.

**Union Square Park,** situated between 14th and 17th streets along Broadway, has seen a complete renovation that turned it into an open and airy space with handsome subway kiosks and small patches of flowers. The sculpture of Lafayette is by Felix Bartholdi, better known for his *Liberty Enlightening the World*—the Statue of Liberty.

A former vacant lot along Greenwich Street, between Chambers and Duane streets, has been landscaped into **Washington Market Park,** 1½ acres of lawn and meandering paths with an adventure playground and an airy Victorian gazebo-cum-bandstand.

At the foot of Fifth Avenue stands **Washington Square Park,** a former potter's field and hanging ground that now bustles with families, kids, chess players, street musicians, students, and even a few aging hippies. Neighborhood watchdogs have battled to keep out the drug dealers, making this once again a pleasant spot for people watching on Sunday afternoons. At the park's center is the landmark arch designed by Stanford White in 1892 to replicate an earlier structure commemorating the centennial of George Washington's inauguration. Around the park's perimeter are redbrick town houses that such luminaries as Henry James, Edith Wharton, and John Dos Passos once called home.

**Pelham Bay Park** This 2,764-acre Bronx park, the city's largest, is one of the great surprises of New York. Once the fishing and hunting grounds of the Siwanoy Indians, it was named for Englishman Thomas Pell, who made peace with them in 1654. Its recreational areas include golf courses and popular Orchard Beach.

Although its perimeters are crowded by high-rise housing projects, it is also a large and complex environment for wildlife: fish and egrets, salamanders and frogs, insects, raccoons and rabbits, owls, and even red fox. Many people consider its ragged 13-mile shoreline one of the most scenic of all public lands along the Atlantic. Along the shore, migrating ospreys dive for winter flounder, harbor seals dine on mollusks and crustaceans, and, in spring, fiddler crabs—one of several types that live here—lay their eggs on the pebbly beaches of Long Island Sound. Pelham Bay's salt marshes are the targets of another recent parks restoration program.

For more information, contact the Pelham Bay Park Environmental Center near Orchard Beach (tel. 212/885–3466), the park administrator's office (tel. 212/430–1890), or the Urban Park Rangers (tel. 212/548–7070).

*Where to Explore*  As you travel from south to north, these are the major landmarks:

**Rodman's Neck,** a meadow-and-scrub area southwest of Orchard Beach, is a favorite destination of bird-watchers and baseball players alike. It also contains a forest of European alder, a large concentration of white poplar, and nearly five acres of bayberry bushes.

**Thomas Pell Wildlife Refuge and Sanctuary** is one of the city's great outdoor classrooms for the study of nature, established in 1967. In addition to many acres of woodlands, it is the site of **Goose Creek Marsh,** the last 50 acres of ancient marshlands that once extended over 5,000 acres. **Split Rock Trail,** which winds through and around the marsh, passes the landmark **Split Rock,** a massive glacier-split boulder where poet Anne Hutchinson died in 1643 at the hands of marauding Siwanoy Indians.

The **Central Woodlands,** full of red oak, black birch, and boxelder maples, shelter ruby-throated hummingbirds and other bird life.

**Glover's Rock** bears a plaque commemorating the Battle of Pell Point, a Revolutionary War skirmish in which Colonel John Glover ambushed British and Hessian troops lying in wait for General George Washington.

**Bartow-Pell Mansion** (*see* Museums and the Visual Arts).

**Hunter Island** is a beach area full of natural pleasures: tidal wetlands, towering old oaks, uncommon native plants such as wild geraniums and wood betony, and the park's largest continuous forest. Huge rock outcrops incised by glaciers' movements 10,000 years ago, part of the Hunter Island Marine Zoology and Geology Sanctuary, can be seen along the Kazimiroff Nature Trail.

**Van Cortlandt Park**  What's remarkable about this Bronx park is that all but 146 of its 1,146 acres are forests and wetlands. The pileated woodpecker feeds on insects in dead trees; the great horned owl hunts rabbits; and three types of bedrock jut out majestically: Fordham gneiss, Yonkers granite, and softer Inwood marble. And everything is getting in better shape, thanks to an ongoing $16 million rehabilitation.

For more information, call the Urban Park Rangers (tel. 212/548–7070) or the administrator's office (tel. 212/430–1890).

*Where to Explore*  **Van Cortlandt Mansion** (*see* Chapter 4).

**Memorial and Constitution groves** are each pleasant stands of trees. The former, of immense pin oaks, honors World War II soldiers; the latter, 13 American lindens, commemorates the bicentennial of the U.S. Constitution.

**Vault Hill,** the burial ground of the Van Cortlandt family, rises 169 feet above sea level, offering a fine view of the recreation areas at the Parade Ground.

**Van Cortlandt Lake,** the largest expanse of fresh water (13 acres) in the borough was formed when Jacobus Van Cortlandt dammed Tibbetts Brook in 1699 to power two mills.

**Tibbetts Brook** flows through marshy areas that make for fine bird-watching; follow the new mile-long **John Kieran Nature Trail** along Van Cortlandt Lake or the **Old Putnam Railroad Track,** abandoned since the early 1980s. The most notable denizens here are downy wood ducks.

**Aqueduct Trail,** another good walking path, was formed in the 1830s by workers who built the aqueduct to tap the Croton watershed north of the city. (The aqueduct itself was abandoned in 1897.) Fine forests of oak, maples, and tulip trees shade the trail.

**Northwest Forest** contains great stands of hemlocks and tulip trees interspersed with stunning outcroppings of Fordham gneiss. It can be explored on the **Cass Gallagher Nature Trail.**

**Prospect Park** Frederick Law Olmsted and Calvert Vaux, who collaborated on this 526-acre Brooklyn expanse of meadows, bluffs, boulders, glens, streams, and ponds, considered it even better than Central Park, their previous project. Located west of Flatbush Avenue and south of Grand Army Plaza, it is a beautiful place, with its 15,000 trees and shrubs and a network of winding roads and paths. With more than $18 million poured into it since 1980, it's looking better than ever. As in Central Park, roads are closed to motor vehicles all weekend.

For information on volunteer activities, including half-day park cleanups and bulb-planting marathons for which the whole community turns out, call 718/788–8960. Call the Prospect Park Environmental Center (tel. 718/788–8500 or 718/788–8589 for a recorded message) to find out more about the park's wildlife.

*Where to Explore* From north to south, the principal destinations are these:

**Grand Army Plaza** (intersection of Flatbush Ave. and Eastern Pkwy.), the stately and imposing northern entrance to the park, was designed by the architect Stanford White. The interior of the arch is open only on Sundays during warm weather; a spiral staircase to the top gives you a wonderful panorama of the park, south Brooklyn, and lower Manhattan.

**Long Meadow** (west side of the park) is the largest open space in an urban park in the entire United States. Many recreational facilities are located here (*see* Sports and Recreation, below).

**Vale of Cashmere** (center of the park), a natural amphitheater full of free-form ponds, offers cover for small birds amid its rhododendrons and azaleas.

**Prospect Park Zoo** (*see* Zoos, below).

**Prospect Park Carousel** (near the zoo) was created by a Russian immigrant, with horses representing the work of some of Brooklyn's finest carousel carvers.

**Music Grove,** a pagoda-shaped bandstand, is the site of concerts in summer.

**The Boathouse** (*see* Chapter 4).

**Camperdown Elm** (near the Boathouse), one of the city's biggest trees, is immense, gnarled, and redolent of antiquity. When endangered by neglect in the mid-1960s, it was saved by a public campaign during which Marianne Moore published a notable poem about the tree.

**Quaker Cemetery** (*see* Cemeteries, below).

**Lefferts Homestead** (*see* Chapter 4).

**Alley Pond Environmental Center** This is what the Long Island sections of Queens looked like before suburbia: reed-edged glacial kettles, creeks, oak woodlands, and salt- and freshwater marshes. Although some of the metropolitan area's busiest highways surround you, they seem far away as you follow the three short marked trails in search of small mammals—rabbits, muskrats, opossums—and identify migrating birds by the hundred in the wetlands in the fall. The center proper displays live snakes and stuffed birds and hosts lively weekend programs for youngsters.

For details, contact the center (228-06 Northern Blvd., Douglaston, Queens, tel. 718/229–4000).

**Jamaica Bay Wildlife Refuge** Despite the fact that this part of Queens is a stone's throw from Kennedy Airport and within sight of Manhattan, during the past 25 years some 320 species of birds have been recorded on these 9,155 acres of salt marshes, fresh and brackish ponds, and open water. A wildlife refuge since 1953, it is now part of the Gateway National Recreation Area.

It's most exciting in spring, when hundreds of thousands of birds are nesting—including the great egret, snowy egret, and glossy ibis—and in fall, when thousands of ducks and geese making their way southward along the Atlantic flyway stop over on the two refuge ponds. Floyd Bennett Field, the city's first municipal airport, is the base for park visitor programs (tel. 718/474–0613).

**The Greenbelt** Covering 2,500 acres of public and private land on Staten Island, the Greenbelt was conceived by great parks designer Frederick Law Olmsted, who owned a farm here. Although Staten Island has been getting progressively more built up since the Verrazano-Narrows bridge was completed in 1964, the preserve still protects five different kinds of owls and shelters the most northerly example known of the sweet-bay magnolia tree. Encompassing woods and meadows, ponds and wetlands, golf courses, cemeteries, and a couple of museums (Richmondtown Restoration and the Jacques Marchais Center of Tibetan Art; *see* Chapter 4), the area has nearly 35 miles of trails, with plants identified and footways spread with wood chips.

For particulars, contact the main Greenbelt office (300 Altamont St., Staten Island, tel. 718/667–2165) or Conservation and the Outdoors (Box 284, New York, NY 10031).

*Where to Explore* **Todt Hill,** the high point (409 feet) of the park, is the highest tidewater elevation on the Atlantic seaboard south of Maine.
**Hiking trails** include the 13-mile Greenbelt Circular Trail, the 7.1-mile La Tourette Trail, the 5.2-mile Richmondtown Circular Trail, the 4.4-mile Willowbrook Trail, and the 5.5-mile Great Kills Trail.
**Reeds Basket Willow Swamp,** 30 acres of trees, ferns, vines, and shrubs, flourishes in what used to be a glacial pond. It's administered by the Staten Island Institute of Arts and Sciences (tel. 718/727–1135 for guided tours).
**Clove Lakes Park** (tel. 718/390–8000), created by the damming of an ancient glacial valley, has a quartet of lakes, several waterfalls, and forests of mature oaks and beeches covering 195 acres.
**High Rock Park** (tel. 718/987–6233), 87 acres of woodlands, swamps, and freshwater ponds, has its own network of six walking trails. The Staten Island Institute of Arts and Sciences sponsors regular guided walks here on Sundays. There's also a Sensory Garden planted with fragrant and textured herbs and identified with Braille markers and a Centennial Wildflower Garden full of native plants.
**Great Kills Park,** on the Atlantic, is a good place for seaside walking and for spotting shorebirds like killdeer, plover, and

teal. Monarch butterflies stop here during their migrations to and from Mexico.

**Moravian Cemetery** (*see* Cemeteries, below).

## Gardens

New Yorkers who like to see nature pruned, planted, and blooming turn out on weekends to stroll, chat, and smell the flowers in the city's great gardens. Horticultural novices will no doubt encounter expert gardeners who are happy to share their passion and offer a tip or two.

**Brooklyn Botanic Garden** With just 50 acres, this favorite New York green spot is smaller than its Bronx counterpart but no less wonderful. In spring, its Daffodil Hill is like sunshine turned into flowers; when the 30 varieties of cherry and crab apple trees bloom, the Cherry Esplanade is one of the best shows in town. Lilacs burst forth when the cherries fade, followed by wisteria, azaleas, peonies, irises, viburnum, and roses in a thousand different varieties. The Japanese Hill and Pond Garden has a lakeful of goldfish and turtles, the Shakespeare garden is full of plants immortalized by the Bard, and the Ryoanji Temple Stone Garden mixes raked sand and large stones. Note also the Celebrity Path, Brooklyn's answer to Hollywood's famous sidewalk, where the names of homegrown stars—Mel Brooks, Woody Allen, Zero Mostel, Mae West—are inscribed on stepping stones. The new $25 million Steinhardt Conservatory lays out the Trail of Evolution through three domed and cupola-topped greenhouses, showing how plant life developed from the mosses and horsetails of billions of years ago to the plants of present-day deserts, temperate lands, and tropics. *1000 Washington Ave., Brooklyn, tel. 718/622–4433. Suggested donation: $2. Open Sun. 10–6 (Oct.–Mar., 10–4:30).*

**The Cloisters Gardens** At the heart of this ersatz medieval monastery (*see* Chapter 4), some 250 species of plants and flowers that would have been found in monastery gardens centuries ago flourish against the most colorful of backdrops: the Romanesque Cuxa Cloister, with its pink-and-white marble columns and octagonal fountain. The more austere Bonnefont Cloister has a fine view of the Palisades across the Hudson River. The Gothic Trie Cloister contains plantings of the 50 species identified in the museum's Unicorn Tapestries, with names like black hellebore, Good King Henry, honesty, samphire, woad, and St. John's wort. The Saint-Guilhem Cloister, covered with a skylight, displays flowering bulbs and other greens year-round. Detour into Fort Tryon Park nearby to see the recently restored **Heather Garden,** just 600 feet long but wonderfully colorful thanks to original designs by Frederick Law Olmsted, Jr. *Fort Tryon Park, tel. 212/923–3700. Admission: $5 adults, $2.50 students and senior citizens. Open Mar.–Oct., Sun. 9:30–5:15 (Nov.–Feb., Sun. 9:30–4:45).*

**Conservatory Garden** A leafy Central Park retreat, established as part of a WPA project in the 1930s but neglected for many years, this is now one of the park's showplaces. Just which of its three sections is loveliest is hard to say. Is it the central half-acre of verdant lawn flanked by allées of crab apple trees leading to a wisteria-twined pergola? Or the geometrically planted French parterre with its fountain of frolicking nymphs? Or the intimate, naturalistic area full of magnolias, lilacs, annuals, and perennials, named the Secret Garden after the Frances Hodgson Burnett children's classic? This is a gorgeous place, especially in May when the lilacs and crab apples are in bloom. The wrought-iron gates, from a now-demolished Vanderbilt mansion, make a stunning entrance. *5th Ave. at 105th St., tel. 212/397–3081. Admission free. Open Sun. 8 AM–dusk.*

**New York Botanical Garden** These 250 wonderfully landscaped and carefully tended acres are among New York City's most underappreciated delights. The Enid A. Haupt Conservatory, that C-shape acre of greenhouses, would, by itself, warrant a trip to the Bronx for its splendid Victorian Palm Court, its leafy Fern Forest, and its arid New World Desert House. Special exhibitions are particularly enjoyable in the dead of winter; poinsettias by the thousand make for a colorful Yuletide. But beyond the conservatory's pleasures are the great outdoors: formal gardens full of clematis, daylilies, and other perennials; the geometrically planted Herb Garden with some 50 species; and the Chemurgic Garden, which shows off plants with scientific uses. There are pines, spruce, and fir from all over the world; gardens of seasonal flowers; Rhododendron Valley, a blizzard of color in late May and early June; the Murray Liasson Narcissus Collection; an Azalea Way; Cherry Valley; the T. A. Havemeyer Lilac Collection, whose huge white, pink, and lavender flower clusters perfume the air in May; and much more. The recently restored Peggy Rockefeller Rose Garden, reconstructed on its 1916 model, blooms from early May until the first hard frosts. The surprising center of it all is the 40-acre NYBG Forest—the only uncut woodland in all New York City. Weekend walks and lectures are available on a regular basis. *Fordham Rd. and Bronx River Pkwy., the Bronx, tel. 212/220–8700. Admission to grounds: voluntary contribution; to conservatory: $3.50 adults, $1.25 students and senior citizens, under 6 free during seasonal exhibits (lower at other times). Grounds open Oct.–Mar., Sun. 8–6 Apr.–Oct., Sun. 8–7; conservatory open 10–5 (last admission at 4).*

**Queens Botanical Garden** Brides, their attendants, and their mothers make summer Sundays a constant swirl of ruffles, petticoats, and smiles at the Wedding Garden, with its weeping willows and waterlily pool; beyond that little corner, you can stroll through a Bee Garden, Bird Garden, Herb Garden, formal gardens of annuals, and more. The Rose Garden is one of the largest in the Northeast, with more than 8,000 plants, and in late April and early May more than 10,000 tulips create a dazzling mass of color. *43–50 Main St., Flushing, Queens, tel. 718/886–3800. Admission free. Open Sun. 9–dusk.*

**Staten Island Botanical Garden** Situated on the 83-acre grounds of the Snug Harbor Cultural Center, this lush spread of sloping lawns and shapely trees has a Victorian air. The perennial garden changes with every season; many other small gardens follow specific themes—one is for herbs, another for annuals, another to attract butterflies, and yet another full of roses. Tours are available. *1000 Richmond Terr., Staten Island, tel. 718/273–8200. Admission free. Open Sun. dawn–dusk.*

**Wave Hill** Located on the Hudson River in Riverdale, the Bronx, this 28-acre estate, with 13 acres of gardens and 10 acres of woodlands, is a high point of horticultural New York. Directors of other public gardens come from all over the country to admire the plants and their unusual juxtapositions, which change from year to year. Free greenhouse and garden walks take place on Sunday afternoons at 2:15; there are also occasional bird walks, art shows, and concerts. Henry Moore, Louise Nevelson, and Isamu Noguchi are represented in the sculpture garden. *Independence Ave. at 249th St., Riverdale, the Bronx, tel. 212/549–2055. Admission: $2 adults, $1 students and senior citizens, children under 6 free. Open Sun. 1–4:30; summer, Sun. 1–7.*

## Zoos

The city's six zoos are home to many, many species of mammals, birds, and reptiles. A $72 million capital modernization program is gradually making them all the more attractive and comfortable, for residents and visitors alike.

**Bronx Zoo**  Only in a big zoo like this one, the largest urban zoo in the country, could you ride a camel, explore a jungle world of crocodiles and slumbering pythons, see snow leopards prowl Himalayan peaks, and penetrate the world of animal nightlife—all in the same afternoon. Some 700 species of animals are assembled here on 265 acres of woods, meadows, ponds, and streams, much of the grounds planted and contoured to re-create the landscapes of far-away places. Wild Asia, where elephants and tigers roam free, is nearly 40 acres of open meadows and dark forests; in Jungle World, where only ravines, streams, and cliffs separate you from the narrow-nosed crocs and the 750-pound Malayan tapirs, waterfalls and lush plantings add up to an indoor tropical forest. The long-closed Elephant Pool has been reopened with pool, wallows, and moats. The Skyfari Ride is a child-pleasing way to get off your feet and enjoy an overview. And don't forget the 2 PM thunderstorm in the World of Birds! *Fordham Rd., the Bronx, tel. 212/367–1010 or 212/220–5141 for Friends of the Zoo walking tours). Admission: $3.75 adults, $1.50 children under 13, senior citizens free, plus $4 for parking. Open Jan.–Oct., Sun. 10–5:30; Nov.–Jan., Sun. 10–4:30.*

**Central Park Zoo**  The country's oldest public zoo, first opened in 1864, is preening itself since the 1988 completion of a $30 million reconstruction. It's state-of-the-art all the way: Animals live in man-made biomes that re-create their home habitats—even the lighting simulates the seasons. The focal point is an enlarged and redesigned 100,000-gallon Sea Lion pool. Flanking it, and linked by a brick-and-glass colonnade, are three other substantial areas: the sky-lighted Tropic Zone building, which explores life in the rain forest on various levels from ground to treetops, amid ferns, moss, and steamy mists; the Temperate Territory, with its snow monkeys, Asian red pandas, and North American river otters; and the frosty Polar Circle, where you can watch the polar bears and penguins sporting below the water line as well as above. Artificial streams and fences hidden by vegetation replace bars, and there are more animals and more kinds of animals than in the old zoo—and only those that can be properly cared for in the limited space available. *Near 5th Ave. at 64th St. in Central Park, tel. 212/861–6030. Admission: $1 adults, 50¢ senior citizens, 25¢ children 3–12. Open Mar.–Oct., Sun. 10–5:30; Nov.–Mar., Sun. 10–4:30.*

**Flushing Meadows Zoo**  A $16 million reconstruction of the 13-acre Queens Zoo and Children's Farm, scheduled for a summer 1991 completion, will retain the zoo's focus on North American animals, but bobcats and pumas may be added to its present population of buffalo, deer, wolves, and sea lions. *Flushing Meadows-Corona Park, Queens, tel. 718/507-3117. Admission fees and hours not available at press time.*

**New York Aquarium** This great institution on Coney Island's famous boardwalk is the perfect place to be in love. Just ask Winston and Natasha, two Beluga whales captured separately off Canada's west coast, flown to Brooklyn, and put in the same 180,000-gallon tank. In the ensuing months, aquarium visitors were treated to water ballet of the highest order, as the happy couple frolicked in an apparent ecstasy of infatuation. With 22,000 specimens representing 225 different species of vertebrates and invertebrates, there's always something going on in the 54 indoor and outdoor exhibits on the aquarium's 14 acres. Each of the re-created habitats in which these sea creatures live has something special: The Cold Water Gallery is inhabited by the rare giant Pacific octopus; the Red Sea presents the spectacle of a reef full of the brightest colored fish imaginable; sandtiger, nurse sharks, and horn sharks glide silently through the 90,000-gallon Shark Tank. Nuka, New York's only Pacific walrus, performs regular feeding-time shows in the domain she shares with her companion, a sea lion named Breezy. Currently under way are two projects that will nearly double the number of exhibits: Discovery Cove, a complex of coastal environments and specialized live animal exhibits mixed with interactive and audiovisual displays, and Sea Cliffs, a sequence of coastal habitats for seals, walruses, sea otters, and penguins where animals can be viewed from above and below water level, from indoor as well as outdoor walkways. Sundays are busy—which means that if something special happens, there will always be an excited kid around to send up the alarm: "Hey, Dad, lookit this!" *Surf Ave. at W. 8th St., Coney Island, Brooklyn, tel. 718/265-3474. Admission: $3.75 adults, $1.50 children 2–13. Open Labor Day–Memorial Day, Sun. 10–4:45; Memorial Day–Labor Day, Sun. 10–5:45.*

**Prospect Park Zoo** By July 1991, this old-fashioned 19-acre zoo, noted for its WPA bas-reliefs and murals from Rudyard Kipling's *Jungle Books*, will wrap up a three-year renovation and emerge with new natural habitats for its creatures, both wild and domestic. *Prospect Park, Brooklyn, tel. 718/965-6560. Admission fees and hours not available at press time.*

**Staten Island Zoo** The excellent collection of snakes is the highlight of this smallish (8-acre) zoo, where the emphasis is on lively smaller animals, such as prairie dogs and otters, raccoons and birds. Children are enchanted by the animal hospital and its nursery viewing area, as well as by the children's zoo full of farm animals that can be petted and fed. *614 Broadway, Sunnyside (in Barrett Park), Staten Island, tel. 718/442-3100. Admission: $1, children under 3 free. Open Sun. 10–4:45.*

## Cemeteries

No description of the city's green places is complete without a mention of its cemeteries, where the shrub-scattered, tree-shaded lawns are punctuated at regular intervals by memorial headstones, monuments, and miniature temples. More peaceful than the parks on weekends, these graveyards also have fascinating stories to tell.

*Manhattan* **New York Marble Cemetery** (between 1st Ave. and the Bowery, 2nd and 3rd Sts.) is the last of more than three dozen cemeteries of Manhattan's early years. It's not open to the public, but through the gates you can read on its headstones names such as Roosevelt, Varick, Scribner, and Beekman.

**St. Mark's in-the-Bowery** (10th St. at 2nd Ave.) claims Peter Stuyvesant as the most famous resident of its cobbled early 19th-century churchyard.

**St. Paul's Chapel** (Broadway at Fulton St., tel. 212/602–0874), a Georgian-style structure (circa 1766), once George Washington's place of worship and now Manhattan's oldest public building, is surrounded by a mossy, grassy, ivied churchyard. Its tumble of blackened headstones and monuments are incised with weeping willows and other funereal motifs of the day.

**Shearith Israel,** a Jewish congregation, has created three cemeteries over the years. The oldest (55 James Pl., opposite Chatham Sq., tel. 212/873–0300 for appointment to view), in use 1682–1828, is full of faded inscriptions in Hebrew, English, and a Spanish-Hebrew known as Ladino. The second (76 W. 11 St., between Sixth and Seventh Aves.) was used 1805–1829. The third (21st St. between 6th and 7th Aves.) was used 1829–1851.

**Trinity Cemetery** (between Amsterdam Ave. and Riverside Dr., 153rd to 155th Sts., tel. 212/283–6200) was established by Trinity Church (*see* below) in the 19th century, when this uptown site was farmland once owned by naturalist-artist John James Audubon. Rural peace still prevails on the grounds, which climb from the Hudson River up to Amsterdam Avenue. Audubon's grave is here, as are those of the colorful Eliza Brown Jumel (who owned the Morris-Jumel Mansion; *see* Chapter 4); Charles Dickens's son, Alfred Tennyson Dickens; philanthropist John Jacob Astor; and clergyman Clement Clarke Moore, author of *'Twas the Night before Christmas*. The cemetery's walls, gates, and keeper's lodge were designed by the firm of Calvert Vaux, who worked with Frederick Law Olmsted on Central Park. The cemetery adjoins Trinity's former rural chapel, now the baronial Church of the Intercession.

**Trinity Church** (Broadway at Wall St., tel. 212/602–0800), in the heart of downtown, is home to frequent concerts on weekdays; Sundays are best for savoring the churchyard's peace and for contemplating the sweep of New York City history revealed by the graves of Alexander Hamilton, William Bradford, steamship creator Robert Fulton, and Captain James Lawrence, the War of 1812 hero who exhorted, "Don't give up the ship!"

*The Bronx* **Woodlawn** (233rd St. and Webster Ave., tel. 212/920–0500) is considered by some people to be the most beautiful cemetery in the country; its 400 acres show off an incredible variety of trees—huge white oak and weeping beech, golden rain trees, and Kentucky coffee trees—and shelter some 120 species of birds. However, it's perhaps best known as the last resting place of a roster of tycoons, celebrities, and politicos so extensive that the cemetery actually publishes a map. The names read like a Who's Who of American civilization: meat-packer H. D. Armour, stockbroker Jules Bache, evaporated milk maker Gail Borden, Roaring '20s dancers Irene and Vernon Castle, patriotic song-and-dance man George M. Cohan, jazz great Duke

Ellington, Admiral David Farragut, tycoon Jay Gould, impresario Oscar Hammerstein (the lyricist's father), bluesman W. C. Handy, composer Victor Herbert, railroad magnate Collis P. Huntington, dimestore kings Samuel H. Kress and Frank W. Woolworth, longtime New York City mayor Fiorello La Guardia, merchants R. H. Macy and J. C. Penney, newspaperman Joseph Pulitzer, women's rights crusader Elizabeth Cady Stanton, inventor Henry H. Westinghouse, and many others. The headstone of *Moby Dick* author Herman Melville, which bears the image of a blank slate, is near the oak where kidnapper Bruno Hauptmann received the $50,000 ransom for the Lindbergh baby. Woodlawn is unexpectedly lively, with a dozen or so Sunday concerts every year—jazz, choral music, George M. Cohan songs, Duke Ellington jazz, and more.

*Brooklyn*  **Green-Wood** (5th Ave. at 25th St., tel. 718/768–7300) was designed by Henry Pierrepont, who laid out the streets of Brooklyn in 1835, a year after it was incorporated. He provided not only 11 parks for the new city but also, inspired by the rolling greenness of Paris's famous Père Lachaise and Boston's Mount Auburn, created a cemetery full of hills, ponds, lakes, and meandering drives—a "Garden City of the Dead" that eventually became a model for cemetery planners everywhere. Its 478 acres have remained among the city's greenest and still offer some of the best bird-watching in the city. Along 22 miles of lanes and 209 paths bearing names like Sylvan Water, Lawn Avenue, Glade Hill, and Grassy Dell, the stones tell tales. An Indian princess said to have died from overeating when feted by New York society is buried here, as is the mad poet McDonald Clark, who is believed by some to have drowned himself in jail by letting a faucet drip down his throat. Better-known denizens are Governor De Witt Clinton; William Marcy "Boss" Tweed; piano manufacturer Henry Engelhard Steinway; soap magnate William Colgate; pharmaceutical kings Edward Squibb and Charles Pfizer; pencil man Eberhard Faber; tobacco millionaire Pierre Lorillard; artists Nathaniel Currier, James Merrit Ives, Louis Comfort Tiffany, George Wesley Bellows, and George Catlin; furniture craftsman Duncan Phyfe; architects James Renwick, Jr., who designed St. Patrick's Cathedral and Grace Church, and Richard Upjohn, who designed today's Trinity Church; abolitionist minister Henry Ward Beecher; newspapermen Henry J. Raymond (of the *New York Times*), Horace Greeley (of the *Tribune*), and James Gordon Bennett, Jr. (of the *Evening Telegram*); inventors Samuel F. B. Morse (the telegraph), Peter Cooper (the steam locomotive), Elias Howe (the sewing machine), and "Soda Fountain King" John Matthews (carbonated water); as well as gangsters Albert Anastasia and Joey Gallo (gunned down at Umberto's Clam House), and scattered secretaries of the navy, Civil War generals, U.S. senators, and entertainers.

**Quaker Cemetery** (Prospect Park) is a landscape of big trees, old gravestones, and pleasant hills; it's also the burial place of actor Montgomery Clift, who died in 1966 at the age of 45.

*Staten Island*  **Moravian Cemetery** (Richmond Rd. at Otis Ave. between Todt Hill Rd. and Altamont) boasts the tenancy of Commodore Cornelius Vanderbilt, who germinated the seed of his great fortune by operating a ferry from Staten Island to Manhattan before the War of 1812. He spent a million dollars here on an imposing bronze-embellished mausoleum designed by the noted Richard

Morris Hunt. His ancestor, Jacob Van Der Bilt, became a Moravian in the 18th century and is buried on an adjacent plot; many others of the sect are buried here, segregated according to sex. However, the cemetery wasn't always a property of the United Brethren, and many graves—including the first, of one Colonel Nicholas Britten, dated 1740—are nonsectarian.

## Group Outings

For what's coming up, check out Other Events in the "Cue" listings section at the back of *New York* magazine or the "Weekend" listings in the Friday *New York Times*.

**New York City Audubon Society** (71 W. 23rd St., tel. 212/691–7483) offers weekend outings to local bird habitats in town and country.
**Outdoors Club** (Box 227, Lenox Hill Station, New York 10021, tel. 212/876–6688 evenings before 10) has a variety of programs that cover shoreline, residential areas, and parks on foot and by bike, by day and by night.
**Parks & Recreation Department Tours** are outings with a variety of nature themes led by the Urban Park Rangers, a decade-old uniformed division of the parks department. Contact them in the **Bronx** at Van Cortlandt Park, tel. 212/548–7070; Crotona Park, tel. 212/589–0096; and Pelham Bay Park, tel. 212/885–3466. In **Brooklyn,** they're at Prospect Park, tel. 718/287–3400; and Fort Greene Park, tel. 718/858–3709. In **Manhattan,** call Central Park, tel. 212/397–3080; and Inwood Hill Park, tel. 212/304–3629. In **Queens,** contact them at Flushing Meadows-Corona Park, tel. 718/699–4204; and Kissena Park, tel. 718/353–1047. On **Staten Island,** call Cromwell Recreation Center, tel. 718/816–5456.
**Shorewalkers** (tel. 718/463–5729) put the emphasis on covering the waterfront.
**Torrey Botanical Club** (tel. 212/220–8700) leads free trips to various parks, in town and out.
**Urban Trail Conference** (Box 264, New York, NY 10274) organizes city walks as well as country walks.
**Wild Foods Walks** (tel. 718/291–6825) introduce participants to the city parks' wealth of edible plants—burdocks, oyster mushrooms, elderberry and mulberry, lamb's quarters, wild sorrel, water mint, and much more.

# Sports and Recreation

There's nothing quite like the exhilaration of victory, the agony of defeat, and the thrill of the game for completely obliterating all the worries of the workweek. The competitive spirit so dear to New Yorkers flourishes on Sundays in dozens of private facilities and public parks.

A permit is required for the use of many of the recreational facilities in the city parks. To get one, contact designated Parks & Recreation Department offices on weekdays (tel. 212/408–0209 for Manhattan, 212/430–1830 for the Bronx, 718/965–8939 for Brooklyn, 718/520–5932 for Queens, and 718/816–6529 for Staten Island).

## Baseball

Playing fields in almost every park are largely reserved for use by leagues playing either softball or baseball. To guarantee playing time, you need a permit, but there are also pickup games here and there in every park. Sometimes the game happens by chance, the teams made up of anyone within earshot, so take your mitt, show up, and ask whether the players on hand need an extra.

## Basketball

Shooting and dribbling action takes place at hundreds of public outdoor courts in the city parks. The courts at **Sixth Avenue near 8th Street** draw real hotshots—and amazed onlookers. There's also lively play in **Riverside Park,** at the five-court complex between 104th and 114th streets or another complex near 76th Street.

## Bicycling

One or two Sundays every month, some 50 to 85 members of the Century Road Club Association turn out early—usually around 7 AM—for four- or five-lap races around the 6-mile circular drive in Central Park. Smaller packs of racing cyclists streak along at practically any hour on Sundays, although the park roads, closed to auto traffic, also have plenty of room for those who pedal at a more sedate speed. And on Sunday mornings, when there's little traffic and most of the rest of the world is still abed, city streets lend themselves perfectly to exploring by bike.

*Manhattan*  While **Central Park** is the focal point of the city cycling scene, the **Riverside Park** promenade, between 72nd and 110th streets, with its Hudson River view, gets a more easygoing crowd. Weekends are a good time to explore the deserted canyons of lower Manhattan; end up on the **Battery Park Esplanade** where you can rest on a park bench and watch the sun set over the Hudson River. Or circle through the winding streets of upper Manhattan in **Inwood Hill** or **Marble Hill,** where there are some terrific old brownstones and town houses and imposing apartment buildings.

*Brooklyn*  The trip across the **Brooklyn Bridge,** with its superb views of Manhattan, is one of the most exhilarating in the city. The winding, sylvan roads in **Prospect Park,** closed to auto traffic as in Central Park, are also popular. Another good bet: the 2.2-mile-long bikeway currently being created along neighboring **Eastern Parkway,** once known as the Champs-Elysées of Brooklyn. The **Ocean Parkway** bicycle path, which runs from Church Avenue, near Prospect Park to Sea Breeze Avenue at Coney Island, is lined with benches, high-rise apartment complexes, and spreading maples, sycamores, and gingkos. The **Shore Parkway** bicycle path, a narrow strip of green from Owls Head Park in Bay Ridge to Kennedy Airport in Queens, offers a constantly changing vista—now the Verrazano-Narrows Bridge and Manhattan skyline, later Jamaica Bay and the Rockaways—but glittering water is always your companion. The **Coney Island Boardwalk** makes for a good ride provided you get there before the crowds, so in summertime plan your

pedal accordingly—before 10 AM if you prefer solitude, later for
good people watching.

*Staten Island* Make tracks around the reservoir and on the roads in 209-acre
**Silver Lake Park** (tel. 718/447–5686), which is closed to motor
vehicles on Sundays and holidays. The golf course sets forth
emerald vistas.

*Rentals* **AAA Bikes** (in Central Park's Loeb Boathouse, near E. 74th
St., tel. 212/861–4137; open Sun. 9–7).
**Bicycles Plus** (85th St. and 3rd Ave., tel. 212/794–2201; open
Sun. 10–7).
**Gene's Bicycles** (242 E. 79th St., tel. 212/249–9218; open Sun.
9:15–7).
**Metro Bicycles** (1311 Lexington Ave. at 88th St., tel. 212/427–
4450; open Sun. 9:30–6:30).
**Pedal Pusher** (1306 2nd Ave. between 68th and 69th Sts., tel.
212/288–5592; open Sun. 10–6).

*Group Trips* **American Youth Hostels** (891 Amsterdam Ave., tel. 212/932–
2300) organizes day trips in the metropolitan area and out of it,
often free. A move to 891 Amsterdam Avenue (at 103rd St.) is in
the offing.
**Central Park Cycling & Sports Association** (tel. c/o Errol Toran
at 212/956–5920) plans a full weekend schedule of races, 15- to
30-mile beginners' rides, training rides, and repair clinics;
rides venture as far as 100 miles from Manhattan.
**Hungry Pedalers Gourmet Bicycle Tours** (771 West End Ave.,
tel. 212/595–5542) offers 20- to 50-mile pedals organized around
the city's different ethnic cuisines.
**Staten Island Bicycling Association** (Box 141016, Staten Island,
10314, tel. 718/273–0805) runs group tours on and off the island.

## Bird-watching

When you think of Manhattan bird life, you may think first of
pigeons, but in fact the city's green parks and woodlands provide a habitat for everything from Canada geese, summer
tanagers, and fork-tailed flycatchers to buffleheads, Kentucky
warblers, and common nighthawks. Since the city is on the Atlantic flyway, one of the country's four major spring and fall
migratory routes, you can see birds that nest as far north as the
High Arctic. May is the best season, when the songbirds are in
their freshest colors, with so many singing at once that you can
hardly distinguish their songs. To find out what's been seen
where, call the Rare Bird Alert (tel. 212/832–6523).

*Manhattan* **Central Park** has four prime birding areas: the promontory of
the Pond near the southeast entrance, the Reservoir, the Loch
at 104th Street, and the wild-and-woodsy Ramble on the north
shore of the lake. Some 20 species of birds nest in the park, including brown thrashers, cardinals, downy woodpeckers,
eastern kingbirds, gray catbirds, and mallard ducks; others
come through during migrations. The spring migration begins
in March and climaxes in mid-May. You may see fish crows and
iridescent common grackles in February; American robins and
American woodcocks in March; ruby-crowned kinglets, blue-
gray gnatcatchers, yellow-rumped warblers, brown creepers,
black-and-white warblers, and hermit thrushes in April; and
orioles, scarlet tanagers, rose-breasted grosbeaks, indigo
buntings, and some 25 brightly colored species of warblers in

May. The fall migration is less concentrated and less colorful because the birds aren't in their mating plumage.

Other good spots are in 323-acre **Riverside Park,** especially the bird sanctuary between 114th and 120th streets, and the Heather Garden in 66-acre **Fort Tryon Park,** north of Fort Washington Avenue (call Urban Park Rangers at 212/397–3191 for both).

*The Bronx*    The best spots are the saltwater marsh and the lagoon in 2,764-acre **Pelham Bay Park** and the freshwater marshes and upland woods in 1,146-acre **Van Cortlandt Park.**

*Brooklyn*    Try the 798-acre **Marine Park** marsh (near Ave. U, tel. 718/965–6551), on Rockaway Inlet into Jamaica Bay, near Sheepshead Bay; 526-acre **Prospect Park,** particularly the Rose Garden, the Vale of Cashmere, Midwood, the shores of Prospect Lake, and Lookout Hill; and **Green-Wood Cemetery.**

*Queens*    The woodlands and wetlands in the 623-acre **Alley Pond Environmental Center** host a diverse population that includes shorebirds like egrets, herons, and Canada geese, as well as a fantastic array of small birds. This is the site of monthly outings of the **Queens County Bird Club** (tel. 718/229–1094). Other good spots are in **Flushing Meadows-Corona Park,** especially Meadow and Willow lakes; **Jamaica Bay Wildlife Refuge,** a prime habitat for waterfowl; and the trails in 235-acre **Kissena Park,** which begin at the Nature Center (tel. 718/353–1047).

*Staten Island*    The **William T. Davis Wildlife Refuge** (off Travis Ave., New Springville, tel. 718/727–1135 for tours and trail maps), a 260-acre preserve, occupies a transition zone between salt marshes and glacial terrain full of hardwood forests, so it offers a wide range of birds, animals, and insects. Shrubby growths of viburnum and marsh roses provide cover for warblers and woodpeckers. This is an especially good place to sight hawks—red-tails, sharp-shinned, Coopers, and marsh hawks.

**Wolfe's Pond Park,** a fairly undeveloped 224 acres of wetlands, stretches around a pond that may be covered from shore to shore with ducks and geese during a seasonal migration; a stone's throw away, at the ocean, 200–300 birds—grebes, cormorants, and ducks—may land in front of you all at once. The park is also the best place on Staten Island for herons, including the yellow-crowned night heron, a Florida native that is rarely sighted in these parts. Upland and shrub growth shelters small birds as well.

Other Staten Island sites include **Clove Lakes Park,** for a good variety of ducks, geese, and wading birds; **High Rock Park,** where herons and ibis frequent the Lower Pond and small birds the brush; and **Heyedahl Hill** (accessible from a small parking area at the intersection of Meisner and Rockland Aves.), where, especially in fall, it's occasionally possible to see as many as 25 hawks in a two-hour period. For more information on Staten Island birding sites, call the Staten Island Urban Park Rangers (tel. 718/846–5456) or contact the Greenbelt park administration (tel. 718/667–2165).

## Boating

The idea of boating around New York City conjures up images of a 19th-century lady twirling her parasol while her elegantly suited swain rows her across still waters. Only the costumes have changed, although the participants often have radios to serenade them when conversation palls. Boating is hugely popular on weekends, so go early or be prepared to wait your turn.

In **Central Park**, the boats are rowboats (plus one authentic Venetian gondola!) and the rowing terrain is the 18-acre lake. *Loeb Boathouse, near 74th St., tel. 212/517–2233. Open Sun. 11–6; closed in winter.*

In **Prospect Park**, the two- and four-seater boats that scuttle across the 60-acre Prospect Lake and Lullwater are pedal powered. *Pelican Boat Rentals, near Wollman Skating Rink, tel. 718/287–9824. Open Sun. 11–7:30.*

## Boccie

There's more boccie than bowling in New York—100 city courts in the five boroughs. Of these, the easiest to get to from Midtown are at 96th Street and First Avenue, at East River Drive and 42nd Street, and at the Thompson Street Playground at Thompson and Houston streets in Greenwich Village. You'll also find boccie courts on Randalls and Wards islands and in Prospect Park, Brooklyn.

## Bowling

Leagues are popular, so call before you come to make sure that open bowling is available.

**Beacon Lanes** has 10 lanes. *344 Amsterdam Ave. between 76th and 77th Sts. tel. 212/496–8180. Open Sun. 1 PM–midnight.*
**Bowlmor** has 44 lanes and a colorful Village crowd. *110 University Pl. between 12th & 13th Sts., tel. 212/255–8188. Open Sun. 10 AM–1 AM.*

## Croquet

Anglophiles go for the fine croquet courts north of the Sheep Meadow in Central Park. Season permits are necessary for play (tel. 212/360–8133 for information), but onlookers are welcome to peer over the hedge.

## Cross-Country Skiing

In **Central Park**, the Sheep Meadow, the Great Lawn, and the North Meadow are flat enough for even beginners to handle. In **Prospect Park**, Long Meadow and Nethermead are favorite destinations. Better skiers tackle various city nature trails: Bucks Hollow in **La Tourette Park**, Staten Island (tel. 718/816–5456), winding through a former farm; the hardwood forests traversed by the Cass Gallagher Nature Trail in **Van Cortlandt Park**; and the woods in **Pelham Bay Park**.

For rentals, try **Scandinavian Ski & Sport** (40 W. 57th St., tel. 212/757–8524), open Sun. 11–5.

## Dancing

**Folk Dancing** **Central Park** (east of Belvedere Castle mid-park at 81st St.; tel. 212/673–3930 for dance information) attracts any and all ethnic dance lovers to the foot of the statue of King Jagiello of Poland, Sundays from 2 to 6.

**Ballroom Dancing**  No longer limited to the blue-haired set, ballroom dancing is catching on with younger people—and there are some real fanatics out there.

**Marc Ballroom** (27 Union Sq. W, between 15th and 16th Sts., tel. 212/924–4085), an unpretentious, old-time Manhattan ballroom, gets a very chic crowd of professionals and dedicated amateurs of all ages. Dances are held every other Sunday night at 7.

**Roseland** (239 W. 52nd St., tel. 212/247–0200), a glossy dance palace from back when, attracts a good Sunday crowd, mostly men and women over 50, but there's a sprinkling of younger newcomers. The bands play on from 2:30 to midnight.

**Sandra Cameron Dance Center** (439 Lafayette St. at Astor Pl., tel. 212/674–0505), a focal point for the resurgence of ballroom dancing, is owned by a three-time U.S. champion.

**Stepping Out** (1845 Broadway, tel. 212/245–5200), another teaching studio that draws a crowd of ballroom specialists, devotes Sundays to private lessons, by appointment, with personable instructors.

## Fishing

**Party Boats**  Brooklyn's **Sheepshead Bay**, a grand and stylish neighborhood at the turn of the century, is today salty, fish happy, and proud of its fleet, which is among the country's largest: Some 32 party boats go out every day year-round and take evening trips in summer as well. The prime destination is the Mudhole, one of the world's great fishing grounds. Piers are along shore-hugging Emmons Avenue, and departure times are posted in the area—typically at 6, 7, 8, and 10 AM for full-day trips, noon and 1 PM for half-day outings. Tackle rentals and bait are provided. Call **Mike's Tackle & Bait Shop** (tel. 718/646–9261) for more information. No charter boats are available.

**Small Boats**  On the Bronx's quaint City Island, **Jack's Bait & Tackle** (Cross St. and City Island Ave., tel. 212/885–2042) rents small boats with 6 HP motors to go out for flounder and blackfish, Sundays 5 AM—8 PM.

**Shore Fishing**  In the Bronx's **Pelham Bay Park,** regulars cast for black bass, flounder, fluke, and small blues from Orchard Beach (tel. 212/885–2275), before and after the swimmers take over, and from nearby Hunter's and Twin islands. In Queens, **Rockaway Beach** (tel. 718/318–4000) can be good for bass, flounder, and porgies.

In Brooklyn, you can sometimes catch a big one from the **Breezy Point Jetty** or the **Canarsie Pier** in the Gateway National Recreation Area (tel. 718/474–4600). Occasionally the park management sponsors surf fishing master classes on weekends.

## Golf

**Courses**  The city's hundreds of avid golfers jam the area's handful of well-kept city courses—layouts so verdant that residents are always surprised to find them.

*Long Island*  **Bethpage State Park,** devoted exclusively to golf, is about an hour and 20 minutes from Manhattan. Probably the best public golf facility in the area, it's home to no less than five courses, and the 7,065-yard par-71 Black is generally rated among the nation's top 25 public courses. Golfers without well-honed skills will find themselves in deep trouble on its narrow fairways and small, well-bunkered greens. Reservations for starting times are not accepted; the line starts forming at midnight for tee time tickets to go on sale at 4 AM. But things aren't so congested on the other courses on the property: the 6,537-yard Red, full of doglegs and long par 4s; the 6,513-yard par-72 Blue, with a tough front nine; the more forgiving 6,171-yard par-71 Yellow, a good beginner's course; and the 6,267-yard par-71 Green, the original course on the estate, which was acquired by the state in the early 1930s.

*The Bronx* **Pelham Bay Park** has two unexpectedly scenic 18-hole courses adjoining the Thomas Pell Wildlife Refuge and Sanctuary: the 6,405-yard Pelham course, noted for its wide fairways and gentle slopes, and the 6,492-yard Split Rock, with narrower fairways, more woods, and denser roughs (tel. 212/885–1258 or 718/225–4653 for tee times).

**Van Cortlandt Park** is the home of the nation's first municipal golf course, established in 1895: the rolling 6,052-yard Van Cortlandt Golf Course (tel. 212/543–4595). There's also the flatter, 5,231-yard Mosholu Golf Course (tel. 212/655–9164).

*Brooklyn* The 6,500-yard **Dyker Beach** course (7th Ave. and 86th St. tel. 718/836–9722 or 718/225–4653 for tee times) is a nice little layout.

The **Marine Park Golf Course** (2880 Flatbush Ave. near Belt Pkwy., tel. 718/338–7113) may not be as well kept as it could be, but the location adjoining Floyd Bennett Field in the Gateway National Recreation Area gives you a chance to fill your lungs with sea breezes as you play.

*Queens* The 5,431-yard course at **Forest Park** (Forest Park West Dr. and 80th St., tel. 718/296–0999) is challenging and full of character.

The flat, 6,263-yard **Clearview** course (202–12 Willets Point Blvd., tel. 718/229–2570 or 718/225–4653 for tee times) sees a lot of activity.

The 5,482-yard layout at **Douglaston** (6320 Marathon Pkwy. and Commonwealth Blvd., tel. 718/224–6566) is rolling, with small greens and narrow fairways.

**Kissena** (Booth Memorial Ave. and 164th St., tel. 718/939–4594) is relatively short at 4,600 yards, but it holds its own with decent-size hills and tight fairways.

*Staten Island* At the 5,891-yard **Silver Lake** Course (915 Victory Blvd. near Forest Ave., tel. 718/447–5686), hills and tight fairways pose respectable challenges to good golfers.

The 6,315-yard **South Shore** course (Huguenot Ave. and Raily St., tel. 718/984–0101) is woodsy, though with a major housing development blooming on its perimeter.

Historic 6,600-yard **La Tourette** (100 London Rd., at Forest Hill and Richmond Hill Aves., tel. 718/351–1889) has long, wide, pretty fairways.

Tee times may be reserved at any of the city's courses by calling 718/225–4653.

**Driving Ranges**  In the Bronx, visit those at Turtle Cove Golf Complex in **Pelham Bay Park** and at the Mosholu Course in **Van Cortlandt Park**. In Brooklyn, there's **Gateway Golf and Tennis** (3200 Flatbush Ave., tel. 718/253–6816), a concessionaire of the Gateway National Recreation Area, open Sundays 10 AM–11 PM.

**Miniature Golf**  The newest course in Manhattan is **Gotham Miniature Golf** (at Wollman Rink, Central Park near 64th St., tel. 212/517–4800; open Sun. 10–9:30), where putters maneuver around scale models of city landmarks. **Putter's Paradise** (48 W. 21st St., tel. 212/727–7888; open Sun. noon–10) is a fun, if gimmicky, layout created by two investment bankers. Miniature golf can also be found at the **Turtle Cove Golf Complex** and **Gateway Golf and Tennis** (*see* Driving Ranges, above).

## Handball

Many of the city's 854 playgrounds have handball courts, including those in **Central Park** at North Meadow Center (mid-park at about 97th St.) and in **Riverside Park** at 72nd Street and 101st Street.

In the Bronx, you'll find courts in the **Orchard Beach** games area, among other locations. In Queens, go to Victory Field in pretty **Forest Park** (Myrtle Ave. and Woodhaven Blvd.).

## Horseshoes

Pitches are at the Parade Ground in **Prospect Park** (tel. 718/287–3400) and at Victory Field in **Forest Park** (Myrtle Ave. and Woodhaven Blvd., tel. 718/520–5900)—but you've got to bring your own horseshoes.

## Ice Skating

Everyone becomes a country kid when whirling and twirling across the ice of the city's rinks. All schedule Sunday sessions and provide lockers, skate rentals, music, and snack bars.

**Kate Wollman Rink** (Prospect Park, Brooklyn, tel. 718/965–6561) features Caribbean Winter at the Rink and sessions for figure skaters, besides public skating.
**Lasker Rink** (Central Park, 110th St. and Lenox Ave., tel. 212/996–1184), recently restored, is a well-kept secret. It has recently offered ice hockey as well as free-style skating areas, plus demonstrations and clinics.
**Rivergate Ice Rink** (34th St. and 1st Ave., tel. 212/689–0035) is a handsome little rink that draws a lively crowd of children.
**Rockefeller Center** (50th St. at 5th Ave., tel. 212/757–5730) may be postage-stamp-size, but skating in the shadow of golden Prometheus may be the ultimate Manhattan skating experience. It's open long hours, but rates tend to be higher than elsewhere.
**Sky Rink** (450 W. 33rd St., 16th floor, tel. 212/695–6555 or, for lessons, 212/239–8385), improbably located in the penthouse of a far West Side building near the Javits Center, is the city's biggest indoor skating spot and its only year-round rink. There are special sessions for adults and families.
**Staten Island War Memorial Rink** (Clove Lakes Park, Staten Is-

land, tel. 718/720–1010) is probably the best place to skate on Staten Island.

**Wollman Memorial Rink** (Central Park near 64th St., tel. 212/517–4800) is the largest city-owned skating facility, and there's no more beautiful spot on a clear day—or a snowy one, for that matter.

**World's Fair Ice Skating Rink** (Flushing Meadows-Corona Park, Queens, tel. 718/271–1996) is a city-owned facility that encourages ice hockey.

## Jogging and Racewalking

The only essential for jogging is something the city has plenty of: pavement. And with less competition from cars and pedestrians on Sunday, a jogger can tick off the miles just about anywhere.

*Manhattan*   In **Central Park,** the route circling the Reservoir is long enough to give a good workout but short enough that those who wish to can do several loops and compare their times. It's also a sociable place, busy from early in the morning until dark. You can do the upper track (1.58 miles) for water-and-woods views or the through-the-woods bridle path (1.66 miles) on the lower level. The park roads, closed to traffic on weekends, offer a more varied passing scene, with bicyclists and roller skaters as well as joggers. You can go longer distances on the roads without repeating your route—up to 6 miles if you go around the northern end of the park. A shorter route (1.72 miles) takes you via Tavern on the Green, the West Drive, the southernmost road through the park to the East Drive, and the 72nd Street park road back to your starting point. Crime is not a problem as long as you jog when and where plenty of others do, which is nearly everywhere almost all day long on Sunday.

**Riverside Park** is gorgeous at sunset and at any time of day when the cherry blossoms bloom in May. From 72nd Street to 116th Street and back is about 4½ miles. There is also an outdoor track near 74th Street (8 laps equal 1 mile).

There is a quarter-mile track in **East River Park** (E. 6th St. at FDR Dr.). Other good routes are around **Gramercy Park** (one-fifth mile), **City Hall Park** (a half mile), and along the **Battery Park Esplanade** (about 2 miles), and around off-shore **Roosevelt Island** (3.6 miles).

*Brooklyn*   For Brooklyn joggers, the prime destination is **Prospect Park,** where the roads are closed to traffic on Sundays. Also good are the 3-mile-long **Coney Island Boardwalk** to Brighton Beach and the 5-mile-long **Shore Road Promenade** along the Narrows in Bay Ridge.

*The Bronx*   **Pelham Bay Park** has a track-and-field facility that includes a quarter-mile oval and a multistation exercise trail. **Van Cortlandt Park** has a quarter-miler as well as a cross-country course, whose 3.1- and 5-mile loops begin and end at the Parade Ground.

**Races and**   The **New York Road Runners Club** (9 E. 89th St., tel. 212/860–
**Group Runs**   4455) offers a complete schedule of races and fun runs; Sunday races draw the biggest crowds of all. A handful of New York City Marathon Long Training Runs are also available. You don't have to be a member to participate, and registration is usually available right up until starting time.

**New York Walkers Club** (Box M, Livingston Manor, NY 12758, tel. 914/439–5155) organizes regular clinics and group workouts.

## Lawn Bowling

There's a beautiful green for this antique sport just north of the Sheep Meadow in **Central Park.** The required permits are available only by the season, which runs May–November (tel. 212/360–8133 for permit information). You can also contact the New York Lawn Bowling Club (tel. 212/988–3962), whose members play in the park on Sundays at 10 AM and 1 PM; they welcome participants as well as interested bystanders.

## Model Airplane Flying

Designated fields are in the Bronx at **Ferry Point Park** (north of the Bronx–Whitestone Bridge) and in **Pelham Bay Park,** in Queens around Meadow Lake at **Flushing Meadows-Corona Park** and in **Forest Park,** and in **Great Kills Park** in the Greenbelt on Staten Island.

## Riding

Sundays in the city's stables are busy, as riders turn out to enjoy the city's parks from a somewhat loftier perch on the back of a horse. Spring and fall are the busy seasons; horses are usually freshest in the mornings.

*Manhattan* There are 4.4 miles of bridle paths in Central Park, including the one around the Reservoir, renovated in 1987. Experienced English riders can rent a variety of mounts at the carefully run **Claremont Riding Academy** (173–177 W. 89th St., tel. 212/724–5100), the city's largest and oldest riding academy and the only stable for riding horses left in Manhattan. A National Historic Site, it's been in the same location since 1892, and it's the longtime home of the Central Park Hunt, an equestrian group that stages annual rides on certain holidays. Private lessons are available from beginner through advanced level, including dressage. Sundays are the busiest days of the week. The stable opens at 6 AM.

*The Bronx* At the **Van Cortlandt Park Riding Academy** (254th St. at Broadway, tel. 212/543–4433), you can cover the park's wooded and wide-open trails using Eastern or Western saddles. On Sundays, the stable is open from 9 AM to an hour before dusk.

In Pelham Bay Park, you can ride along woodsy, recently restored bridle paths with horses (saddled Eastern or Western style) from the **Pelham Bit Stable** (Pelham Bay Park, tel. 212/885–0551), open Sundays 8–8.

*Brooklyn* On mounts from **Culmitt Stables** (51 Caton Pl., tel. 718/438–8849), you can ride solo in the ring or take a guide to go out into Prospect Park. The stable is open Sundays 9–8.

**Jamaica Bay Riding Academy** (7000 Shore Pkwy., tel. 718/531–8949) rents horses for beach riding and provides lessons in a large indoor ring. It's open Sundays 8–6.

*Queens* To take trail rides through 538-acre Forest Park, try **Dixie Dew Stables** (88–11 70th Rd., tel. 718/263–3500), open Sundays 7:30

AM–7 PM, or **Lynnes Riding School** (88–03 70th Rd., tel. 718/261–7679), open Sundays 9–4.

*Staten Island* **V&S Stables** (715 Sharrotts Rd., tel. 718/317–7777) uses the trails of lonely 240-acre Clay Pit Pond State Reserve, which some people call Staten Island's Wild West.

## Roller Skating

Dozens of skaters streak through **Central Park** every Sunday. Wired via headphones to music they alone can hear, they trace circles and loops on the pavement east of the Sheep Meadow; in front of the Tavern on the Green, they sometimes set up obstacle courses. Rentals are available at smooth **Wollman Rink,** which is given over to roller skating from the beginning of warm weather to November (tel. 212/517–4800).

It's also fun on weekends to roll through **Riverside Park** from 72nd to 95th streets along the river, past the Boat Basin and along the Promenade; around **Roosevelt Island;** and along the deserted concrete canyons and wide-open plazas downtown, particularly **Wall Street.** If you don't have your own skates, you can rent from **Peck & Goodie** (919 8th Ave., between 54th and 55th Sts., tel. 212/246–6123), open Sundays noon–5.

## Sailing

**City Island,** a nautical village in the jaws of Long Island Sound, is where many who can afford it dock their own boats. The Minneford Yacht Club here built Ted Turner's *Courageous* and many another America's Cup winner.

**Offshore Sailing School** (c/o Kretzer Boat Works, 459 City Island Ave., City Island, 10464, tel. 212/885–3200) offers a variety of instruction programs, including a basic learn-to-sail course. Intensive classroom study and on-the-water work are part of all courses. Other programs are available from the equally well-established **New York Sailing School** (560 Minneford Ave., City Island, 10464, tel. 212/885–3103), whose basic sailing programs run Friday through Sunday or on four consecutive Sundays. Advanced sailors can sign up for refresher programs or courses on racing, big-boat sailing, navigation, and other special topics. Both schools also have programs that allow qualified sailors to rent boats for the day.

## Scuba Diving

The coast of New York, New Jersey, and Connecticut keeps divers busy with reefs, wrecks, and sunken subs. Dozens of head boats go out every weekend. Two local dive shops can tell you about these: **Richard's Aqua Lung Center** (233 W. 42nd St., tel. 212/947–5018), the country's oldest and largest dive shop, which also sells books and charts; and **Scuba World** (167 W. 72nd St., tel. 212/496–6983), which packages its own group dives. The shops themselves are closed on Sundays, so call on weekdays.

## Skateboarding

Junior hotshots will tell you that Sunday in New York is heaven; the obstacles and challenges that make the city so much fun for skateboarders are still there, but minus weekday crowds. Top spots include the banks underneath the Brooklyn Bridge on the Manhattan side, around the great buildings downtown by Battery Park City, and the banked plazas of various apartment towers near 95th Street and Columbus Avenue. For gear, visit **SoHo Skateboards** (80 Varick St., between Grand and Watts Sts., tel. 212/925–7868), open Sundays noon–5.

## Sledding

After a good snowfall, New York City children do what children do the world over: They head for the nearest sledding hill. In **Central Park,** top spots are Pilgrim Hill, south of the Conservatory Water, and Cedar Hill, near 78th Street on the east side of the park. In **Riverside Park,** there's a good steep hill at 105th Street.

Brooklyn's **Fort Greene Park** has Monument Hill, which is long and smooth. **Prospect Park's** best slope is Paine Hill.

Sledders in Queens head for **Crocheron Park** (Little Neck Bay, tel. 718/520–5367) or **Juniper Valley Park** (tel. 718/520–5362); in Staten Island, try the rolling **La Tourette Golf Course** (tel. 718/351–1889).

## Surfing

**Rockaway Beach** draws the crowds. To find out if the surf's up, call the local park beach (tel. 718/318–4000) or the **Rockaway Beach Surf Shop** (177 Beach 116th St., Rockaway Beach, tel. 718/474–9345), which has a huge stock of sailboards, surfboards, and wet suits and is open Sundays 11–5.

## Tennis

**City Courts** Permits are required for play; modestly priced at $35 a year, they're easy to get and are sold in every borough (tel. 212/430–1838 for information).

*Manhattan* **Central Park** (mid-park near 94th St., tel. 212/397–3190) has 26 clay courts. Single-play admissions are available for $4 at the Tennis House adjoining the courts; play is free to season permit holders, who can make court reservations by telephone weekdays 1–4. You don't need a permit to take lessons, which are given on four adjoining hard courts (tel. 212/289–3133).
**East River Park** (FDR Dr. at Broome St., tel. 212/397–3102) has 12 hard courts.
**Riverside Park** (96th St. at Riverside Dr., tel. 212/397–3180) has 10 red clay courts.
**Fred Johnson Memorial Park** (151st St. at 7th Ave., tel. 212/397–3134) has eight hard courts, the only ones in Manhattan that are lighted for night play. On Sundays they're open 8 AM–11 PM.
**Inwood Park** (207th St. and Seaman Ave., tel. 212/397–3199) has nine hard courts open Sundays 7 AM–8 PM.
**Randall's Island** (east of Downing Stadium, tel. 212/860–1827) has seven clay courts and four hard courts. Open Sundays 8–8, the courts are busy after noon, but waits don't usually exceed an hour. From November to April, the hard courts are covered and are privately run (tel. 212/534–4845).

*The Bronx*    **Pelham Bay Park** (Rice Stadium, Middletown Rd. and Bruckner Blvd., tel. 212/885–3369) has 10 recently renovated courts. **Van Cortlandt Park** (beside Van Cortlandt Stadium, tel. 212/430–1800) offers eight clay courts and four all-weather courts, open Sundays 8 AM–dusk.

*Queens*    **USTA National Tennis Center** (Flushing Meadows Corona Park, tel. 718/592–8000) the site of the U.S. Open since 1978, has 23 outdoor courts and nine indoor courts, all Deco Turf II and all lighted for night play. On Sundays they're open 8 AM–midnight.

*Staten Island*    **Walker Park** (50 Bard Ave., Livingston, tel. 718/442–9696), where tennis has been played since it was brought here from Bermuda in 1874, now has six well-kept hard courts; single-play permits are available. The courts are open Sundays 8 AM–9 PM.

*Clubs*    Many private tennis clubs are open to nonmembers as well. Sundays are busy, but it's usually possible to reserve a court in advance. Rates range up to $80 an hour.

*Manhattan*    **Columbus Racquet Club** (795 Columbus Ave. near 97th St., tel. 212/663–6900) has nine outdoor Har-Tru courts, open April–October, from 8 to 6 on Sundays.
**Crosstown Tennis** (14 W. 31st St., tel. 212/947–5780) offers four indoor hard courts that are air-conditioned in summer. Open Sundays 6 AM–midnight.
**HRC Tennis** (Pier 13 and 14, East River at Wall St., tel. 212/422–9300) has eight Har-Tru courts under two bubbles, air-conditioned in summer. Open Sundays 6 AM–midnight.
**Manhattan Plaza Racquet Club** (450 W. 43rd St., tel. 212/594–0554) offers five courts—one Poly Plex, one Deco Turf II, and the others Elastaturf—which are open-air in summer, under a bubble in winter, and lighted for play after dark. They're open Sundays 6 AM–midnight.
**Midtown Tennis Club** (341 8th Ave. at 27th St., tel. 212/989–8572) has eight Har-Tru courts—all under a bubble in winter and half under a bubble (and air-conditioned) in summer. Open Sundays 8 AM–10 PM.
**Sutton East Tennis** (488 E. 60th St., tel. 212/751–3452) has eight indoor red clay courts; an additional 10 red clay courts are available year-round on Roosevelt Island. The club is open mid-October to April, Sundays 7 AM–midnight; tennis parties are held on Sunday nights.
**Tennis Club at Grand Central Terminal** (15 Vanderbilt Ave. at 42nd St., tel. 212/687–3841) has two Deco Turf courts that are not usually too busy on Sunday, when they're open mid-September–May, 7 AM–5 PM.
**Tower Tennis Courts** (1725 York Ave., between 88th and 89th Sts., tel. 212/860–2464) has two indoor courts under a bubble, open Sundays 7 AM–11 PM. They can be very hot in summer.
**Turtle Bay Tennis Club** (UN Plaza Hotel, 44th St. at 1st Ave., tel. 212/355–3400) has only one air-conditioned Uni-Turf court at its 38th-floor health club, but there's a fine view and court time is easy to get. Open Sundays 7 AM–11 PM.
**Village Courts** (110 University Pl. at 12th St., tel. 212/989–2300) has two indoor Supreme-surface courts and a ball machine alley. Open Sundays 7 AM–11 PM.

*The Bronx*    **Century Racquet Club** (2600 Netherland Ave. at Kappock St., tel. 212/548–4700) has four indoor Sprit-surface courts. Open September–May, Sundays 8 AM–10 PM.

*Brooklyn*  **Gateway Golf & Tennis** (3200 Flatbush Ave., tel. 718/253–6816) offers eight hard courts, open Sundays 10 AM–11 PM.

*Queens*  **Boulevard Gardens Tennis Club** (51–26 Broadway, Woodside, tel. 718/545–7774) has six good red clay courts, bubble covered in winter. Open Sundays 8 AM–11 PM.
**Expressway Health & Tennis Club** (53–01 74th St. at Grand Ave., Elmhurst, tel. 718/651–8313) has four indoor Elastaturf courts open Sundays 7 AM–midnight.
**Long Island City Indoor Tennis** (50–01 2nd St. at 50th Ave., Long Island City, tel. 718/784–9677) has two indoor Har-Tru courts open Sundays 8 AM–9 PM.
**Tennisport** (Borden Ave. at 2nd St., Long Island City, tel. 718/392–1880) has 16 indoor red clay courts and 13 outdoor Har-Tru courts open Sundays 8–8.

## Windsurfing

The New York area is blessed with both smooth water for beginners and ocean surf for experts. Plumb Beach, Breezy Point, and Sandy Hook—all part of the Gateway National Recreation Area—offer excellent conditions. **Island Windsurfing** (1623 York Ave., tel. 212/744–2000) goes out to Southampton, a couple of hours from Manhattan on the south shore of Long Island, every day for day-long instructional sessions, with rental equipment provided.

# Spectator Sports

Fans root for the home team with gusto on weekends, when, freed from the office grind, they can throw themselves into the thrill of the game. Peanuts, hot dogs, and a cold beer are great tastes to savor in the middle of a lazy afternoon.

The city's greatest spot for sports fans is probably **Madison Square Garden** (7th Ave. between 31st and 33rd Sts., tel. 212/563–8300), an institution that, in various buildings, has been a fixture of New York life since 1879. A jack-of-all-trades of the city's sports and entertainment scene (the writer O. Henry called it "the center of the Universe"), the Garden hosts everything from Ringling Bros. Circus and the Ice Capades to the Westminster Kennel Club Dog Show and the National Horse Show, most of which begin or end on a Sunday. Basketball, hockey, and many other sports are played here as well, also often on Saturday and Sunday. The box office is open 11–8 on Sundays; call there for tickets by phone or order through Ticketmaster (tel. 212/307–7171) at a slight surcharge.

## Baseball

The **New York Mets** play at Shea Stadium (Flushing Meadows-Corona Park, Queens, tel. 718/507–8499). The **New York Yankees** play at Yankee Stadium (E. 161st St. and River Ave., the Bronx, tel. 212/293–6000). Tickets are usually available at the box office; the best usually go to season ticket-holders, but sometimes good seats are available from sports fans peddling their extras at game time.

## Basketball

The **New York Knickerbockers** play home games in Madison Square Garden during the late-October–April season. Knicks tickets recently have become hot and hard to come by at the box office (tel. 212/563–8300 for information); often you can pick up tickets on the street before the game. For the scoop on the latest action, phone the New York Knicks Hot Line (tel. 212/751–6310).

## Boxing and Wrestling

The *Daily News*'s annual Golden Gloves bout and other major boxing competitions are occasionally staged in Madison Square Garden. Wrestling, a more frequent presence at the Garden, is stagey and outrageous, drawing a rowdy and enthusiastic crowd.

## Football

The **New York Giants** play at Giants Stadium (East Rutherford, NJ, tel. 201/935–8111), as do the **New York Jets** (tel. 212/421–6600). All seats for Giants games and most for Jets games are sold on a season-ticket basis, and there's a waiting list for those; remaining Jets tickets for scattered singles sell out almost as soon as they go on sale in August.

## Hockey

The **New York Rangers** play at Madison Square Garden (tel. 212/563–8300), the **New York Islanders** at Nassau Veterans Memorial Coliseum in Uniondale, Long Island (tel. 516/794–4100), and the **New Jersey Devils** at the Byrne Arena in East Rutherford, New Jersey (tel. 201/935–6050). Tickets are usually available.

## Horse Racing

A trip to the tracks, which are busiest on weekends, shows off another side of New York City life—the horse-mad side, which is half passionate gamblers and half blue-blood types who invest thousands in a share of the thoroughbreds. Stroll to the saddle enclosure for a beguiling look at the parading entries.

**Aqueduct Racetrack** (Rockaway Blvd. at 108th St. off Belt Pkwy., Ozone Park, Queens, tel. 718/641–7400), the largest thoroughbred race track in the United States, is a modern facility with a spate of new lawns and gardens. The season here runs from late October to early May.

**Belmont Park** (Hempstead Ave., Elmont, Long Island, tel. 718/641–7400), the grande dame of New York thoroughbred racing, is home of the third jewel in horse racing's triple crown, the Belmont Stakes. During its seasons (May–June and late August–Oct.), breakfast at Belmont and afternoon tram tours provide pleasant Sunday interludes.

The **Meadowlands** (East Rutherford, NJ, tel. 201/935–8500) has a trotter and pacer season January through mid-August and a flat track season Labor Day through December.

**Yonkers Raceway** (Central Ave., Yonkers, NY, tel. 212/562–9500) has a year-round trotter season.

## Running

The city's biggest Sunday spectator sports event may be the **New York City Marathon,** which takes place annually on a Sunday in late October or early November. The pack has grown from 127 (with 55 finishers) to 22,000 (some 16,000 of them finishing) since the race's inception in 1970. Participants now include racewalkers, "jogglers" (who juggle their way through the 26 miles), oldsters, and youngsters, cheered on by the spectators lining rooftops and sidewalks, promenades and terraces all along the course. If you relish mob scenes, try to get near the finish line in Central Park.

## Tennis

The **U.S. Open,** a high point of the tennis buff's year, is held at the National Tennis Center in Queens's Flushing Meadows-Corona Park annually from late August through early September. The first Sunday falls at the midpoint of the tournament, usually over Labor Day weekend, and the second Sunday sees the men's finals. Finals tickets are available only to those who have planned well in advance or are willing to pay sky-high prices to scalpers, and the best seats—the ones down below, where you can actually see more than specks on the court—go only to those who order box seats for the entire tourney. In the early rounds, however, tickets are easier to get, and there's action on almost all the courts, all day long. Strolling from one court to another is the real pleasure of a trip to the Open, which shows off the enthusiasm of the juniors and the aplomb of the over-30 players as well as the competitive spirit of players in their prime—the only group that TV covers. Buy a draw sheet as you enter the complex and decide which matches you want to see; your reserved-seat ticket to the stadium also admits you to all the other courts. People come and go all the time during the changeovers, and waiting patiently will reward you with a vantage point so close up, you can count the sweat beads on the players' foreheads. For details, call the U.S. Open ticket office (tel. 718/271-5100). Tickets go on sale in late spring by mail or through Teletron (tel. 212/947-4840 or 800/922-2030 outside NY).

The **Tournament of Champions** takes place on the Har-Tru courts of the West Side Tennis Club in Forest Hills, Queens, where the U.S. Open got its start. Beginning in 1990, it takes place in August just before the U.S. Open. Tickets go on sale a few months ahead (tel. 718/268-2300).

The tennis year winds up with two tourneys in Madison Square Garden, both of which end on Sundays: the **Virginia Slims** in mid-November and the **Nabisco Masters** at the end of November. Slims tickets go on sale beginning in September (tel. 212/563-8954); Masters tickets can be ordered beginning in October (437 Madison Ave., 17th floor, New York 10022, tel. 212/752-7777 for information).

## Track and Field

The **Millrose Games,** the top indoor track and field competition in the United States, take place at Madison Square Garden every year in February (tel. 212/563-8300).

The **New York Track and Field Games** are held in late July at Wein Stadium, Columbia University (call the Road Runners Club, tel. 212/860–4455, for information).

# Best Bets for Children

**Parks**  In Central Park, favorite destinations include the **Carousel** and the **Conservatory Water**, with its huge remote-controlled model boats and the nearby statues of *Alice in Wonderland* and *Hans Christian Andersen*. Older children will enjoy roller skating or ice skating, depending on the season, at **Wollman Rink**. Hands-on activities at both the **Dairy** and **Belvedere Castle** entertain curious young explorers, and the Urban Park Rangers' summer **Junior Ranger Naturalists** program is fun.

In Brooklyn's **Prospect Park,** kite-flying on the Long Meadow is a great way to spend a spring Sunday with your kids; afterwards, head to the **Brooklyn Botanic Garden** and its fascinating Trail of Evolution in the Steinhardt Conservatory. Short marked nature trails suitable for younger hikers can be found at the **Alley Pond Environmental Center** and **Jamaica Bay Wildlife Refuge** in Queens and **Van Cortlandt Park** in the Bronx.

**Playgrounds**  Playgrounds in the parks are all that many New York City youngsters ever know of the outdoors. The city has made an effort, therefore, to provide lots of play space and to make it state-of-the-art. The result is so successful that even country kids can't get enough of their fanciful swings and slides.

**Abingdon Square Park** (Bleecker and Hudson Sts.), where West Village kids slide, climb, and play in the sandbox, is a friendly place, although perhaps not sophisticated enough to keep older brothers and sisters entertained.

**Carl Schurz Park** (near East End Ave. and 84th St.) offers play equipment on two green blocks within sight of the East River esplanade.

**Central Park** has benefited from an active playground-building program, creating "adventure playgrounds" full of slides, bridges, bars, swings, towers, and tunnels, usually carpeted with sand or soft rubber matting and often cooled in summer by sprinklers and running water. Playgrounds can be found along Fifth Avenue at 67th Street, 71st Street, 77th Street, 85th Street, and 95th Street. Along Central Park West, they're at 68th Street, 81st Street, 85th Street, 93rd Street, and 100th Street. The large Heckscher playground, mid-park at 62nd Street, has been designed expressly for toddlers.

**John Jay Park** (off York Ave. near 77th St.), very big and busy, offers great swinging bridges, curving slides, a sprinkler, and a big sandbox.

**Pearl Street Playground** (Fulton, Water, and Pearl Sts.) is a postmodern playground with a couple of giant-size and multi-colored capitals and a wall of glass blocks.

**Playground for All Children** (Flushing Meadows-Corona Park, Corona Ave. and 111th St., Queens, tel. 718/699–8283) is a 3½-acre playground that puts handicapped and able-bodied children on an equal footing. Nature trails feature plaques in Braille as well as print, sandboxes are at wheelchair height, swings have extra-large seats and hand cords so swingers don't have to pump with their legs; there's even a track for wheelchair racing.

**77th St. at Amsterdam Ave.**, a fanciful schoolyard park featuring a log castle, fortress, slides, and tire swings was built by parents and designed by kids working with a professional playground designer.

**Zoos**　The **Central Park Zoo** is pleasant to visit for all ages, although smaller citizens may get more of a kick out of the whimsical **Children's Zoo.** The **Bronx Zoo** is more satisfying than Central Park's for older kids with a yen for jungle cats and other huge beasts; the Bronx Zoo's **Children's Zoo** area, which charges an additional admission, is a well-planned educational layout. The **New York Aquarium** is a perennial favorite with children; leave time for a walk along **Coney Island** boardwalk as well.

# 7 Performing Arts

With heads clear of the week's concerns, audiences are ready to settle in and appreciate some of the finer things that New York has in such abundance.

Saturday has always been a big day on New York's arts scene, with as many as two evening performances at most theaters and concert halls. And while Sunday may be a day of rest for some performers, there are more than enough matinees scheduled to take up the slack. And there are movies, lectures, readings, comedy, jazz, and much more. Come summer, the city's artists take to the open spaces, joining in special music festivals or playing sporadic gigs in the parks. And because Sunday means that strollers are out and about, street entertainers turn up on practically every corner—Michael Jackson imitators, barbershop quartets, mimes and jugglers, and performance artists doing things that defy description.

**How to Find Out What's On**    The major local publications are an excellent source of information. Consult the *Village Voice, New York Newsday*, the *New Yorker, 7 Days*, the *New York Observer*, the *New York Times* (particularly Friday's "Weekend" section), or the Cue listings at the back of *New York* magazine. Several additional publications covering specific arts are noted below as well.

One fabulous source of information is the Theatre Development Fund's **New York City on Stage** hotline (tel. 212/587–1111). Callers using touch-tone phones can choose from a menu that includes theater, dance and music, children's entertainment, and events accepting the TDF voucher. With a little patience you can get not only listings but also lively descriptions of, for example, a particular play's plot, cast, and crew. That goes equally for box office hits on Broadway and for obscure dance shows in church basements.

The other essential phone number to know is the **Department of Parks & Recreation's Events Hotline** (tel. 212/360–1333), which announces all kinds of goings-on in the parks a few days beforehand—music, dance, theater, circuses, and what have you. To plan further ahead, write for a copy of the complete Special Events Calendar (c/o City of New York Department of Parks & Recreation, The Arsenal, Central Park, New York, NY 10021, tel. 212/360–1309).

**Lincoln Center** has a hotline for current information about performances there (tel. 212/877–2011). Two other arts organizations publish valuable calendars: the **Lower Manhattan Cultural Council** (42 Broadway, New York, NY 10004) and the **Queens Council on the Arts** (161–04 Jamaica Ave., Jamaica, NY 11432, tel. 718/291–1100).

On weekdays, the New York Convention and Visitors Bureau can also supply information (2 Columbus Circle, tel. 212/397–8222 weekdays).

**Ticket Sources**    *Box Offices*    This is almost always the best source: Ticket sellers there make it their business to know their theaters and don't mind pointing out on a chart where you'll be seated. On Sundays, box offices open around noon, though it's often advisable to buy your tickets before the day of the performance. For advance purchase, send the box office a certified check or money order, several alternate dates, and a self-addressed stamped envelope.

If you're charging tickets, call **Tele-Charge** (tel. 212/239–6200), **Teletron** (tel. 212/246–0102), **Hit-Tix** (tel. 212/564–8038), or

Ticketmaster (tel. 212/307–7171)—newspaper ads will specify which you should use for any given show. A $1–3 surcharge will be added to the total, and your tickets will be waiting for you at the theater's box office.

*TKTS*   The Theatre Development Fund's venerable TKTS operation in Duffy Square (Broadway and 47th St.) sells day-of-performance tickets for Broadway plays and some dance and other performing arts events at half price, plus a $1.50 surcharge. For Sunday matinee and evening performances, go to the booth between noon and 8 PM, check out what's offered on the boards up front, and then wait in line. TKTS accepts only cash or traveler's checks—no credit cards.

There are also TKTS booths at 2 World Trade Center and near the intersection of Court and Montague streets in Brooklyn Heights. To buy tickets for Sunday performances at the downtown TKTS, visit the booth between 11 and 5:30 on Saturday; in Brooklyn (for matinees only), Saturday between 11 and 3:30. The lines at these TKTS out-stations are shorter than those at Duffy Square, though the offerings are sometimes limited.

*Bryant Park Music*   What TKTS does for the theater, the ticket booth in Bryant
*and Dance*   Park, on 42nd Street between Fifth and Sixth avenues, does for
*Half-Price Ticket*   music and dance events, including those at Lincoln Center,
*Booth*   Carnegie Hall, City Center, and even a few nightclubs (tel. 212/382–2323 for recorded information from noon on).

*TDF Vouchers*   If you attend a great number of arts events, it will definitely pay to call the Theatre Development Fund (weekdays only; tel. 212/221–0885) to get TDF vouchers, which cost $3 apiece. When redeemed at the box office, the vouchers are worth substantial discounts off the cost of a ticket for dance, theater, and musical events at non-Broadway theaters. It's a good way to see up-and-coming groups at modest cost, and they will also occasionally buy you admittance to performances by better-known companies as well.

# Theater

Of the approximately 250 legitimate theaters in New York, a good many schedule Sunday performances—matinees on Broadway and matinees and evening performances Off- and Off-Off-Broadway. Sundays are the end of a long week for actors and stagehands (Mondays are usually their day of rest), but the quality of the production never slides. If anything, everyone works even harder to win Sunday audiences, which are generally composed of dedicated theater goers. Lines at the TKTS discount tickets booth stretch around the block; under theater marquees, sidewalks buzz with conversation. Serious drama students and working actors catch the evening performance when they're doing a matinee or the matinee if their show goes on at 8.

## Broadway

To most people, American theater is epitomized by Broadway, that region of extremes centered on Times Square. Despite the sleazy elements that surround and occasionally invade the theater district, it's a vibrant place. The neighborhood is at its most benign on Sunday afternoons.

Historically, the nation's entertainment capital was once composed of almost 50 theaters that sprang up around Times Square between 1899 and 1925. Many of those showplaces have been gutted or turned into movie houses; those that remain as legitimate theaters are squeezed into an area bounded by 41st and 53rd streets between Sixth and Ninth avenues. In addition to the wonderful old jewel-box playhouses, you'll find **Theater Row,** six intimate Off-Broadway houses on the south side of 42nd Street between Ninth and Tenth avenues, and **Restaurant Row** (46th St. between 8th and 9th Aves.), where critics, actors, directors, playwrights, and regular starstruck Joes come to dine before and after the show.

Your major challenge will probably be choosing one show from the riches offered. Consider first the long-running smashes, but don't overlook a chance to catch tomorrow's hits and today's flops. Remember, there's something special about seeing a show in previews or seeing a negatively reviewed play before it bites the dust.

**What's Playing**    Broadway is well covered by *The New York Times;* the Friday "Weekend" section notes ticket availability for the weekend, while the Sunday "Arts and Leisure" section covers theater in depth. *Theater Week* and *Stages,* available at many newsstands, canvass Broadway offerings in a more concentrated fashion, with the latter providing samplings of what the critics have said about each show. The League of New York Theatres and Producers publishes a weekly *Broadway Theatre Guide,* available in hotels and from the visitors bureau. One of the best information sources is *Playbill,* which wraps generic Broadway lore around each play's own program notes; it's distributed by ushers at the theater when you see a play, but contains information about other productions as well.

**Tickets**    Discounts on name-brand, long-running shows (*Cats, A Chorus Line,* and the like) are often available if you can lay your hands on a couple of "two-fers"—discount ticket coupons found on cash registers around town, in line at TKTS, at the New York Convention and Visitors Bureau, and the office of the **Hit Show Club** (630 9th Ave., 9th floor, tel. 212/581–4211, open weekdays 9:15–3:45).

Ticket clubs designed to serve frequent theater goers are also helpful. **Advance Entertainment New York** (tel. 212/239–2570), essentially a telemarketing firm whose phones are manned by actors and actresses, provides constant updates on what's hot and gets tickets for members, sometimes at a discount and with special attention to the location of the seats. Membership costs $85 annually; the service can also be used on a onetime, no-obligation-to-join basis, with a $3 per ticket service charge for nonmembers. Another well-known ticket group is **Stubs Preview Club** (tel. 212/398–8370, $35 a year), which specializes in preview showings.

If you're willing to pay top dollar, try a ticket broker. (A $45 ticket will cost about $60 from the typical broker.) Try **Golden/Leblang Ticket Service** (tel. 212/944–8910; open Sun. 9–3) and **American Theatre Service** (tel. 212/581–6660; open Sun. 10–5).

**Broadway**    **Ambassador** (215 W. 49th St., tel. 212/239–6200).
**Theaters**    **Belasco** (111 W. 44th St., tel. 212/239–6200).
**Booth** (222 W. 45th St., tel. 212/239–6200).
**Broadhurst** (235 W. 44th St., tel. 212/239–6200).

**Broadway** (1681 Broadway at 53rd St., tel. 212/239–6200).
**Brooks Atkinson** (256 W. 47th St., tel. 212/719–4099).
**Circle in the Square** (235 W. 50th St., tel. 212/239–6200).
**Cort** (138 W. 48th St., tel. 212/239–6200).
**Criterion Center** (1530 Broadway at 45th St., tel. 212/239–6200).
**Edison** (240 W. 47th St., tel. 212/302–2302).
**Ethel Barrymore** (243 W. 47th St., tel. 212/239–6200).
**Eugene O'Neill** (230 W. 49th St., tel. 212/246–0102).
**46th Street** (226 W. 46th St., tel. 212/221–1211).
**Gershwin** (222 W. 46th St., tel. 246–0102).
**Helen Hayes** (240 W. 44th St., tel. 212/944–9450).
**Imperial** (249 W. 45th St., tel. 212/239–6200).
**John Golden** (252 W. 45th St., tel. 212/239–6200).
**Lincoln Center's Vivian Beaumont and Mitzi E. Newhouse** (W. 62nd–66th Sts., Columbus–Amsterdam Aves., tel. 212/362–7600).
**Longacre** (220 W. 48th St., tel. 212/239–6200).
**Lunt-Fontanne** (205 W. 46th St., tel. 212/575–9200).
**Lyceum** (149 W. 45th St., tel. 212/239–6200).
**Majestic** (247 W. 44th St., tel. 212/239–6200).
**Marquis** (Broadway at 46th St., tel. 212/246–0102).
**Martin Beck** (302 W. 45th St., tel. 212/246–0102).
**Minskoff** (200 W. 45th St., tel. 212/246–0102).
**Music Box** (239 W. 45th St., tel. 212/239–6200).
**Nederlander** (208 W. 41st St., tel. 212/921–8000).
**Neil Simon** (250 W. 52nd St., tel. 212/757–8646).
**Palace** (1564 Broadway at 47th St., tel. 212/530–8200).
**Plymouth** (236 W. 45th St., tel. 212/236–6200).
**Ritz** (225 W. 48th St., tel. 212/246–0102).
**Royale** (242 W. 45th St., tel. 212/239–6200).
**St. James** (246 W. 44th St., tel. 212/246–0102).
**Shubert** (225 W. 44th St., tel. 239–6200).
**Virginia** (245 W. 52nd St., tel. 212/977–9370).
**Winter Garden** (1634 Broadway at 50th St., tel. 212/239–6200).

## Off- and Off-Off-Broadway

Off- and Off-Off-Broadway, Sundays bring matinees at 2 or 3 and evening performances at 7 or 7:30—and there are usually plenty of seats (though this depends entirely on the kind of notices the play is getting from the press and the public).

As Broadway ticket prices climb and the hit mentality takes over, Off-Broadway, which was the 1930s' reaction to Broadway frivolity, is less and less avant-garde. Instead, it's a good place to catch Broadway smashes in the making (like *A Chorus Line*, which opened at the Public Theater, or Wendy Wasserstein's *The Heidi Chronicles*, which first appeared at Playwrights Horizons). Major Off-Broadway enclaves are along Theatre Row—on 42nd Street between Ninth and Tenth avenues—and in the Village, though theaters turn up in out-of-the-way spots all across the municipal map, from Coney Island to Columbia Heights.

The experimental spirit also thrives Off-Off-Broadway, a child of the '60s, in legions of small companies devoted to theater and, on its cutting edge, performance art.

**What's Playing** The beyond-Broadway theater scene is especially well covered by the *Village Voice*, in its helpful "Choices" section. The

League of New York Theatres and Producers' weekly *Broadway Theatre Guide* includes Off-Broadway entries as well.

**Tickets**   Some smaller theaters handle their own ticket sales, either by phone or at the box office. Call ahead if going in person, since hours can be erratic. In addition, about 30 of the Off- and Off-Off-Broadway theaters share **Ticket Central** (416 W. 42nd St., tel. 212/279–4200). Normally, Off- and Off-Off-Broadway ticket prices range from $8 to $25.

Discounted tickets are also available. The **TKTS** booth in Duffy Square (47th St. and Broadway) frequently handles Off-Broadway shows. The **Public Theater** (*see* listing below) regularly sets aside tickets for sale at a discount through its Quiktix program. Quiktix go on sale at 6 PM for Sunday night performances and at 1 PM for matinees, but lines form early—sometimes as early as 2 PM for a popular evening performance.

**Theaters to Watch**   **Theater Row,** a collection of houses of 100 seats or fewer on the downtown side of 42nd Street between Ninth and Tenth avenues, is consistently the home of some very good theatrical experiences. Theaters here include **Harold Clurman Theatre** (412 W. 42nd St., tel. 212/695–5429), **Samuel Beckett Theatre** (410 W. 42nd St., tel. 212/594–2828), **Douglas Fairbanks Theatre** (432 W. 42nd St., tel. 212/239–4321), **Intar Hispanic American Arts Center** (420 W. 42nd St., tel. 212/695–6134), and the **Nat Horne Theatre** (440 W. 42nd St., tel. 212/736–7128). Others scattered on the outskirts of the Theater District include **Lamb's Theatre Company** (130 W. 44th St., tel. 212/997–1780) and **Westside Arts Theatre** (407 W. 43rd St., tel. 212/541–8394).

**Cherry Lane** (38 Commerce St. one block south of Bleecker St., tel. 212/989–2020), one of the original Off-Broadway houses, was the site of American premieres of works by O'Neill, Beckett, Ionesco, and Albee. Productions here are generally of very sound quality.

**Circle in the Square Downtown** (159 Bleecker St., near Thompson St., tel. 212/254–6330), a venerable and warm little house is a close relative of the Circle in the Square uptown. Its offerings—often delightfully quirky—have included the recent "musical high school reunion," *Oil City Symphony*.

**Circle Repertory Company** (199 7th Ave. S at W. 4th St., tel. 212/807–1326), not to be confused with Circle in the Square, was founded 20 years ago by, among others, Lanford Wilson, whose plays have often premiered here. Its September-to-June season provides first looks at works by some of America's brightest young playwrights.

**Classic Stage Company** (136 E. 13th St., between Third and Fourth Aves., tel. 212/677–4210) often commissions fresh translations of classic plays and searches out directors with innovative approaches to well-known material. In recent years CSC has mounted acclaimed productions of works by Sophocles, Racine, Pinter, and Chekhov.

**Ensemble Studio Theater** (549 W. 52nd St., tel. 212/247–3405), a theatrical company in the truest sense of the word, has a stable group of actors, directors, and playwrights who collaborate on works-in-progress. EST actors, some of New York's best, are on view at an annual spring marathon of one-act plays.

**Equity Library Theatre** (Riverside Dr. at 103rd St., tel. 212/663–2028) mounts showcase productions—in particular, revivals of beloved musicals—cast with some of New York's best performers, who work here not for big bucks but simply for the exposure.

**Jewish Repertory Theater** (344 E. 14th St., tel. 212/505–2667) was started in 1974 by Ran Avni to produce plays about Jewish life today. *Crossing Delancey*, which became a major motion picture in 1988, started here as a play.

**La Mama E.T.C.** (74A E. 4th St., between 2nd and 3rd Aves., tel. 212/475–7710) grew from humble seeds—an East Village café opened by Ellen Stewart in 1961—into a grand avant-garde legend. La Mama, which has been called "the MGM of experimental theater," today stages productions in four different spaces: the Annex, First Floor Theater, Club, and La Galleria. La Mama alumni include Sam Shepard, Bette Midler, Andy Warhol, Nick Nolte, and Meatloaf.

**Mabou Mines** (performing in locations throughout the city, with administrative offices at 150 1st Ave., tel. 212/473–0559) numbers director Lee Breuer, composer Philip Glass, and actor David Warrilow among its original members. Their trademarks are the innovative use of stage technology and explorations (some call them "deconstructions") of Samuel Beckett texts.

**Manhattan Punch Line** (Judith Anderson Theatre, 422 W. 42nd St., tel. 212/279–4200) has been devoted to comedy since its founded by an ex-standup comedian ten years ago. Productions include revivals of American comedy classics and an annual festival of new one-act plays.

**Manhattan Theatre Club** (City Center, 131 W. 55th St., tel. 212/645–5848 or 212/581–7907) was started in the mid-1970s by actress Lynne Meadow, then fresh out of Yale School of Drama and just 25. The theater went on to feed *Ain't Misbehavin'*, *Mass Appeal*, and *Crimes of the Heart* to the Broadway stage and continues to produce some of New York's most serious, talked-about plays.

**Musical Theatre Works** (Theatre at St. Peter's Church, 54th St. and Lexington Ave., tel. 212/677–0040 or 212/688–6022), an alternative to the pricey Broadway musical stage, gives audiences a peek at the new works of developing book writers, composers, and lyricists.

**New Theatre of Brooklyn** (465 Dean St., Brooklyn, tel. 718/230–3366), housed in a converted storefront off Flatbush Avenue (near Park Slope), offers New York premieres of unusual but not always newly written plays.

**New York Theatre Workshop** (Perry Street Theatre, 31 Perry St. west of Seventh Ave S,tel. 212/302–7737) launches seldom-produced plays from as far afield as Australia. Its New Directors Series gives young talents a chance to test their wings.

**Pan Asian Repertory** (Apple Corps Theatre, 336 W. 20th St., tel. 212/505–5655) is dedicated to giving stage space to Asian-American artists and plays. Recent seasons included an adaptation of Shakespeare's *Macbeth* set in medieval Japan.

**Playwrights Horizons** (416 W. 42nd St., tel. 212/279–4200), one of the first Theater Row stages, seeks to develop new American playwrights through readings, workshops, and full-scale productions. Stephen Sondheim's *Sunday in the Park with George* and Wendy Wasserstein's *The Heidi Chronicles* both got lift-offs here.

**Promenade Theater** (2162 Broadway, tel. 212/580–1313), on the near Upper West Side, has produced such celebrated works as Sam Shepard's *A Lie of the Mind*, the musical *Godspell*, and Athol Fugard's *The Road to Mecca*. The Promenade is also the

home of Theaterworks/USA (a children's theater company) and
Second Stage (tel. 212/787-8302), which re-produces recent
plays that may not have been given a fair shake the first time
around.

**Provincetown Playhouse** (133 MacDougal St., between W. 3rd
and W. 4th Sts., tel. 212/477-5048) premiered the works of
Eugene O'Neill when he was still unknown. Its current offerings are generally intriguing.

**Public Theater** (425 Lafayette St. off 8th St. and Astor Pl., tel.
212/598-7100), founded by Joseph Papp, is housed in a landmark building that once served as the Astor Library. The
Public is in the midst of a six-year, 36-play Shakespeare Marathon featuring lots of big-name actors. Sunday matinees are at
3 (October–June). Offerings also include new, somewhat experimental plays; an alternative film series; and a Latin arts
festival (August). Tickets may be hard to come by, so plan
ahead.

**Repertorio Español** (Gramercy Arts Theatre, 138 E. 27th St.,
tel. 212/889-2850), an award-winning Spanish arts theater, often mounts productions in Spanish.

**Ridiculous Theatrical Company** (Charles Ludlam Theater, 1
Sheridan Sq., near W. 4th St., tel. 212/691-2271) endures despite the death of its inspired founder, Charles Ludlam, in
1988. The company has been around since 1972, honing its
unique performance style, a blend of classical acting and high
camp.

**Riverside Shakespeare** (West Park Presbyterian Church, 165
W. 86th St., tel. 212/877-6810) has been performing the Bard's
works and plays inspired by them for more than a decade, here
and in parks throughout the five boroughs.

**Roundabout Theatre Company** (100 E. 17th St., tel. 212/420-
1360) began more than 25 years ago in a Chelsea supermarket
basement and now boasts the largest continuing membership of
any New York theater institution. Modern classics (featuring
stars of the New York stage) are the Roundabout's staples—
with a special emphasis on the works of G. B. Shaw.

**Sullivan Street Playhouse** (181 Sullivan St., between Houston
and Bleecker Sts., tel. 212/674-4573) continues to host **The
Fantastiks,** the world's longest-running musical.

**Theater for the New City** (155 1st Ave., between 9th and 10th
Sts., tel. 212/254-1109), another theatrical experimenter with
its roots in the 1960s, now offers 30 to 40 productions a year (on
Sunday, generally, at 7, 8, and 10).

**Vineyard Theater** (Irving Dimson Theatre, 108 E. 15th St., tel.
212/832-1002), which relocated to brand new digs in 1989, is a
small, nonprofit theater founded by a former cabaret singer.
This theater is strong on new and revived musicals; *Lady Day
at Emerson's Bar & Grill,* based on the life of Billie Holiday,
was a 1985 Vineyard hit.

**The Wooster Group** (Performing Garage, 33 Wooster St. at
Grand St., tel. 212/966-3651), an experimental theater
founded in the 1960s, is a SoHo pioneer composed of a small
group of artists who collaborate for long periods of time on each
piece.

**WPA Theatre** (519 W. 23rd St., tel. 212/206-0523) produces neglected American classics by playwrights, such as Tennessee
Williams and Lillian Hellman, and new, realistic American
plays. Six recent WPA offerings have become feature films, including *Key Exchange* and *Steel Magnolias.*

**York Theatre Company** (Church of the Heavenly Rest, 2 E. 90th

St., tel. 212/534–5366) is another good place to sample revivals of notable musicals, such as Stephen Sondheim's *A Little Night Music* and *Sweeney Todd*.

# Music

To music lovers, New York opens like a colossal Stradivarius case. Weekends resound with offerings at the major concert halls, downtown studios, parks, piers, and museums; the smoke even clears at some of the city's clubs, when nocturnal musicians rise and shine for jazz brunch—a distinctively Sunday institution. Although getting tickets to hot events may still be tough, the atmosphere around box offices mellows on Sunday; people waiting in line relax and even turn to their fellows to chat.

Audiences in New York are extremely diverse, which means that there are musical events to satisfy the most eclectic tastes, from classical symphonies to cutting-edge New Music experimenters to ethnic performers flown in from the far corners of the globe.

**What's Playing** The Friday *New York Times* "Weekend" section includes a Weekender listing and the "Sounds Around Town" and "Pop/Jazz" columns, in which one of the paper's critics takes a closer look at some current musical phenomenon. On Sunday, the *Times*'s "Arts and Leisure" section features longer "think pieces" on orchestras, opera stars, cabaret performers, composers, jazz, etc. For New Music and the avant-garde scene, hunt down a copy of *Ear* magazine.

Record and music shops, such as cavernous **Tower Records** (692 Broadway, on the corner of 4th St., tel. 212/505–1500 and 1965 Broadway at 66th St., tel. 212/799–2500) and **Bleecker Bob's Golden Oldies** (118 W. 3rd St., between Sixth Ave. and MacDougal St., tel. 212/475–9677), serve as music information centers, as do the city's radio stations.

**Tickets** Most major music halls have their own box offices. The **Music and Dance Half-Price Ticket Booth** in Bryant Park is open on Sundays noon–6.

With membership in Channel 13, New York's public television station, comes a handy "Ticket to the Arts" card, making you eligible for 15–33% discounts at approximately 40 arts locales around the city, including many concert halls. Public radio station WNYC has a similar discount scheme, the WNYC Artscard.

## Orchestral Music

New York is the home of several major orchestras and a principal stopping point for tours by out-of-town musicians, so every day of the week is lively on the concert scene.

**Major Concert Halls** **Avery Fisher Hall** (Lincoln Center, 65th St. and Broadway, tel. 212/874–2424) brings to its stage the world's great musicians, and to its boxes the black-tie-and-diamond-tiara set. Designed by Max Abramovitz and opened in 1961 as Philharmonic Hall, it underwent a $5-million renovation in 1976, to improve acoustics, resulting in a 2,700-seat auditorium that follows the classic European rectangular pattern. Although the September-to-

May season does not include Sunday, in summertime the Mostly Mozart and the Classical Jazz Festival series are very much in evidence on the seventh day of the week. The box office is open noon–5:45 on Sundays.

**Brooklyn Academy of Music** (30 Lafayette Ave., Brooklyn, tel. 718/636–4100) is America's oldest performing arts center, founded in 1859, though the present building dates from 1908. Isadora Duncan did her famous scarf dance here, Sarah Bernhardt wrung out one of her last Camilles, and Enrico Caruso suffered the throat hemorrhage that almost ended his career. These days, the Brooklyn Philharmonic performs in BAM's 2,000-seat Opera House, and autumn's Next Wave Festival has put Brooklyn at the center of the avant-garde map.

**Carnegie Hall** (57th St. and 7th Ave., tel. 212/247–7800) has witnessed the pianist Ignace Paderewski being attacked by crowds clamoring for kisses and locks of hair, a young Leonard Bernstein triumphing in his 1943 debut as a stand-in for New York Philharmonic conductor Bruno Walter, Jack Benny playing duets with Isaac Stern, and the Beatles taking New York by storm in 1964. In preparation for a 100th-birthday celebration in the 1990–91 season, a multi-million-dollar renovation in 1986 left this international musical landmark in better acoustical and physical shape than ever—not just the Main Concert Hall but the small Weill Recital Hall, where bright young stars make their New York debuts.

**City Center** (131 W. 55th St., tel. 212/581–7907) has a large auditorium under its eccentric, tiled Spanish dome, built in 1924 by the Ancient and Accepted Order of the Mystic Shrine, saved from demolition by Fiorello La Guardia, and recently renovated to sparkling splendor. City Center hosts music of all kinds, lots of dance, opera, and occasional Gilbert and Sullivan forays.

**Colden Center for the Performing Arts** (Kissena Blvd. and the Long Island Expressway, Queens, tel. 718/793–8080), a part of the Queens College complex, brings the music of the Queens Philharmonic and others to the city's largest borough.

**Symphony Space** (2537 Broadway, tel. 212/864–5400) held an ice skating rink, wrestling ring, and movie theater before volunteers from a drug rehabilitation center converted it to a concert space. Metropolitan Opera musical director James Levine has called it "a West Sider's dream," with its fine acoustics and location in one of the city's musical hubs. Everyone from Itzhak Perlman to the Wretched Refuse String Band has appeared here, and in recent years, Symphony Space has become a major venue for dance and New Music as well.

**Town Hall** (123 W. 43rd St., tel. 212/840–2824), built in 1921, was designed by the renowned architectural firm McKim, Mead & White. This 1,500-seat midtown music enclave lets everyone feel close to the stage; in the words of *The New Yorker*, "the acoustics are excellent; the look is right." Its bill is wide and a touch eccentric, with classical entries, ethnic sounds, occasional chamber revivals of dusty musical comedies, and downtown-style New Wave.

## Smaller Ensembles

Sunday and chamber music are one of those happy combinations, like pizza and Friday night. Metropolitan-area concert halls specializing in chamber music echo with applause nearly every Sunday of the year, greeting performances by such groups as the Ad Hoc Players, An die Musik, Beaux Arts Trio, Chamber Music Society of Lincoln Center, Juilliard String Quartet, New York Chamber Orchestra, Orpheus Chamber Ensemble, the Pierrot Consort, Prism Chamber Orchestra, and Speculum Musicae.

**Chamber Music and More**

**Aaron Davis Hall** (City College, W. 134th St., tel. 212/307–7420) hosts the way-uptown scene of iconoclastic musical events staged by the World Music Institute, as well as a variety of classical concerts.

**Alice Tully Hall** (Lincoln Center, 65th St. at Broadway, tel. 212/874–6770), an intimate "little white box" with seats for 1,096, is considered as acoustically perfect as concert houses get. It is the home of the Chamber Music Society of Lincoln Center, founded 20 years ago by William Schuman, Alice Tully, and Charles Wadsworth—a group that almost single-handedly put chamber music on the Manhattan artistic map. Sunday performances are at 5; the box office is open 11–7 on Sundays.

**Bargemusic** (Fulton Ferry Landing, Brooklyn, tel. 718/624–4061) has chamber music bubbling out of an old Erie Lackawanna coffee barge tethered along the East River, on Sunday afternoons at 4.

**Donnell Library Center** (20 W. 53rd St., tel. 212/621–0618). Though most of the libraries in the municipal system are closed on Sundays, this one, in the heart of midtown, hosts a chamber concert series that starts at 2:30. Donnell programs are free and the season runs from September to May in the library's capacious Bankers Trust Company Auditorium.

**The Kitchen** (512 W. 19th St., tel. 212/255–5793) has been, since 1976, a center for the avant-garde arts, including experiments in New Music.

**La Mama La Galleria** (6 E. 1st St., tel. 212/505–2476) is a new feature of the La Mama complex, famed home of the experimental arts. Sunday brings a composer series at 4 featuring the likes of Philip Fraser with the 12 Tone Funk Orchestra.

**Merkin Concert Hall** (Abraham Goodman House, 129 W. 67th St., tel. 212/362–8719), one of the city's newer auditoriums, is developing a reputation nearly as fine as that of its near neighbors at Lincoln Center. Lots of famous soloists claim the stage at this 457-seat hall, which also occasionally hosts the New York Philharmonic Ensemble, Mendelssohn String Quartet, and the Boston Camerata.

**92nd Street Y** (1395 Lexington Ave. at 92nd St., tel. 212/427–4410) is an East Side magnet for music, as the curtain goes up in its Kaufman Concert Hall every Sunday at 3. The Y has been devoted to cultural enrichment since the 1930s, when it welcomed a young dancer named Martha Graham; in the 1960s, Joan Baez came here with her guitar; and its Poetry Center has offered New Yorkers a chance to hear writers such as W. H. Auden, Tennessee Williams, and Dylan Thomas. The Y's 44-piece Chamber Symphony, born in 1977, is considered one of the city's very best abbreviated orchestras.

**Performance Space 122, or P.S. 122** (150 1st Ave. on the corner of 9th St., tel. 212/477–5288), called by the *Village Voice* "the petri dish of downtown culture," was converted from an old elementary school once attended by comedian George Burns. Concerts, exhibits, and productions come and go quickly, but seldom fail in freshness. Look especially for P.S. 122's annual marathon, in which scores of dazzling downtown musicians and artists take part.

**R.A.P.P. Arts Center** (220 E. 4th St., between Avenues A and B, tel. 212/529–5921), an East Village center for New Music, mounts the annual Bang on a Can Festival, showcasing avant-garde styles.

**Wave Hill** (675 W. 252nd St., the Bronx, tel. 212/601–7399), a historic estate and garden with smashing views across the Hudson, holds musicales by the Bronx Arts Ensemble and other groups on Sundays at 3.

**Weill Recital Hall** (Carnegie Hall, 57th St. and 7th Ave., tel. 212/247–7800), formerly the Carnegie Recital Hall, was renamed and renovated in 1986, providing this intimate 268-seat auditorium with its own entrance on 57th Street. Three acoustic chandeliers imported from Holland warm up the sounds here, making it excellent for chamber music. The city's most promising young artists choose it for debuts; soloists, quartets, jazz, and early music are all on the Sunday calendar.

**Winter Garden Atrium** (World Financial Center, Battery Park City, tel. 212/945–0505) frequently offers new works soon to air in larger halls and a "Meet the Moderns" series, among other events. The setting couldn't be prettier: an airy plaza full of polished granite and Italian marble, where 16 palms reach skyward into the barrel-vaulted glass roof. Most Sunday concerts and performances are at 2 and are free.

**The Conservatories**   If you're interested in hearing youthful stars-to-be, check into the following: **Juilliard** recitals, held at Alice Tully Hall (tel. 212/874–6770), Paul Recital Hall (144 W. 66th St., tel. 212/874–7515), and the Juilliard Theater (155 W. 65th St., 212/799–5000); **Manhattan School of Music** (Broadway at 122nd St., tel. 212/749–2802); **Mannes College of Music** (150 W. 85th St., tel. 212/580–0212); **Bloomingdale House of Music** (323 W. 108th St., tel. 212/663–6021); and the **Brooklyn Conservatory of Music** (58 7th Ave., Park Slope, Brooklyn, tel. 718/622–3300).

**Museum Concerts**   **Asia Society** (725 Park Ave. at 70th St., tel. 212/288–6400) features Oriental musicians performing at various dates throughout the year.

**Brooklyn Museum** (200 Eastern Pkwy., Brooklyn, tel. 718/638–5000) hosts occasional chamber concerts and New Music events, as well as a Sunday jazz festival in August. A new auditorium will open in 1990.

**The Cloisters** (Fort Tryon Park, tel. 212/923–3700), the celebrated medieval branch of the Metropolitan Museum of Art, often imports early music and Renaissance music groups. Sunday events are usually at 1:30 and 3, and during the Christmas season the Waverly Consort traditionally holds forth.

**The Frick Collection** (1 E. 70th St., tel. 212/288–0700), one of the city's most splendid little museums, hosts Sunday concerts from October to May. Tickets to these are free but much in demand. Write to the Frick exactly three Mondays before the concert date, requesting up to two tickets; if they're available, they'll come to you by mail.

**Guggenheim Museum** (5th Ave. at 89th St., tel. 212/360–3500) has an interesting Works in Process series, showcasing excerpts from pieces the composer or performance artist is still fine-tuning.

**Jewish Museum** (5th Ave. at 92nd St., tel. 212/860–1888) offers a Sunday program of events that includes classical, pop, and ethnic music.

**Metropolitan Museum of Art** (5th Ave. at 82nd St., tel. 212/879–

5500) offers occasional Sunday classical music concerts at its Grace Rainey Rogers Auditorium.

**Museum of the City of New York** (1220 5th Ave., tel. 212/534–1672) sometimes holds Sunday concerts amid its collection of artifacts from 300 years of New York history.

**Queens Museum** (Flushing Meadows, Queens, tel. 718/592–5555) offers chamber music and jazz on Sunday afternoons, free with paid admission to the museum.

**Studio Museum of Harlem** (144 W. 125th St., tel. 212/864–4500) showcases the works of African-American painters, photographers, and sometimes, musicians.

**Music in Churches** Some of the city's best music takes place every Sunday in its churches—sometimes as part of worship services, sometimes at concerts or vespers held in mid- or late afternoon. A few institutions stand out; watch the newspapers for notices of concerts or call to have your name put on the mailing list.

**Cathedral of St. John the Divine** (112th St. and Amsterdam Ave., tel. 212/316–7540) has a lively musical program that includes weekly choral vespers by candlelight followed by an organ meditation.

**Chapel of the Intercession** (550 W. 155th St., tel. 212/690–3333) features the Emmy Award–winning Harlem Boys' Choir, with a repertoire that moves exuberantly between Vivaldi and Stevie Wonder.

**Church of the Transfiguration** (1 E. 29th St., tel. 212/684–6770) offers late afternoon choral vespers at which you can hear the fine Arnold Schwartz Memorial Organ, the only instrument in the city built by the Massachusetts firm of C. B. Fisk—the first modern American organ builder to abandon 20th-century electro-pneumatic works in favor of the mechanical key action and stop action of historic European instruments.

**Holy Trinity Lutheran Church** (Central Park West at 65th St., tel. 212/877–6815) has one of the most ambitious professional church music programs in the country, starring a Bach Vespers series from late fall through Easter. This remains the only place in the country where cantatas are regularly sung on the days of the liturgical calendar for which they were composed. The Holy Trinity Choir, soloists, and the Bach Orchestra, a resident professional chamber ensemble, perform. In winter, several Bach organ recitals star the church's three-manual 67-rank pipe organ.

**John Street United Methodist Church** (44 John St., tel. 212/269–0014) holds occasional concerts on Sundays.

**Madison Avenue Presbyterian Church** (921 Madison Ave., tel. 212/288–8920) features the St. Andrews Music Society, which has brought major choral works and chamber music to the community, sometimes with talented young soloists. Performances are usually at 4.

**Metropolitan Baptist Church** (151 W. 128th St., tel. 212/663–8990) presents soul-stirring gospel music.

**Riverside Church** (Riverside Dr. at 122nd St., tel. 212/222–5900) rings the 74 bells of the Laura Spelman Rockefeller Memorial Carillon in an hourlong concert every Sunday at 3 PM.

**St. Ann and the Holy Trinity Episcopal Church** (122 Pierrepont St., Brooklyn, tel. 718/834–8794) offers chamber concerts, Bach cantatas, plays, dance, film, and many other events in the Arts at St. Ann's series.

**St. Bartholomew's** (Park Ave. at 50th St., tel. 212/751–1616), home of the fifth largest organ in the Western Hemisphere, presents mid-afternoon concerts by visiting brass ensembles, choirs, opera companies, youth orchestras, organists, and other groups, as well as its own choir and chamber orchestra nearly every Sunday from fall through spring.

**St. Michael's Church** (225 W. 99th St., tel. 212/222–2700) features the Great Organ, a mechanical action instrument with fine, majestic sound, best heard during choral eucharists at 11 AM on the first and third Sundays of every month. The annual Christmas Festival of Lessons and Carols is modeled on the one held in King's College, Cambridge.

**St. Patrick's Cathedral** (5th Ave. at 50th St., tel. 212/753–2261) presents guest organists from New York and around the world every Sunday at 3:45. The choir at the 10:15 AM masses usually numbers at least 100.

**St. Peter's Lutheran Church** (Lexington Ave. at 54th St., tel. 212/753–4318) offers a lively program of jazz masses, vespers, and concerts.

**St. Thomas Church** (5th Ave. at 53rd St., tel. 212/757–7013) stars its celebrated boy's choir at choral evensong recitals most Sundays at 4.

**Washington Square Church** (135 W. 4th St., tel. 212/777–2528) has lively 11 AM Sunday services, thanks to its music director Paul Knopf, a professional jazz-gospel pianist.

## Opera

Although the celebrated Metropolitan Opera is dark on Sundays, the New York City Opera—which most critics agree is the livelier and more adventurous of the two—lights up on Sundays. Smaller opera companies fill the city's other halls, too, and vocal artists from all over the world consider New York *the* place to make an operatic debut.

**After Dinner Opera** (23 Stuyvesant St., between Second and Third Aves., tel. 212/477–6212) has eclectic offerings, produced in halls around town. Performances generally begin at 8 PM on Sundays.

**Amato Opera** (319 Bowery, on the corner of E. 2nd St., tel. 212/228–8200) performs at both its intimate 107-seat downtown house and in venues throughout the city. The season typically includes several classics (such as *The Marriage of Figaro* or *Cavalleria Rusticana*) and American premieres of rarely performed operas.

**Brooklyn Academy of Music** (30 Lafayette Ave., Brooklyn, tel. 718/636–4100), once the stage for all the world's great singers, has recently become active again in the field of opera. In 1988 BAM kicked off its Opera Project series with the Welsh National Opera's production of Verdi's *Falstaff* and a rare revival of Jean-Baptiste Lully's French Baroque *Atys*.

**Brooklyn Lyric Opera** (Hirsch Hall, Temple Ansche Chesed, 251 W. 100th St., Brooklyn, tel. 718/837–1176) boasts a 24-piece orchestra, professional leads, and lots of enthusiasm for a repertoire that includes *The Magic Flute* and *La Traviata*. At intermission singers mingle with the audience in the lobby, and during the summer a free performance is held at Brooklyn's Seaside Park.

**Brooklyn Opera Theater** (58 7th Ave., Brooklyn, 718/638–6563), a showcase for young singers, stages the works of Puccini and Verdi, occasionally in English.

**Carnegie Hall** (57th St. and 7th Ave., tel. 212/247–7800) frequently offers vocal programs in its main concert hall. Weill Recital Hall presents new faces in opera, ready to receive roses on the occasion of their New York debuts.

**City Center** (131 W. 55th St., tel. 212/581-7907) periodically hosts the New Sadler's Wells Opera (specializing in the Gilbert and Sullivan repertoire) and premieres works produced by the **New York Opera Repertory.**

**Light Opera of Manhattan** (Playhouse 91, 316 E. 91st St., tel. 212/831-2000), grounded in the works of Gilbert and Sullivan, also performs English, French, and Viennese light operas; the early American operas of Victor Herbert; and the operas of Sigmund Romberg and Rudolf Friml.

**New York City Opera** (Lincoln Center, Broadway at 65th St., tel. 212/870-5570) performs at the New York State Theater from mid-summer through fall, playing on summer Sundays at 1 and on autumn Sundays in both the afternoon and evening. In past years, the City Opera has widened its repertory to new works (*The Ballad of Baby Doe*, *The Turn of the Screw*), classic musicals (*Brigadoon*, *South Pacific*, and *The Pajama Game*), and time-tested favorites (*La Bohème*, *Madama Butterfly*, and *Rigoletto*). Foreign-language operas are supertitled in English, an ingenious way to help the audience follow complex opera plots.

**New York Gilbert and Sullivan Players** (251 W. 91st St., tel. 212/769-1000) performs the lively operettas of the English masters of the form. Its 1990 season includes *The Gondoliers* and *The Pirates of Penzance*, with Sunday matinees at 3.

**New York Grand Opera** (154 W. 57th St., Suite 125, tel. 212/245-8837) mounts free performances at Central Park's bandshell during the summer, with a full orchestra and professional singers.

**Opera Ebony** (2109 Broadway, Suite 1418, tel. 212/690-4100) was founded 17 years ago to provide exposure for the city's black singers. Last year Opera Ebony co-produced *Porgy and Bess* with the Finnish National Opera and took it on tour to Finland and the Soviet Union.

**Repertorio Español** (138 E. 27th St., tel. 212/889-2850) presents a diverse selection of performances in Spanish, ranging from comedic operas to flamenco dancing.

## Jazz

Somehow jazz seems mostly the province of late Saturday nights, when artists jam away until the wee hours, then pack up their instruments, go home, and conk out. But even jazz musicians can be persuaded to tune up whenever club managers and producers can bring in an audience, and increasingly that means Sunday. As a result, jazz erupts in clubs over brunch, in concert halls uptown and downtown, and at open-air festivals all over the city. Greenwich Village is the city's jazz hub, but you'll find everything from fusion to Dixieland playing at plenty of truly serendipitous sites.

**What's Playing?** On Friday, the *New York Times*'s "Sounds Around Town" column in the "Weekend" section can give you a sounding on the current scene, as can the *Village Voice*. Or stop by **Tower Records** (692 Broadway at 4th St., tel. 212/505-1500, and 1965 Broadway at 66th St., tel. 212/799-2500), where you'll find fliers about upcoming events and club passes stacked outside the doors.

**Tickets**    Jazz concerts and club gigs are usually priced at a fairly reasonable $5–$15, often several dollars less when you pay in advance. Sometimes you'll find there's no charge for the entertainment at the clubs, but a drink minimum instead. Call the box office to obtain tickets, and check whether the club honors credit cards (many don't). Club music regulars offer two further cautions: Once upon a time, one admission fee covered the cost of a whole evening of jazz, but an increasing number of proprietors charge by the set, meaning that after the music temporarily dies down, you'll be herded toward the door. And concerning the matter of start-up, remember that time is surprisingly elastic in the music world. The ad may say the artists begin at 7:30, but that could mean 8 or 8:30—so order a drink and be cool.

**Jazz Concert Spots**    **Apollo Theatre** (253 W. 125th St., tel. 212/749–5838), the legendary Harlem showcase for black musicians and entertainers, occasionally schedules Sunday shows.

**Brooklyn Academy of Music's Majestic Theater** (651 Fulton St., Brooklyn, tel. 718/636–4100 or 718/307–7171) presents a series of jazz concerts on Sundays at 4, featuring groups such as the Jimmy Smith and Dayton Selby trios.

**Brooklyn Museum** (200 Eastern Pkwy., Brooklyn, tel. 718/638–5000) hosts a series of Sunday jazz concerts in August.

**Carnegie Hall** (57th St. and 7th Ave., tel. 212/247–7800), decidedly at the tony (and thus, pricey) end of the New York jazz spectrum, schedules concerts with some of the greats in the field, such as vocalists Ella Fitzgerald or tenor saxophonists Sonny Rollins and Branford Marsalis.

**Classical Jazz** (Lincoln Center, Broadway at 65th St., tel. 212/874–6770) is a hot summertime jazz ticket, with performances at Alice Tully Hall. The *New York Times* called its recent Thelonius Monk tribute "intelligent and not pompous or over-ambitious." Harry Connick, Jr.; Dizzy Gillespie; and Benny Carter have appeared here.

**Harlem Jazz and Gospel Tours** (Harlem Your Way Tours Unlimited, Inc., 129 W. 130th St., tel. 212/690–1687) offers terrific Sunday gospel tours.

**Jazzmobile** (tel. 212/866–4900) is a kind of musical RV that rolls into parks (most often Riverside Park by Grant's Tomb) on balmy summer evenings.

**Jazz Piano at the Y** (92nd St. Y, 1395 Lexington Ave., tel. 212/427–4410) brings Dick Hyman to the stage, discussing jazz piano history and illustrating improvisational techniques with his colleague Derek Smith on summer Sundays at 4.

**JVC Jazz Festival** (tel. 212/787–2020), held in June and July, is the pinnacle of New York's jazz year. Concerts bring jazz greats to halls all over town, including Carnegie, Town, and Avery Fisher halls. For a complete schedule, write JVC Jazz Festival New York, Box 1169, Ansonia Station, New York, NY 10023.

**The Kitchen** (512 W. 19th St., Tel. 212/255–5793), which moved uptown from SoHo to become the Chelsea home of the downtown arts, includes jazz mixed with a little of the New Music and World Beat sounds. Sunday evening shows start at 8:30, September to May.

**Queens Jazz Festival** (Queens County Farm Museum, 73–50 Little Neck Pkwy., Floral Park, Queens, tel. 718/463–7700) brings out an enthusiastic audience of jazz aficionados who may see the likes of Doc Cheatham. The free concerts run Sunday evenings in July.

**Studio Museum of Harlem** (144 W. 125th St., tel. 212/864–4500) offers frequent Sunday concerts that showcase the work of African-American painters, photographers, and sometimes, jazz musicians.

**Symphony Space** (2537 Broadway at 95th St., tel. 212/864–5400) is a main stage for jazz uptown, particularly programs sponsored by the World Music Institute, a group dedicated to bringing music from the far corners of the globe to the Big Apple. The World Music Institute's season runs from September to June (for information call 212/206–1050); its annual blues festival generally takes place in winter.

**Town Hall** (123 W. 43rd St., tel. 212/840–2824) frequently books notables from the experimental jazz scene, such as the sax whiz and world music synthesizer John Zorn.

**Triplex Theater** (199 Chambers St., tel. 212/618–1980) programs some Sunday concerts that run the musical gamut from string-band blues to experimental jazz.

**Winter Garden Atrium** (World Financial Center, Battery Park City, tel. 212/945–0505) has a stylish, palm-lined plaza where the arts flourish. Sunday afternoons focus on the experimental, including jazz.

**Jazz Clubs** The following clubs have sets on Sunday nights.

**Angry Squire** (216 7th Ave., between 22nd and 23rd Sts., tel. 212/242–9066) offers comfortable booths and jazz on tap.

**The Blue Note** (131 W. 3rd St. off Sixth Ave., tel. 212/475–8592) is the quintessial jazz club—cramped, low-ceilinged, dim, and electric with musical excitement.

**Birdland** (2745 Broadway, tel. 212/749–2228) is way up on the West Side (at 105th Street), but still close to the Village at heart. You'll find lots of up-and-coming groups here, and the requisite thick atmosphere.

**Bradley's** (70 University Pl., between 9th and 10th Sts., tel. 212/228–6440) has brighter-than-usual lighting and, generally, jazz piano, for serious jazz/blues imbibers.

**Fortune Garden Pavilion** (209 E. 49th St., tel. 212/753–0101) mixes jazz and Chinese food for two shows on Sunday nights.

**Knickerbocker** (33 University Pl. at 9th St., tel. 212/228–8490) is particularly comfortable and spacious.

**The Knitting Factory** (47 E. Houston St., between Mott and Mulberry Sts., tel. 212/219–3055) looks seedy on the outside, but inside there's often fine avant-garde jazz.

**The Village Gate** (160 Bleecker St., on the corner of Thompson St., tel. 212/475–5120) is a classic Village jazz joint. The music starts at 9:30, and upstairs there's a cabaret/theater.

**The Village Vanguard** (178 7th Ave. S., between 11th and Perry St., tel. 212/255–4037), an old Thelonius Monk haunt in a smoky cellar, became a jazz mecca under the guidance of the late jazz impresario Max Gordon. It's pricey, but worth every penny.

**Zanzibar & Grill** (550 3rd Ave., between 36th and 37th Sts., tel. 212/779–0606) is the East Side's new option.

# Dance

On Sunday, dance lovers gravitate to the city's halls and theaters to enjoy performances by one or another of the city's 140 established dance companies. The wealth of dance events is nearly overwhelming, with everything from aquatic dance (by a troupe called Waterworks) to time-stepping (by the Jazz Tap

Ensemble) to virtuoso acrobatics (by the celebrated Pilobolus company) and beyond. Modern masters like Paul Taylor and Eliot Feld base their companies here as well, along with wonderful classical companies such as the Joffrey Ballet and the New York City Ballet, both of which perform on Sundays. And there are frequent visiting troupes as well: the Bolshoi, the Royal Danish, the Stuttgart, and others.

Two once-a-year events are well worth noting. The first is the spun-sugar-fest provided by the New York City Ballet's production of *The Nutcracker,* which runs from just after Thanksgiving until the first of the year with as many as three performances on Sundays. The Joffrey Ballet recently premiered its own production, for an earlier run. Whichever you choose, plan on ordering tickets well in advance for first choice of dates and seats.

Perhaps more important on the balletomane's calendar are the annual Workshop Performances of the School of American Ballet (tel. 212/877–0600), many of whose students eventually graduate into the New York City Ballet's prestigious corps de ballet. The Workshop Performances, which star the school's older students, are lots of fun; the dancers display impressive technique along with genuine enthusiasm.

**What's Playing?** The local press does a fine job documenting the dance scene. Particularly good is the respected and tireless Anna Kisselgoff, who reviews in the *New York Times.*

**Tickets** You can pay as little as $5 for dance tickets or as much as $45. Remember that in dance, seats close in do not always provide the best vantage point on the intricate patterns that emerge. For discounted tickets, try Bryant Park's Music and Dance booth or the TKTS booths; check whether TDF vouchers are valid for the dance events of your choice.

**Major Dance Venues** **Brooklyn Academy of Music** (30 Lafayette Ave., Brooklyn, tel. 718/636–4100) is increasingly a dance hub, hosting visiting talents such as Pina Bausch and the Central Ballet of China. An American Ballet Festival is held here each summer, and the Dance Africa festival takes place in June.

**City Center** (131 W. 55th St., tel. 212/581–7907) is where the moderns hold sway: the Dance Theatre of Harlem, Alvin Ailey American Dance Theater, Basel Ballet, and Lar Lubovitch, Trisha Brown, Merce Cunningham, and Paul Taylor.

**Dance Theater Workshop** (219 W. 19th St., tel. 212/691–6500) began 25 years ago as a choreographers' cooperative and now showcases some of the city's freshest dance talent. The DTW's year-long season, which includes not only dance but contemporary music, video, theater, and readings, features Sunday performances at 3.

**Danspace Project** (St. Mark's Church in the Bowery, 10th St. and 2nd Ave., tel. 212/674–8112) hosts a festival of avant-garde choreography from October to June.

**Joyce Theater** (175 8th Ave. at the corner of 19th St., tel. 212/242–0800), a former Art Deco movie theater in Chelsea, has become a major New York dance center. It's the permanent home of the Eliot Feld Ballet, founded 15 years ago by an upstart American Ballet Theater dancer, and hosts various other companies throughout the year.

**New York City Ballet** (New York State Theater, Lincoln Center, Broadway at 65th St., tel. 212/496–0600), now under the leadership of Peter Martins, was started by Lincoln Kirstein and George Balanchine in 1948. NYCB stresses the company's identity above that of individual ballet stars, though that hasn't stopped the public from making stars of prima ballerinas such as Patricia McBride, Kyra Nichols, and Darci Kistler. The 110-member company's repertory of 20th-century works is un-matched in the world. Seasons run from November to February and April to June, with Sunday performances at 1 and 7.

**P.S. 122** (150 1st Ave. at 9th St., tel. 212/477–5288) produces dance that borders on performance art. Meredith Monk occasionally cavorts here.

**Radio City Music Hall** (1260 6th Ave. at 50th St., tel. 212/757–3100) presents the Rockettes in the annual Christmas and Easter spectaculars, along with a schedule of visiting artists.

**Repertorio Español** (138 E. 27th St., tel. 212/889–2850) is often visited by the famed Spanish dancer Pilar Rioja.

**Riverside Dance Festival** (Riverside Church, 490 Riverside Dr., tel. 212/864–2929) stages classical, jazz, modern, and ethnic dance programs in its Gothic-style sanctuary.

**Symphony Space** (2537 Broadway at 95th St., tel. 212/864–5400) features ethnic dance on its eclectic calendar of events.

# Performance Art

When dance, drama, music, video, and other visual arts come together, the result is performance art, the enfant terrible of the avant-garde. New York is *the* place to sample the style, since it all started here—specifically downtown, in tattily chic, low-rent corners of SoHo, TriBeCa, and the Lower East Side. Audiences for performance art events are generally serious-minded yet hip—the kind of people who like to spend their days on the artistic cutting edge.

**BACA Downtown** (111 Willoughby St., Brooklyn, tel. 718/596–2222) is a true outpost of the avant-garde, featuring up-and-comers and imported acts.

**Brooklyn Academy of Music** (30 Lafayette Ave., Brooklyn, tel. 718/636–4100) has built its current reputation on its annual Next Wave Festival of performance works, running from October to December and featuring the performance art elite: Robert Wilson, Philip Glass, and Laurie Anderson, among others.

**Brooklyn Anchorage** (Cadman Plaza West, near the Fulton Ferry Landing) is the site for performance art extravaganzas inside the solid-looking expanse of the Brooklyn Bridge's eastern anchorage, which is actually hollow. In 1990 it will host portions of the Antoni Miraldo Honeymoon Project, a grand-scale, multimedia artistic event that celebrates the upcoming 500th anniversary of Christopher Columbus's discovery of the Americas. (For information on this event, call Creative Time, tel. 212/619–1955.)

**Franklin Furnace** (112 Franklin St., between Church St. and W. Broadway, tel. 212/925–4671) has, since 1976, supported off-center arts. Eric Bogosian, author/star of *Talk Radio*, got · his start here.

**The Kitchen** (512 W. 19th St., tel. 212/255–5793) is perhaps *the* Manhattan center for performance art, although video, dance, and music have their moments here, too.

**La Mama E.T.C.** (74A E. 4th St., between 2nd and 3rd Aves., tel. 212/475-7710), a producing facility perpetually in the avant-garde, devotes both its Club and First Floor Theater to performance art.

**P.S. 1** (46–01 21st St., Long Island City, Queens, tel. 718/784–2084), otherwise known as the Institute for Contemporary Art, features occasional theatrical events, with Sunday hours from noon to 6.

**P.S. 122** (150 1st Ave. on the corner of 9th St., tel. 212/477–5288), a vital force in downtown culture, usually has something experimental on tap. Look especially for its annual February marathon, starring scores of dazzling downtowners in several artistic disciplines.

# Readings and Lectures

Writers flock to New York, not only because it offers high-voltage stimulation but because it's one of the world's publishing centers. Lectures, workshops, and readings frequently staged at major auditoriums are attended by the literary and publishing big shots. For those interested in the written word, New York Sundays seldom fail to produce a reading or two—a little Sunday food for the soul.

**Academy of American Poets** (tel. 212/427–5665) organizes readings and lectures at sites around town, including the Guggenheim Museum and public libraries.

**Books & Co.** (939 Madison Ave., between 74th and 75th Sts., tel. 212/737–1450) is a literary bookshop where authors occasionally come to read.

**Endicott Bookstore** (450 Columbus Ave., between 81st and 82nd Sts., tel. 212/787–6300), an Upper West Side writer's haunt, hosts readings generally scheduled to accompany the publication of significant new works.

**Manhattan Theatre Club** (City Center, 131 W. 55th St., tel. 212/645–5848) offers a Writers in Performance series that has welcomed Salman Rushdie, Annie Dillard, Margaret Atwood, Ntozake Shange, and others.

**Metropolitan Museum of Art** (5th Ave. at 82nd St., tel. 212/570–3949), like most museums, has a heavy lecture schedule all day on Sundays. Artists such as David Hockney hold forth, as do the world's eminent art historians, on topics as varied as are the museum's collections.

**PEN** (568 Broadway, between Prince and Houston Sts., tel. 212/334–1660), the New York branch of a worldwide organization of poets, playwrights, essayists, editors, and novelists, frequently sponsors readings and workshops at locations around town.

**The Poetry Center** (92nd St. Y, 1395 Lexington Ave., between 91st and 92nd Sts., tel. 212/996–1100) for 50 years has been a prominent platform for poets, novelists, and playwrights. Sundays bring a popular Biographers and Brunch series.

**The Poetry Project** (St. Mark's Church in the Bowery, 2nd Ave. and 10th St., tel. 212/674–0910) frequently sponsors readings by poets.

# Comedy and Magic

On Sundays, most of the major comedy and magic clubs stand ready to welcome those looking for laughs or sleight of hand. Top comic acts are also traveling more and more often to Broadway and Off-Broadway, so check the theater listings as well.

**Boston Comedy Club** (82 W. 3rd St., between Thompson and Sullivan Sts., tel. 212/477–0622) provides a place for Beantown comedians to test their stuff in the Big Apple. Sunday shows are at 9 PM.

**Caroline's** (89 South St., Pier 17 at South Street Seaport, tel. 212/233–4900), one of Manhattan's original comedy clubs, is still going strong.

**Catch a Rising Star** (1487 1st Ave., between 77th and 78th Sts., tel. 212/794–1906), where Johnny Carson got his start and talent scouts still come to test the comic current, presents Sunday shows at 10 PM.

**Comedy Cellar** (117 MacDougal St., between W. 3rd and Bleecker Sts., tel. 212/254–3630), located for eight years beneath the Olive Tree Cafe, presents a bill that's a good barometer of who's hot. The host here is WNBC's Wild Bill Grundfest; Sunday show time is at 9 PM.

**The Comic Strip** (82nd St. and 2nd Ave., tel. 212/861–9386), with its corner-bar atmosphere and tiny, brilliantly lit stage, has a bill that's unpredictable but definitely worth checking out. The Sunday evening show starts at 9.

**Dangerfield's** (1118 1st Ave. at 61st St., tel. 212/593–1650) has been, since 1969, an important showcase for prime comic talent. It's frequently visited by its owner, Mr. D. himself. On Sundays, show time is at 9:15 PM.

**The Original Improvisation** (358 W. 44th St., tel. 212/765–8268) introduced lots of now-famous comedians, among them Richard Pryor and Robin Williams. Sundays at 9 PM you'll find audition night, so brush up your act and take a number.

**Rags to Riches** (226 E. 54th St., tel. 212/688–5577), a newcomer to the New York comedy scene, features such pleasant innovations as space enough to seat 300. Sunday shows are at 9 PM.

**Stand Up N.Y.** (236 W. 78th St., tel. 212/595–0850), a 175-seat, Upper West Side option for comedy devotees, books lots of bright faces coming off recent TV gigs. Stars drop in on occasion, too. On Sundays the fun starts at 9 PM.

**Steve McGraw's** (158 W. 72nd St., tel. 212/595–7400), on the site of the former Palsson's Supper Club, has been renovated to accommodate an audience of 130. The bill is sophisticated comic revues, on Sundays at 3 and 7:30.

# Movies

The cinematic splendors glowing on screens in the dark of New York's movie theaters go far beyond the star vehicles and made-for-the-masses action-adventure films that monopolize auditoriums in most other towns. Unusual foreign offerings, small independent films, and classics both renowned and arcane—you can see them all on any day of the week, but Sunday is prime time for film goers. Be prepared for lines that stretch around the block, especially for exclusive showings of newly premiered hits.

**What's Playing?**   All local publications give a complete local film picture. *7 Days* gives very brief reviews and schedules with show times for all movie theaters and revival houses in Manhattan; the "Movie Clock" in the "Weekend" section of the Friday *New York Times* gives weekend showing times (but not reviews) for cinemas in all five boroughs. Listings in *New York* magazine tell what's playing at every movie theater in the five boroughs and the nearby suburbs, and there are reviews for most films currently playing (but no show times). The *New Yorker* covers Manhattan movie theaters and selectively excerpts reviews.

**Tickets**   Go to the first show of the day, and you'll seldom have a wait. When buying tickets for a box office hit early in its run, you may want to guarantee a seat by arriving at the box office an hour or so before show time. A good strategy is to pass by the theater, pick up tickets, have a meal and a stroll, and come back (a half hour before show time) to claim a place in the ticket holders' line.

**Cinema Museums**   **American Museum of the Moving Image** (36–01 35th Ave., Astoria, Queens, tel. 718/784–4520), housed in a building belonging to the historic Kaufman-Astoria Studios, presents more than 700 programs annually, including major artist-oriented retrospectives (sometimes with personal appearances), Hollywood classics, experimental videos, and documentaries. *See* Chapter 4.
   **Museum of Modern Art** (11 W. 53rd St., tel. 212/708–9490 for film information) is a treasure house, with a 10,000-film archive founded by former museum director Alfred H. Barr, Jr., who believed that film is one of the most important art forms of the 20th century. Half a dozen Sunday screenings in two small, acoustically perfect auditoriums include offerings from cinema's earliest days to the present, encompassing films of all types, from all nations. *See* Chapter 4.

**Festivals**   **New Directors/New Films** (Museum of Modern Art's Roy and Niuta Titus Theatre, 11 W. 53rd St., tel. 212/877–1800, ext. 489), a joint project of MOMA and the Film Society of Lincoln Center, presents each March the best work by up-and-coming directors.
   **New York Film Festival** (Alice Tully and Avery Fisher halls, Lincoln Center, Broadway at 65th St., tel. 212/877–1800), the city's numero uno film series, screens each September as many as 50 hot independent movies that may or may not wind up on screens anyplace else.

**Revival houses**   **The Biograph Cinema** (225 W. 57th St., tel. 212/582–4582).
   **Cinema Village** (22 E. 12th St., between Fifth Ave. and University Pl., tel. 212/924–3363).
   **Thalia Soho** (15 Vandam St., between 6th and 7th Aves., tel. 212/675–0498).
   **Theatre 80 St. Mark's** (80 St. Marks Pl., between First and Second Aves., tel. 212/254–7400).
   **Trans-Lux Seaport Cinema** (210 Front St., between Beekman and South Sts., tel. 212/608–7888).

**Big Screens**   **Radio City Music Hall** (1260 6th Ave. at 50th St., tel. 212/247–4777).
   **The Ziegfeld** (141 W. 54th St., tel. 212/765–7600).

**Foreign Films**   **Bleecker Street Cinemas** (144 Bleecker St., between Thompson St. and LaGuardia Pl., tel. 212/674–2560).

**Cinemas I and II** (1001 3rd Ave. at 60th St., tel. for I, 212/753–6022; for II, 212/753–0774).
**Cinema 3** (Plaza Hotel, 2 W. 59th St., tel. 212/752–5959).
**Lincoln Plaza Cinemas** (30 Lincoln Plaza, Broadway at 62nd St., tel. 212/757–2280).
**Paris** (4 W. 58th St., tel. 212/688–2013).
**68th Street Playhouse** (1164 3rd Ave. at 68th St., tel. 212/734–0302).
**RKO Art Greenwich** (93 Greenwich Ave. at 12th St., tel. 212/929–3350).

**Experimental Films** **Anthology Film Archives** (32–34 2nd Ave. at 2nd St., tel. 212/505–5181).
**Collective for Living Cinema** (41 White St., between Broadway and Church St., tel. 212/925–2111).
**Millenium Film Workshop** (66 E. 4th St., between Bowery and 2nd Ave., tel. 212/673–0090).
**Public Theater** (425 Lafayette St., between Broadway and 8th St., tel. 212/598–7171).

# Summer Arts

On weekends, particularly in summer, urban open spaces yield a Fort Knox of cultural events, giving city folk plenty of reasons to stay in town and suburbanites plenty of reasons to visit. You might find the Big Apple Circus, the Metropolitan Opera, the Bread and Puppet Theatre, or a Korean-American fest. The curtain goes up on Shakespeare in many a city park, not only Central Park—where the New York Shakespeare Festival has long been the focal point of the city's summer theater—but in Brooklyn's Prospect Park, the Bronx's Van Cortlandt Park, Fort Tryon Park at Manhattan's northern tip, and Riverside Park at its western edge.

Note: Parks events are popular, so claim your parcel of lawn an hour or so before curtain time, then while away the time with wine and cheese and some fascinating people watching.

## Outdoors

**Celebrate Brooklyn** (9th St. Bandshell, Prospect Park, Brooklyn, tel. 718/788–0055) presents dance events, Shakespeare, and classical, pop, and ethnic music from July to September. Programs begin at 8 PM, and there's a suggested contribution of $1 for each adult.
**Hot Prospects** (Picnic House, Prospect Park, Brooklyn, tel. 718/788–0055) is a summer series of arts events geared to children. Its adult counterpart, the fall-through-winter New Prospects series, presents eclectic avant-garde events, including virtuoso monologues, readings, performance art, and ethnic dance.
**Lincoln Center Out-of-Doors** (Broadway at 65th Street, tel. 212/877–2011) transforms Manhattan's performing arts centerpiece into a virtual state fair of the arts. In recent years, as many as 300,000 people have attended some 100 events per summer. Stages set up in the plaza accommodate jazz dancers, chamber orchestras, Broadway lyricists and composers, mimes, children's theater, and more.
**Metropolitan Opera in the Parks** (tel. 212/362–6000), a wonderful free series of concerts performed in parks throughout the

five boroughs, usually takes place on weeknights, but it's worth a call to check on the occasional Sunday rain date.

**New York Shakespeare Festival** (Delacorte Theater, Central Park at 81st St., tel. 212/861–PAPP after mid-June, or contact Public Theater, 425 Lafayette St., tel. 212/598–7150) stages two plays every summer. Park breezes keep the Delacorte Theater cool on hot summer nights, as big-name stars such as Kevin Kline and Michelle Pfeiffer appear beneath the starry sky. Since 1954, when producer Joseph Papp launched the program, innovative productions of all kinds of classics have gone under the Shakespeare rubric. The focus now and for the immediate future is on the Shakespeare marathon undertaken by the parent group, the Public Theater, which will mount every one of the Bard's plays during a six-year period. Although a certain portion of the tickets is sold in advance, most tickets are distributed free at 6 for the 8 PM performance. Lines form early in the afternoon, beginning near the Delacorte box office and stretching around the southern end of the Great Lawn. Bring a blanket or lawn chairs, get a number, take your place in the line, and pass the afternoon relaxing and watching the Central Park panorama.

**Summersounds** (South Meadow, Snug Harbor Cultural Center, Staten Island, tel. 718/448–2500) brings a series of concerts to this gem of an arts complex, a quick ferry and bus ride from Manhattan. Recent years have brought Arlo Guthrie, the Preservation Hall Jazz Band, and Nelson Riddle and his orchestra. Tickets can be ordered in advance from the center's ticket office.

**Summerstage** (Naumburg Bandshell, Central Park at 72nd St., tel. 212/860–1335) fills this Roman-temple-like edifice with free programs of music, dance, theater, and comedy, ranging from grand opera to polka to experimental rock. Performances are generally at 3 on Sundays, from June to September.

**Other Parks** Elsewhere on municipal greenswards, Sundays bring the **Bronx Arts Ensemble Concert Series** (with performances at 2 in the Bronx's Van Cortlandt Park), the **Orchard Beach Weekend Concert Series** (with musical groups tuning up at 2 at Pelham Bay Park's Orchard Beach), occasional musicalizing by the **Brooklyn Philharmonic** at Brooklyn's Seaside Park, and a **Starlight Concert Series** at Forest Park in Queens.

## Indoors

**Classical Jazz** (Alice Tully Hall, Lincoln Center, Broadway at 65th St., tel. 212/874–6770) helps to keep August cool (*see* Jazz, above).

**Festival Latino** (Public Theater, 425 Lafayette St., between Astor Pl. and 8th St., tel. 212/598–7182), dedicated to south-of-the-border music, theater, dance, and film, takes place annually in August.

**Mostly Mozart** (Avery Fisher Hall, Lincoln Center, Broadway at 65th St., tel. 212/874–2424) enlivens city life for seven weeks during July and August with classical artists, such as Trevor Pinnock, Kathleen Battle, and Jean-Pierre Rampal, performing the music of Mozart and his contemporaries.

**The New York International Festival of the Arts** (tel. 212/472–1490), scheduled for four weeks in June 1991, will present hundreds of events in all the arts, all over town. The emphasis is on foreign artists and companies rarely or never seen before in

New York, and on new works commissioned specifically for the festival.

**Queens Theatre in the Park** (Flushing Meadows-Corona Park, Queens, tel. 718/291–1100), a 500-seat performing arts center on the site of the 1964 World's Fair's New York State Pavilion, is being renovated at this writing, with the objective of hosting even better programs in the future.

**Serious Fun** (Alice Tully Hall, Lincoln Center, Broadway at 65th St., tel. 212/877–2011) brings the way-out arts to staid Lincoln Center for three weeks in July and August. Look for talents such as monologuists Eric Bogosian and Spalding Gray, theatrical experimenter Laurie Anderson, and composer Philip Glass.

# Best Bets for Children

Sunday is youngsters' time to claim the Big Apple for their own, as concerts and theater presentations abound, parks and museums stage special programs, and children's performing arts groups burst into life. Many of these events are modestly priced or even free.

**Arts in the Parks**  **Big Apple Circus** pitches its big top in Damrosch Park in Lincoln Center. Call for schedules and ticket information (tel. 212/391–0767).

**Hot Prospects** (Picnic House, Prospect Park, Brooklyn, tel. 718/788–0055), a summer arts series designed for families, takes the stage on Sundays at 3 (*see* also Summer Arts, above).

**Arts in Museums**  Children's museums are extra-lively on Sundays, with all kinds of special events. Check into the **Brooklyn Children's Museum,** the **Manhattan Children's Museum,** and the **Staten Island Children's Museum.** Frequent programs for young visitors, often centered on the arts, are also offered at the **Museum of the City of New York, South Street Seaport,** the **Jewish Museum,** and the **Queens Museum,** among others. *See* Chapter 4 for addresses, phone numbers, and hours.

**Children's Theater**  **Don Quijote Experimental Theatre** (Lincoln Sq. Theater, 250 W. 65th St., tel. 212/496–8009), dedicated to exposing kids to realistic theater, explores topics, such as literacy and aging, with occasional Sunday performances—usually in fall and winter.

**Henry Street Settlement, Louis Abrons Arts for Living Center** (466 Grand St., between Pitt and Willett Sts., tel. 212/598–0400), founded by a nurse in 1893 to care for the Lower East Side's sick and disadvantaged, now covers the arts and mounts plays in its Arts for Family Series on Sundays at 2.

**Little People's Theatre** (The Courtyard Playhouse, 39 Grove St., between W. 4th St. and 7th Ave., tel. 212/765–9540) brings nursery rhymes like Humpty Dumpty and other child-pleasers to life on Sundays at 1:30 and 3, September through June.

**The Paper Bag Players** (tel. 212/362–0431) perform frequently at Symphony Space and Town Hall, presenting original plays like *I Won't Take a Bath*—great fun for all ages. Sellout crowds make advance ticket orders a good idea.

**Penny Bridge Players** (Undercroft of the Assumption Church, 59 Cranberry St., Brooklyn Heights, tel. 718/855–6346) put on weekend performances of adapted fairy tales.

**Theaterworks/USA** (Promenade Theater, Broadway at 76th St., tel. 212/677–5959), honored by the American Theater Association for "sustained and exceptional accomplishment in children's theater," serves up terrific original children's plays, like one looking into the life of suffragette Susan B. Anthony. These magical performances are on Sundays at 12:30.

**13th Street Theater** (50 W. 13th St., between 5th and 6th Aves., tel. 212/675–6677) presents programs for kids on Sundays at 1 and 3.

**Story Hours**   **Eeyore's Books for Children** (2212 Broadway at 79th St., tel. 212/362–0634, and 25 E. 83rd St., tel. 212/988–3404) offers Sunday story hours and invites authors and illustrators to come and chat with small fry.

**Storyland** (1369 3rd Ave. at 78th St., tel. 212/517–6951, and 379 Amsterdam Ave. at 78th St.) has appearances by authors and illustrators on Sundays at 1:30, except during the summer.

**Other Organizations**   The **92nd Street Y** (1395 Lexington Ave. at 92nd St., tel. 212/427–4410) is tireless about offering special programs for kids.

**Lincoln Center** offers a neat Family Sampler, which includes some Sunday tickets in a packet that takes in the Metropolitan Opera (as part of the Opera Guild's **Growing Up with Opera** series) and the New York Philharmonic's **Young Peoples' Concerts** (tel. 212/877–1800). In addition, performances of the **Little Orchestra Society** in Avery Fisher Hall (tel. 212/704–2100) are ideal for families. The free summer arts festival, Lincoln Center Out-of-Doors, contains many offerings with child appeal. And don't forget December's great event, *The Nutcracker*, at the New York City Ballet.

# Index

Map page numbers are in *boldface italics*.

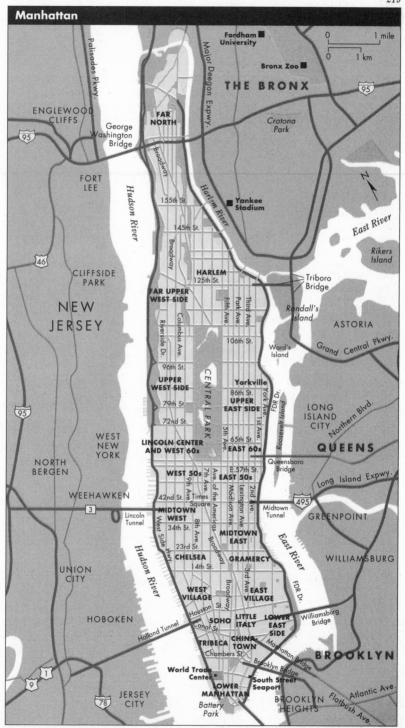

# Manhattan

**THE BRONX**

Fordham University

Bronx Zoo

ENGLEWOOD CLIFFS

Palisades Pkwy.

Major Deegan Expwy.

FAR NORTH

George Washington Bridge

Broadway

Crotona Park

FORT LEE

Hudson River

Harlem River

Yankee Stadium

East River

155th St.

Rikers Island

CLIFFSIDE PARK

145th St.

NEW JERSEY

Broadway

HARLEM
125th St.

Triboro Bridge

FAR UPPER WEST SIDE

Randall's Island

ASTORIA

Riverside Dr.

Columbus Ave.

Fifth Ave.

Park Ave.

Third Ave.

Grand Central Pkwy.

106th St.

Ward's Island

96th St.

CENTRAL PARK

Yorkville

UPPER WEST SIDE

86th St.

UPPER EAST SIDE

York Ave.

FDR Dr.

1st Ave.

LONG ISLAND CITY

Northern Blvd.

79th St.

72nd St.

LINCOLN CENTER AND WEST 60s

65th St.

5th Ave.

EAST 60s

Roosevelt Island

QUEENS

Queensboro Bridge

WEST NEW YORK

WEST 50s

7th Ave.

EAST 50s

E.57th St.

Long Island Expwy.

NORTH BERGEN

Ave. of the Americas

Madison Ave.

Lexington Ave.

2nd Ave.

WEEHAWKEN

42nd St.

Times Square

9th Ave.

8th Ave.

Midtown Tunnel

GREENPOINT

Lincoln Tunnel

West Side Hwy.

MIDTOWN WEST

34th St.

MIDTOWN EAST

East River

FDR Dr.

23rd St.

Broadway

UNION CITY

CHELSEA

14th St.

GRAMERCY

3rd Ave.

WILLIAMSBURG

HOBOKEN

WEST VILLAGE

EAST VILLAGE

Houston St.

Hudson River

SOHO

Canal St.

LITTLE ITALY

LOWER EAST SIDE

Williamsburg Bridge

Holland Tunnel

TRIBECA

CHINA-TOWN

Manhattan Bridge

Chambers St.

World Trade Center

LOWER MANHATTAN

South Street Seaport

Brooklyn Bridge

**BROOKLYN**

JERSEY CITY

Battery Park

BROOKLYN HEIGHTS

Atlantic Ave.

Flatbush Ave.

0 ———— 1 mile
0 ———— 1 km

# New York City Area

**Scale:**
0 — 5 miles
0 — 5 km

N

## LONG ISLAND SOUND

PORT WASHINGTON

NASSAU

GREAT NECK
GREAT NECK ESTATES

KINGS POINT

*Manhasset Bay*

LITTLE NECK

*Little Neck Bay*

Cross Island Pkwy.

BAYSIDE Pkwy.

Clearview Expwy.

Long Island Expwy.

Grand Central Pkwy.

ST. ALBANS

Pelham Bay Park

Hart I.

City I.

*Eastchester Bay*

Throgs Neck

Throgs Neck Bridge

*East River*

Whitestone Bridge

COLLEGE POINT

FLUSHING

Shea Stadium

USTA Nat'l Tennis Center

Flushing Meadow–Corona Park

FOREST

QUEENS

WESTCHESTER

MT. VERNON

YONKERS

95

Van Cortlandt Park

RIVERDALE

Spuyten Duyvil

THE BRONX

Ferdham University

Bronx Park

Bronx Zoo

Crotona Park

HUNTS POINT

Rikers I.

La Guardia Airport

*Flushing Bay*

Northern Blvd.

JACKSON HEIGHTS

ASTORIA

Grand Central Pkwy.

Yankee Stadium

Tribor Bridge

Randall's I.

Roosevelt I.

LONG ISLAND CITY

Queensboro Bridge

Columbia University

Harlem R.

Central Park

MANHATTAN

Lincoln Center

Hudson River

Palisades Pkwy.

FORT LEE

George Washington Bridge

CLIFFSIDE PARK

WEST NEW YORK

NORTH BERGEN

TENAFLY

ENGLEWOOD CLIFFS

ENGLEWOOD

BERGEN

PARAMUS

NEW JERSEY

4

95

80

46

17

EAST RUTHERFORD

Meadowlands Sports Complex

95

2

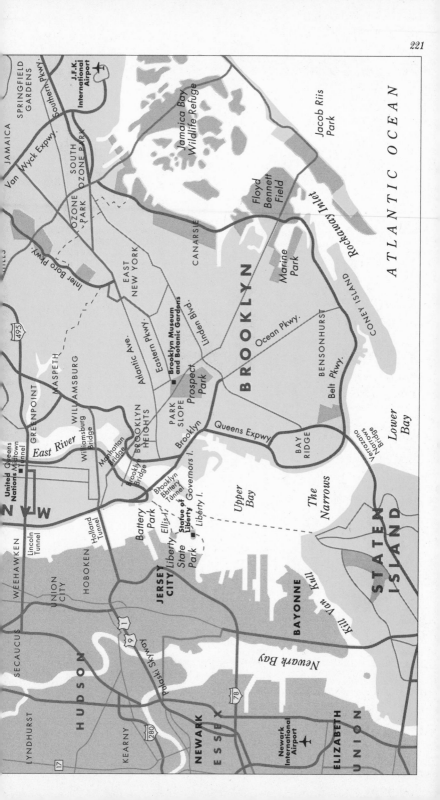

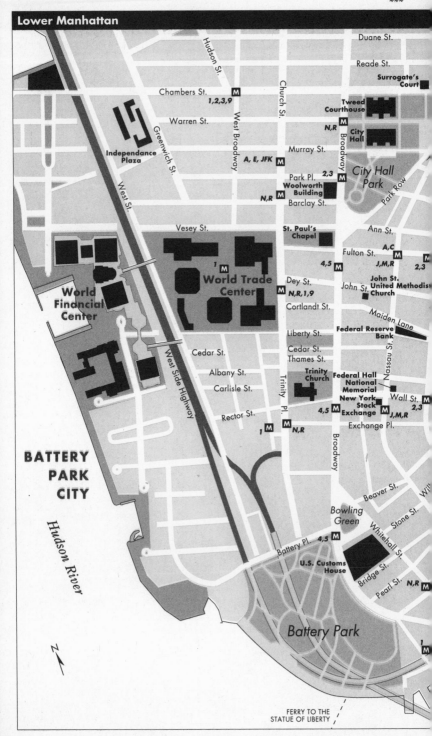

Centre St.

**M** 4,5,6

**M** J,M,Z

**Municipal Building**

Pearl St.

Madison St.

Catherine St.

St. James Pl.

FDR Drive

Spruce St.

Beekman St.

Gold St.

Dover St.

Peck Slip

Pearl St.

Beekman St.

**Fulton Fish Market**

Brooklyn Bridge

Fulton St.

John St.

**South Street Seaport**

Burling Slip

Cedar St.

Maiden Lane

Depyster St.

Pine St.

Water St.

Front St.

South St.

Pearl St.

Hanover Sq.

Old Slip

*East River*

Broad St.

Jeanette Park

Vietnam Veterans Plaza

ater St.

GOVERNOR'S ISLAND FERRY

STATEN ISLAND FERRY

Brooklyn-Battery Tunnel

0             440 yards

0             400 meters

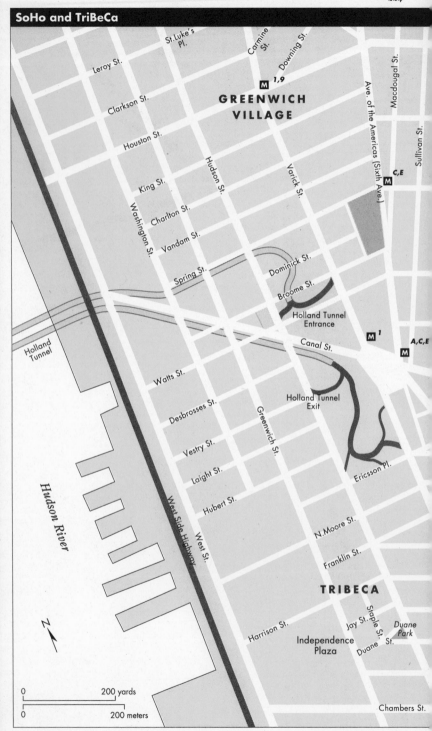

GREENWICH VILLAGE

TRIBECA

Hudson River

Holland Tunnel

Holland Tunnel Entrance

Holland Tunnel Exit

Independence Plaza

Duane Park

St. Luke's Pl.

Carmine St.

Downing St.

Macdougal St.

Leroy St.

Clarkson St.

Houston St.

King St.

Charlton St.

Vandam St.

Spring St.

Hudson St.

Varick St.

Ave. of the Americas (Sixth Ave.)

Sullivan St.

Washington St.

Dominick St.

Broome St.

Canal St.

Watts St.

Desbrosses St.

Vestry St.

Laight St.

Hubert St.

Greenwich St.

West Side Highway

West St.

N. Moore St.

Franklin St.

Harrison St.

Jay St.

Staple St.

Duane St.

Ericsson Pl.

Chambers St.

1,9

C, E

1

A, C, E

0    200 yards

0    200 meters

# Chinatown, Little Italy, and the Lower East Side

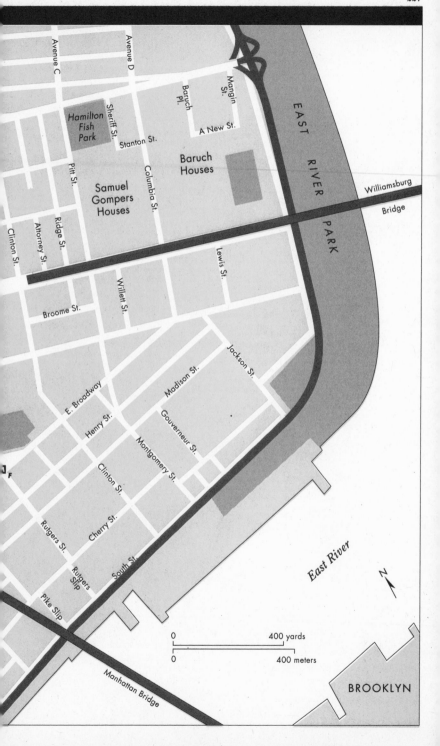

Avenue C

Avenue D

Mangin St.

Baruch Pl.

Hamilton Fish Park

Sheriff St.

A New St.

Stanton St.

Baruch Houses

E A S T

Pitt St.

Columbia St.

R I V E R

Samuel Gompers Houses

Williamsburg

Clinton St.

Attorney St.

Ridge St.

Bridge

P A R K

Lewis St.

Broome St.

Willett St.

Jackson St.

Madison St.

E. Broadway

Gouverneur St.

Henry St.

Montgomery St.

Clinton St.

East River

N

Rutgers St.

Cherry St.

Rutgers Slip

South St.

Pike Slip

0                    400 yards

0                    400 meters

Manhattan Bridge

BROOKLYN

# West Village

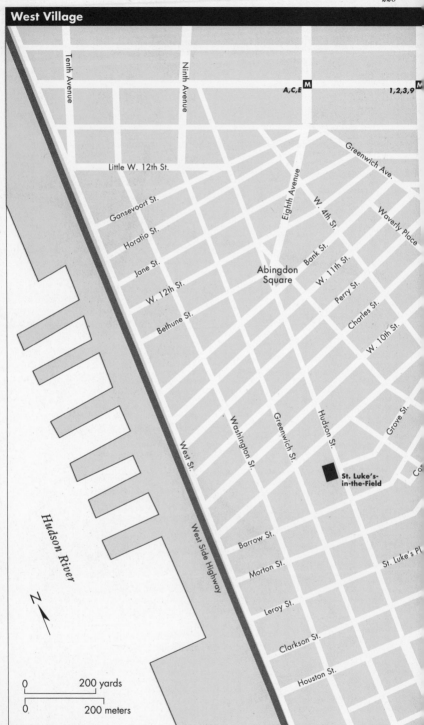

Tenth Avenue

Ninth Avenue

A,C,E 1,2,3,9

Greenwich Ave.

Little W. 12th St.

Eighth Avenue

W. 4th St.

Waverly Place

Gansevoort St.

Horatio St.

Bank St.

Jane St.

Abingdon
Square

W. 11th St.

Perry St.

W. 12th St.

Charles St.

W. 10th St.

Bethune St.

Grove St.

Washington St.

Greenwich St.

Hudson St.

Co

St. Luke's-
in-the-Field

Hudson River

Barrow St.

West St.

Morton St.

St. Luke's Pl

Leroy St.

West Side Highway

Clarkson St.

N

Houston St.

0        200 yards

0        200 meters

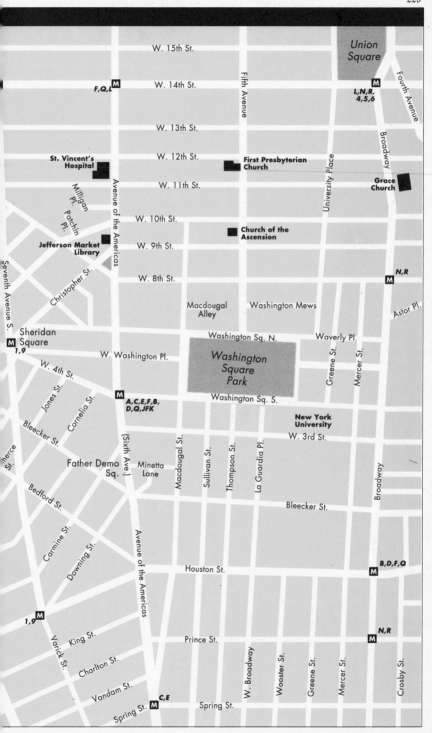

# East Village

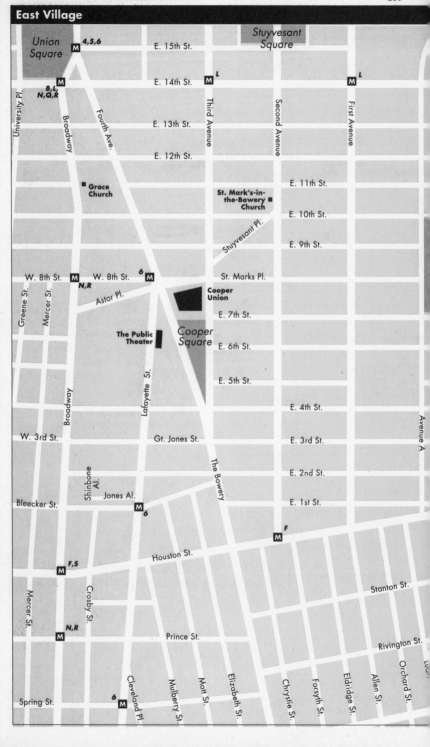

Union Square

4,5,6

E. 15th St.

Stuyvesant Square

E. 14th St.  L  L

B,L,
N,Q,R

University Pl.

Broadway

Fourth Ave.

Third Avenue

Second Avenue

First Avenue

E. 13th St.

E. 12th St.

E. 11th St.

Grace Church

St. Mark's-in-the-Bowery Church

E. 10th St.

E. 9th St.

Stuyvesant Pl.

W. 8th St.  W. 8th St.  6

N,R

Astor Pl.

St. Marks Pl.

Cooper Union

E. 7th St.

Greene St.

Mercer St.

The Public Theater

Cooper Square

E. 6th St.

E. 5th St.

Broadway

Lafayette St.

E. 4th St.

W. 3rd St.

Gt. Jones St.

E. 3rd St.

Avenue A

The Bowery

E. 2nd St.

Shinbone Al.

Jones Al.

6

E. 1st St.

Bleecker St.

F

Houston St.

F,S

Stanton St.

Mercer St.

Crosby St.

N,R

Prince St.

Rivington St.

6

Cleveland Pl.

Mulberry St.

Mott St.

Elizabeth St.

Chrysie St.

Forsyth St.

Eldridge St.

Allen St.

Orchard St.

Spring St.

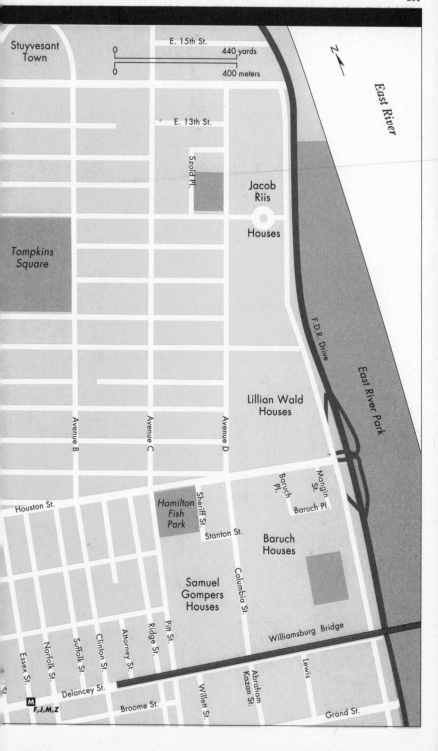

Stuyvesant
Town

E. 15th St.

0          440 yards

0          400 meters

E. 13th St.

N

East River

Szold Pl.

Jacob
Riis

Houses

Tompkins
Square

F.D.R. Drive

East River Park

Lillian Wald
Houses

Magin St.

Baruch Pl.

Baruch Pl.

Houston St.

Avenue B

Avenue C

Avenue D

Hamilton
Fish
Park

Sheriff St.

Stanton St.

Baruch
Houses

Samuel
Gompers
Houses

Columbia St.

Williamsburg Bridge

Essex St.

Norfolk St.

Suffolk St.

Clinton St.

Attorney St.

Ridge St.

Pitt St.

Lewis

Willett St.

Abraham
Kazan St.

St.

Delancey St.

Broome St.

Grand St.

M
F, J, M, Z

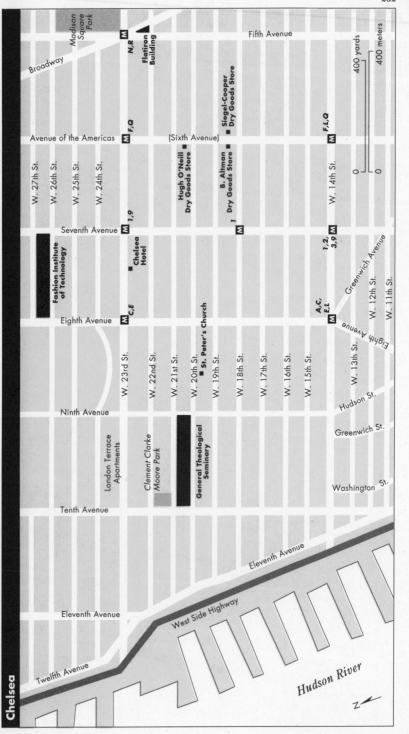

**Chelsea**

Madison Square Park

Broadway

Fifth Avenue

N,R

Flatiron Building

M F,Q

Avenue of the Americas

(Sixth Avenue)

Siegel-Cooper Dry Goods Store

M F,L,Q

W. 27th St.

W. 26th St.

W. 25th St.

W. 24th St.

Hugh O'Neill Dry Goods Store

B. Altman Dry Goods Store

M 1,9

Seventh Avenue

M

W. 14th St.

Fashion Institute of Technology

Chelsea Hotel

M C,E

Eighth Avenue

St. Peter's Church

1,2, 3,9 M

Greenwich Avenue

A,C, E,L M

Eighth Avenue

W. 23rd St.

W. 22nd St.

W. 21st St.

W. 20th St.

W. 19th St.

W. 18th St.

W. 17th St.

W. 16th St.

W. 15th St.

W. 13th St.

W. 12th St.

W. 11th St.

Ninth Avenue

London Terrace Apartments

Clement Clarke Moore Park

General Theological Seminary

Hudson St.

Greenwich St.

Washington St.

Tenth Avenue

Eleventh Avenue

West Side Highway

Eleventh Avenue

Twelfth Avenue

Hudson River

N

400 yards

400 meters

0

0

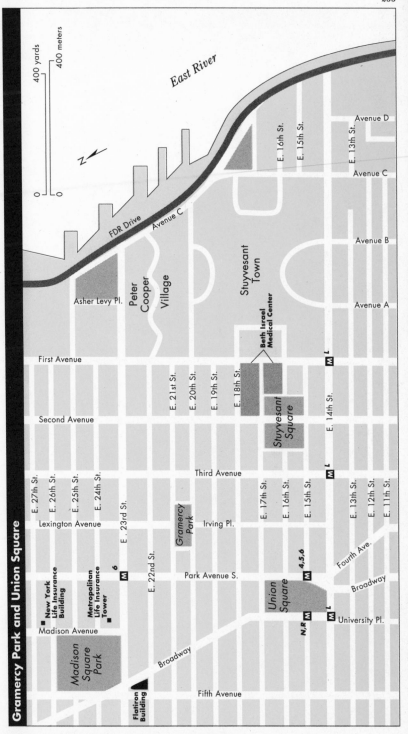

Gramercy Park and Union Square

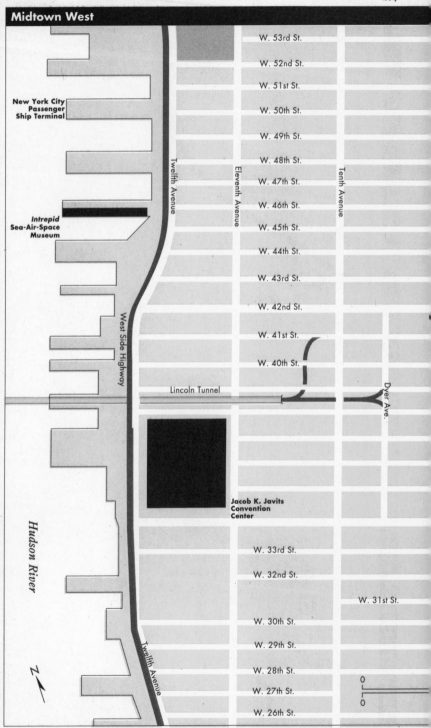

B,D,E M

**THEATER DISTRICT**

Rockefeller Center

M C,E    M 1,9

B,D,F,Q, JFK M

Radio City Music Hall

Rockefeller Plaza

M N,R

Skating Rink

Ninth Avenue

Eighth Avenue

Duffy Square

TKTS Booth

Seventh Avenue

Avenue of the Americas

Times Square

A,C, E M

M 1,2,3,N,R, 7,9,S

M B,D, F,Q

N.Y. Public Library (Main)

Port Authority Bus Terminal

Bryant Park

W. 39th St.

W. 38th St.

W. 37th St.

W. 36th St.

W. 35th St.

W. 34th St.

Broadway

(Sixth Avenue)

Fifth Avenue

**GARMENT DISTRICT**

Macy's

Herald Square

Empire State Building

A,C, E M

M 1,2,3,9

B,D,F, N,Q,R

**Penn Plaza**

Penn Plaza Dr.

Penn Station

Post Office

Madison Square Garden

Broadway

400 yards

400 meters

M 1,9

M N,R

236

Midtown East

East River

Queens-Midtown Tunnel

United Nations Headquarters

Conference Bldg.

Hammarskjold Library

General Assembly

Secretariat Bldg.

MacArthur Plaza

Mitchell Pl.

Beekman Pl.

First Avenue

United Nations Plaza

Tudor City Place

Dag Hammarskjold Plaza

TURTLE BAY

Second Avenue

Private Drive

Third Avenue

E. 53rd St.
E. 52nd St.
E. 51st St.
E. 50th St.
E. 49th St.
E. 48th St.
E. 47th St.
E. 46th St.
E. 45th St.
E. 44th St.
E. 43rd St.
E. 42nd St.
E. 41st St.
E. 40th St.

Chrysler Building

E, F
M E, F

Lexington Avenue

E, F
M 6

Grand Central Terminal

M 4,5,6

St. Batholemew's Church

Park Avenue

Vanderbilt Ave.

M S

Madison Avenue

St. Patrick's Cathedral

E. 45th St.
E. 44th St.
E. 43rd St.
E. 42nd St.

M E, F

Fifth Avenue

Rockefeller Center

Skating Rink

Rockefeller Plaza

Radio City Music Hall

New York Public Library (Main)

S M

Bryant Park

FDR Drive

New York University Medical Center

Bellevue Hospital

First Avenue

Tunnel Entrance St.

Kips Bay Plaza

Second Avenue

Tunnel Exit St.

Third Avenue

E. 39th St.

E. 38th St.

MURRAY HILL

Lexington Avenue

400 yards

400 meters

0

0

Park Avenue

Pierpont Morgan Library

Church of the Incarnation

E. 34th St.

E. 33rd St.

M 6

E. 32nd St.

E. 31st St.

E. 30th St.

Park Avenue South

M 6

E. 29th St.

E. 28th St.

E. 27th St.

E. 26th St.

Madison Avenue

E. 37th St.

E. 36th St.

E. 35th St.

Church of the Transfiguration

Fifth Avenue

Empire State Building

Marble Collegiate Church

N,R

M

Broadway

West 50s

Fifth Avenue

Grand Army Plaza

N,R

Plaza Hotel

E,F

Museum of Modern Art

American Craft Museum

Rockefeller Plaza

Skating Rink

Radio City Music Hall

Rockefeller Center

B,Q,JFK

Avenue of the Americas (Sixth Avenue)

B,D,F,Q, JFK

CENTRAL PARK

Central Park South

Carnegie Hall

Equitable Center

Seventh Avenue

N,R

N,R

TKTS Booth

B,D,E

Duffy Square

Broadway

1,9

THEATER

A,B,C,D, 1,9

Eighth Avenue

C,E

DISTRICT

Broadway

Columbus Circle

Worldwide Plaza

Ninth Avenue

W. 60th St.
W. 59th St.
W. 58th St.
W. 57th St.
W. 56th St.
W. 55th St.
W. 54th St.
W. 53rd St.
W. 52nd St.
W. 51st St.
W. 50th St.
W. 49th St.
W. 48th St.
W. 47th St.

Tenth Avenue

N

300 yards

300 meters

Eleventh Avenue

0

0

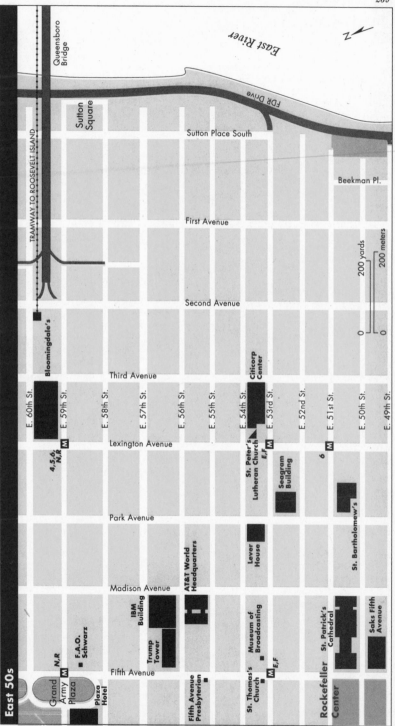

East 60s

East River

FDR Drive

New York Hospital

York Avenue

Rockefeller University

First Avenue

Second Avenue

Third Avenue

St. Vincent Ferrer Church

Lexington Avenue

**M** 6

Hunter College

E. 72nd St.
E. 71st St.
E. 70th St.
E. 69th St.
E. 68th St.
E. 67th St.
E. 66th St.
E. 65th St.
E. 64th St.
E. 63rd St.
E. 62nd St.
E. 61st St.
E. 60th St.
E. 59th St.

Seventh Regiment Armory

Park Avenue

Asia Society

Frick Collection

Madison Avenue

Christ Church United Methodist

Bloomingdale's

**M** N,R,4, 5,6

Temple Emanu-el

Fifth Avenue

Grand Army Plaza

**M** N,R

CENTRAL PARK

Bandshell

Central Park Zoo

Wollman Rink

The Pond

Central Park South

TRAMWAY TO ROOSEVELT ISLAND

Queensboro Bridge

400 yards
400 meters
0
0

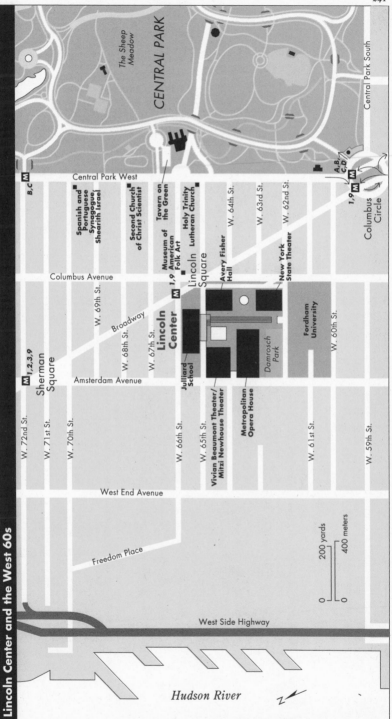

## Lincoln Center and the West 60s

CENTRAL PARK

The Sheep Meadow

Central Park South

Central Park West

Tavern on the Green

Spanish and Portuguese Synagogue Shearith Israel

Second Church of Christ Scientist

Museum of American Folk Art

Holy Trinity Lutheran Church

W. 64th St.

W. 63rd St.

W. 62nd St.

Columbus Circle

B,C

A,B, C,D

1,9

Columbus Avenue

Lincoln Square

Avery Fisher Hall

New York State Theater

W. 69th St.

Broadway

W. 68th St.

W. 67th St.

Lincoln Center

Fordham University

W. 60th St.

Damrosch Park

1,9

Sherman Square

1,2,3,9

Amsterdam Avenue

Julliard School

Vivian Beaumont Theater/ Mitzi Newhouse Theater

Metropolitan Opera House

W. 72nd St.

W. 71st St.

W. 70th St.

W. 66th St.

W. 65th St.

W. 61st St.

W. 59th St.

West End Avenue

Freedom Place

200 yards

400 meters

West Side Highway

Hudson River

N

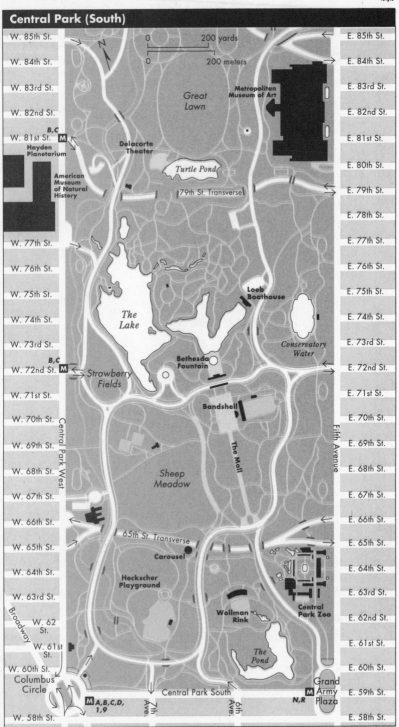

242

# Central Park (South)

W. 85th St. — E. 85th St.
W. 84th St. — E. 84th St.
W. 83rd St. — E. 83rd St.
W. 82nd St. — E. 82nd St.
W. 81st St. — E. 81st St.
— E. 80th St.
— E. 79th St.
— E. 78th St.
W. 77th St. — E. 77th St.
W. 76th St. — E. 76th St.
W. 75th St. — E. 75th St.
W. 74th St. — E. 74th St.
W. 73rd St. — E. 73rd St.
W. 72nd St. — E. 72nd St.
W. 71st St. — E. 71st St.
W. 70th St. — E. 70th St.
W. 69th St. — E. 69th St.
W. 68th St. — E. 68th St.
W. 67th St. — E. 67th St.
W. 66th St. — E. 66th St.
W. 65th St. — E. 65th St.
W. 64th St. — E. 64th St.
W. 63rd St. — E. 63rd St.
W. 62 St. — E. 62nd St.
W. 61st St. — E. 61st St.
W. 60th St. — E. 60th St.
Columbus Circle
W. 58th St. — E. 58th St.

0 200 yards
0 200 meters

Metropolitan Museum of Art

Great Lawn

B,C
Hayden Planetarium
American Museum of Natural History

Delacorte Theater
Turtle Pond
79th St. Transverse

The Lake
Loeb Boathouse
Conservatory Water

B,C
Strawberry Fields
Bethesda Fountain

Bandshell

Sheep Meadow
The Mall

Central Park West
Fifth Avenue

65th St. Transverse
Carousel
Heckscher Playground
Wollman Rink
Central Park Zoo

Broadway
The Pond

Central Park South
Columbus Circle
M A,B,C,D, 1,9
7th Ave.
6th Ave.
Grand Army Plaza
N,R

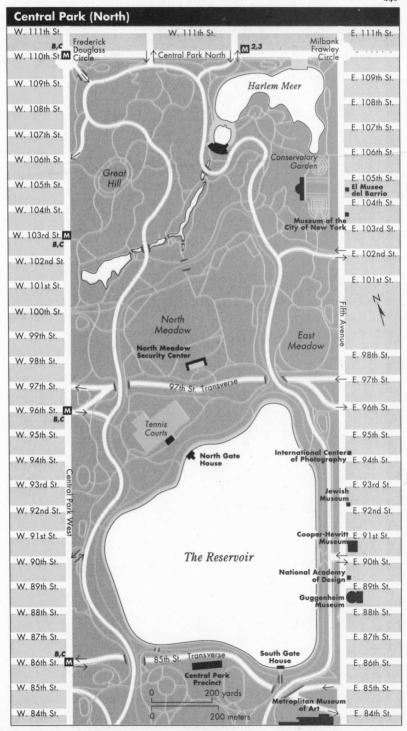

# Central Park (North)

W. 111th St.    W. 111th St.    E. 111th St.

Frederick Douglass Circle

Central Park North

Milbank Frawley Circle

W. 110th St.

M   2,3

W. 109th St.    E. 109th St.

W. 108th St.    E. 108th St.

Harlem Meer

W. 107th St.    E. 107th St.

W. 106th St.    E. 106th St.

Conservatory Garden

Great Hill

W. 105th St.    E. 105th St.

El Museo del Barrio

W. 104th St.    E. 104th St.

Museum of the City of New York

W. 103rd St. M    E. 103rd St.

B,C

W. 102nd St.    E. 102nd St.

W. 101st St.    E. 101st St.

W. 100th St.    N

W. 99th St.

North Meadow

East Meadow

W. 98th St.    E. 98th St.

North Meadow Security Center

Fifth Avenue

W. 97th St.    97th St. Transverse    E. 97th St.

W. 96th St. M    E. 96th St.

B,C

W. 95th St.    E. 95th St.

Tennis Courts

W. 94th St.    International Center of Photography   E. 94th St.

North Gate House

W. 93rd St.    E. 93rd St.

Jewish Museum

W. 92nd St.    E. 92nd St.

Central Park West

Cooper-Hewitt Museum

W. 91st St.    E. 91st St.

W. 90th St.    E. 90th St.

The Reservoir

National Academy of Design

W. 89th St.    E. 89th St.

Guggenheim Museum

W. 88th St.    E. 88th St.

W. 87th St.    E. 87th St.

W. 86th St. M    E. 86th St.

B,C

South Gate House

W. 85th St.    85th St. Transverse    E. 85th St.

Central Park Precinct

0   200 yards

0   200 meters

W. 84th St.    Metropolitan Museum of Art   E. 84th St.

Upper East Side, including Yorkville

East River

Gracie Mansion

Carl Schurz Park

East End Avenue

York Avenue

Henderson Place Historic District

Y O R K V I L L E

First Avenue

Second Avenue

Third Avenue

Lexington Avenue

M 6

E. 92nd St. YMHA

M 4,5,6

Park Avenue Methodist Church

Park Avenue

Madison Avenue

St. Ignatius

Cooper-Hewitt Museum

Guggenheim Museum

Fifth Avenue

Reservoir

E. 97th St.
E. 96th St.
E. 95th St.
E. 94th St.
E. 93rd St.
E. 92nd St.
E. 91st St.
E. 90th St.
E. 89th St.
E. 88th St.
E. 87th St.
E. 86th St.
E. 85th St.
E. 84th St.

FDR Drive

John Jay Park

Cherokee Pl.

York Ave.

First Ave.

E. 83rd St.
E. 82nd St.
E. 81st St.
E. 80th St.
E. 79th St.
E. 78th St.
E. 77th St.
E. 76th St.
E. 75th St.
E. 74th St.
E. 73rd St.
E. 72nd St.
E. 71st St.
E. 70th St.

Second Ave.

Archdiocesan Cathedral of the Holy Trinity

Third Ave.

200 yards
200 meters
0
0

Lexington Ave.

Lenox Hill Hospital

Whitney Museum of American Art

Madison Avenue Presbyterian Church

Asia Society

Park Ave.

Loyola Church

Carlyle Hotel

St. James's Church

Madison Ave.

Metropolitan Museum of Art

Frick Collection

Fifth Ave.

CENTRAL PARK

The Reservoir

CENTRAL

TO TENNIS → COURTS

Central Park West

B.C M

Columbus Avenue

West 89th St. Community Garden

W. 97th St.

W. 96th St.

W. 95th St.

W. 94th St.

W. 93rd St.

W. 92nd St.

W. 91st St.

W. 90th St.

W. 89th St.

W. 88th St.

W. 87th St.

W. 86th St.

W. 85th St.

W. 84th St.

Claremont Riding Academy ■

Amsterdam Avenue

M 1,2,3,9

■ Symphony Space

M 1,9

Broadway

Pomander Walk

West End Avenue

Joan of Arc Park

Soldiers' and Sailors' Monument ■

Riverside Drive

RIVERSIDE PARK

The Promenade

Henry Hudson Parkway

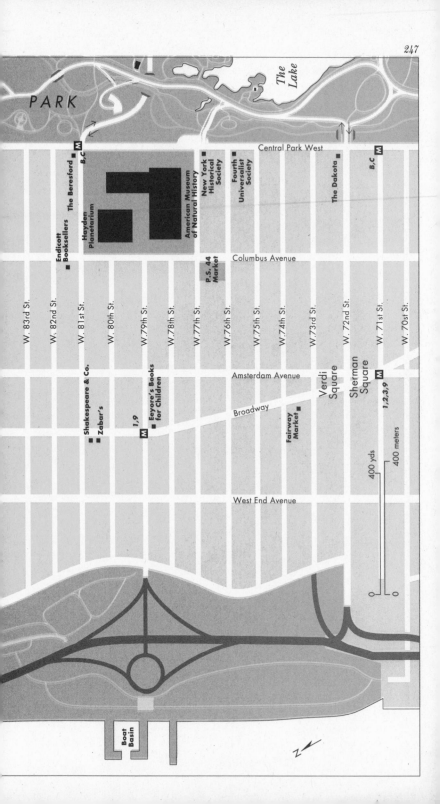

PARK

The Lake

Central Park West

B,C M

B,C M

The Beresford

Endicott
Booksellers

Hayden
Planetarium

American Museum
of Natural History

New York
Historical
Society

Fourth
Universalist
Society

The Dakota

Columbus Avenue

P.S. 44
Market

W. 83rd St.

W. 82nd St.

W. 81st St.

W. 80th St.

W. 79th St.

W. 78th St.

W. 77th St.

W. 76th St.

W. 75th St.

W. 74th St.

W. 73rd St.

W. 72nd St.

W. 71st St.

W. 70st St.

Amsterdam Avenue

Verdi
Square

Sherman
Square

M 1,2,3,9

Shakespeare & Co.

Zabar's

M 1,9

Eeyore's Books
for Children

Broadway

Fairway
Market

West End Avenue

400 yds

400 meters

0

0

Boat
Basin

N

# Far Upper West Side

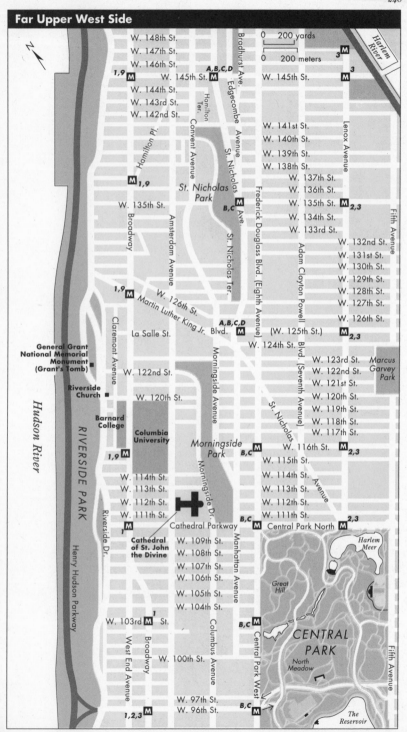

W. 148th St.
W. 147th St.
W. 146th St.
W. 145th St.
W. 144th St.
W. 143rd St.
W. 142nd St.

A,B,C,D

1,9 M

Bradhurst Ave.
Edgecombe Avenue
Hamilton Ter.
Convent Avenue
St. Nicholas Ter.

Harlem River

0    200 yards
0    200 meters

3 M

W. 145th St.

3 M

W. 141st St.
W. 140th St.
W. 139th St.
W. 138th St.
W. 137th St.
W. 136th St.
W. 135th St.
W. 134th St.
W. 133rd St.

Lenox Avenue
Frederick Douglass Blvd. (Eighth Avenue)
Adam Clayton Powell
Fifth Avenue

1,9 M

St. Nicholas Park

B,C M

St. Nicholas Ave.

2,3 M

W. 135th St.

W. 132nd St.
W. 131st St.
W. 130th St.
W. 129th St.
W. 128th St.
W. 127th St.
W. 126th St.

Hamilton Pl.
Broadway
Amsterdam Avenue

1,9 M
W. 126th St.
Martin Luther King Jr. Blvd.

A,B,C,D M
La Salle St.

(W. 125th St.)
W. 124th St.

2,3 M

Blvd. (Seventh Avenue)

General Grant
National Memorial
Monument
(Grant's Tomb)

Riverside Church

Barnard College

W. 122nd St.
W. 120th St.

Claremont Avenue
Morningside Avenue
Morningside Drive

W. 123rd St.
W. 122nd St.
W. 121st St.
W. 120th St.
W. 119th St.
W. 118th St.
W. 117th St.

St. Nicholas

Marcus Garvey Park

1,9 M

Columbia University

Morningside Park

B,C M

W. 116th St.

2,3 M

Hudson River

RIVERSIDE PARK

W. 114th St.
W. 113th St.
W. 112th St.
W. 111th St.

Riverside Dr.

W. 115th St.
W. 114th St.
W. 113th St.
W. 112th St.
W. 111th St.

Avenue

1 M

B,C M

Central Park North

2,3 M

Cathedral of St. John the Divine

Cathedral Parkway
W. 109th St.
W. 108th St.
W. 107th St.
W. 106th St.
W. 105th St.
W. 104th St.

Manhattan Avenue

Harlem Meer

Great Hill

1 M

W. 103rd St.

B,C M

CENTRAL PARK

Henry Hudson Parkway

West End Avenue

Broadway

W. 100th St.

Columbus Avenue

North Meadow

Central Park West

Fifth Avenue

1,2,3 M

W. 97th St.
W. 96th St.

B,C M

The Reservoir

# Harlem

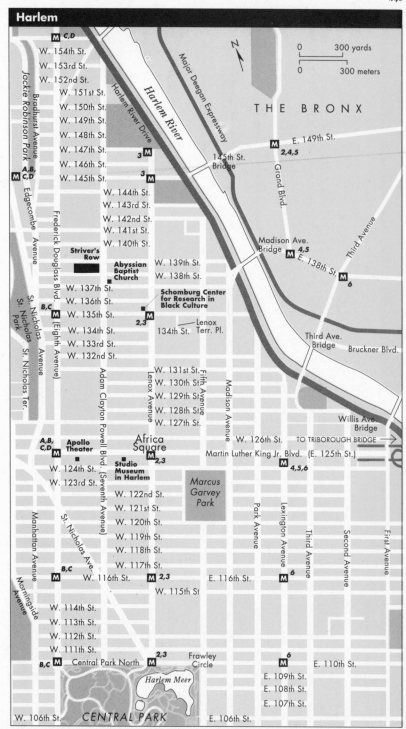

THE BRONX

Harlem River

Harlem River Drive

Major Deegan Expressway

Jackie Robinson Park

Bradhurst Avenue

Edgecombe Avenue

Frederick Douglass Blvd. (Eighth Avenue)

St. Nicholas Avenue

St. Nicholas Park

St. Nicholas Ter.

Adam Clayton Powell Blvd. (Seventh Avenue)

Lenox Avenue

Fifth Avenue

Madison Avenue

Park Avenue

Lexington Avenue

Third Avenue

Second Avenue

First Avenue

Grand Blvd.

Third Avenue

Manhattan Avenue

St. Nicholas Ave.

Morningside Avenue

W. 154th St.
W. 153rd St.
W. 152nd St.
W. 151st St.
W. 150th St.
W. 149th St.
W. 148th St.
W. 147th St.
W. 146th St.
W. 145th St.
W. 144th St.
W. 143rd St.
W. 142nd St.
W. 141st St.
W. 140th St.
W. 139th St.
W. 138th St.
W. 137th St.
W. 136th St.
W. 135th St.
W. 134th St.
W. 133rd St.
W. 132nd St.
W. 131st St.
W. 130th St.
W. 129th St.
W. 128th St.
W. 127th St.
W. 126th St.
W. 124th St.
W. 123rd St.
W. 122nd St.
W. 121st St.
W. 120th St.
W. 119th St.
W. 118th St.
W. 117th St.
W. 116th St.
W. 115th St
W. 114th St.
W. 113th St.
W. 112th St.
W. 111th St.
W. 106th St.

E. 149th St.
E. 138th St.
E. 126th St.
E. 116th St.
E. 110th St.
E. 109th St.
E. 108th St.
E. 107th St.
E. 106th St.

0       300 yards
0       300 meters

145th St. Bridge
Madison Ave. Bridge
Third Ave. Bridge
Bruckner Blvd.
Willis Ave. Bridge
TO TRIBOROUGH BRIDGE
Martin Luther King Jr. Blvd. (E. 125th St.)

Striver's Row
Abyssian Baptist Church
Schomburg Center for Research in Black Culture
Lenox Terr. Pl.
134th St.

Africa Square
Apollo Theater
Studio Museum in Harlem
Marcus Garvey Park

Central Park North
Frawley Circle
Harlem Meer
CENTRAL PARK

M C,D
M A,B, C,D
M B,C
M A,B, C,D
M B,C
M B,C
M 2,4,5
M 4,5
M 6
M 4,5,6
M 6
M 2,3
M 2,3
M 2,3
M 2,3
3 M
3 M

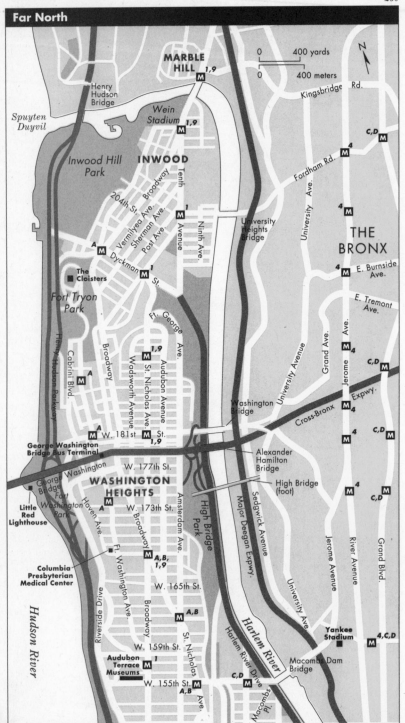

MARBLE HILL

M 1,9

Henry Hudson Bridge

*Spuyten Duyvil*

*Wein Stadium* M 1,9

0 ___ 400 yards
0 ___ 400 meters

N

Kingsbridge Rd.

C,D M

*Inwood Hill Park*

INWOOD

Fordham Rd.

4 M

204th St.

Broadway

Vermilyea Ave.

Sherman Ave.

Post Ave.

Tenth

1 Avenue

Ninth Ave.

University Heights Bridge

University Ave.

THE BRONX

4 M

A M

Dyckman St.

1 St.

M

The Cloisters

*Fort Tryon Park*

4 M E. Burnside Ave.

E. Tremont Ave.

Henry Hudson Parkway

Cabrini Blvd.

A M

Broadway

Ft. George Ave.

Wadsworth Avenue

St. Nicholas Ave.

Audubon Avenue

1,9 M

University Avenue

Grand Ave.

Ave.

Jerome

M 4

C,D M

Cross-Bronx Expwy.

M 4

Washington Bridge

A M W. 181st M St. 1,9

C,D M

M 4

George Washington Bridge Bus Terminal

George Bridge

Fort Washington Park

Little Red Lighthouse

A M

W. 177th St.

WASHINGTON HEIGHTS

Washington

Haven Ave.

Broadway

Amsterdam Ave.

High Bridge Park

Alexander Hamilton Bridge

High Bridge (foot)

Sedgwick Avenue

Major Deegan Expwy.

M 4

C,D M

W. 173rd St.

Columbia Presbyterian Medical Center

Ft. Washington Ave.

M A,B, 1,9

Broadway

W. 165th St.

M A,B

St. Nicholas

University Ave.

Jerome Avenue

River Avenue

Grand Blvd.

*Hudson River*

Riverside Drive

W. 159th St.

1

Audubon Terrace Museums

*Harlem River*

Harlem River Drive

Yankee Stadium

4,C,D M

Macombs Dam Bridge

C,D M

W. 155th St.

M A,B

Ave.

Macombs Pl.

*Help us evaluate hotels and restaurants for the next edition of this guide, and we will send you a free issue of Fodor's newsletter, TravelSense.*

## Title of this guide:

**1 Hotel** ❑   **Restaurant** ❑   *(check one)*

Name

Number/Street

City/State/Country

Comments

**2 Hotel** ❑   **Restaurant** ❑   *(check one)*

Name

Number/Street

City/State/Country

Comments

**3 Hotel** ❑   **Restaurant** ❑   *(check one)*

Name

Number/Street

City/State/Country

Comments

## General Comments

*Please complete for a free copy of TravelSense*

**Name**

**Number/Street**

**City/State/Zip**

# Business Reply Mail

*First Class*     *Permit N⁰ 7775*     *New York, NY*

*Postage will be paid by addressee*

## Fodor's Travel Publications

*201 East 50th Street*
*New York, NY 10022*